INTELLECTUAL MORONS

INTELLECTUAL MORONS

How Ideology Makes

Smart People

Fall for

Stupid

Ideas

Daniel J. Flynn

CROWN FORUM
New York

Published by Crown Forum, New York, New York.
Member of the Crown Publishing Group, a division of Random House, Inc.
www.crownpublishing.com

CROWN FORUM and the Crown Forum colophon are trademarks of
Random House, Inc.

Printed in the United States of America

Design by Karen Minster

Library of Congress Cataloging-in-Publication Data
Flynn, Daniel J.
Intellectual morons : how ideology makes smart people fall for stupid ideas / Daniel J. Flynn.
Includes bibliographical references and index.
1. Ideology—United States. 2. Radicalism—United States. I. Title.
HM641.F59   2004
303.48'4—dc22   2004016871

ISBN 1-4000-5355-2

10 9 8 7 6 5 4 3 2 1

First Edition

To my mother, Janet Flynn,
who read to me.

~

To my father, Ronald Flynn,
who led a reader's life.

Contents

INTELLECTUAL MORONS

"THE TRUE BELIEVER"

*A faith is not acquired by reasoning. One does not fall in love with
a woman, or enter the womb of a church, as a result of logical persuasion.
Reason may defend an act of faith—but only after the act has
been committed, and the man committed to the act.*

—Arthur Koestler,
The God That Failed

WHEN IDEOLOGY IS YOUR GUIDE, YOU'RE BOUND TO GET LOST.
Ideology deludes, inspires dishonesty, and breeds fanaticism. Facts, experience, and logic are much better at leading you to truth. Truth, however, is not everyone's intended destination.

This is a book about morons. The morons that we'll meet don't have tobacco juice dripping from their chins, sunburned necks, or any other stereotypical manifestations of dimness. As the title suggests, *Intellectual Morons* focuses on cognitive elites who embarrass themselves by championing idiotic theories, beliefs, and opinions. It is a quite pedestrian occurrence for stupid people to fall for stupid ideas. More interesting, and of greater harm to society, is the phenomenon of smart people falling for stupid ideas. Ph.D.s, high IQs, and intellectual honors are not antidotes to thickheadedness.

It doesn't matter how smart you are if you don't use your mind. Ideologues forgo independent judgment in favor of having their views handed to them. To succumb to ideology is to put your brain on autopilot. Ideology preordains your reaction to issues, ideas, and people, your view of politics, philosophy, economics, and history. For the true believer, ideology is the Rosetta Stone of everything. It provides stock answers, conditions responses, and delivers one-size-fits-all explanations for complex political and cultural questions. Despite the conviction and seeming depth of knowledge with which ideologues speak, they are intellectual weaklings—joiners—who defer to systems of belief and charismatic gurus for their ideas. Why bother thinking when the guru provides all the answers? What's the use of examining the facts when the system has already determined the real truth?

When you submit to a guru, allow a system to predetermine your views, or become a knee-jerk party-liner, you abdicate your responsibility to think. For an intellectual, this is the unforgivable sin. Intellectuals think. This is what they do. When intellectuals let ideology do their thinking, we can't with any justification continue to label them intellectuals. This is not an anti-intellectual book. It is an antipseudo-intellectual book.

And many obviously bright political leaders, academicians, journalists, and artists reveal themselves as pseudo-intellectuals.

Why does Al Gore believe that cars pose "a mortal threat to the security of every nation"?[1] Why do feminist leaders defend accused wife-killer Scott Peterson against charges of killing his unborn son?[2] Why do seemingly well-educated antiwar activists see President George W. Bush "exactly as a Hitler," argue that the U.S. government orchestrated the 9/11 attacks, and liken America to "a stuck-up little bitch"?[3] Why does the intellectual godfather of the animal-rights movement, Princeton professor Peter Singer, object to humans eating animals but not to humans having sex with them—and why does the activist group PETA defend that position?[4]

In other words, why do smart people fall for stupid ideas?

The answer is ideology.

SYSTEMS

Communism, environmentalism, animal rights, sexual anarchism, feminism, postmodernism, multiculturalism, relativism, deconstructionism—foreign ideologies to most people—have been embraced without scrutiny by intellectuals at various points during the past century. The intelligentsia's enthusiasm for these isms has made it easier for them to overlook the shortcomings of those most closely identified with these systems. The ideologies themselves also get a pass, since their advocates dominate the fields that generally hold ideas up to scrutiny. Since this book argues against formulas, it is fitting that several of the systems and gurus discussed don't fit into this formula. Both Objectivists and Straussians, ideologues on the political Right, operate outside of normal intellectual circles. But like the other ideologues discussed, they function inside a cloistered environment shielded from outside criticism. Society should be so lucky as to be guarded from these isms as the isms are from society, but an ideology's blockers only seem to screen incoming ideas.

The primary and most obvious reason people join mass movements and follow ideology is the issues they address. To view all ideologues as entirely tricked or self-deluded overlooks the fact that at the core of many ideologies is a laudable idea, whether it is the need for a clean environment, a better understanding of other cultures, or equality of opportunity for the sexes. Naturally, people want to correct the failings they see around them. But dangers arise when the perceived morality of the mission allows immorality—lying for the cause, forcing the "good" upon society, self-righteousness, and so on—to corrupt the crusaders. Problems also occur when activists mistake any cause bearing their ideology's name for a noble one. It is intentions rather than outcomes that matter for such people. Thus we must separate the ideological nonsense from the good idea it clings to.

Can't we support equality of opportunity for women while opposing Andrea Yates–style "fourth-trimester" abortions? Does support for a multicultural outlook mean holding your tongue regarding the practice of female genital mutilation, AIDS-curing sex with virgins in South Africa, and Middle Eastern "honor" killings? Can't one be against cruelty to animals and still enjoy a tunafish sandwich?

To the ideologue, the answer is no. All the ideology—the good, the bad, and the ugly—is a package deal.

Defining one's position based on what serves the cause makes the party line triumphant. Allegations of sexual impropriety against Senator Bob Packwood, Supreme Court nominee Clarence Thomas, and California gubernatorial candidate Arnold Schwarzenegger—all Republicans—sparked angry campaigns to oust these men from political life. When women accused Bill Clinton of sexual harassment, indecent exposure, and even rape, the same Democrats who rabidly attacked Packwood, Thomas, and Schwarzenegger reflexively defended the president. Hypocrisy is, of course, bipartisan. One president with a (D) next to his name sponsors humanitarian missions in Haiti, Bosnia, and Somalia and the opposition blasts him for "nation building." His successor, who sports an (R) next to his name, does the same thing to a greater degree in Afghanistan, Iraq, and Haiti and his party's stalwarts cheer him. What matters to the party-liners in both cases is not the issue involved but how that issue can be used to damage political opponents. "The issue is not the issue," 1960s radicals famously remarked.[5] It still isn't, unfortunately.

Ideologues are prone to mistaking their ideal for the real. Whether consciously or not, they tend to see what they want to see and to find what they want to find. The impulse to evaluate reality by how it vindicates the greater theory leads to a selective use of facts, cooking the books, and simply making things up when the facts don't cooperate. In other words, ideologues draw conclusions prior to investigating. Smaller truths pale in comparison with the importance of the larger "truth," the ideology.

What never fails inside the mind of an intellectual never works outside the confines of his head. The world's stubborn refusal to vindicate the intellectual's theories serves as proof of humanity's irrationality, not his own. Thus, the true believer retrenches rather than rethinks; he launches a war on the world, denying reality because it fails to conform to his theories. If intellectuals are not prepared to reconcile theory and practice, then why do they bother to venture outside the ivory tower or the coffeehouse? Why not stay in the world of abstractions and fantasy?

From an early age, smart people are reminded of their intelligence, separated from their peers in gifted classes, and presented with opportunities unavailable to others. For these and other reasons, intellectuals tend to have an inflated sense of their own wisdom. It is thus arrogance, and not intelligence, that leads them into trouble. They're so smart, hubris compels them to believe, that they can run everyone else's life. But no one is that smart. What's more, theorists devising systems for the rest of us to live under often have a difficult time running their own lives. Mundane tasks are to them what quantum physics is to the rest of us.

"To make of human affairs a coherent, precise, predictable whole one must ignore or suppress man as he really is," social theorist Eric Hoffer observed. "It is by eliminating man from their equation that the makers of history can predict the future, and the writers of history can give a pattern to the past."[6]

Systems fail because the notion of a single idea directing, ordering, and planning the lives of vast numbers of people is an absurd one. Human beings are too independent, and the fact that there are more than 6 billion of us makes applying one system to all of mankind an idiot's endeavor. Tolerance for the failed idea rarely wanes. Tolerance for the humans invariably does. When the masses balk, elites impose their will. After all, they know what's best for us.

The same impulse that pushes men to believe arrogantly that a system can plan the affairs of whole nations leads them to think that a theory can explain all of history. Single-bullet theories of history rarely pan out. The attraction of such explanations is their simplicity. They relieve adherents from any obligation to think. The answers are preordained. "Human nature," sociologist Raymond Aron reminds us, "is not very amenable to the wishes of the ideologists."[7]

Why has ideology taken such a powerful hold over so many smart people? Humans desire meaning in their life. With the decline of religion among the well-educated, intellectuals increasingly look for meaning outside the church, temple, and mosque. Ideology can fill this void. It bestows an easy-to-understand explanation for the way the world works. It supplies a moral code, membership in a community, and a vocation. The new religions exalt secular saints, enforce dogma, punish heretics, value self-sacrifice, and sanctify writings. In short, ideology serves as a proxy religion for people who view themselves as too smart for traditional religion. And since worshiping a god is an impossible task for the self-obsessed, the intellectual moron worships himself—man—and the ideas that will deliver us all into salvation.

Seeing ideology in this light—as a substitute for religion—explains quite a bit. The ideologue believes he possesses a truth others have missed—for the more audacious true believers, the key to earthly redemption. Ideology contains no such power, but if you believed that it did, dishonesty, repression, murder, and other sins might be seen as a mere pittance to pay when you're providing deliverance to humanity. When you're saving the world, what's wrong with telling a few lies? If you're making heaven on earth, what's wrong with sacrificing a few people to save the rest? But heaven is in heaven and not on earth, and demands for human sacrifice necessarily make any cause suspect.

GURUS

Behind the bad ideas that have poisoned politics and culture stands ideology. Behind ideology stand gurus—the popularizers and founders of the theoretical systems that have done great mischief by misleading people. These are the ones who have planted the many harmful and false ideas that have taken root in our society. We must naturally go back to these gurus to examine the roots of those bad ideas. Only by looking at the ideas and those who propagated them—and when, where, why, and how they did so—can we begin to clean up the mess that the ideas have unleashed.

Intellectual Morons examines the mendacity and foolishness of those who have had a far-reaching impact on the world through ideas. The progenitors of these stupid ideas are in some cases the leaders of massive popular movements. Others have had monuments erected in their honor. The majority have authored books that have sold in excess of a million copies. They are not bohemians relegated to the fringes of society. They are the paragons of establishment respectability.

So who are the generals leading armies of intellectual morons?

Alfred Kinsey, Margaret Sanger, and Michel Foucault propagated a notion of sex without consequences. Those "liberated" from antiquarian ideas regarding sex soon found themselves chained to unplanned offspring, incurable diseases, and personal emptiness. Kinsey, Sanger, and Foucault peddled falsehoods to alter the prevailing morality to accommodate their own unconventional behavior. They needn't change; the world should. Kinsey knowingly perpetrated a fraud, shouting "Science!" to silence skeptics. Similarly, Planned Parenthood founder Sanger simplistically branded any opponent of her agenda as a tool of the Catholic Church. Like Icarus flying too close to the sun, Foucault pushed the limits of sexuality and paid for it with his life. All three shared a penchant for damning their critics as troglodytes standing athwart progress.

Feminist matriarch Betty Friedan covered up her life in the Communist fold and fabricated an everywoman, housewife persona to legitimize her ideas. Years later, when victimhood became all the rage in feminist circles, she leveled, then retracted, a charge of spousal abuse. Despite her celebrity status, many of her claims went unchecked by journalists and academics for decades.

Soviet spy Alger Hiss lied for the most primal of reasons: to save his skin. It is hardly unusual for someone facing years in a federal penitentiary to obfuscate the crimes he has committed. What are we to make of his supporters?

Noam Chomsky, Howard Zinn, and Gore Vidal have spent the better part of their long lives portraying the nation that has protected their freedoms as the base of worldwide oppression. The self-refuting nature of their work has never dawned on them. Vidal's jaundiced view sees America operating behind the curtains during the 9/11 attacks and the Oklahoma City bombing. Zinn penned a million-selling America-bashing history that reads more like fiction. Chomsky overlooked the very real sins of anti-American governments but saw with amazing clarity nonexistent offenses committed by the United States. The MIT professor denied Pol Pot's mass killings in Cambodia, for example, but imagined a "silent genocide" conducted by the United States against Afghanistan. The trio has never lost faith in their theories, only in reality.

Nobel Peace Prize winner Rigoberta Menchu peddled falsehoods to enhance her credibility as spokeswoman of the oppressed. When caught, she simply dismissed her accusers as racists. This was a sufficient explanation for her academic admirers, who continue to assign her book as if nothing has changed.

Like the street-corner evangelist, biologist Paul Ehrlich warns of the proximity of doomsday. Giving Ehrlich the benefit of the doubt, one could say that he never intended to deceive others. Perhaps his many predictions for environmental apocalypse were merely wrong. That he continued to issue such dire forecasts after deadlines for earlier predictions came and went is a sign that Ehrlich should have been dismissed. He wasn't. He gained celebrity and credibility from the media, higher education, and the world of philanthropy. The more wild and inaccurate his declarations, the greater his stature became. Since Ehrlich issues his proclamations from Stanford University, and not from a sidewalk pulpit, the intelligentsia confuses his delusional fanaticism for wisdom.

W.E.B. Du Bois looked for heaven on earth behind the Iron Curtain and, like most ideologically motivated searchers, found what he was looking for. At one time or another, the NAACP cofounder offered praise for just about every bad idea that came along in the twentieth century—Communism, Nazism, racial separatism, and eugenics, to name but a few. Du Bois's academic cheerleaders revise history to manufacture a civil rights hero who never existed.

In a more enlightened time, advocating infanticide as humane while condemning Thanksgiving dinner as something akin to murder might have suggested a mild form of insanity. Today, it earns Peter Singer an endowed professorship at Princeton University.

Ayn Rand launched a philosophy that elevated her own opinion to holy writ, immodestly naming it Objectivism. In the process, she sold tens of millions of books and established a global following. The best Objectivists ironically were the ones who imitated Rand most closely, right down to her Russian accent. Rand liked smoking, so lighting up became obligatory for her acolytes. Rand hated Shakespeare, so her followers denounced the Bard while partaking in *Charlie's Angels*, what she called "tiddlywink music," Ian Fleming spy novels, and any other low-church indulgence that Rand found pleasurable. Rand sought to prove the perfectibility of man, but her life instead demonstrated how human we all are.

Europeans Jacques Derrida, Leo Strauss, and Herbert Marcuse put forth theoretical frameworks that attempted to legitimize dishonesty as a form of expression. The topsy-turvy world of Marcuse directed readers to see intolerance as tolerance, violence as nonviolence, and totalitarianism as freedom. Derrida leads a gang of literary critics that exhorts connoisseurs of the written word to read into texts any meaning desired, regardless of the author's intent. Leo Strauss, the Right's house deconstructionist, remains the only figure associated with contemporary conservatism to gain a major following within academia. Strauss purported to discover hidden meanings in the works of great philosophers by relying on numerology and encoded silences. When several of his followers occupied key positions within the executive branch of the U.S. government prior to 2003's Iraq war, the consequences of this crackpot ideology proved greater than fostering ignorance of long-dead philosophers.

"If you're on the wrong road," C. S. Lewis famously wrote, "progress means doing an about-turn and walking back to the right road; and in that case the man who turns back soonest is the most progressive man."[8] For too long, intellectuals have been traveling briskly down the wrong paths, taking the rest of us along for the ride. It's time to get off and turn back, quickly.

To fix what's wrong with politics and culture by laboring for the victory or defeat of a particular candidate or piece of legislation is merely to chop away at branches that will grow back. Real change will come only when we unearth the roots of the bad ideas holding sway over countless academics, journalists, artists, government officials, and other elites.

JOINERS

Joiners rarely have more than a surface knowledge of the issues in which they involve themselves. What they lack in knowledge, they make up for in passion. Every reader has come across the joiner, the person who shifts every conversation to the favored cause of the moment, attends massive group-therapy sessions commonly referred to as protests, and decorates his car with various bumper stickers. To the automobile's owner, pithy lines like "Keep Your Rosaries Out of Our Ovaries" and "Hate Is Not a Family Value" clearly express his views. To everyone else, the myriad slogans blur, and only one message stands out: The owner of this car is a screwball.

The celebrity joiner is always sure to wear the appropriate ribbon, use an acceptance speech to ramble on about a political cause, and serially affix his name to diverse petitions. Susan Sarandon, Michael Stipe, Alec Baldwin, Ed Asner, Jane Fonda, and Yoko Ono are a few who qualify for the celebrity joiner hall of fame.

Even the joiner's inability to abide by the ideology's dictates fails to persuade her of possible flaws in the secular faith.

- "I think the only people in this nation who should be allowed to own guns are the police officers," proclaimed Rosie O'Donnell. "I don't care if you want to hunt. I don't care if you think it's your right. I say, 'Sorry. It is 1999. We have had enough as a nation. You are not allowed to own a gun,' and if you do own a gun I think you should go to prison."[9] After making these remarks, Million Mom Marcher Number One made headlines when her bodyguards sought concealed-weapons permits to protect her children when they went to school.[10]

- Megabucks populist Arianna Huffington ran for governor of California charging that "corporate fat cats get away with not paying their fair share of taxes." She should know. The tightfisted Huffington paid no state income taxes in 2001 and 2002 and handed over a meager $771 to the Internal Revenue Service during the same period.[11]

- Michael Moore excoriates big business for exporting jobs, weakening unions, and offering miserly pay and benefits. In his own business dealings, Moore proves more flexible. The *Roger and Me* director outsourced the design and hosting of his website to Canadian companies. Sporting the poseur fashion of scruffy jeans and his trademark baseball cap, the man behind *Fahrenheit 9/11* lives in a multimillion-dollar Manhattan condo, demands first-class flights and five-star hotels, and sends his daughter to a posh school. One Hollywood source states, "Michael's the greediest man I've ever met." Former employees describe the work environment Moore created as "a sweatshop," "indentured servitude," and a "concentration camp." According to former workers, union scale, health care, humane hours, and even pay for services rendered were at times hard to come by for some in Moore's shop. A writer for the short-lived *TV Nation* remembered Moore explaining to a pair of writers, "[I]f you want to be in this union, only one of you can work here."[12] For GM's Roger Smith, such behavior warranted an attackumentary.

- Self-proclaimed environmentalist Barbra Streisand laments our "unsustainable way of life" and declares that decreasing "fossil fuel emissions" is "the most important thing that we can do today."[13] But Streisand owns an SUV, trades shares in the oil and gas company Halliburton, and occasionally travels in a forty-five-foot mobile home that gets less than ten miles to the gallon.[14] In a case thrown out of court, Streisand actually sued an environmental activist for posting a picture of her beachfront home on the Internet to document coastal erosion.[15]

They're excessive, but can we blame Rosie for providing safety to her children, Arianna for keeping the money she earned, Moore for preferring Big Apple glitz to factory-town tedium, or Babs for living in comfort? But if the advocate can't live under the system, why must we? The cognitive dissonance should spark the joiner to reassess the tenability of her position, but it rarely does.

Joiners mistake great passion for great wisdom. They are more persuaded by the volume and pitch of an argument than by the logic and facts behind it. The bolder and brasher the pronouncement, the better it sounds in the true believer's ears. Initiates speak an insider language. The ideologically elect demonstrate more concern for proving their ideological bona fides than for effectively communicating ideas to outsiders. *Patriarchy, proletariat, whim-worshiper,* words that would be about as meaningful to most listeners if spoken in Martian, are liberally tossed about by the joiner to enhance his credibility within his particular circle. In addition to buzzwords, the ideologue peppers his speech with mantras, slogans, and other mindless bromides.

Movements attract misfits. The desire to change the world usually corresponds with personal unhappiness. The frustrated man, not the self-contented one, goes about altering his surroundings. He would do better changing himself, but egomania prevails and fosters a less rational cure for his troubles. Mass movements also attract misfits because they take all comers. Someone who finds it difficult to make friends, or to fill in any of the 365 empty dates on his social calendar, is relieved of these problems by remaining obedient to the Cause. The individual who doesn't thrive as an individual longs to be part of something bigger. The Cause allows him to belong to the group, but naturally takes his individuality in the process. As the joiner loses his identity amid the mass, adversaries lose their individuality—their humanity—in the eyes of the joiner.

Apostate Communist Stephen Spender, writing in *The God That Failed*, recognized this aspect of mass movements. "[W]hen men have decided to pursue a course of action," Spender wrote, "everything which seems to support this seems vivid and real; everything which stands against it becomes abstraction. Your friends are allies and therefore real human beings with flesh and blood and sympathies like yourself. Your opponents are just tiresome, unreasonable, unnecessary theses, whose lives are so many false statements which you would like to strike out with a lead bullet as you would put the stroke of a lead pencil through a bungled paragraph."[16] In other words, in pursuit of ostensibly humanitarian ends, the true believer sees no contradiction in wiping out other humans.

The religious nature of ideology spawns an odd character—the ismist, the true believer who floats from one ideology to the next. For the ismist, the ideas expressed hardly matter in comparison with being a part of something, belonging. Hence, we witness the spectacle of rabid Communists transforming into virulent anti-Communists, Objectivists becoming Scientologists, and religious conservatives morphing into gay activists—any cause will do.

To question the joiner's faith is to mark oneself as an enemy. Mocking the guru or challenging the system puts the ideologue on the defensive, and not merely regarding his worldview. The joiner, whose submission to the guru's teaching is often rewarded with automatic friends, a newfound social life, and restored purpose, views the heretic as a threat to all this and defends accordingly.

"To rely on the evidence of the senses and of reason is heresy and treason," Eric Hoffer noted regarding the ways of fanatics. "It is startling to realize how much unbelief is necessary to make belief possible."[17] In his midcentury classic *The True Believer*, Hoffer depicted the mass-movement fanatic as one seeking to escape from the self by means of enlisting in a world-saving cause, one that he would kill or die for. His glorious ends justify his despicable means. The ideologue's faith seems impenetrable: "At the root of [the fanatic's] cockiness is the conviction that life and the universe conform to a simple formula—his formula."[18] The true believers Hoffer described are just like the ones we find today. Times have changed but not much else.

THE COSTS

It is folly to blame "bad" ideology for the current degraded state of the public square. The problem isn't necessarily Left ideology or Right ideology, but all ideology. Anyone who abandons rational analysis for the dictates of a governing philosophy is bound to be led astray. To the ideologue, what matters is not whether an idea is good or bad, harmful or beneficial, or true or false. What matters is whether it can serve the Cause.

There is great danger when lies are institutionalized as truth. Ideas, Richard Weaver famously wrote, have consequences. Men of action adopt ideas and put them into practice. Civilization suffers the repercussions of bad ideas. The evils this past century witnessed are not historical constants. The concentration camps and the gulag, total war, and Big Brother's garrison state came about because bad ideas wrought bad consequences. These were anything but accidents. Closer to our time and place, unparented children, well-traveled venereal diseases, and dissipating freedoms—to smoke, to own firearms, to drive without the government's robotic paparazzi tracking you—result from the implementation of some scribbler's fantasy of how the rest of us should live. Ideology makes us susceptible to pernicious and false ideas, because true believers never view evidence of the system's failure as just that. In the face of failure, ideologues have a vested interest to claim success.

Ideology acts as a mental straitjacket. It prevents adherents from seeing reality, encourages zealotry, and justifies dishonesty. It makes smart people stupid.

In Plato's *Phaedrus*, the unjustified warnings regarding book learning seem more appropriate to the intellectual morons we find today: "They will appear omniscient and will generally know nothing; they will be tiresome, having the reputation of knowledge without the reality."[19] This is a fitting epigraph for those discussed in the following pages.

"FICTION CALLS THE FACTS BY THEIR NAME"

The New Left's Pop Philosopher

There is, indeed, a very close analogy between words and coins,
both quintessentially human creations. A word, when fresh-minted,
has the objectivity and innocence of a legal penny. Handled by men,
it is soon subjected to the processes of inflation or deflation,
and acquires moral or immoral characteristics.

— PAUL JOHNSON,
Enemies of Society

ALMOST HALFWAY THROUGH THE TWENTIETH CENTURY, GEORGE
Orwell published his classic novel, *1984.* Orwell described a society that
exhibited an extreme form of political correctness before such a phrase
had entered common parlance. At the time of its printing, *1984*'s futuris-
tic dystopia of Oceania mirrored the totalitarianism that had swept across
Eastern Europe.

Orwell's biting prose, which had earlier made him a hero of the intelligentsia when he penned such vehement denunciations of British colo-
nialism as "Shooting an Elephant" and "A Hanging," now transformed
him into an object of hate among those who still believed that a City upon
a Hill existed between the Carpathians and the Urals. Winston Smith, the
protagonist of *1984,* finds himself in a society where euphemisms are the
staple of language. The Ministry of Truth's main purpose is to spread lies.
Forced labor camps are renamed "joycamps." The party's slogans—WAR
IS PEACE, FREEDOM IS SLAVERY, IGNORANCE IS STRENGTH—reflect a world
where the meaning of words is topsy-turvy. There is even a name for this
new language: Newspeak.

Real-life Oceanias are not hard to find. Walk onto any of a great number of college campuses today and life imitates art. University administrators and professors preach the gospel of "tolerance" but are completely intolerant of anyone who might challenge the liberal orthodoxy.

Examples abound. At Cornell University, when a mob of student activists burned hundreds of copies of the conservative campus newspaper—copies they had stolen—the dean of students attended the newspaper burning to show his support for torching free speech. Moreover, a Cornell spokesperson defended not the conservative newspaper's right to free speech but rather the liberal activists' right to theft and newspaper torching: "The students who oppose the *Cornell Review* have claimed their First Amendment right to be able to have symbolic burnings of the *Cornell Review.*"[1] Administrator John Smeaton banned displays of the American flag by Lehigh University employees after glimpsing the Stars and Stripes adorning a campus bus on 9/11. Speaking fluent Newspeak, the insensitive vice provost maintained, "The message was supposed to be that we are sensitive to everyone."[2] At Minnesota's St. Cloud State University, the university president forced a student journalist to undergo "multicultural sensitivity training conducted by Multicultural Student Services" merely for arguing, perhaps illogically, that banning credit card companies from campus is illegal in the same way that banning blacks is illegal. The public condemnation of the student and the punishment meted out would "teach others the lesson of tolerance," said the intolerant school leader.[3]

The ancient university mottoes *veritas* and *lux et veritas* weren't always empty slogans. But today they've yielded to intolerance advertised as tolerance, politics disguised as scholarship, indoctrination calling itself education, and other phenomena that inhibit the search for truth. In some classrooms, ignorance is indeed strength.

The person most responsible for this development is a German émigré named Herbert Marcuse (1898–1979), who preached that freedom is totalitarianism, democracy is dictatorship, education is indoctrination, violence is nonviolence, and fiction is truth. Nothing better sums up the modern academic Left's Orwellian dishonesty than what Marcuse called "liberating tolerance," which he defined as "intolerance against movements from the Right, and toleration of movements from the Left."[4] Even if today's professors, administrators, and campus activists haven't read anything Herbert Marcuse wrote—and many of them haven't—his ideas are nonetheless pervasive. His influence is so profound that the denizens of academe carry out his marching orders without ever getting them from the original source.

It is not terribly unusual to hear lies told in the service of ideology. Far more extraordinary is forming an ideology that serves to codify lying as a legitimate form of discourse. This is precisely what Herbert Marcuse did.

Marcuse was the pop philosopher of the New Left. He allegedly coined the catchphrase "Make Love, Not War," but even if he didn't, that spirit certainly dripped off the pages of several of his books.[5] When Parisian students revolted in May of 1968, they carried signs reading "Marx/Mao/Marcuse" as they tore apart the city.[6] In America he came to even more renown—or notoriety, depending on one's perspective—as the mentor of Angela Davis, the militant fugitive whose manhunt, capture, and trial on charges of murder and conspiracy created a media sensation. One Marcuse admirer ventured to guess that "among pure scholars he had the most direct and profound effect on historical events of any individual in the twentieth century."[7]

THE FRANKFURT SCHOOL

The sage of campus radicals in '60s America got his start in Weimar Germany, developing his outlook at the Institute of Social Research. Established in 1923, the institute was to be called the Institute for Marxism, but its founders quickly saw the political disadvantages in such a blatantly ideological name for a scholarly endeavor. In addition to Marcuse, the group boasted a circle of intellectual luminaries that included Max Horkheimer, Walter Benjamin, Erich Fromm, Theodor Adorno, Leo Lowenthal, and Georg Lukacs. Although his colleagues viewed him for many years as an inferior, Marcuse's star would in time eclipse the institute's entire constellation.

By the 1960s, outsiders had begun referring to this gang of scholars as the Frankfurt School, in deference to the German city, and university, whence they came. The Frankfurt School was multidisciplinary. Sociologists, philosophers, literary critics, psychologists, and specialists in numerous fields made up its ranks. The common denominator linking its followers was Critical Theory, a term that Horkheimer first used in his 1937 essay "Traditional and Critical Theory." Critical Theory, as its name implies, criticizes. What deconstruction does to literature, Critical Theory does to societies. Critical Theory does not offer a positive alternative to what it is criticizing and thus itself avoids criticism—except, of course, the inevitable complaints about its reliance on accentuating the negative regarding societies, people, and ideas critical theorists don't like.

Marcuse and his cohorts expanded Marx's fetishization of the worker to include minorities, women, homosexuals, and other "outsider" groups. Mixing Freud with Marx, they psychoanalyzed Western civilization from a socialist outlook and recommended overhauling not just the economic system, but the family, patriotism, and organized religion too. By applying the principles of Communism to matters beyond economics, the Frankfurt School ensured that Marx's ideas wouldn't die if traditional Communism lost its luster.

Herbert Marcuse formally became associated with the Institute of Social Research in 1932. Shortly thereafter, the Nazis ascended to power in Germany. If not for the near-universal Jewish identity of the institute's members, then certainly for their association with Marxism, most of those connected with the Frankfurt School wisely fled Germany. The Nazis seized the house shared by two critical theorists and converted it into a barracks; they turned the institute itself over to the Nazi Student League.[8] The institute relocated, first to Geneva, then to Columbia University in New York City. The Frankfurt School's emigration to the United States and not to the Soviet Union, and its return after the defeat of the Nazis to capitalist West Germany and not to one of the multitude of Communist nations, speaks volumes about the divide between theory and practice among its leaders.

Other contradictions arose. Even while they railed against capitalism, the Cultural Marxists had difficulty applying to themselves the ideas they wanted to impose on others. For all the talk of Marxist systems, the institute severed its ties with Leo Lowenthal because he dared ask for a pension, and by 1950 the institute's director enjoyed a salary seven times higher than what lower-level employees made.[9] In fact, nearly all of the Frankfurt School's major players personally enjoyed the perks of capitalism. Stock quotes adorned a whole wall in Friedrich Pollack's office.[10] Meanwhile, Herbert Marcuse lived a life of leisure because he was subsidized by his father, who owned a construction company; his father paid for his apartment and provided him with part ownership of a book business. Likewise, Theodor Adorno enjoyed the generous support of his parents well into adulthood. Max Horkheimer was the son of a millionaire industrialist. Jurgen Habermas's father served as the director of the local chamber of commerce.[11] Were these men rebelling against the bourgeoisie, or their parents? Their lavish upbringings do much to explain why these trust-fund revolutionaries never really connected with the workers. Worse, the institute gladly took capitalist blood money from the Rockefeller Foundation, and it even accepted a contract from a company that had generously contributed to the Nazi Party and had helped take over factories in conquered nations. A sympathetic historian of the Frankfurt School somewhat understatedly labels this a "serious lapse."[12]

Traditional Communists found the institute's unorthodox Marxism heretical. The Cultural Marxists, however, were hardly political free spirits. Many associates of the Frankfurt School were committed Communist Party members, a few even Soviet spies.[13] The Communist Party directed Georg Lukacs, whose wife was a terrorist in czarist Russia, to denounce his book *History and Class Consciousness* after its publication in 1923 because portions of it offended powerful ears in Moscow.[14] When another institute scholar dared criticize Hitler during the Nazi-Soviet pact, historian Martin Jay notes that his book "was suppressed by its own publishers and copies already printed were recovered if at all possible."[15] Rarely did the practitioners of Critical Theory focus their criticism on the Communist world. Prior to World War II, Theodor Adorno advised, "in the current situation, which is truly desperate, one should really maintain discipline at any cost (and no one knows the cost better than I!) and not publish anything which might damage Russia."[16]

Marcuse himself was even more deferential to the Soviets. In 1947, he argued that the Nazi defeat in World War II didn't change the precarious situation:

> The Communist Parties are, and will remain, the sole anti-fascist power. Denunciation of them must be purely theoretical. Such denunciation is conscious of the fact that the realization of the theory is only possible through the Communist Parties, and requires the assistance of the Soviet Union. This awareness must be contained in each of its words. Further: in each of its words, the denunciation of neo-fascism and Social Democracy must outweigh denunciation of Communist policy. The bourgeois freedom of democracy is better than totalitarian regimentation, but it has literally been bought at the price of decades of prolonged exploitation and by the obstruction of socialist freedom.[17]

Deviationists paid a price. One unfortunate exponent of Critical Theory who had spent time in Stalin's gulag and Hitler's concentration camps did speak out against Communist subversion in the United States. Karl Wittfogel named names. His longtime colleagues subsequently shunned him.[18]

In its most ambitious project, the Frankfurt School took advantage of the postwar zeitgeist that mistook social science for real science. Arguably the Frankfurt School's most famous work, the 1950 book *The Authoritarian Personality*, reported that America was potentially on the brink of fascism because of personality traits within individuals that had been developed by the family, religion, capitalism, and patriotism. The authors' methods were hardly scientific. Relying on Americans' responses to a special questionnaire to prove their thesis, they maintained that agreement with certain statements on the questionnaire indicated an affinity for authoritarianism. One such statement was "Now that a new world organization is set up, America must be sure that she loses none of her independence and complete power as a separate nation."[19] But what the authors took to be signs of fascism were merely indications of conservatism. In fact, they inadvertently betrayed this bias, for in one instance they argued that agreement with a particular statement indicated potential fascism, but elsewhere they said that agreement with the same statement was a sign of conservatism.[20] Writing about *The Authoritarian Personality*, a historian of the Frankfurt School asked, "Was it not, therefore, merely the prejudices of left-wing academics, who wanted to discredit political and economic conservatism by demonstrating a correlation between ethnocentrism and fascist character structures, which were being disproved?"[21]

This was the "scientific" background out of which Herbert Marcuse emerged. But over time, Marcuse would do much to separate himself from his Frankfurt School brethren. Most members of the Institute of Social Research, and the institute itself, returned to Germany after World War II, but Marcuse stayed in America. There, he would go on to greater fame and influence than his fellow critical theorists.

SEX, DRUGS, AND ROCK 'N' ROLL

Before becoming the savant of the New Left ragtag, Marcuse tried his hand at a number of pursuits. He had served in the German military during World War I, in the U.S. Office of War Information and the Office of Strategic Services during the Second World War, and in the U.S. State Department for several years after the war. Still, he attained his greatest influence in the world of academia. In the 1950s he held positions at

Harvard, Yale, and Columbia, and in 1954 he began an eleven-year stint at the infant Brandeis University. There he would publish his two most famous works, *Eros and Civilization* and *One-Dimensional Man*. By the time he arrived in Southern California to begin teaching at the University of California at San Diego in 1965, he was already being viewed as the intellectual guru of the counterculture.

And for good reason. He taught his followers the virtues of poor hygiene and a "body unsoiled by plastic cleanliness."[22] To practice nonviolence in the age of the Black Panthers, the Weathermen, and the Symbionese Liberation Army, he proclaimed, was to commit acts of violence against the establishment. Speaking of such groups, Marcuse contended, "If they use violence, they do not start a new chain of violence but try to break an established one."[23] He spoke directly to radical firebrands, sometimes being careful to rescind earlier commands. For example, in 1972's *Counterrevolution and Revolt* he informed readers that his earlier emphasis on the "political potential" of swearwords had perhaps been misguided. "The verbalization of the genital and anal sphere, which has become a ritual in left-radical speech (the 'obligatory' use of 'fuck,' 'shit') is a *debasement* of sexuality," he castigated. "If a radical says, 'Fuck Nixon,' he associates the word for highest genital gratification with the highest representative of the oppressive Establishment, and 'shit' for the products of the Enemy takes over the bourgeois rejection of anal eroticism."[24] Heavy stuff!

It isn't just the Newspeak of *1984* that Marcuse's writings evoke. The famous Orwell witticism—that some ideas are so absurd that only an intellectual could believe them—often comes to mind when one tumbles through a Marcuse essay. Yet intellectuals were not the only ones reading Marcuse's work. His message had broader appeal, for he called for something the counterculture could relate to: the pursuit of pleasure.

Marx argued against the exploitation of labor; Marcuse, against labor itself. Don't work, have sex. This was the simple message of *Eros and Civilization*, released in 1955. Its ideas proved to be extraordinarily popular among the fledgling hippie culture of the following decade. It provided a rationale for laziness and transformed degrading personal vices into virtues.

The book took Freud and turned him on his head. Marcuse agreed with the German psychologist that civilization is the result of the repression of animal instincts, like the sex drive. He disagreed, however, that civilization is a good thing. What the author mined from Freud he mixed with his unique interpretation of Marx. "To each according to his needs" was updated to include not just material needs but pleasure's "needs" as well.

In a later book, whose literary style was much more conducive to being understood by his youthful audience, Marcuse described his reinterpretation of Marx:

> In Marxian theory, originally, impoverishment meant privation, unsatisfied vital needs, first of all material needs. When this concept no longer described the condition of the working classes in the advanced industrial countries, it was reinterpreted in terms of relative deprivation: relative to the available social wealth, cultural impoverishment. However, this reinterpretation suggests a fallacious continuity in the transition to socialism, namely, the amelioration of life within the existing universe of needs. But what is at stake in the socialist revolution is not merely the extension of satisfaction within the existing universe of needs, nor the shift of satisfaction from one (lower) level to a higher one, but the rupture with this universe, the *qualitative leap*. The revolution involves a radical transformation of the needs and aspirations themselves, cultural as well as material; of consciousness and sensibility; of the work process as well as leisure.[25]

Doctrinaire Communists cringed at Marcuse's application of Marxist thought to issues that Marx never addressed. In the late 1960s, Marcuse was even forced into hiding because of threats against his life from orthodox Marxists who disdained his call to abandon the workers as the catalyst of the coming revolution (which Marcuse didn't see as coming in the near future anyhow).[26] In the place of the workers—who despised the Marxists, after all—the professor called for a mélange of "victims": racial minorities, women, homosexuals, and so on.

Eros and Civilization posits that man's "labor time, which is the largest part of the individual's life time, is painful time, for alienated labor is absence of gratification, negation of the pleasure principle."[27] The culprit ruining the lives of the citizenry was the technological capitalism that had created the many products that seemed to improve the lives of consumers. The products didn't. They merely forced consumers to work more and more to consume an even greater number of unnecessary vendibles.

The solution was for people to stop working and start doing what felt nice. Marcuse called for "polymorphous sexuality" and "a *transformation* of the libido: from sexuality constrained under genital supremacy to eroticization of the entire personality."[28] Some work would be necessary, he conceded, but only a bare minimum. "Since the length of the working day is itself one of the principal repressive factors imposed upon the pleasure principle by the reality principle," *Eros and Civilization* proclaims, "the reduction of the working day to a point where the mere quantum of labor time no longer arrests human development is the first prerequisite for freedom."[29] Automation would allow for the reduction of toil without losing the benefits of that toil, and the "exchangeability of functions" would make labor all the more tolerable.[30] Marcuse conceded that "a vastly lower standard of living [would occur] if social productivity were redirected toward the universal gratification of individual needs: many would have to give up manipulated comforts if all were to live a human life."[31] This bit of realism amid a scribbler's fantasyland demonstrates the ridiculousness of the whole scenario.

The fantasyland, however, was very popular among academics, and Marcuse's works, particularly *Eros and Civilization*, became a staple of the curriculum in a wide variety of fields. On the book's final page, he preached that "the struggle" for the sexualization of culture "has to be turned into a spiritual and moral struggle."[32] The recent substitution of glandular for intellectual pursuits in such courses as the University of Michigan's "How to Be Gay: Homosexuality and Initiation," Berkeley's "Pornographies On/Scene," and Antioch's "Queer Acts," in which "Drag will be encouraged but not required," is proof that Marcuse's call to arms did not fall on deaf ears in higher education.[33] A parade of MTV tarts, a lecherous cad's eight-year occupation of the White House, and court demands that society endorse relationships between couples of the same sex indicate that Marcuse's "spiritual and moral struggle" has moved beyond academia's ivy-covered walls.

ONE-DIMENSIONAL MAN

A major theme of Marcuse's work, most clearly stated in 1964's *One-Dimensional Man*, is that reality is false and fantasy is truth. The one-dimensional man can only conceptualize the tangible world around him. The enlightened, two-dimensional man can see, in addition to the experienced world, a world of potentiality. The perfect world viewed by two-dimensional man fulfills all the promises of the Marxist ideal. It is this utopia, Marcuse theorized, that is the true universe.

Paintings, novels, poems, plays, and other works of art play a prime role in injecting "true consciousness" into connoisseurs: "Fiction calls the facts by their name and their reign collapses; fiction subverts everyday experience and shows it to be mutilated and false."[34] Examples of the rebellion against reality that Marcuse suggested aren't difficult to find, especially in Hollywood. The noble inmates and sadistic guards in *The Shawshank Redemption*, the virtuous prostitutes in *Pretty Woman*, and the treasonous Marines in *The Rock* evoke a notion of reality so foreign to the dictates of common sense as to make celluloid simian Dr. Cornelius and Tatooine bad-guy Jabba the Hut seem realistic in comparison. If you're a leftist, your life story need be only mildly interesting to warrant a lionizing Tinseltown biopic. *Reds*, *The People v. Larry Flynt*, *Patch Adams*, *Dead Man Walking*, *Malcolm X*, *Frida*, *Born on the Fourth of July*, *Silkwood*, *Gorillas in the Mist*, *Norma Rae*, and *Evita* are just a few examples of Hollywood's hagiography of leftist icons. Where are the movies about Pope John Paul II, Whittaker Chambers, Mother Teresa, and Aleksandr Solzhenitsyn? Is it that they've led less interesting lives than, say, Patch Adams?*

---

*While Hollywood propaganda certainly predated Marcuse's preaching (consider, for example, *Birth of a Nation* and *Mission to Moscow*), its role today as an ingredient in films is often more highly valued than entertainment's role. Take the five films nominated for the Academy Award's Best Picture in 1999. All but one force-fed audiences a heavy-handed political message. *The Green Mile* bemoans the death penalty, while *The Insider*, which lionizes Marcuse by name, tells the story of a left-wing reporter and his source's fight against an evil tobacco corporation. *The Cider House Rules* is the story of a gentle abortionist whose unenlightened apprentice finally gets over his hang-up of being an orphan and learns the virtues of infanticide. Upon receiving an Oscar, its writer thanked Planned Parenthood and the National Abortion Rights Action League. *American Beauty*, an excellent movie that took home the award for best picture, is more effective in its propaganda because it actually entertains. The film is a venomous indictment of American society that skewers the life-draining corporate conformity faced by the husband, the Tony Robbins–style self-improvement of salesmanship adopted by his wife, and the high school inhabited by their daughter that serves to manufacture such people. The only normal family in their neighborhood is a homosexual couple, and the film's villain is a repressed Marine colonel. That the movie's writer and producers were gay activists shocked no one. More recently, Oscar nominees have included the class-warfare whodunit *Gosford Park*, crusading environmentalist biopic *Erin Brockovich*, the boring feminist film *The Hours*, and *Gangs of New York*, yet another cinematic ode to class warfare.

Fictional expression is so appealing to utopians precisely because anything, no matter how ridiculous, can be made to seem realistic. (It's no coincidence that two members of the Frankfurt School actually settled in Hollywood to write for the film industry.) What fails in real-world practice is often an unmitigated success in film, on the stage, or in the pages of a novel. Because the stated goal of a work of fiction is entertainment, the cultural message might be subtle, and as a result it can have a greater impact. Propaganda can be particularly effective in entertainment because people are supposed to suspend reality when they watch sitcoms, movies, plays, and other dramatic performances. With enough theatrical repetition, the abnormal becomes normal, and far-fetched ideas seem plausible.

In Marcuse's world, critical thinking, and even logic, is the enemy. In *One-Dimensional Man* he condemned "the process by which logic became the logic of domination."[35] If an ideal is devoid of sound logic, Marcuse argued, the problem is not always the idea but sometimes logic itself. To Marcuse, logic is a tool of oppression, in no small measure because it can be used to debunk many ideas that he thinks are good ones.

According to Marcuse, *nothing* can debunk his claims. That's the beauty of the system he foisted on his followers. He claimed that the senses distort reality by portraying reality as that which is experienced, and that is why the one-dimensional man, slave to his senses, cannot visualize the Marxist utopia. Thus, he argued, "True knowledge and reason demand domination over—if not liberation from—the senses."[36] Experience and the senses work against true reality. To become enlightened, he reasoned, one must emancipate oneself from these chains of oppression.

Another enemy is the scientific method, which, through its claims of objectivity, denies the reality of utopia. "[T]here is no such thing as a purely rational scientific order; the process of technological rationality is a political process," Marcuse wrote.[37] He reserved special contempt for science, because he deemed it responsible for man's "ever-more-effective domination of nature" and the "ever-more-effective domination of man by man *through* the domination of nature," which brought ecological pollution, military destructiveness, assembly-line conformity, and other maladies.[38]

In keeping with the theme of Critical Theory, Marcuse rationalized that he didn't need to come up with a positive alternative to explain what should replace logic, reason, objectivity, experience, and the other truth-finding methods that he denounced. "We are still confronted with the demand to state the 'concrete alternative,'" he complained years later.

"The demand is meaningless if it asks for a blueprint of the specific institutions and relationships which would be those of the new society."[39]

LIBERATING TOLERANCE

Distraught by the inability of Cultural Marxism to grab hold of the masses in the West, Herbert Marcuse searched for new solutions to bring about the social change he longed for. "[F]ree competition and free exchange of ideas have become a farce," he concluded in the 1960s.[40] Under such a system, Marcuse realized, Marxism didn't fare well. What was needed was "the cancellation of the liberal creed of free and equal discussion."[41] "Not 'equal' but more representation of the Left would be the equalization of the prevailing inequality."[42] This is when he proclaimed his doctrine of "liberating tolerance," the Orwellian call for "intolerance against movements from the Right, and toleration of movements from the Left."[43]

Shunning the protocols of Critical Theory, Marcuse laid out a vision for his tolerant society of the future. What actions did he recommend to achieve "true tolerance"?

> They would include the withdrawal of toleration of speech and assembly from groups and movements which promote aggressive policies, armament, chauvinism, discrimination on the grounds of race and religion, or which oppose the extension of public services, social security, medical care, etc. Moreover, the restoration of freedom of thought may necessitate new and rigid restrictions on teachings and practices in the educational institutions which, by their very methods and concepts, serve to enclose the mind within the established universe of discourse and behavior—thereby precluding *a priori* a rational evaluation of the alternatives.[44]

It would be justifiable, then, to revoke free speech rights from anyone who opposed socialism. Later, he called for restricting speech even further, arguing for "[w]ithdrawal of tolerance from regressive movements before they can become active; intolerance even toward thought, opinion, and word, and finally, intolerance . . . toward the self-styled conservatives, to the political Right."[45]

Marcuse's mutterings on tolerance call to mind yet another of Orwell's observations: "All animals are equal, but some animals are more equal than others."[46]

Marcuse was careful to assure liberals, who traditionally opposed censorship, particularly suppression of creative expression, that "censorship of art and literature is regressive under all circumstances." His very next sentence, however, revealed that he had no problem censoring literature and art that he didn't like. "The authentic oeuvre is not and cannot be a prop for oppression, and pseudo art (which can be such a prop) is not art," he wrote.[47] In his fantasy world, he would be suppressing not art or literature in banning such material, but pseudo-art and pseudo-literature.

Tolerating what you like and censoring what you don't like, of course, had a name before Marcuse came along. It was called intolerance. Intolerance had an unpopular ring to it, so Marcuse called it by its more popular antonym, tolerance. This word was often modified by *liberating*, *discriminating*, and *true*. Further corruption of language came via his criticism of practitioners of free speech as "intolerant."

Proponents of government policing of the marketplace of ideas are often accused of an elitism that assumes people are too dumb to think for themselves and need the state to think for them. But in Marcuse's case, the opposite is true. Because people *do* think for themselves—and reject what Marcuse is offering—he is compelled to limit options. If he didn't do so, people would make choices he opposed.

Marcuse's pedantic prose gave the intelligentsia a highfalutin academic justification for intolerance. It gave moral sanction—indeed, a sense of self-righteousness—to liberals acting in the most illiberal way. The modern university, with its speech codes and general "intolerance against movements from the Right," is the most graphic example of what Marcuse has wrought. But we see the pernicious influence of this ideology elsewhere in our culture. Calls for John Rocker to be banned from baseball for making impolite remarks, efforts to remove Dr. Laura from the airwaves for her religious conviction against homosexuality, and attacks on Mel Gibson for making a movie about Jesus Christ are all manifestations of the new "liberal" sensibility on censorship. While a remnant of old-style liberals exist—Nat Hentoff, Harvey Silverglate, Tammy Bruce, and Camille Paglia, to name but a few—many of those known as liberals today are merely leftists who have co-opted a name. Those who walked down the path set by Marcuse ceased in all but name to be liberals.

FREEDOM AND DEMOCRACY

Marcuse's view of freedom and democracy was similarly skewed. As with his interesting interpretation of tolerance, Marcuse reversed the meanings of *freedom* and *democracy* and then assigned the labels *antifreedom* and *antidemocratic* to those who actually believed in liberty and popular sovereignty. Marcuse's followers once again had to borrow Alice's looking glass to concur.

It is instructive to see which nations embodied freedom and which ones exemplified tyranny in Marcuse's view. "[I]s there today, in the orbit of advanced industrial civilization," he asked in 1964, "a society which is not under an authoritarian regime?"[48] The question answered itself. Western societies, like the United States, Canada, and the United Kingdom, were really "authoritarian" states. Vietnam, Cuba, and Red China, according to Marcuse, represented freedom.[49] "For a whole generation, 'freedom,' 'socialism,' and 'liberation' are inseparable from Fidel and Che and the guerrillas," he wrote; "they have recaptured . . . the day-to-day fight of men and women for a life as human beings."[50]

Marcuse and his confederates knew totalitarianism. The perverse lesson that they gleaned from their experiences in Germany was not to fight against tyranny but to be the tyrants. If totalitarianism undermined their goals, they spoke the language of human rights and liberation. If the total state served their ends, they adopted an apologist's accent.

Marcuse simultaneously condemned "the repressive ideology of freedom" and affirmed Rousseau's oxymoron that people "must be 'forced to be free.'"[51] When Westerners were asked if they were free, inevitably they would answer in the affirmative. This answer was irrelevant, according to Marcuse, who contended that the people would be free "if and when they are free to give their own answer. As long as they are kept incapable of being autonomous, as long as they are indoctrinated and manipulated (down to their very instincts), their answer to this question cannot be taken as their own."[52] One suspects that until the people agreed with Marcuse, they would always be deemed lacking in independence.

For Marcuse, democracy is a worthy form of government only if it facilitates the arrival of socialism, and it is to be discarded when it turns against the Left. In the last years of his life, Marcuse quite openly acknowledged the Left's inability to win through the democratic process. He affirmed in *Counterrevolution and Revolt*, for instance, the depressing fact that the "radicals are confronted with violent hostility on the part of the people."[53] Che Guevera was killed in Bolivia because the very peasants he claimed to be aiding turned him in to the authorities. In America, groups of working-class men known as the "hard hats" engaged radical activists in fistfights. Unique among Marxists, Marcuse recognized the wide chasm between leftist rhetoric extolling the workingman and the reality of the workingman's contempt for the people employing such rhetoric. "The prevalence of a non-revolutionary—nay, antirevolutionary—consciousness among the majority of the working class is conspicuous," he noted.[54]

The foremost impediment to achieving Marcuse's utopia was not kings or dictators or the aristocracy, but the people themselves. The people were suffering from "false consciousness" and couldn't recognize what was good for them, Marcuse maintained. Democracy was dangerous, because where it appeared to be carrying out the will of the people, it really subverted their will. At least people who lived under tyrannies did not suffer under such illusions. By giving people supposed political rights, Western democracies made "the traditional ways and means of protest ineffective—perhaps even dangerous because they preserve the illusion of popular sovereignty."[55]

The German émigré railed against democratic systems, saying, "The *immediate* expression of the opinion and will of the workers, farmers, neighbors—in brief, of the people—is not, per se, progressive and a force of social change: it may be the opposite. The councils will be organs of revolution only to the degree to which they represent the people *in revolt.*"[56]

Democracy was good when it benefited the Left, but bad—and therefore not real democracy—when it went against the Left. He wrote:

> Direct democracy, the subjection of all delegation of authority to effective control "from below," is an essential demand of Leftist strategy. The demand is necessarily ambivalent. To take an example from the student movement: effective student participation in the administration of the university. In political terms, this demand presupposes that the majority of the student body is more progressive than the faculty and the administration. If the contrary is the case, the change would turn against the Left.[57]

By his admission, democracy is merely a part of strategy, a means to an end. It possesses no inherent value other than its ability to, from time to time, bring the Left political power. When it has served its purpose, or when the people are against the Left, democracy should be abandoned.

It was an ideology of convenience—do what works for you when it works for you. Sadly, the Left has adopted Marcuse's teachings. Different rules applied to Western democracies than to Communist countries, Middle Eastern dictatorships, and Third World outposts. The standard carried to the battlefield of ideas by Marcuse would be picked up by Howard Zinn, Noam Chomsky, and countless other culturally alienated scribes in the years to come.

REAL EDUCATION IS INDOCTRINATION

"All authentic education," Marcuse wrote, "is political education."[58] Education's antithesis, indoctrination, he disguised as education. It was the familiar formula: assign a word with positive connotations, in this case *education*, to an ugly practice—*indoctrination*.

The Frankfurt School's aim was not enlightenment but attitudinal adjustment. Psychological conditioning through entertainment, the classroom, linguistic taboos, and other means would transmit their ideology through osmosis. The scientific method, logic, reasoning, debate, and other staples of a classically liberal education they deemed bourgeois. Why go through all of that nonsense when the Marxist truth has already been revealed? The educator of the future would teach students *what* to think, not *how* to think.

Of specific interest to Marcuse was higher education—and not coincidentally, that is where he has had his most profound influence. "The development of a true consciousness is still the professional function of the universities," he stated.[59] In Marcuse's heyday of the late 1960s and early 1970s, the Left took over campuses, further promoting violence, the stop-the-war effort, black nationalism, the women's movement, the drug culture, sexual licentiousness, and other phenomena. And they retained their control of the universities. Protestors who took over administration buildings in the 1960s were calling the shots from those very same administration buildings a few decades later. Marcuse foresaw this development:

> What appears as extraneous "politicization" of the university by disrupting radicals is today (as it was so often in the past) the "logical," internal dynamic of education: translation of knowledge into

reality, of humanistic values into humane conditions of existence. This dynamic, arrested by the pseudo-academic features of academia, would, for example, be released by the inclusion into the curriculum of courses giving adequate treatment to the great nonconformist movements in civilization to the critical analysis of contemporary societies.[60]

When Marcuse wrote this, the college campus was almost entirely innocent of such departments as women's studies, environmental studies, and peace studies, let alone more recent creations like gay and lesbian studies. Today, more than six hundred programs grant degrees in women's studies.[61] At schools like Duke, Harvard, and Cornell, there are more classes listed in the course catalogue for women's studies than for economics.[62] Programs in gay and lesbian studies (or sex studies, queer studies, or any of its other manifestations) exist at the University of Massachusetts, Brown, the University of North Carolina, the University of California at Santa Cruz, Bowdoin, and dozens of other schools. According to one of the most popular readers in gay and lesbian studies, the subject "straddles scholarship and politics" and it "intends to establish the analytical centrality of sex and sexuality within many different fields of inquiry, to express and advance the interests of lesbians, bisexuals, and gay men, and to contribute culturally and intellectually to the contemporary lesbian/gay movement."[63] Other fields of this ilk are similarly pervasive and aggressively political.

What unites these seemingly disparate fields of study is a condemnation of Western civilization. The various victim-studies concentrations are Critical Theory broken down into specific components, each bemoaning a particular aspect of society. Peruse the course descriptions of these departments and Herbert Marcuse's name continually pops up.

DUMB AND DISHONEST IDEAS

In the late 1960s, the monster unleashed by the Frankfurt School turned on its creators. University campuses and city streets erupted.

The disorder hit close to home for the Institute of Social Research. In 1968, one of Theodor Adorno's students led a chaotic takeover of Frankfurt University, during which Jurgen Habermas's research assistants conducted teach-ins. The protestors renamed the school Karl Marx

University. The sociology department became the Spartacus Department.[64] In January 1969, students invaded the building that housed the Institute of Social Research, prompting the institute's directors to call the police. To their embarrassment, the directors learned that the students were just looking for a place to hold a discussion. Of this incident, Marcuse wrote Adorno, "We cannot ignore the fact that these students have been influenced by us (and not least by you)."[65]

The rebellions continued. During one lecture by Adorno, by then the leader of the Institute of Social Research, a gang of disruptive women who forgot to wear their tops barged into his classroom. Habermas displayed to historian Martin Jay the lock he put on his phone to impede radical students who would break into his office from running up long-distance bills.[66]

All this disorder caught the Frankfurt School's leadership off-guard. Incredulous, Adorno admitted, "When I made my theoretical model, I could not have guessed that people would try to realize it with Molotov cocktails."[67]

People did, unfortunately, try to realize the Frankfurt School's societal blueprint. They still do. They do so because Cultural Marxism's evangelist, Herbert Marcuse, effectively transmitted the blueprint to the masses. Ideas aren't contained in a vacuum.

Marcuse is significant, first, because he helped save Marxism by divorcing it from its association with economics and applying its tenets to any number of "victim" categories. The worker was erased and in his place came an endless stream of variables: the homosexual, the woman, the black, the immigrant. The enemy was no longer capitalism, but racism, sexism, xenophobia, anti-Semitism, homophobia, ableism, and a host of other isms and alleged pathologies. By appropriating Marxist analyses to issues unrelated to economics, Marcuse exhibited either great prescience or great luck. Within a few decades, faith in the Marxist economic model had largely collapsed along with the Iron Curtain. Cultural Marxism still thrives.

A second legacy is his role in legitimizing scholarly pursuits pertaining to matters less of the mind than of the groin. Sex-obsessed philosophical books such as *Eros and Civilization* and *An Essay on Liberation*, novel for their time, now flood the academic market. What was once relegated to the walls of bathroom stalls is now common fare in the pages of scholarly journals or on the printing plates of university publishing houses.

Even more significant than Marcuse's contributions to establishing "victim studies" and an intellectualism based on sexuality was his impact on discourse. The impact was especially profound in the university.

Appropriately, we embark upon an investigation of dumb and dishonest ideas by conducting an examination of the thought of Herbert Marcuse. Unlike many others discussed in this book, Marcuse did something more pernicious than simply tell a few lies to further a cause. He created a theoretical framework that endorsed double standards and the separation of words from their meanings for the purpose of granting positive connotations to negative practices. This verbal legerdemain created a real-life Newspeak. "If a National Museum of Double Standards is ever built," journalist John Leo humorously proposes, "we should name it for Marcuse and put a huge statue of him on the roof. Maybe he should be shown holding up two fingers, one for each standard."[68] Marcuse quite clearly had two standards on violence, democracy, freedom, education, tolerance, and any other issue that he wished to distort.

In the final chapter of *1984*, Winston Smith is told by O'Brian, a high-ranking party official:

> You believe that reality is something objective, external, existing in its own right. You also believe that the nature of reality is self-evident. When you delude yourself into thinking that you see something, you assume that everyone else sees the same thing as you. But I tell you, Winston, that reality is not external. Reality exists in the human mind, and nowhere else. Not in the individual mind, which can make mistakes, and in any case soon perishes; only in the mind of the Party, which is collective and immortal. Whatever the Party holds to be truth is truth. It is impossible to see reality except by looking through the eyes of the Party.[69]

Academics looking through the jaundiced eyes of Marcuse see anything that they want to see. "Diversity" describes a faculty that looks like the United Nations but thinks like a San Francisco coffeehouse. Women who don manly garb, never shave their legs or underarms, and imitate males by dating other women are labeled "feminists." "Tolerance" is defined as saying anything you want, so long as it agrees with prevailing campus dictates. "Multiculturalism" shuns an exploration of foreign cultures in favor of bashing America. "Equality" means treating individuals differently through race and gender preferences.

Far too often, present-day ideologues mask their agenda with sweet-sounding words when their real goal is to wage war on the concepts embodied by those words. The twenty-first century rolls onward, but the campuses are perpetually stuck in *1984*. The result is a corruption of language that threatens meaningful discourse. Participants in debate can at once be speaking the same language but effectively be speaking different languages. Words that have fixed definitions, like *democracy* and *tolerance*, now come to mean something entirely different in the vernacular of the intellectuals.

In the dénouement of *1984*, Winston Smith, his spirit broken, traces "2 + 2 = 5" on a table. When we are taught to use such words as *tolerance*, *diversity*, and *sensitivity* in an Orwellian—or, perhaps more appropriately, Marcusean—fashion, two plus two begins to equal five.

"SCIENCE!"

How a Pervert Launched the Sexual Revolution

A man must be something of a moralist if he is to preach,
even if he is to preach unmorality.

—G. K. CHESTERTON,
Heretics

WHAT MOTIVATES SOCIAL REVOLUTIONARIES? DO THEY SELF-lessly long for an elevation of society onto a higher plane, or is it their selfish design to bring the world down to their own degraded level?

Jean-Jacques Rousseau was incapable of holding a job and sponged off women his entire life. He spawned five children, not one of whom he bothered to name, all of whom he abandoned to almost certain death at an asylum. He was a sexual pervert and enjoyed physical punishment and exposing himself to women.[1] Should it surprise us, then, that he advocated a philosophy of sexual anarchy, state ownership of children, and the subsidization of those unwilling to work?

British writer Paul Johnson reminds us that so far as we know, "Marx never set foot in a mill, factory, mine, or other industrial workplace in the whole of his life."[2] His war against free enterprise stemmed not from solidarity with the workers but from his constant debts, unemployment, and inability to support his family. His mother complained, "Karl should accumulate capital instead of just writing about it."[3]

More recently, apostles of the drug culture—Allen Ginsberg, Timothy Leary, Abbie Hoffman—have preached what they practiced. It was only after these men became drug users that they also became apologists for substance abuse.

Halfway through the twentieth century, Indiana University professor Alfred Kinsey launched what was perhaps the first salvo in the Sexual Revolution. The Kinsey Reports hit postwar America like a sucker punch. Claiming that more people than America was willing to admit engaged in premarital sex, homosexuality, adultery, and various other frowned-upon pursuits, 1948's *Sexual Behavior in the Human Male* and 1953's *Sexual Behavior in the Human Female* revolutionized American law, culture, education, and a host of other areas. Critics of the best-sellers, the media informed America, were to Kinsey what the Church was to Galileo. Kinsey, after all, was a "scientist."

At midcentury, Kinsey's fame rivaled that of Harry Truman, Joe DiMaggio, and Douglas MacArthur. Today, the IU professor is perhaps best known for putting forward the idea that 10 percent of the population is gay, with "1 in 10" becoming something of a mantra for homosexual activists.

By the twilight of the 1960s, the Sexual Revolution that Alfred Kinsey helped father was in full bloom. The Pill, the advent of *Playboy* magazine, increased sexuality in entertainment, male dislocation from decades of near-nonstop warfare, and the women's and gay rights movements all changed the moral fabric. Kinsey, more than any other human being, can be said to be responsible for the change. His detractors point to the increased rates of abortion, illegitimacy, rape, divorce, and sexually transmitted disease as his legacy. His supporters claim that a more sexually open and tolerant society has improved the lives of nearly everyone, particularly gays, who are no longer forced to keep their lives hidden. As evidenced by the controversy surrounding the 2004 release of the biopic *Kinsey*, starring Liam Neeson, he is a polarizing figure to this day.

Partisans and detractors agree that Kinsey changed the world. While time obscures his name, Kinsey's spirit looms large in a world much more indulgent of unsettling sexual behavior:

- A March 2000 state-funded conference in Massachusetts instructed high school students how to engage in a sexual practice called "fisting" and dispensed bandages for "when the sex got really rough."[4]

- Videos aired by MTV after school, by performers like Christina Aguilera and Britney Spears, increasingly resemble soft-core porn on late-night pay television.

- In 2003, *Rolling Stone* explored the homosexual subculture of "bug chasers" and "gift givers." The labels refer to gays who actively seek HIV, and the men who grant their wish. One bug chaser, who ironically volunteered as an AIDS educator, explained, "I think it turns the other guy on to know that I'm still negative and that they're bringing me into their brotherhood. That gets me off, too." The moment he is infected, he confessed, will be "the most erotic thing I can imagine."[5] The piece seems to have exaggerated the popularity of such pursuits, but this sensationalism didn't negate the fact that something this sick actually occurs.

- Some institutions have begun constructing third bathrooms for transgender people. The Massachusetts Bay Transit Authority, for instance, doled out $8,000 to build a bathroom for a single employee.[6]

- A Florida group hosts a nudist camp for children, featuring such activities as a naked talent show and eating s'mores nude around a campfire.[7]

- After tying up and gagging a blindfolded classmate, a San Francisco Art Institute student performed a class project with him in front of students, two professors, and security. This is how the "artist" described the outdoor event: "I engaged in oral sex with him and he engaged in oral sex with me. I had given him an enema, and I had taken a shit and stuffed it in his ass. That goes on, he shits all over me, I shit in him."[8]

Post-Kinseyan America is very different from pre-Kinseyan America. The Indiana University professor set into motion radical societal changes. No less a sexual revolutionary than Hugh Hefner, founder of *Playboy*, has labeled himself "Kinsey's pamphleteer."[9] Though it is too simplistic to pin the blame or credit for any social trend on one person, Alfred Kinsey has had extraordinary influence.

In fact, he is more relevant now than when he lived. Proponents of relaxed attitudes toward sex and sexuality still trumpet Kinsey's findings to show the "truth" about sex that supposedly puritanical Americans don't want us to know. It is quite an achievement for a supposed scientist whose work was an utter fraud. Of course, the intellectual morons who promote

Kinsey's work aren't interested in whether the research bears any relation to reality. As long as his work forms the foundation for claims that "anything goes" when it comes to sex, it doesn't matter if Alfred Kinsey was a fraud and a pervert. Bogus scientific findings can serve the ideologue's cause.

A "SECOND DARWIN"?

Born in Hoboken, New Jersey, to middle-class parents on June 23, 1894, Alfred Charles Kinsey was the first of three children. From the age of ten onward, Kinsey grew up in the more suburban South Orange, where, biographer James Jones notes, "he did not make a single close friend."[10] As peers played, Kinsey spent most of his early years indoors as a result of a heart condition and bouts with rickets, measles, typhoid, chicken pox, and rheumatic fever. His bookish nature denied him opportunities to develop normal relationships. He was the only boy in his high school class not to play at least one varsity sport.

Kinsey excelled in academics, however. His high school yearbook's "class prophecy" predicted that Kinsey, the class valedictorian, would become the "second Darwin."[11] At elite Bowdoin College, he was one of two students to graduate magna cum laude. Kinsey went on to do graduate work in biology at Harvard, where he came under the sway of Dean William Morton Wheeler. "Thanks to Wheeler's influence," Jones observes, "Kinsey left Boston believing that biologists should become social engineers, shaping public policy and altering private attitudes on a variety of issues, ranging from eugenics, to private morality."[12]

Yet Kinsey's metamorphosis had come long before he had set foot on the Cambridge, Massachusetts, campus. From an early age, the superficially austere Kinsey had begun to engage in a variety of bizarre activities. "For a boy like Kinsey, a righteous boy whose sense of self-worth depended upon rigid self-control, nothing needed to be kept more hidden than the fact that he masturbated and that he did so with a foreign object inserted up his penis," Jones writes. "By late adolescence, his masochism was well advanced. He had progressed beyond straws and was inserting a brush back up his penis, a practice he would continue for life, at times changing the instrument of self-torture, but never the point of attack."[13] Rather than control his destructive behavior, Kinsey projected his perversions upon society through "science."

Kinsey picked up another peculiar habit in these years. After earning honors as one of America's first Eagle Scouts, Kinsey devoted an unnatural amount of time to mentoring boys. He taught Sunday school, served as a counselor for the YMCA and the Boy Scouts, and helped start organizations for boys where none existed. At Bowdoin he involved himself in the Brunswick Boys Association.[14] At Harvard he helped found a boys' club at his Methodist church.[15] Even as a professor at Indiana University, he left his wife of three years to spend the summer as a camp counselor for boys.[16] In total, Kinsey would devote more than ten summers to working at boys' camps.[17] Kinsey compensated for his unrealized boyhood by partaking in male adolescent pursuits well into adulthood.

He quickly accepted a teaching position at Indiana University in 1920 after completing graduate work at Harvard. The new professor of zoology began dating a student, Clara McMillen. After a two-month courtship, he proposed, and six months later they married. At their wedding there was no best man, nor did Kinsey have any family in attendance.[18] The academic's voracious sexual appetites were not so wide as to include much of a taste for women, leaving the marriage unconsummated for months.[19]

Kinsey's early years as a professor were marked by his authorship of several lucrative textbooks and by long field trips in remote parts of the country searching for gall wasps. On these trips he would bring along male assistants, who would be startled by Kinsey's work attire of various stages of undress, as well as his regimented demand for continual bathing by them. "For Kinsey not only ordered his students to bathe; he routinely checked while they were showering, ostensibly to make certain they were complying with his orders," Jones notes. If this were not strange enough, Kinsey insisted on showering with his students. One befuddled student was left to confess to his diary, "Such a mania for baths I've never seen."[20]

In the classroom, Jones says, "Kinsey made no effort to conceal his desire to politicize young people."[21] But Kinsey's primary interest was not the classroom. It was sex. In July 1938 Kinsey collected his first sexual history. He collected thousands more over the next few years, oblivious to the war that had engulfed the world around him. In 1945 he quit teaching entirely to focus exclusively on his research. He released his first report within three years and became one of the most recognizable names on the planet.

"THE VERY EMBODIMENT OF MIDDLE AMERICAN SQUARE"?

The Kinsey that has been passed on by college texts and popular histories is that of the disinterested scientist whose research is unimpeachable. In David Halberstam's *The Fifties*, Kinsey is "prudish," "old fashioned," and "the very embodiment of Middle American square."[22] Rutgers University professor William O'Neill praises Kinsey in *American High* as a "hero of science"; those who pressured the Rockefeller Foundation to cut Kinsey's funding won "a victory for small mindedness."[23] Paul Johnson's *History of the American People* affirms Kinsey's statistics and explains that his "findings . . . confirmed much other evidence that, even in the 1950s, the Norman Rockwell images no longer told the full story."[24] William Manchester's Kinsey in *The Glory and the Dream* is "an objective investigator," "a stickler for explicit detail," and a "disciple of truth." "As a scientist," Manchester informs readers, "he had naturally played no favorites."[25]

But Kinsey, as we know now, was a very different kind of "scientist." He was a homosexual, a wife-swapper, a sadomasochist, and, some suspect, a pedophile—much more involved in his work than the keepers of the tablets would have us believe.

The real Kinsey lent his wife to other men. His attic served as a personal pornographic movie studio. His fellow researchers, Wardell Pomeroy and Clyde Martin, also acted as his sex partners. One Kinsey researcher bragged about having bedded a dog. Others were committed sadomasochists. The common denominator among the staff at the Institute for Sex Research was a pursuit of sex that was outside of societal conventions.

In large part because of their zeal for abnormal sex, the Kinsey team focused their research on people who deviated from community standards—pimps, prostitutes, homosexuals, and imprisoned sex offenders. Kinsey's "methodology and sampling technique virtually guaranteed that he would find what he was looking for," writes Jones.[26]

Kinsey's perversion was often self-destructive. For most of his life, he masturbated with a toothbrush inserted in his urethra. At one point, Kinsey crawled into a bathtub, pulled out his pocketknife, and, says Jones, "circumcised himself without benefit of anesthesia."[27] He engaged in auto-asphyxiation while masturbating and pierced his genitals to such an extent that by the end, biographer Jonathan Gathorne-Hardy reveals, there was "nothing left to pierce."[28] Jones describes perhaps the most disturbing occurrence, from Kinsey's final years: "[H]e tied a strong, tight knot around his scrotum with one end of the rope dangling from the pipe overhead. The other end he wrapped around his hand. Then, he climbed up on a chair and jumped off, suspending himself in midair."[29] This particular self-inflicted torture hospitalized Kinsey for weeks and was part of a pattern of behavior that, ironically, had caused impotence for this champion of "sexual freedom."[30]

Kinsey's need for control manifested itself in demands to know the sexual histories of his workers and their families. He regulated the sexual behavior of those on his staff and demanded access to them and, occasionally, their wives. The pressure, recalled one wife, was "sickening." She "felt like my husband's career at the Institute depended on it."[31] So great was his dominance that Pomeroy and Martin felt compelled to ask his permission to engage in extramarital affairs. Another Kinsey researcher, Paul Gebhard, was once ordered to cease an affair by his apologetic boss, who normally preferred to order his underlings to have sex, not to stop having it.[32] Kinsey's work environment was more Spahn Ranch than Menlo Park.

Kinsey used a bizarre litmus test for prospective employees and almost without fail hired those with sexual histories falling well outside the mainstream. When one employee, Vincent Nowlis, showed squeamishness toward a sexual case history, Kinsey, Pomeroy, and Martin cornered him in a hotel room. Jones writes, "As near as Nowlis could tell, his boss was offering to provide 'seductive instruction' that would involve 'learning plus pleasure.'" Nowlis explained that his boss's advances "obviously would involve some kind of sexual activity on my part." But, he said, "I didn't see my wife or any desirable partners, shall we say, around, and I wasn't interested." The sexual harassment persuaded Nowlis to announce his resignation the following day.[33]

Jones describes the Indiana University professor as a "secular evangelist," "a scolding preacher rather than a disinterested scientist," and a "covert revolutionary" who "used science to lay siege to middle class morality."[34] Kinsey, explains Jones, engaged in "a public crusade for private reasons."[35] At every turn these "private reasons"—perversion and a need to dominate others—permeated his "scientific" work.

QUEER FINDINGS

It would be one thing if Alfred Kinsey's perverted "science" had been dismissed for what it was—nonsense. But Kinsey's research, flawed as it was, fundamentally altered perceptions of sexuality and sexual behavior and ultimately forced changes in our laws.

The first Kinsey Report announced that the moral code Americans preached was far different from the one that governed their private lives. By Kinsey's estimation, more than nine out of ten American males were, by definition, sex offenders. The former Eagle Scout believed that there were "only three kind of sexual abnormalities: abstinence, celibacy, and delayed marriage."[36] With his first report, Kinsey set out to eradicate the perception that anything outside these three categories was an abnormality. To Kinsey, the problem was not so-called abnormal sexual practices but the attitudes toward, and laws against, such practices.

What Kinsey reported to the American public was likened to a sexual A-bomb. About eight out of every ten men had engaged in the marital act prior to their wedding day.[37] Sixty-nine percent had had sexual relations with prostitutes.[38] Half of all married men were adulterers.[39] Homosexual sex to the point of orgasm was an experience of 37 percent of males.[40] A full 8 percent had engaged in some form of sexual relations with an animal.[41]

Or so the Kinsey Report claimed.

Kinsey was a propagandist, not a scientist. He recognized that he had to make his operation *appear* to be a paragon of scientific objectivity. So, for instance, he paid a friend $500 to pretend to be the institute's statistician, which shielded him from criticism of his own ignorance of the most rudimentary statistical methods (for example, he often confused the mean with the median).[42] In reality, though, Kinsey showed no concern for honest statistics.

By disregarding random sampling of the population, Kinsey had license to stack his survey with some groups to the exclusion of others. More than three-fourths of *Sexual Behavior in the Human Male*'s sample group of men twenty and over were single, even though only three-tenths of the U.S. adult male population was single at that time.[43] In an era when the dissolution of marriages was not common, Kinsey's research subjects included 3,000 divorced men.[44] Sixty-four percent of his subjects were what Kinsey ambiguously labeled "college level" at a time when only 12 percent of American males were college educated.[45] Old people, whose staid and curtailed sex lives bored Kinsey, were almost wholly excluded. His sample group of several thousand males, for instance, contained only 87 white males over the age of sixty.[46] The sample's heavy Eastern bias made its extrapolations irrelevant to the entire American population.[47] Blacks were entirely omitted. Those with strong religious views were excluded too. Eight out of every ten males in the survey were "inactive" Protestants, Catholics, or Jews.[48]

Other homosexuals were of particular interest to Kinsey. In late 1939 he wrote to a favorite former graduate student, "Now have a total, from all sources, of 120 H–histories."[49] The *H* refers to homosexuals. This was at a time when he had collected 590 histories, meaning that histories from individuals he knew to be gay constituted about 20 percent of his total sample group.[50] There is no specific record of the number of homosexual histories after this point, but we do know that Kinsey continued to track down gay men to interview. Kinsey actively sought out homosexuals by developing key contacts in the urban gay subcultures of Chicago, Philadelphia, St. Louis, and other cities. In New York, for instance, Kinsey stayed at the Astor in Times Square because its street-level bar was a hangout for gays seeking anonymous sex.[51] Within the pages of *Sexual Behavior in the Human Male*, Kinsey candidly admits that "several hundred male prostitutes contributed their histories" to the survey.[52]

Seeking out homosexuals not only weighted Kinsey's study toward his predrawn conclusions but provided him sexual liaisons as well. Kinsey was anything but the detached researcher. At times he had sex with subjects he was supposed to be interviewing. For one interview in 1946, Kinsey invited a Dr. Earle Marsh to his hotel room. Jonathan Gathorne-Hardy writes, "While they chatted, Marsh suddenly told him he'd had a fantasy of having sex with him. '[I told him] with no idea in mind except to report it.'" Kinsey then turned to Marsh and decreed, "Take off your clothes." They had sex and would do so every subsequent time they met.[53] On some occasions the professor would surreptitiously view others engaging in intercourse.[54]

Preselecting homosexuals was only part of the equation to bias the results. Kinsey also stacked the sample group with prison inmates. In 1941, for instance, Kinsey visited forty penal farms—more than three times the amount of campuses where he collected histories (an early complaint was that Kinsey focused his interviews too much on students).[55] A Kinsey staff member claimed years later that 44 percent of the inmates Kinsey interviewed had had homosexual experiences, while the authors themselves placed the figure in a higher range.[56] Whatever the real number, one need not be a sexologist to know that prisons are a breeding ground for homosexual activity and that prisoners normally have rebelled against societal norms not just in their criminal activities. Yet padding the sample group with inmates was not enough. The researchers pursued a particular type of inmate, the sex offender, to skew the survey's results further. This still was insufficient, as a particular type of sex offender, the most perverse and abnormal, became the focus of interviews. All three of Kinsey's coauthors have since admitted that their prison histories ignored scientific sampling techniques and focused on the most perverse sex offenders, including those who had practiced incest, rape, and pedophilia. Paul Gebhard—a coauthor of the *Female* volume, an institute staff member at the time of the *Male* volume's release, and later a director of the institute—candidly states that the focus on sexual deviants was quite deliberate: "At the Indiana State Farm we had no plan of sampling—we simply sought out sex offenders and, after a time, avoided the more common types of offense (e.g., statutory rape) and directed our efforts toward the rarer types."[57] *Male* volume coauthor Wardell Pomeroy concurs: "We went to the [prison] records and got lists of the inmates who were in for various kinds of sex offenses. If the list was short for some offenses—as in incest, for example—we took the history of everybody on it. If it was a long list, as for statutory rape, we might take the history of every fifth or tenth man."[58] A third coauthor, Kinsey's gardener-turned-colleague Clyde Martin, notes that the institute team sought out sex offenders serving time for "contributing to the delinquency" of minors.[59]

While it is clear that the institute staff took thousands of inmate histories, it is not known how many made it into the data used for *Sexual Behavior in the Human Male*. Credible estimates based on remarks by Kinsey and others place the total amount used at around 20 percent to 25 percent.[60] Until the institute opens up its files for scholarly examination—provided that the records exist, as they claim—the number of prisoners surveyed can only be estimated.

SEXUAL BEHAVIOR IN THE HUMAN FEMALE

Kinsey's findings in his 1953 study, *Sexual Behavior in the Human Female*, were just as startling as those in his 1948 *Male* study. Among the women that Kinsey used for his survey, about half had partaken in sex prior to marriage.[61] Thirteen percent had engaged in lesbian sex to the point of orgasm, with a higher percentage of women having taken part in some form of lesbian activity.[62] Among married women, the survey's authors deduced, more than one-fourth would cheat on their husbands at some point.[63] A small percentage had even had sex with animals.[64]

Critics claimed that volunteers who tell their sexual histories to complete strangers naturally would be more sexually adventurous. Others criticized not the subjects being interviewed but those conducting the interrogation. Two angry Indiana University nurses interviewed by Kinsey charged that "he could provoke any answer that he might want from the students involved."[65] More often than not, however, observers praised Kinsey for adapting his style to the individual answering his questions. For an underworld figure he might use street lingo; for a graduate student he might employ technical terms. By maximizing the comfort level of those revealing their most closely guarded secrets, he was able to unearth minute details of people's sex lives.

Although Kinsey collected the sexual histories of more than 16,000 people, he used slightly less than 6,000 cases for *Sexual Behavior in the Human Female*. Worse still, different statistical tables and graphs contained different totals of women without explaining why. As in the *Male* report, he excluded blacks. But in a departure from *Male*, he did not include the histories that he had collected from prison inmates, because, he said, "the sexual histories which we have of white females who had served prison sentences (915 cases) prove, upon analysis, to differ as a group from the histories of the females who have not become involved with the law."[66] Kinsey calculated that between 50 percent and 75 percent of prison inmates engaged in homosexual relations behind bars, which he concluded "would have seriously distorted the calculations on the total sample."[67] Yet if Kinsey contended that rampant homosexuality in correctional institutions made inmate data invalid, why hadn't he excluded prison data from the *Male* volume too?

More telling than those excluded from the second Kinsey Report were the women included. Kinsey skewed his female sample group just as he did with the male group. Nonmarried women dominated the ranks of those surveyed. The ages of the women surveyed did not come close to mirroring the diverse generational makeup of American women. Three-fourths of the women in the *Female* volume had attended college at a time when a much smaller percentage had done so.[68] Kinsey thus skewed the survey toward sexual libertinism, since his survey showed that as the education level rose for females, so did rates of adultery, premarital sex, masturbation, and homosexuality.* Jewish women were overrepresented by a factor of almost ten. As in the *Male* volume, the majority of those surveyed were "inactive" religiously, and the "inactive" category was not coincidentally the most adventurous sexually. When looking at *Sexual Behavior in the Human Female*'s charts that break down the sexual practices of those surveyed, one has no way of knowing that the "inactive" religious group dominates and thus skews the results. Kinsey conveniently leaves out the total number in each religious classification's subgroup—inactive, moderate, and devout—at the bottom of the chart, where such information is usually found.[69] This key omission is evidence that the Kinsey team buried data that would bring discredit on their statistical practices.

Kinsey assured readers that his team had not skewed results by preselecting groups for his survey. "For our general sample," he wrote, "we have avoided groups that had been brought together by some particular sexual interest."[70]

He lied.

Kinsey actually sought out prostitutes and interviewed a massive number of them, which slanted the results more than the overrepresentation of any particular religious subgroup had done. *Sexual Behavior in the Human Female* claimed, "None of the activities which females have had as prostitutes are included in any of the calculations in the present volume."[71] But there is no evidence that supports this save Kinsey's word. Nor does it seem plausible that this information could have been scientifically weeded out.

Kinsey complicated the survey even more by categorizing many of these prostitutes as "married women" even though he knew they were not. Ostensibly, married women made up 30 percent of the female sample group. Even at that figure they would have been greatly underrepresented, but in reality, married women represented an even smaller percentage of his survey group. According to the Kinsey Report, women "were identified as married if they were living with their spouses either in

---

*Among men, the reverse was true. The lower the level of education, the more libidinous the male. This was probably because of the infusion of massive numbers of prison inmates—specifically imprisoned sex offenders—in the first volume.

formally consummated legal marriages, or in common-law relationships which had lasted for at least a year." Kinsey added, "These definitions are more or less in accord with those used in the U.S. Census for 1950, except that common-law relationships have been more frequently accepted as marriages in our data."[72]

Why did Kinsey change the meaning of the word *marriage* for the purposes of his survey? American wives (including his own spouse) did not excite him. He wanted to slip into his sample group "professional" women who lived with their pimps and sexually "liberated" women who cohabited with boyfriends (an uncommon phenomenon in the 1940s and '50s). Yet he also knew that the number of married women in his survey was low, so he found a way to boost that number artificially to a respectable figure.

Throughout his two volumes, one would be hard-pressed to find more than a few mentions of *pregnancy, mother, father,* or any other word or phrase conveying the message that sex has consequences. The reader is struck by the paucity of utterances of *abortion, rape,* and *venereal disease.* Anything that reminds the book's audience of a dark side of sexuality is airbrushed out. Sexually transmitted diseases, he contends, are "a relatively unimportant matter today in regards to premarital sex."[73] At other points, he asks that the reader suspend reality and believe him when he writes that he found just one case of violent sexual abuse of a child among the 4,441 females included in the survey.[74] He scoffs at other reports of rape as well, invoking the notion that observations of monkeys reveal females seeking out males for sex and then attacking them once their primary partners caught them. "A high proportion of the human 'rape' cases which we have had the opportunity to examine involve something of the same motifs," *Sexual Behavior in the Human Female* imparts.[75] Note the use of scare quotes.

AMERICAN MENGELE?

In 1981, Judith Reisman addressed the Fifth World Congress of Sexology in Jerusalem. Her speech accused one of the most respected academics of the twentieth century of complicity in the rape and abuse of children, and of pawning off fraudulent data as legitimate scholarly material. The subject of her earth-shattering talk was Alfred Kinsey. Of Kinsey's famous reports, Dr. Reisman announced, "such mercantile pseudo-science eventually defames the entire scholarly community, and tends to implicate us all as popularizers of whatever 'truth' is paying dividends at the moment."[76]

In *Sexual Behavior in the Human Male* and *Sexual Behavior in the Human Female*, Kinsey's team claimed that children were sexual beings essentially from birth, meaning that even infants were capable of orgasm. Until Reisman came along in 1981, it apparently did not occur to anyone to question publicly how Kinsey and his men came to this conclusion.

Kinsey collected data on at least 317 male children and numerous additional female children. Infants as young as five months old, said Kinsey, achieve "orgasm" after being stimulated from "partners." Symptoms of sexual climax for young children, claimed Kinsey, often included "sobbing," "violent cries," "loss of color," and an "abundance of tears." He added that often the child "will fight away from the partner and may make violent attempts to avoid climax." From all this he deduced that the child derived "definite pleasure" from the situation.[77]

For a man who gained joy from hanging himself by his testicles, circumcising himself with a pocketknife, and inserting toothbrushes into his urinary tract, the children's responses might very well have been interpreted as pleasure. For almost everyone else it is clear that the expressions of these babies were not of delight but of extreme terror.

Kinsey's charts show how an eleven-year-old was supposedly brought to orgasm nineteen times in one hour and how a two-year-old was brought to orgasm eleven times in sixty-five minutes. One unfortunate four-year-old boy was manipulated to "climax" twenty-six times in a twenty-four-hour period by someone Kinsey labeled a scientifically "trained observer."[78] In Kinsey's sanitized jargon, Reisman pointed out, these unfortunate kids were no longer children—referred to as such on only one occasion—but "individuals" (five references) and "preadolescent" (seven references). Their tormentors were not rapists or molesters, but "partners" or "scientifically trained observers."[79]

That Kinsey allowed child molesters to dictate whether these children enjoyed being molested speaks volumes not only about his character but about his interest in real science as well. His methods were something akin to relying on tobacco executives to determine the addictiveness of nicotine, or allowing a rapist to discern whether his victim really "wanted" sex.

Dripping from every page of his work on preadolescent sexuality is the notion that sex between children and adults is natural and healthy. Child-adult sexual contacts, Kinsey writes, "had often involved considerable affection, and some of the older females in the sample felt that their pre-adolescent experience had contributed favorably to their later socio-sexual development."[80] At another point, he puts the blame of adult-child sexual contact on kids: "Children, out of curiosity, sometimes initiate the manipulation of male genitalia, even before the male has made any exposure."[81] Are children harmed by such contacts? According to Kinsey, yes and no. He writes:

[S]ome 80 per cent of the children had been emotionally upset or frightened by their contacts with adults. A small portion had been seriously disturbed; but in most instances the reported fright was nearer the level that children will show when they see insects, spiders, or other objects against which they have been adversely conditioned. If a child were not culturally conditioned, it is doubtful if it would be disturbed by sexual approaches of the sort which had usually been involved in these histories.[82]

Kinsey adds that to the extent that a child is damaged after having sexual contact with an adult, the rapist is not to blame; rather, the child is harmed by the "hysteria" created by police, parents, and others.[83]

How Kinsey obtained his data on children is a point of contention. Current Kinsey Institute director John Bancroft and past director June Reinisch have attested that the data came from a lone pedophile.[84] The authors of the *Male* report claimed that nine scientifically inclined pedophiles observed preadolescent orgasm.[85] Kinsey confidant and colleague Paul Gebhard states that the Indiana University researchers got their data from pedophile organizations, sex offenders, and numerous individuals who had volunteered information.[86] Someone isn't telling the truth, but why?

Was Kinsey himself a pedophile?

It is quite possible that Kinsey—who privately condoned child-adult sexual encounters and acted as a longtime counselor for such groups as the Boy Scouts and the YMCA—was a prime "observer" and source of information. The fact that hundreds of children were molested to generate data is not the evidence. Kinsey also bragged of his large collection of early adolescent sperm. "You can only collect early adolescent ejaculate by being pretty close to the adolescent," Reisman points out. "Early adolescent sperm is not collected by *recall.*"[87] Although there is no direct proof that Kinsey raped any of these children, it is irresponsible not to raise the question. If it wasn't Kinsey, then who raped hundreds of children in the name of science?

One child rapist Kinsey relied on for "research" was a Mr. Rex King, who, in addition to bedding his grandmother and most other members of his family, had about eight hundred sexual contacts with children. King continued to molest children and report back to the Institute for Sex Research, with the full knowledge of Kinsey, until 1954, after both volumes had been released. "I congratulate you on the research spirit which has led you to collect data over these many years," Kinsey admiringly wrote to King. "Everything that you've accumulated must find its way into scientific channels."[88]

Another child molester who assisted Kinsey was a Nazi party official and former Waffen S.S. officer, Fritz von Balluseck. As the Nazi commandant of the Polish town of Jedrzejow, von Balluseck used his position of power to abuse children sexually. He reportedly told the Jewish children under his watch, "It is either the gas chamber or me."[89] They got both. In 1957 von Balluseck was put on trial for murdering a child and was convicted of molesting scores of others long after the war had ended. The West German press reported von Balluseck's collaboration with Kinsey. One paper noted that von Balluseck had been "encouraged to continue his research" by Kinsey.[90] The presiding judge in von Balluseck's trial said to the defendant, "I got the impression that you got to the children in order to impress Kinsey and to deliver him material." Von Balluseck responded, "Kinsey himself asked me for that."[91]

Kinsey's child molesters are beyond the reach of justice. Their victims, however, are for the most part still with us and can be helped if they are found. Unfortunately, Indiana University's Kinsey Institute remains clouded in secrecy. Concerning "interviews" with small girls, Reisman wonders, "If, as the Kinsey team claimed, a parent was always present during the interview between 'Uncle Kinsey' and 'Uncle Pomeroy' and the small girl, and if all of the names of every subject is in secret code in the Institute data base, as they claimed, why are these children not traceable?"[92]

One victim who has come forward is Esther White.* As a child in 1940s Ohio, she was repeatedly molested by her father. "It was for years,"

---

*Esther White is not her real name.

she said. "He was not physically abusive, maybe psychologically abusive, [treating me] like a slave."[93] Even among child molesters, Esther's dad was peculiar. He consulted his watch after he finished raping his daughter. He filled out charts and questionnaires. And he apparently shared the fact that he was forcing sex upon his daughter with members of his family and other acquaintances.[94]

In the mid-1940s, Esther traveled from her home to Columbus, Ohio. She remembers the trip as "a big deal." In Columbus she met some scientists. One of them was Alfred Kinsey, she says. "There was a meeting between Alfred Kinsey and myself and two other men from the Kinsey Institute, my father, and my grandfather, and my great-grandmother," she remembers. "I was a child. I didn't understand any of it." Kinsey's connection to her childhood trauma didn't dawn on her until the early 1990s. "I basically buried it until I heard Judith [Reisman]. . . . I knew I had met Alfred Kinsey, but it didn't mean anything. He was introduced to me. My grandfather was very proud of knowing him. My grandfather went to Indiana University."[95] Records confirm that the Kinsey team stopped in Columbus to interview young children during that time period.[96]

When asked if Kinsey's research was worth it, considering the cost of obtaining such data, current Kinsey Institute president John Bancroft curtly responded, "Consider the cost of remaining ignorant."[97]

To that, White quietly responds, "Remaining ignorant would have meant I would have been a virgin when I married my husband. [Kinsey] took away my virginity by brainwashing my father."[98]

ALL THE NEWS THAT'S FIT TO PRINT

On the first day that journalists were allowed to print stories on Kinsey's initial report, more than 70 percent of the nation's daily newspapers did so, according to *Editor and Publisher* magazine.[99] The reaction to *Sexual Behavior in the Human Female* was overwhelmingly positive: "Analysis of the leading magazines found all but one *(Cosmopolitan)* favourable, and of the 124 leading newspapers 64 per cent favourable to 31 per cent not."[100]

"[T]hey are presenting facts," *Look* magazine insisted before the release of the first volume. "They are revealing not what should be, but what is."[101] *Reader's Scope* labeled the work "the most complete and objectively scientific report ever assembled on the sex life of American men."[102] *Harper's* assured readers that the book was "a soberly documented report," adding, "Experts who have closely scrutinized the interviewing techniques of Kinsey and his associates indorse the scientific validity and state further that the people so far interviewed represent a fair cross section of the American population."[103] A *San Francisco Chronicle* reviewer labeled the *Male* report the "least biased piece of research" that he had ever seen.[104] Five and a half years later, the *Chronicle* also praised the *Female* report as "a highly scientific piece of research" whose authors were "open-minded" and harbored "no preconceived ideas that the results should be one way or another."[105]

Kinsey controlled the public flow of information by forcing members of the Fourth Estate to sign a thirteen-point contract. Journalists had to agree to come to Bloomington to review Kinsey's work or receive a summary by the authors. "In addition," writes James Jones, "they had to consent to submit copies of their articles prior to publication to Kinsey, who would review them for factual accuracy" and correct any "errors."[106] What was "error" and what was criticism was often indistinguishable for the hypersensitive zoologist.

In scholarly journals, Kinsey corrupted the process of the traditional, and ethical, practice of peer review.[107] Although journal editors typically assign neutral scholars to review academic books, Kinsey directed a network of hacks to submit reviews. James Jones describes how "several scholars actually submitted drafts to [Kinsey] for comment before their reviews were published."[108]

When writers did take issue with his work, a wrathful Kinsey fumed. "*Any* criticism was both a personal attack on him, a rejection of him, and the result of deep emotional and psychological flaws and prejudices in the critic," Gathorne-Hardy observes.[109] Kinsey invariably responded in two ways: He wondered aloud if he could sue his critics, and he responded— even to ancillary objections—with shouts of "Science!"[110]

His heirs within the Kinsey Institute operate in much the same manner. When Indianapolis radio station WNDE announced that it would be discussing *Kinsey, Sex, and Fraud,* a book critical of Kinsey, the institute implied legal action, leading the station to pull the plug on the program.[111] A 1983 Pat Buchanan opinion piece mentioning the sex films made by Kinsey and his colleagues elicited a more direct legal threat from the Kinsey Institute. In a letter, the institute denied, incredibly, that such films were ever made. Not intimidated, the pugnacious columnist retorted with yet another column. The institute backed down.[112] When National Institutes of Health scientist Walter Stewart endorsed *Kinsey, Sex, and Fraud,* Kinsey Institute president June Reinisch wrote to the organization's leadership in a not-so-subtle attempt at intimidation. "If such a scientist does exist and is on the staff of NIH," she wrote, "I thought you would like to know he is making these kinds of statements."[113]

Journalists gave, and some continue to give, the Kinsey Reports a free ride. Whether the result of laziness or behavioral solidarity, the effect was the same: The American public accepted Kinsey's work as pure science. His books were beyond criticism. This journalistic ineptitude laid the groundwork for the unquestioned acceptance of his findings by historians, sex educators, lawmakers, sociologists, scientists, and other opinion shapers. The early words of praise for Kinsey's work retain their impact today, despite the severe flaws that have been revealed in his research. Those who uphold Kinsey today still laud him for supposed scientific breakthroughs.

KINSEY'S PROGENY

Decades have passed since Kinsey's death in 1957. Kinsey's is no longer a household name, nor has it been for some time. Yet his legacy looms larger than ever. The Kinseyan model serves as the basis for most modern sex education. Historians like Halberstam, Johnson, O'Neil, and Manchester uncritically accept his findings and pass on to readers that Kinsey was a high priest of science. Law students base their understanding of sex crimes on Indiana University's Institute for Sex Research, now called the Kinsey Institute. Westlaw, the most widely used legal database, has more than 650 Kinsey citations in law journals from 1980 to 2000. He is cited more than any other sex researcher.[114] The Science Citation Index and the Social Science Citation Index list Kinsey as a source almost 6,000 times during this same time period, with 2,000 more citations than the more current Masters and Johnson. The academic journals listed in these two indices cite Kinsey more than twice as often as they do Sigmund Freud and Margaret Mead.[115]

Kinsey's influence, however, is greatest among a small but growing number of anthropologists, professors of gay and lesbian studies, and sociologists who view sex between children and adults as beneficial to both parties. Kinsey is the first and usually the only man of "science" invoked to gain legitimacy for arguments in favor of what most people view as child rape.

In an essay in *Lavender Culture*, which has been used as a text in many college courses, the author maintains that Americans must work to dismantle "two archaic concepts." What are these "archaic concepts"? The first is "the innocence of children," and the second is "the potential harmfulness of sex."[116] The author calls to overturn "repressive, ageist legislation."[117] To do this, he advises his student readers to "proselytize," to reach "young gay people with the message that gay is good, that they are not diseased or sinful, that they should get out of their families as soon as they can, that they should organize with other gay people," and "that it's all right to be having sex." He adds, "If we don't proselytize with our message, they're going to with theirs and we will have future generations of gay people who wait until their twenties before they start to live."[118]

Kinsey is the source on which this whole argument rests. How do we know this? The author says so. He writes, "[T]he myth that children are not sexual beings . . . is maintained, after all, in the face of massive evidence to the contrary. . . . Infants in their cribs have orgasms—Kinsey documented them in babies less than a year old."[119]

The very first essay in *The Lesbian and Gay Studies Reader*, a textbook that Princeton, Dartmouth, Cornell, and many other prestigious colleges have used in course offerings, also gives "cross-generational" encounters the stamp of approval—with Kinsey once more providing the supporting "scientific" evidence. Feminist anthropologist Gayle Rubin writes:

> Like communists and homosexuals in the 1950s, boy lovers are so stigmatized that it is difficult to find defenders for their civil liberties, let alone erotic orientation. Consequently, the police have feasted on them. Local police, the FBI and watchdog postal inspectors have joined to build a huge apparatus whose sole aim is to wipe out the community of men who love underaged youth. In twenty years or so, when some of the smoke has cleared, it will be much easier to show that these men have been the victims of a savage and undeserved witch hunt. A lot of people will be embarrassed by their collaboration with this persecution, but it will be too late to do much good for those men who have spent their lives in prison.[120]

Rubin characterizes viewpoints opposing sex between children and adults as having "more in common with ideologies of racism than with true ethics."[121]

Rubin cites the work of Indiana University's Institute for Sex Research several times in her essay. She writes, "Alfred Kinsey approached the study of sex with the same uninhibited curiosity he had previously applied to examining species of wasp. His scientific detachment gave his work a refreshing neutrality."[122] By writing of Kinsey's "scientific detachment" and "refreshing neutrality," Rubin gives her propedophilia screed an objective, analytical air.

Cornell University has offered a whole course that, critics claim, promotes pedophilia. According to the professor who teaches "The Sexual Child," the class's mission is "to undermine preconceived notions about what a child is." As part of its required reading, the course features books and essays that seek to change the way we view sex between children and adults.[123] In *Public Sex*, for example, self-proclaimed "sexual outlaw" Pat Califa scolds parents for denying children their "sexual freedom." She* writes, "Culturally induced schizophrenia allows parents to make sentimental speeches about the fleeting innocence of childhood and the happiness of years unbroken by carnal lust—and exhaust themselves policing the sex lives of their children. Children are celibate because their parents prevent them from playing with other little kids or adults."[124]

Kinsey is used to justify the author's rants in favor of pedophilia. Califa states, "Even though many prominent sex researchers have documented the existence of sexual capacity in children (for instance Kinsey verified the occurrence of orgasm in girls and boys at less than six months of age), our society is fanatically determined to deny it."[125]

SCIENCE'S FIFTH COLUMN

"The whole army of religion," Kinsey once confessed to a confidant, "is our central enemy."[126] Kinsey's weapon of choice to defeat superstition was the club of "science," which he promiscuously wielded to silence critics without having to answer their charges. Yet Kinsey was not just an adversary of the established order of religion. He was an enemy of science as well.

Perhaps the most basic premise of the scientific method is that a theory can be proven true if others can replicate its findings. Despite his popularity, Kinsey's findings have not been matched in any study on sexuality before or since. Kinsey was fond of blasting the inadequacy of all sex

---

*Califa, who at the time of the release of *Public Sex* was a woman, has since undergone "gender reassignment surgery."

researchers who came before him.[127] The German Magnus Hirschfeld found a homosexuality rate of 2 percent among his fellow countrymen, a figure seconded for Americans by Havelock Ellis.[128] Louis Terman came up with a 4 percent figure for an admittedly unique sample group of men, while tabulations of the earlier calculations of Selective Service Boards and others noticed homosexuality in about 1 percent of servicemen or inductees during World War I.[129] A 1994 University of Chicago study reported that about three-fourths of married men and more than four-fifths of married women were faithful to their spouses and just 2 percent of the population was homosexual.[130] The fact that numerous recent studies have also come out with similar figures, according to one admirer, "is a measure of how they were all equally wrong, not that Kinsey was."[131]

The sophists of ancient Greece are said to have created a false air of intellectualism by growing solemn beards and relying on multisyllabic verbiage. Their look and speech demanded an undeserved authority, immune from criticism. A similar modus operandi was at work at the Institute for Sex Research. Kinsey's bowtie and lab coat took the place of the sophist's elongated beard. His "I-am-a-scientist" self-righteousness at any questioning of his findings substituted for the Greeks' highfalutin gibberish. These methods are an admission of intellectual cowardice and seek to scare skeptics away from examining the facts.

Kinsey's rejection of the scientific method; his contempt for statistical sampling; his stacking sample groups with prostitutes, homosexuals, and prison inmates; and his reliance on the word of pedophiles to determine whether young children enjoyed sex with adults are all examples of how the Harvard-trained zoologist was, at base, a propagandist.

Kinsey sought to democratize sex. All sex, he decreed, is equal. Bestiality, adultery, masturbation, procreation, and incest were all, in the vernacular of Kinsey, merely "outlets." What gave sex value was neither the love between the two participants nor the greater good that it served, but the attainment of orgasm. If the end result was the same, any way of getting there was of equal worth. Yet even in Kinsey's egalitarian utopia, as evidenced by the length of his chapters on homosexuality or his Kinsey Scale—which awarded a 0 to heterosexuality and a 6 to homosexuality at the favored end of the continuum—some sex was more equal than others.[132]

As in any democracy, King Numbers ruled. Since his tables, graphs, and charts showed that millions of Americans engaged in what was deemed immoral activity, Kinsey made clear that sexual mores needed to be changed. Everyone's sin, the old saying dictates, is no one's sin.

By presenting a false picture of human sexual practices, Kinsey exerted a negative peer pressure on Americans—but from peers who didn't exist. Since no one can ever truly know the frequency or variety of this most private of matters, how could readers in the 1950s categorically discount the validity of Kinsey's survey? This was the genius of Kinsey's hoax. However much it flew in the face of common sense, no one could really say for sure if the neighbors' bedroom turned into a bacchanalia once the lights went out. If the new perception was that everyone else was doing it—paying for sex, sleeping with coworkers' wives, seeking anonymous encounters—societal constraints could no longer prevent individuals from engaging in pleasurable activities that ultimately had a social cost. Hence came the Sexual Revolution.

The Kinsey Reports weren't a mirror of society held up to its face. They were a reflection of its chief author. The Kinsey Reports were Alfred Kinsey's pathologies writ large upon America. They were rationalizations of Kinsey's own perverse behavior. He wasn't sick, he convinced himself. Society was. It couldn't be cured until it conformed to him. His "science" would be a particularly effective tool to make sure that it did.

The Kinsey Reports of the 1940s and '50s tell us next to nothing about the sexual practices of Americans. What they tell us about Alfred Kinsey, and the intellectuals who continue to promote his findings, is far more revealing.

"COERCION IN A GOOD CAUSE"

Environmentalism's False Prophet

Sometimes lying is okay, like when you know
what's good for people more than they do.

—SOUTH PARK'S
"Rob Reiner"

IN THE PREDAWN HOURS OF AUGUST 1, 2003, TERRORISTS DESTROYED
a 1,500-unit condominium complex under construction in University
Town Center, California, outside San Diego. The inferno reportedly
climbed two hundred feet into the sky, rained down softball-sized fire-
balls, and melted plastic lawn furniture blocks away. One disgusted car-
penter remarked, "I am out of work now. Thank you, arsonist." Though
no lives were lost, the economic costs were staggering. The conflagration
carried an estimated $50 million price tag, reducing wood to ash, felling
a $7 million construction crane, and imploding a 500-gallon fuel farm.

Who were the terrorists who caused this devastation? The group
claiming responsibility was a radical environmentalist operation called the
Earth Liberation Front. How, exactly, setting this fire helped the planet
was left unexplained.[1]

The San Diego arson was by no means an isolated outburst from environmentalist radicals. In late 1999, environmentalists axed 180 trees at
the University of Washington. The Washington Tree Improvement Association killed the trees in protest of the school's experiment cultivating
hybrid poplar trees. The 180 trees, however, weren't the modified poplar
trees. They were ordinary raspberry bushes.[2]

Even mainstream voices can do substantial damage when fueled by emotion rather than knowledge. After the Exxon *Valdez* spilled more than a quarter million barrels of oil into Alaska's Prince William Sound, the public demanded an artificial cleanup despite warnings from experts. The experts, it turns out, were right to voice objections to pressure-washing the Alaskan coast. Danish academic Bjorn Lomborg notes in his landmark 2001 book *The Skeptical Environmentalist* that the cleanup actually killed marine life. "By way of experiment," Lomborg writes, "some stretches of beach were left uncleaned, and it transpired that life there returned after just 18 months, whereas it did not do so to the cleaned beaches for three to four years. The oil experts said this would be the case time and time again during the cleanup—but in vain, as this did not harmonize with the public view of things, i.e. that a cleanup had to be better for animals."[3]

Cutting down trees, committing arson, and exacerbating ecological catastrophes may have made people feel better. But these actions didn't help the environment. They harmed it.

Wanting to help the environment and helping the environment are two different things. Too many activists mistake great ardor for great wisdom. It matters little how passionate one is for a cause when one hasn't the slightest clue how to serve that cause effectively.

The intellectuals of the movement propagate extremist doctrines that their followers accept as dogma. And *dogma* is certainly the right word, as environmentalism has become, for many, a new religion.

The faithful accept the teachings of the environmentalist high priests, no matter how hyperbolic or antihuman those pronouncements might be. Insane declarations deserving scorn instead receive welcome within the movements:

- "Human beings, as a species, have no more value than slugs," contends *Earth First! Journal* editor John Davis.[4]

- "Don't bring any more humans into being." So begins Paul Watson's Ten Commandments. A founder of Greenpeace and a director of the Sierra Club, Watson believes "earthworms are *far* more valuable than people" and the "world will be a much nicer place without us."[5] The pioneer of tree-spiking showed no repentance after a spike maimed a mill worker. "Those loggers don't give a damn for future generations,"

Watson remarked. "And if they don't have any compassion for the future, I don't have any compassion for them."[6]

- "To feed a starving child is to exacerbate the world population problem," maintained Yale professor Lamont Cole.[7]

- "The only hope for the world is to make sure there is not another United States," says the Environmental Defense Fund's Michael Oppenheimer. "We can't let other countries have the same number of cars, the amount of industrialization, we have in the U.S. We have to stop these Third World countries right where they are."[8]

- The Worldwatch Institute ominously observes, "The twentieth century has been extraordinarily successful for the human species—perhaps too successful."[9]

One of the most influential environmentalist preachers of recent decades is Professor Paul Ehrlich of Stanford University. Ehrlich shares much in common with another professor, Alfred Kinsey. Like Kinsey, Ehrlich grew up in the suburbs of northern New Jersey. Both men amassed giant collections of bugs; Kinsey's winged insect of choice was the gall wasp, while Ehrlich's passion lay in butterflies. More important, however, was their shared interest in human beings—specifically, in reshaping society according to their own tastes. When their work drew criticism, they both dismissed their critics as enemies of science. The more unfounded Ehrlich's and Kinsey's assertions, the louder their scientific boasting became.

In Paul Ehrlich's case, his "scientific" pronouncements consist of doomsday scenarios that have been proven wrong again and again. Still, like other environmentalist intellectuals, Ehrlich has continued to issue dire warnings about the future of the planet. And many followers continue to accept his proclamations as gospel.

Looking at Ehrlich's career reveals why the environmentalist movement has bred such fanaticism, stupidity, and dishonesty.

THE BET

At the dawn of the 1980s, two men made a bet. Both were scholars, they were the same age, and both had grown up around Newark, New Jersey. In just about every other way, they differed. Paul Ehrlich, Stanford's environmentalist crusader, argued that the world was running out of natural resources. Julian Simon, a proponent of laissez-faire economics who later taught business administration at the University of Maryland, countered that new technologies would help find previously undiscovered deposits of resources. The optimist challenged the pessimist to name any five natural resources, and, the optimist said, by the end of the decade there would be a greater abundance of all five. Ehrlich mocked the free-market scholar's challenge, boasting that he would quickly "accept Simon's astonishing offer before other greedy people jump in."[10]

Each man put $1,000 on the line. If prices depreciated (Ehrlich picked chrome, copper, nickel, tin, and tungsten as his resources), Simon would win and collect the difference between the depreciated amount and $1,000. If prices escalated, Ehrlich would win and pocket the increase on the value of the metals. Rising prices, the professors agreed, would indicate problems with supply meeting demand; falling prices would indicate that supply outpaced demand.

In the wake of numerous oil crises and an economically disastrous decade, Ehrlich's wager was regarded as a sure bet by many of his colleagues. Several even joined him in making the same agreement with the eccentric Simon. It seemed a no-lose proposition for the environmentalists, especially since Simon had allowed his adversaries to choose which resources to bet on. The libertarian had seemingly stacked the deck against himself.

Ten years after they made their bet, Ehrlich conceded defeat. The prices of chrome, copper, nickel, tin, and tungsten had all fallen. So had the prices of oil, gold, silver, and so many of the world's other precious resources. This was neither the first time nor the last that Paul Ehrlich would make an embarrassingly wrong forecast about the world.

THE POPULATION BOMB

"The battle to feed all of humanity is over," Ehrlich memorably declared in his 1968 book *The Population Bomb.* "In the 1970's the world will undergo famines—hundreds of millions of people are going to starve to death."[11] He promised readers that "a minimum of ten million people, most of them children, will starve to death during each year of the 1970s. But this is a mere handful compared to the number that will be starving before the end of the century. And it is now too late to take action to save many of those people."[12]

Ehrlich's tome contained many predictions about the future of what he called "Spaceship Earth." Starvation wouldn't be the only problem, for by "1984 the United States will quite literally be dying of thirst."[13]

Didn't happen.

Leaving open the possibility of global warming, he also contended, "With a few degrees of cooling, a new ice age might be upon us, with rapid and drastic effects on the agricultural productivity of the temperate regions."[14]

Didn't happen.

"I predict that the rate of soil deterioration will accelerate as the food crisis intensifies," he continued, also opining that "meat will get more and more expensive, and most of us will become vegetarians."[15]

Didn't happen.

"Will our gross national product soon be reduced to no national product?" Ehrlich answered in the affirmative.[16]

Didn't happen.

He spoke favorably about a book called *Famine—1975!*, "which may be remembered as one of the most important books of our age."[17]

Didn't happen.

With regard to disease, he informed, "A net result of 1.2 billion deaths—one out of every three people—is not inconceivable."[18]

Didn't happen.

Nuclear conflict, too, was likely. "It seems inevitable that world political tensions will increase," he noted.[19]

Didn't happen.

All this from a man who described himself as "an eternal optimist."[20]

Ehrlich's predictions missed the mark. Living conditions improved. There was more food for everyone. Drinking water became cleaner and there was enough to go around. Life expectancy rates rose dramatically. Economic growth, which Ehrlich and other environmentalists see as a negative thing, continued at a sprinter's pace during the 1980s and 1990s. An ice age didn't befall the planet; in fact, others began to talk of global warming. New technology effectively combated diseases that once meant certain death. The Cold War ended, there was no nuclear war, and international tensions decreased.

Ehrlich's predictions weren't merely wrong. They were absurd.

Although *The Population Bomb* factored population growth projections into its equations, the book assumed no growth in the human capacity to deal with increasing needs for food, water, precious metals, and other resources. It might have seemed that the world was running out of copper, for instance, because that metal was being used increasingly in electrical wiring. But then someone invented fiber-optic technology, which relies on sand, a much more abundant material. Ehrlich, like Thomas Malthus and other population doomsayers before him, disregarded what Julian Simon would call "the ultimate resource," the human mind.

The Population Bomb offered up a number of fictional scenarios that made the author's predictions seem reasonable by comparison. Scenario #1 depicted an America of food riots, ration cards, and street-corner "Breath-a-life" machines. Billions die of starvation.[21] In Scenario #2, one-third of the world's population—more than a billion people—died of a mysterious disease called Lassa Fever. With an air of I-told-you-so, Ehrlich concluded the chapter by writing, "[T]he lessons of overpopulation were clear for all to see."[22] Alas, in this scenario, we didn't listen to wise men like Ehrlich. Scenario #3 was the "optimistic" scenario. In this final conjecture, "World action came too late for almost one billion people."[23] The world, however, adopted the program Ehrlich was pushing and averted even greater catastrophe.

With impending doom on the horizon, what could we do to prevent environmental disaster? Ehrlich implored his readers to "reverse the government's present system of encouraging reproduction and replace it with a series of financial rewards and penalties designed to discourage reproduction."[24] To do this he called for "luxury taxes . . . placed on layettes, cribs, diapers, diaper services, expensive toys," and other seemingly benign items.[25] Responsibility Prizes would be awarded to couples who stayed childless for five years or more and to men who underwent vasectomies, and a cash lottery would be organized with prize eligibility limited to small families.[26] More sex education, unlimited access to abortion, and easy availability of sterilization were additional programs that would supposedly push society in the right direction: "Obviously, such measures should be coordinated by a powerful government agency. A federal Bureau of Population and Environment should be set up to determine the optimum population size for the United States and devise measures to establish it. . . . [T]he BPE also would encourage more research on human sex determination."[27]

Internationally, he saw it as the role of the United States to combat population with the same vigor its military used abroad to combat enemies. In India, for instance, he demanded forced sterilization for men with three or more children. "Coercion? Perhaps, but coercion in a good cause."[28]

He confessed about his entire program, "The operation will demand many apparently brutal and heartless decisions."[29] This honest utterance was a rarity in a book that butchered the facts.

THE PROFESSOR WHO CRIED WOLF

The doomsday that Paul Ehrlich envisioned for the 1970s never came to pass. This was, for him, a minor inconvenience. The Stanford professor simply revised his apocalyptic forecast for a few years later. When, yet again, his predictions missed both bull's-eye and target, he made still more predictions that delayed the day of reckoning even further.

"It seems certain," he remarked six years after his initial predictions, "that before 1985, mankind will enter a genuine age of scarcity in which many things . . . will be in short supply."[30] In 1990, Ehrlich, along with a colleague, pushed back the time of worldwide catastrophe a few more years: "Several hundreds of millions to a billion or so could die of hunger in future decades."[31] "One thing seems safe to predict," he wrote with more certainty that same year, "starvation and epidemic disease will raise the death rates over most of the planet" and humanity will incur the "deaths of many hundreds of millions of people in famines."[32] Midway through the 1990s, he warned, "If population continues to grow at the rate it's growing now, I think by the year 2050 civilization will have largely disappeared."[33] At the end of that decade he again predicted the end of days: "We're facing an extinction crisis worse than that of the dinosaurs."[34]

The grim outlook Ehrlich depicts for mankind seems like a fairy tale in comparison with the bleak fate that supposedly awaits our friends in the plant and animal kingdoms. In 1981, Ehrlich announced that the planet was losing 250,000 species per annum. If this were true, life on Earth would be completely extinct within a few decades. While it's impossible to know exactly how many species perish every year, reasonable estimates ascertain that the planet has lost 25 species every decade since 1600.[35] Ehrlich's calculations exaggerate by about a factor of 100,000.

Things are getting better, but this is the last thing that Ehrlich and other Chicken Littles want the public to know. Globally, forest cover saw a slight increase over the latter half of the twentieth century.[36] Since 1970, the six pollutants indicating outdoor air quality tracked by the Environmental Protection Agency are down 48 percent.[37] Since 1930, London's air pollution has declined 90 percent and New York City's untreated sewage has decreased 99.9 percent.[38] Since 1973, mileage has improved 60 percent on cars made by American manufacturers.[39] Americans produced an average of three pounds of waste daily in 1985. By 2000, the weight had dropped to 2.5 pounds.[40]

One daring to challenge Ehrlich with such evidence, or with the obvious fact that his predictions have been wildly inaccurate, invites trouble. The professor fiercely protects his reputation by attacking anyone who questions his "scientific" arguments, just as Alfred Kinsey did. Refusing to publicly debate critics like Julian Simon, Ehrlich has preferred to call them names. In their 1996 book *Betrayal of Science and Reason*, Ehrlich and his wife warned that an antienvironmentalist backlash had "acquired an aura of credibility." With chapter titles such as "Fables About Population and Food," the Ehrlichs contended that critics of environmentalism had "produced what amounts to a body of anti-science—a twisting of the findings of empirical science—to bolster a predetermined worldview and to support a political agenda."[41] In other words, the very sins Ehrlich was so blatantly guilty of he projected on his enemies. The Ehrlichs also challenged the credentials of scientists who disagreed with their perspective, noting that their opponents were in the minority. Even as they benefited from several million dollars of largesse from environmental charities, the Ehrlichs wondered if their critics had been paid off. The couple even argued that many who questioned global warming, human culpability in the ozone hole, or overpopulation were "right-wing," pointing out that one opponent, gasp, "happened to share" his opinion "with radio talk-show host Rush Limbaugh."[42]

Ehrlich has perceived threats not just from the "right wing," but from within his own movement as well. In the 1970s, when fellow environmentalist Barry Commoner wrote a book claiming that pollution, not overpopulation, was the environment's worst enemy, Ehrlich attempted to prevent the book from being published, Commoner alleged. "Ehrlich is so intent upon population control as to be unwilling to tolerate open discussion of data that might weaken the argument for it," Commoner claimed.[43]

By attacking those who call him on his research and forecasts, Paul Ehrlich has preserved his reputation as a man of science. Retaining his respectability has helped ensure that he can go on making outrageous claims like the ones he made in *The Population Bomb*.

One might ask, though, how a serial exaggerator and prophet of false divinations can continue to enjoy the popularity he does. The fact is, in the polluted sty of the intellectuals, Ehrlich's scare tactics have enhanced his standing. Foundations kept the money flowing his way. After all, grants and contributions dry up for groups that say everything is okay. Without the feeling of an emergency, ecological concerns run the risk of getting placed on the back burner. Journalists, who don't cover good news with the fervor they devote to bad news, anointed him the population "expert." Scholars cited his work on population.

However ridiculous Ehrlich's ruminations appear in hindsight, their desired effect of frightening people into changing their lifestyles and governments into changing their laws justifies the whole endeavor, his supporters reason. Ehrlich's Stanford colleague Stephen Schneider exemplified how the green movement is willing to betray science for the larger cause. "Scientists should consider stretching the truth to get some broad based support, to capture the public's imagination," proclaimed Schneider. He added, "[W]e have to offer up scary scenarios, make simplified dramatic statements, and make little mention of any doubts we might have."[44]

Promoting untruths is a perfectly worthy undertaking, green fanatics hold, so long as those untruths further the correct causes.

WHERE SCIENCE AND PROPAGANDA MEET

Paul Ehrlich's scare stories are just some of the catastrophic scenarios that environmentalists have been putting forward for decades that have never materialized. An unusually hot or cool summer, an abundance or dearth of hurricanes, too much or too little snow—all can evoke cries of impending doom. Although Ehrlich and other environmentalists seem to have done more than "stretch the truth," their devotees remain fervently committed to their crusade. The fact that what Ehrlich said was wildly off is of little importance to a true believer. The true believer's commitment is based not on facts, logic, or reason but on blind faith. Environmentalism's relation to religion is not just metaphorical. It is in some cases literal. Eco-feminists have invented a religion that worships Gaia, or Mother

Earth, while other environmentalists have reverted to pagan earth worship. Many of those who haven't gone so far to formally adopt an earth-centered faith practice environmentalism as their de facto religion.

Oddly, the educated devotees of environmentalism are often the same people who scoff at the unscientific and superstitious who built earthen Y2K shelters from old school buses in Idaho, or at the primitive peoples who trembled at the sight of any astronomical phenomenon such as a comet or eclipse. The educated classes also look down on doomsday groups from the distant past such as the Millerites, who determined precisely that Jesus Christ would return on October 22, 1844. Yet radical environmentalists have much in common with millenarians. Both groups alter their lives for something that is extremely unlikely to occur. For hard-core environmentalists, this means having few children, shunning effective laundry detergents, flushing only occasionally, and going vegetarian, among other things.

Radical environmentalists aren't content to make these changes themselves. They want the rest of us to obey their dictates. Like all ideologues, environmentalists believe themselves to be the beneficiaries of an enlightenment not revealed to everyone else. They carry the burden of knowing what is good for the public and knowing that the public does not know what is good for itself. Paul Ehrlich and other like-minded people argue that if their proposals are rejected, we risk environmental disaster. If their proposals are accepted, the worst that could happen is that we prepare for something that will never occur. Better safe than sorry, they say.

But consider the grave costs in kowtowing to environmentalist fear-mongering:

- Banning the pesticide DDT has had dreadful consequences. The pseudo-science of Rachel Carson's *Silent Spring* sparked the crusade to prohibit DDT, which became the *de rigueur* cause of the 1960s. Despite the fact that no study has ever shown that the pesticide harms humans, scores of countries around the world heeded the call to ban DDT. Millions of people died as a result. So effective is DDT as a combatant of malaria that its inventor, Dr. Paul Muller, was honored with the Nobel Prize for medicine in 1948. After the chemical was introduced in Sri Lanka, for instance, cases of malaria dropped from 3 million in 1946 to just 29 in 1964. That year, Sri Lanka banned DDT, and within just five years, the number of malarial infections had jumped back up to a half million.[45] In Zanzibar, malaria cases plummeted from afflicting 70 percent of the populace in 1958 to less than 5 percent only six years later. When the pesticide was later banned, the malaria rate ballooned, to the point that by the mid-1980s more than half of the population was infected. In 1984, the chief malariologist for the U.S. Agency for International Development remarked, "If Zanzibar's [DDT spraying] program hadn't been suspended in the 1960s, malaria would now be 98% eradicated." It was estimated that 3 million Africans died of malaria that same year.[46]

- Acid rain served as the environmental scare story of the 1980s. Describing acid rain as an "ecological Hiroshima," the "experts" warned that forests would die off and that lakes would become giant death pools for the fish inhabiting them. "Acid rain," one author maintained, "has become one of the most serious threats to life here on earth." It wasn't a threat to life at all. In time, lakes grew less acidic. Some studies indicated that trees experiencing moderate levels of acid rain grew more quickly. The United Nations even conceded in 1997 that "the widespread death of European forests due to air pollution which was predicted by many in the 1980's did not occur."[47] Once an incessant grievance in classrooms, legislatures, and newspapers, acid rain has simply disappeared from discussion.

- Like tales of acid rain's tree-eating destruction a decade earlier, the threat of ozone depletion—quite literally, the sky-is-falling story of the 1990s—is now almost universally regarded as wildly exaggerated. In the late fall of 2000, NASA announced that the ozone hole was shrinking. The hole, the agency predicted, would be entirely gone within a few decades.[48] Some scientists claimed that the fortunate development was a result of mankind's rapid rejection of environmentally damaging products. Others, who had rejected the human-causation theory of ozone depletion all along, were skeptical of that conclusion. Regardless of who was right, predictions of the ozone layer's imminent demise were wrong.

And those are just some of the green proposals that have caused grave harm. When the hysteria over the pesticide Alar gripped the media in the late 1980s, many apple farmers were ruined—all over a pesticide that posed no threat to humans unless one imbibed it in massive doses.[49] Many believe that removing bigger cars from the highways resulted in unnecessary fatalities in auto accidents involving lighter, fuel-efficient cars. Not only did mileage standards result in this unforeseen cost, the argument goes, but they had the unintended consequence of boosting the sale of gas-guzzling sport utility vehicles, which do not have to abide by the same gas mileage standards as cars. Nuclear power, among the cleanest and most cost-efficient energy sources, has been curtailed in the West not by sound science but by political protestors.

For the environmentalists, too, there is a danger in continually employing scare tactics. While garnering support in the short term, the hyperbolic claims of extremists can dissipate support in the long term. As Ehrlich and other doomsayers have been discredited among segments of the public, popular support has naturally eroded for sound environmental protections. Legitimate conservation advocates are lumped together with Ehrlich and his ilk by an indiscriminate public. When real concerns arise over the ecosystem, a portion of the population will, not surprisingly, resist making the sacrifices necessary to preserve our natural surroundings because of an evolving skepticism of environmentalists' claims. As evidenced by the smog in Houston or Mexico City, much still needs to be done to clean up the Earth and pass on to the next generation a more healthful living space. Ehrlich's wild declarations, despite his intentions, have hurt these efforts.

THE PROPHET AND THE PARIAH

In 1990, Paul Ehrlich made good on his bet with Julian Simon. He sent Simon a check for $576.07, the difference between $1,000 in 1980 dollars and the 1990 depreciated value of the resources named in the wager. So overwhelming were the results in Simon's favor that had the bet's participants not agreed to take inflation into account, Simon still would have won. "I got schnookered," Ehrlich complained of his bet. Yet, given that the entomologist was afforded the luxury of picking the very things that constituted the subject of the bet, it is hard to see how anyone but Ehrlich himself "schnookered" Ehrlich. The best-selling author wore his bitterness on his sleeve. Simon, Ehrlich remarked, was "clueless." After Simon offered double-or-nothing, Ehrlich proposed guidelines for a new wager—for example, that the gap between rich and poor will widen, AIDS will spread to greater numbers, and global temperatures will rise. Predicting a victory, the Stanford professor declared, "This time, we are going to ram it down his throat."[50] Simon rejected the overture. Many of

Ehrlich's social barometers were poor indicators of the health of mankind, he believed. There would be no second bet.

As misguided as his claims have been, Ehrlich has maintained the admiration of a sequacious herd of academics, journalists, and foundation heads. Losing his famous bet with Julian Simon was a mere pittance to pay compared with the massive sums of money he amassed in prizes for his environmental writings. In 1990, the Royal Swedish Academy of Sciences bestowed on him the Crafoord Prize, and the MacArthur Foundation gave him a $345,000 "genius grant." In 1993, he joined past recipients John Denver and Jacques Cousteau as a winner of the World Ecology Award. Ehrlich and his wife, Anne, received a $250,000 prize in honor of the late senator and ketchup king John Heinz in 1995. In 1998, the couple was awarded the Tyler Prize for Environmental Achievement, which carried with it a purse of $200,000. In 1999, he was honored with the Blue Planet Prize from the Asahi Glass Foundation of Japan, for which he took home 50 million yen, or $422,000. Other awards during the decade include the Volvo Environmental Prize, the Sierra Club's John Muir Award, the United Nations' Sasakawa Environment Prize, and the Heineken Prize for Environmental Science. During his career, he has pocketed several million dollars from these and other awards.

Beyond money, Ehrlich has earned respect and even adulation in some circles. Although Paul Ehrlich has authored or coauthored more than thirty-five books, his fame has come about almost solely because of *The Population Bomb*. The book's popularity helped spark paid speaking tours throughout the world and twenty-five appearances on Johnny Carson's late-night television show. Along with such books as Rachel Carson's *Silent Spring* and Al Gore's *Earth in the Balance*, *The Population Bomb* continues to have an enormous impact on the way individuals think about the world around them. As with other books in the genre, its influence is due largely to the apocalyptic scenarios it foretold for the future world. Rather than appealing to the reader's intellect, it sought from him a more primal response: fear. Fortunately for us, unfortunately for its author's credibility, the warnings of *The Population Bomb* were off, way off. This did little, however, to affect the judgment of other academics, who continued to assign the book to students long after its doomsday scenarios had been proven wrong. Its popularity among professors who would require their students to read the book helped account for a good chunk of the 3 million copies sold. The media, too, were complicit in furthering *The Population Bomb*'s mythology. For instance, in 1990—by which point the

United States should have been "dying of thirst," according to Ehrlich's predictions—NBC's *Today* show invited the Stanford professor to produce a twelve-part program on the environment. The series garnered an Emmy nomination. Later in the 1990s, PBS aired a documentary on his life's work.

"Picture a mutual fund manager whose bad investments have caused his fund to lose value for each of the last 30 years, but who nonetheless has built the reputation of fundmeister Peter Lynch. If you can do so, you can envision Paul Ehrlich," observes science writer Michael Fumento.[51] Indeed, however damning this abysmal track record is for Ehrlich personally, it is even more discrediting for the hordes of intellectuals who worship him. Quite clearly, accuracy, the facts, and truth are utterly meaningless to such people.

By contrast, Julian Simon was considered a pariah. The mainstream adulation heaped upon Paul Ehrlich escaped him. Simon occasionally even glued devil's horns to his head when speaking in front of audiences to affirm that, yes, he was the same man about whom so many awful things had been said. The Lucifer garb, he reasoned, made it easier for audience members who had only heard about him to identify him. By the time he died in the winter of 1998, Simon was shown to have been correct on population, natural resources, and so many other questions. Still, according to the intelligentsia, Simon, and not Ehrlich, was the one on the fringe. The reason was that he was not politically correct.

His betting partner, on the other hand, was. Ehrlich was wrong on just about everything, but because his ideology was deemed "right," he became a media darling and the subject of tribute. The intellectual class's verdict on each man is less a reflection of the judged then of their judges.

At his death, Simon may have lacked the prestige of his betting partner. He did, however, have the comfort of vindication—and $576.07 of Ehrlich's money.

"SPECIESISM"

Animal Rights, Human Wrongs

I love animals. They're delicious.

—Bumper sticker
seen on a Ford Taurus

THEY ARE THE ANIMAL-RIGHTS MOVEMENT. THEIR ENEMIES INCLUDE Ronald McDonald, Mayor McCheese, and Grimace; Mrs. Aldini, your seventh-grade biology teacher who has long presided over a frog Holocaust; and the diabolical Captain Ahab. Foremost on their list of villains, it goes without saying, is the deceptively slight Takeru Kobayashi, whose athletic talents have granted him the coveted title World Hot Dog Eating Champion.

Their hero is Peter Singer.

Peter Singer is the Paul Ehrlich of the animal-rights movement—and more. Whereas Ehrlich shares environmentalism's stage with Rachel Carson, John Muir, and others, Singer's act is basically a one-man performance. Singer's 1975 manifesto *Animal Liberation* is the bible of the animal-rights movement. Activist Ingrid Newkirk has said that it inspired her to start the People for the Ethical Treatment of Animals (PETA).[1] To this day every new PETA member receives an abridged version. The character Elle Woods even could be spotted boning up on the book in the 2003 film *Legally Blonde II: Red, White, and Blonde.*

Singer is the movement's intellectual par excellence. It really shows. Animal-rights activists have embarked on a global rampage, spurred on by Singer. Like their ideological siblings the environmentalists, they view their cause as so noble that no action can be considered ignoble in its service.

Their attention-grabbing exploits include torching fast-food restaurants, mailing bombs, sinking whaling ships, dousing fur-wearing women with red paint, and threatening to poison supermarket turkeys during Thanksgiving.[2] In 2000, PETA launched an ill-fated campaign imploring college students to replace their daily intake of milk with beer.[3] After British journalist Graham Hall made an unflattering documentary about the Animal Liberation Front (ALF), terrorists from that group kidnapped him and branded the letters "ALF" onto his back.[4]

They abhor what the rest of us admire. PETA, for instance, demonizes the March of Dimes.[5] They admire what the rest of us abhor. PETA vice president Dan Mathews includes serial killer Andrew Cunanan as one of the people he reveres most "because he got Versace to stop doing fur."[6] After a tiger mauled magician Roy Horn during a Siegfried & Roy performance in October 2003, Mathews sent a particularly nasty note to Horn as he lay in a Las Vegas hospital bed fighting for his life.[7] Ingrid Newkirk, PETA's president, longs for foot-and-mouth disease to afflict American cattle country. "I openly hope that it comes here," the PETA cofounder stated. "It will bring economic harm only for those who profit from giving people heart attacks."[8]

In various cities in 2003, PETA staged public displays featuring large posters juxtaposing Nazi concentration camp victims with turkeys and chickens. The "Holocaust on Your Plate" display contended that "the leather sofa and handbag are the modern equivalent of the lampshades made from the people killed in the death camps."[9] One passerby, cornered by a pamphleteer accompanying a similar exhibit on the streets of Boston, declined PETA's brochure, saying, "I don't take things from insane people."[10]

And "insane" is the proper adjective for such people. Weaned on anthropomorphic cartoons and '70s movies with sidekick monkeys, animal liberationists often mistake animals for people and people for animals. They are the sort of individuals who assign human qualities to teddy bears and pet rocks, expecting the rest of us to interpret this as a sign of heightened sensitivity rather than mild insanity. Confused feelings substitute for clear thought.

Most animal lovers, it goes without saying, are not militant nuts. Few of us begrudge the autonomous individual who chooses vegetarianism for herself or the man who punches his neighbor for kicking his dog. It is the preachy extremist (usually with sunken, blank eyes, a pallid complexion, and the muscle tone of an amoeba), who hopes to force everyone to live as he does, who generally perturbs the uninitiated.

As with the environmentalists, zeal clouds the animal-rights activists' judgment. Their efforts are therefore often counterproductive. It's not just that they repulse potential sympathizers with unhinged rhetoric or violence. Rash activists frequently end up harming the very creatures they purport to help.

This is especially applicable, for instance, to the crusade to "liberate" animals. Out of the 2,103 dogs and cats PETA took in or "rescued" in 1999, they put down 1,325. Ingrid Newkirk defended euthanizing more than half the pets PETA supposedly saved by claiming that "the only kind option for some animals is to put them to sleep forever."[11] In 2002, fanatics raided a mink farm in the Netherlands and liberated more than 16,000 animals. Rather than realizing their destiny as some old woman's coat, scores of mink became roadkill. For some unexplained reason, activists deemed this a better outcome. An earlier clandestine operation in Oregon resulted in the deaths of 4,000 mink, including tiny kits mistakenly squashed by clumsy activists.[12] In a 2003 emancipation of 10,000 mink from a Washington farm, the casualties weren't mainly mink but unfortunate animals the newly freed omnivores preyed on. "Over half our livestock was shredded," lamented local farmer Jeff Weaver. In addition to a wounded dog, Weaver's geese and ducks sustained fatal injuries. Dianne Sallee, another small farmer, picked up the pieces after the mink ate numerous hens and chickens. Sallee surmised, "The people who do these things don't think it through."[13] No, they don't.

These are Peter Singer's ideas in action. He doesn't think things through either.

BIZARRE PHILOSOPHY

Peter Singer has taught at the most prestigious universities on three continents. He is the author of more than a dozen books and three hundred articles. He serves on the editorial boards of numerous journals of philosophy and as president of two animal-rights organizations. His work has been published in Bengali, Turkish, Korean, and several other languages. The *Encyclopaedia Britannica* even commissioned him to pen its entry on ethics.

So when Princeton University named the disheveled Aussie as its first Ira W. DeCamp Professor of Bioethics, it could *claim* that it was hiring someone very much within the mainstream.

Singer's ideology is a mélange of animal-rights activism, environmentalism, and Marxism, with a very casual view of the value of human life thrown into the mix. He claims to be an adherent of utilitarianism, which aspires for a society in which the happiness of the greatest number of people trumps all other concerns. Jeremy Bentham, an Industrial Age Englishman who composed a "hedonistic calculus" that determines whether an action is good by determining whether it causes more pleasure than pain, was the philosophy's first exponent. John Stuart Mill, who is known more for his views on freedom of expression, was a later proponent of utilitarianism. Critics of utilitarianism note that it attempts to transform moral questions into mathematical ones—something that might sound nice in a classroom or a book but rarely works in the real world.

Immediately upon his arrival at Princeton, Singer asserted his opinions on a range of issues. He gave public lectures and wrote articles in the student paper praising Dutch euthanasia, and condemning America for shunning universal health care and not giving enough foreign aid.[14] Singer's style of jumping from one cause to the next certainly predates his employment at Princeton. Peruse one of his books and amid a discussion on animal rights you'll find him warning, "Cattle fart large quantities of methane, the most potent of all greenhouse gases. . . . By eating so many animals and animal products we are helping to heat up our planet."[15] Read one of his articles in the *New York Times Magazine* and you're asked, "[W]hat is the ethical distinction between a Brazilian who sells a homeless child to organ peddlers and an American who already has a TV and upgrades to a better one—knowing that the money could be donated to an organization that would use it to save the lives of kids in need?"[16] Neither common sense nor focus is his strong suit.

Singer's positions on life and death have sparked controversy. Singer advocates euthanasia, encourages sterilization in Third World countries, and endorses abortion even for "the most trivial reasons."[17] Perhaps more controversial are his views on infanticide. "When the death of a disabled infant will lead to the birth of another infant with better prospects of a happy life," he writes in *Practical Ethics*, "the total amount of happiness will be greater if the disabled infant is killed."[18] Killing the disabled infant, Singer suggests, should not only be allowed, it should be considered "right."[19] Singer is uniquely honest among proponents of late-term abortions in his open proclamations that there are no real differences between killing a newborn lying in a crib and killing a fully developed baby lying in its mother's womb. His advocacy of infanticide injects a new concept into the pro-choice/pro-life debate: the postbirth abortion.

He rationalizes this position by asserting that "beings who cannot see themselves as entities with a future cannot have any preferences about their own future existence."[20] Therefore, it would be wrong to kill, for example, "a professor of philosophy [who] may hope to write a book demonstrating the objective nature of ethics. . . . Killing a snail or a day-old infant does not thwart any desires of this kind, because snails and new-born infants are incapable of having such desires."[21]

Singer's promotion of infanticide extends to healthy babies as well. In his book *Rethinking Life and Death*, Singer argues that "newborn-infants, especially if unwanted, are not yet full members of the moral community," and thus it is acceptable to kill them.[22] He offers a plan in which "a period of twenty-eight days after birth might be allowed before an infant is accepted as having the same right to life as others."[23] During this time, parents would be allowed to kill their baby. Singer believes that there is "wide support for medical infanticide" and that "the world already has enough human beings."[24]

Women killing their offspring, he writes, "does not prevent them [from] being loving mothers."[25] The West, the bioethics professor posits, is culturally deficient in its taboo on such behavior and "in the case of infanticide, it is our culture that has something to learn from others, especially now that we, like them, are in a situation where we must limit family size."[26]

BARNYARD CONCENTRATION CAMPS?

Singer's views concerning the "tyranny of human over nonhuman animals," if not as controversial, are perhaps more influential.[27] He compares scientists who engage in research on animals to Nazi doctors and likens the lives of animals on farms to the lives of enslaved blacks on plantations.[28] Central to his argument is the notion of "speciesism," a form of discrimination toward animals that he equates with racism, sexism, and various other forms of oppression. At first glance, the term Singer has coined might seem to be a parody of political correctness. It is not. The professor is deadly serious. "Speciesism—the word is not an attractive one, but I can think of no better term—is a prejudice or attitude of bias in favor of the interests of members of one's own species and against those of members of other species," he writes in *Animal Liberation*, the animal-rights movement's seminal work.[29]

"It should be obvious that the fundamental objections to racism and sexism made by Thomas Jefferson and Sojourner Truth apply equally to speciesism," declares Singer.[30] He elaborates: "Racists violate the principle of equality by giving greater weight to the interests of members of their own race. . . . Sexists violate the principle of equality by favoring the interests of their own sex. Similarly, speciesists allow the interests of their own species to override the greater interests of members of other species. The pattern is identical in each case."[31]

Many enamored with the fight against racism, sexism, classism, ableism, ageism, and sizeism have welcomed the opportunity to add another category of oppression to fight against. Others have concluded that comparing blacks and women to animals is degrading.

Critics accuse Singer of using the classroom as a soapbox to preach his bizarre ideas. The tone of his supposedly scholarly works, they say, is more fitting for a fanatic's pamphlet. Of course, many of his arguments *have been* incorporated into fanatics' pamphlets.

"Should one break in and free the animals?" Singer asks in *Animal Liberation*. "That is illegal, but the obligation to obey the law is not absolute. It was justifiably broken by those who helped runaway slaves in the American South."[32] Later in the book—which, again, is distributed to all new PETA members in abridged form—he reveals the names of scientists who experiment on animals. "I see no reason to protect experimenters behind a cloak of anonymity," he remarks.[33]

Hunting, fishing, farming, experimenting on animals, even an act as benign as eating a hamburger—each is compared to murder in Singer's worldview. Do hunters, Singer wonders, "consider that the animal might have a spouse who will suffer"?[34] Probably not, because hunters know something that the Ivy League professor doesn't: Animals don't have spouses.

The "tyranny" against animals, Singer writes in *Animal Liberation*, "can only be compared with that which resulted from the centuries of tyranny by white humans over black humans."[35] Singer also freely invokes other human tragedies to hammer his point home. "Hens, like humans in concentration camps, will cling tenaciously to life under the most miserable conditions," he emotionally argues.[36] Similarly, he likens medical research on animals to Nazi experiments on humans.[37]

While eating animals is strictly off-limits in Singer's ideal world, having sex with them is not. In an article in a dark corner of the Internet, Singer graphically describes an octopus performing sex acts upon a woman. Elsewhere in the piece he details men engaging in the marital act with barnyard hens. Of this latter practice, the Ivy League prof proclaimed, "But is it worse for the hen than living for a year or more crowded with four or five other hens in [a] barren wire cage so small that they can never stretch their wings, and then being stuffed into crates to be taken to the slaughterhouse, strung upside down on a conveyor belt and killed?"[38]

Contemplating that humans, like dogs, monkeys, apes, and elephants, are mammals, Singer concludes, "This does not make sex across the species barrier normal, or natural, whatever those much-misused words may mean, but it does imply that it ceases to be an offence to our status and dignity as human beings."[39]

PRINCETON LABELS SINGER "MAINSTREAM"

Aristotle ridiculed the pre-Socratic philosophers Melissus and Parmenides by humorously pointing out that "their premises are false, and their conclusions do not follow."[40] Much of the same neglect of logic is at work in the writings of Peter Singer. His premises aren't true, and the conclusions he draws from these false premises don't always follow his faulty starting points.

His argument, for instance, that abortion, infanticide, and euthanasia are good because the world already has too many people (and that more people means more misery) is subjective at best. By what standard are there too many people? Population *has* exploded in recent decades. Yet a great many people are living healthier, happier, and longer lives and are facing less hunger, disease, and warfare than previous generations did. Despite what Jeremiahs Ehrlich and Singer tell us, life is better now than ever.

Singer contends that "speciesism" is equivalent to racism and sexism. Racism and sexism, however, evoke opposition because all human beings are equal before the eyes of God. For "speciesism" to be tantamount to these societal afflictions, Singer assumes that all creatures are equal. They are not, and thus the moral equivalency that he ascribes to quite different behavior patterns—for example, snacking on beef jerky and denying a black man a job because of his skin color—doesn't stand up to scrutiny.

Singer also maintains that if killing a baby leads to the happiness of a greater number of people than if that baby lived, then it should be killed. Implicit in this argument is the idea that there is a way of predicting how an infant will turn out. But there isn't. If Singer's formula had been adopted, there probably would have been no Jesus Christ, Ludwig von Beethoven, or Stephen Hawking.

Peter Singer is mainly guilty of being a bad philosopher by peddling logical fallacies. But what is one to make of his defenders who run Princeton University?

Many at Princeton share Singer's views. Unlike Singer, however, they are not comfortable being associated with views that are almost universally recognized as part of the crackpot fringe. Thus, they claim that Singer really didn't say the things he is credited with saying, but was misquoted. Similarly, faculty and administrators attack Singer's critics in an attempt to silence them. Here again we see the legacy of Herbert Marcuse in the academy: Those who speak passionately of the need for "free speech" and "academic freedom" often deny free speech to others with whom they disagree. Singer's supporters are also in the habit of using candy-coated terms—such as *humanitarian* and *bioethicist*—to describe a man whose beliefs have earned him the moniker "Professor Death."

Princeton appointed Singer its first bioethics professor in 1998. Naming a proponent of legalized infanticide and euthanasia for many disabled people to a "bioethics" position in a "Center for Human Values" understandably strikes many observers as Orwellian. Princeton president Harold Shapiro, who chaired a bioethics panel appointed by President Clinton, approved bringing the Australian on board at the prestigious university. Shapiro defended his decision by saying, "You wouldn't want to come to a university where only certain views are allowed."[41] Yet many contend that that is exactly what Princeton is, noting that the school's faculty is dominated by leftists.

The director of Princeton's Center for Human Values, Amy Gutmann, explained her belief that Singer's view is "a mainstream philosophical view."[42] *Mainstream?* Perhaps among Gutmann's friends or in the faculty lounge. But among nonintellectuals Singer's views are considered extreme. Gutmann insisted, "I don't think any University can deny tenure to any individual who's done first-rate work."[43] Yet in the past, Gutmann has been vocal about banning faculty who exhibit "ethnic, sexist, homophobic and other forms of offensive speech directed against members of a disadvantaged group." Just what constitutes such speech, she has left vague. She explained in 1992 that views displaying "misogyny, racial and ethnic hatred, or rationalization of self-interest and group interest parading as historical or scientific knowledge" should not be given a hearing on campus.[44] Apparently, Gutmann does not believe that Singer falls into any of these categories.

Likewise, a Princeton University speech code seems to bar the utterances of Peter Singer. The school's "Commitment to the Community" specifically decrees, "Abusive or harassing behavior, verbal or physical, which demeans, intimidates, threatens, or injures another because of his or her personal characteristics or beliefs is subject to University disciplinary sanctions. Examples of personal characteristics or beliefs include but are not limited to sex, sexual orientation, race, ethnicity, national origin, religion, and handicap."[45] Administrators who might normally pounce on violators of the misguided edict refrained from enforcing their "Commitment to the Community" when it stood to harm one of their own. All that mattered was whose ox was being gored.

The controversy caused at least one Princeton official, school trustee and billionaire Steve Forbes, to declare that the school's hiring of Singer had forced him to withhold his monetary support from the university. "I have given no money to Princeton since Peter Singer was appointed to be a professor of bioethics," Forbes announced in 1999, "and I pledge to you today that so long as Peter Singer remains a tenured professor there, I will not financially contribute to Princeton University."[46] The magazine publisher's outspokenness sparked an angry response from his fellow trustees. "The trustees have a special and overarching responsibility to advance and protect the core values of the University, which include the essential principles of academic freedom," board chairman Robert Rawson wrote in a public letter. "We sincerely regret that one of our members apparently is not willing to accept this fundamental responsibility of trusteeship."[47] In the same breath that they praised Singer exercising his right to express himself, they blasted Forbes for doing the same. Speaking for his fellow trustees, Rawson announced that he and his colleagues were "extremely disappointed" in Forbes: "The trustees have not, and will not, apply any ideological litmus test to the appointment of distinguished scholars and teachers who are recommended to the board by the faculty, the faculty's elected Advisory Committee on Appointments and Advancement, and the president."[48]

However deluded Peter Singer is, he at least has the bravery to champion ideas openly that are commonly met with justified contempt. Princeton's administrators, who fawn over so much of what Singer advocates, would be less despicable if they embraced his honesty as well.

DEVOTED FOLLOWERS

In contrast to other intellectual morons, Peter Singer actually has more influence outside of the academy than within it. It is his writings on animal rights that his sectaries have latched onto, and because many of them call Hollywood home, they have popularized his views in the larger culture.

By lending support to the cause, celebrities such as Pink, Pamela Anderson, Alicia Silverstone, Moby, and Kim Basinger have added star power to the animal-rights movement. While they may not be cerebral heavyweights, they bring something to the issue that the frumpy professor lacks: glitz. Whereas the general public might overlook Peter Singer, they don't overlook his ideas when show-biz types offer a dumbed-down version of them. "Cruelty is cruelty," music mogul Russell Simmons asserted in a letter to a KFC executive, "whether it's cruelty to children, to the elderly, to dogs and cats, or to chickens, animals who are as least as intelligent as dogs or cats and are interesting individuals in their own rights."[49] Actor Joaquin Phoenix appeared in a PETA ad that declared, "Thanksgiving Is Murder on Turkeys."[50] Prior to the publication of *Animal Liberation*, it is difficult to think of any public figure unglued enough to lend his name to such off-the-wall statements.

For Peter Singer, milking a cow is "speciesist," but having sex with one can be really groovy; eating a Big Mac makes you complicit in murder, but killing your newborn daughter doesn't necessarily make you a bad parent. His followers take his logic to further extremes. Good: sending a Revlon executive a mail-bomb that maims him. Bad: going to the circus.

An academic crank has convinced a platoon of overpaid entertainers and an army of impressionable students that animals are people too. The rest of us, thankfully, are not that dumb yet.

"AND THAT IS MY TRUTH"

Liars and the Intellectuals Who Enable Them

Quid est veritas?

—PONTIUS PILATE

HERBERT MARCUSE TAUGHT AT SOME OF AMERICA'S MOST PRESTI-gious universities, including three Ivy League schools. Alfred Kinsey's work bore the imprimatur of Indiana University, where a research insti-tute today carries his name. Paul Ehrlich is a longtime professor at Stan-ford, the "Harvard of the West." Peter Singer has held professorships at the most prestigious universities on three continents.

Marcuse, Kinsey, Ehrlich, and Singer are just a few of the crackpots for whom our institutions of higher learning have provided mainstream acceptance. The intellectuals who rule the ivory tower are far too often beholden to ideology. It is troubling that these intellectuals so easily deny the truth when it impedes their ideological goals. Nothing in recent his-tory reflects this unsettling reality better than the long and sordid saga of Rigoberta Menchu.

In 1982, an unlettered Guatemalan peasant exiled in Paris told her story to a Marxist scholar. The book she dictated, *I, Rigoberta Menchu*, would be published in twelve languages and assigned at thousands of col-leges. She would become the Shakespeare of the emerging multicultural canon. With such chapters as "Women and the Political Commitment: Rigoberta Denounces Marriage and Motherhood" and "The Natural World: The Earth, Mother of Man," the book indicates that Central American peasants and North American academics share amazingly sim-ilar social attitudes and political views. As Menchu herself points out,

"There have been 15,000 theses written about me all over the world by people who have read the book and made commentaries about it."[1] The academic who "discovered" Menchu writes in the book's introduction that the word of this indigenous Guatemalan "allows the defeated to speak." Menchu's book goes beyond the power of a mere autobiography and "speaks for all the Indians of the American continent."[2]

The Marxist refugee soon enjoyed audiences with Pope John Paul II, the Dalai Lama, Nelson Mandela, and UN Secretary-General Boutros Boutros-Ghali. In spite of the fact—or perhaps because—she had made so much of her past illiteracy, the United Nations Educational, Scientific, and Cultural Organization made her a goodwill ambassador and schools awarded her more than a dozen honorary degrees. On the quincentennial of Columbus's voyage to the New World, the indigenous Menchu won the Nobel Peace Prize. "What a miracle that someone like us who eats tortillas and chili arrived at the Nobel Prize," a Guatemalan peasant remarked. "How I would like to know how that happened!"[3]

How it happened isn't quite the "miracle" it seemed. More earthly forces were at work. Specifically, dishonesty and the gullibility of intellectuals willing to buy into any story so long as it fit their ideological needs. In the late 1990s, Middlebury College anthropologist David Stoll revealed Menchu to be a fraud. In something of an understatement, Stoll noted that "the nature of my findings is inopportune for many scholars."[4]

RIGOBERTA MENCHU'S HOMELAND

The setting of *I, Rigoberta Menchu* is an impoverished, war-torn country beset by ethnic strife and government repression. Bordered on the north by Mexico, on the east by Belize, on the south by El Salvador, and on the southeast by Honduras, Guatemala is a nation of more than 10 million people. Its capital, Guatemala City, is the largest city between Mexico and South America. With indigenous Indians constituting more than half the population, Rigoberta Menchu's homeland is multicultural, multiethnic, and multilingual. It's also quite poor.

On December 29, 1996, Guatemala's civil war officially ended. The violence that had begun thirty-six years earlier—one year after Rigoberta Menchu's birth—was hardly an aberration in the tempestuous history of this mountainous land. Prior to the European conquest of the Americas, the Mayas of Guatemala were part of one of the most advanced civilizations in the Western Hemisphere, with a written language, a calendar more accurate than Gregory's, mathematics that grasped the concept of "zero," and majestic architecture marveled at to this day. At the same time, Mayan civilization was beset by incessant warfare, slavery, and human sacrifice. Then in the sixteenth century came the Spanish, who by the mid-1520s had vanquished their aboriginal foes and instituted colonial rule. Spain did not relinquish authority until 1821. After briefly becoming part of the Mexican empire, Guatemala became an independent nation in 1839. For much of the next century, it engaged in numerous conflicts over territory with its neighbors, particularly British Honduras (Belize). Dictatorships, assassination, and oppression marred much of Guatemala's modern history.

In 1954, the seeds were planted for the civil war that dominated most of Rigoberta Menchu's life. That year, in the midst of the Cold War, Jacobo Arbenz's government, which had come under the influence of Communists, decided to nationalize the property of the wealthy. When the Guatemalans seized about four-fifths of the United Fruit Company's land, the United States reacted by supporting a successful, albeit controversial, coup. The man the Americans helped install in power was voted out of office with a bullet three years later. Three years after that, civil war broke out.

The fighting pitted the anti-Communist government against leftist rebels. In 1962, the leftists established the Rebel Armed Forces (FAR) to overthrow the government. Deriving support from Castro, the FAR advocated Che Guevara's theory of revolution, in which the peasants would immediately recognize the justice of their cause and fill the ranks of their guerrilla army. This didn't happen. Instead the FAR, as well as later spin-off groups like the Guerrilla Army of the Poor (EGP) and the Revolutionary Organization of the People in Arms (ORPA), extorted military service and financial tribute from peasants. They deemed peasants who disagreed with their aims as suffering from "false consciousness" and sometimes killed them. Likewise, the government conscripted troops, demanded tribute, and even killed Guatemalans. The conflict cost 180,000 people their lives. Countless others were maimed or wounded. Thousands simply "disappeared." Hundreds of thousands fled north to Mexico and the United States.[5]

Even as the war ended, the violence continued. In 1996, rebel leaders kidnapped an eighty-six-year-old woman.[6] After war's official end, peasants doused eight enemies with gasoline and set them ablaze.[7] The crimes of government soldiers and militiamen have largely gone unpunished. President Vinicio Cerezo Arevala explained his reluctance to investigate brutalities by government forces by noting that if the matter were looked into, "we would have to put the whole army in jail."[8]

"Guatemala suffers from a mutilated official memory," writer Eduardo Galeano observed as the war ended, "as if remembering is dangerous, because to remember is to relive the past like a nightmare."[9] The "mutilated official memory" that plagued the war-torn country also affected its most famous citizen.

THE SHAKESPEARE OF THE MULTICULTURAL CANON

After Rigoberta Menchu's book was published in 1982, it became a sensation in the academic world. Here, it seemed, was a poor, illiterate, indigenous woman who told of the violence and devastation in her homeland. Her champions proclaimed that she spoke for the oppressed. Not surprisingly, her book wound up as required reading in many courses.

As academics embraced the book, however, *I, Rigoberta Menchu* came under sharp criticism from opponents of political correctness. In the late 1980s and early 1990s these critics began to see Menchu's book as part of a larger, disturbing trend on America's college campuses: Professors were replacing the "great books" with contemporary works that were assigned not because of educational merit but because of the author's skin color, economic class, sexual orientation, or any other category that elevated his or her victim status. So symbolic of the change in higher education was Rigoberta Menchu that a *Wall Street Journal* article entitled "Stanford Slights the Great Books for Not-So-Greats"cited *I, Rigoberta Menchu* as one of the "not-so-greats."[10] Dinesh D'Souza even called one of the eight chapters in his 1991 bestseller *Illiberal Education* "Travels with Rigoberta."

To the critics, it was clear that *I, Rigoberta Menchu* was not being celebrated for its literary quality. When Menchu claimed not to have undergone any formal education, many readers accepted that statement, for her book seemed monotonous and unreadable. The book is repetitive and includes a great deal of irrelevant material. Scattered throughout the text are obscure terms that are apt to cause a great deal of confusion to readers outside the author's homeland. In one passage, Rigoberta states, "I remember that my clothes were worn out because I'd been working in the *finca*: my *corte* was really dirty and my *hupil* very old. I had a little *perraje*, the only one I owned."[11] The likes of Menchu, in short, was not worthy of inclusion within a canon that included Aristotle, Shakespeare, and Sir Isaac Newton.

If the book had such flaws, why did so many academics fawn over it? Many political conservatives felt that Rigoberta Menchu became a heroine on the campuses not simply because she was a member of an oppressed minority group, though that helped. More important was that she was propagating the various isms being peddled by the academic Left. Dinesh D'Souza observed that professors are "quite happy to teach *I, Rigoberta Menchu* since [it] represents not the zenith in Third World achievement but rather caters to the ideological proclivities of American activists."[12] In *Illiberal Education* he charged that Menchu "embodies a projection of Marxist and feminist views onto South American Indian culture. . . . She is really a mouthpiece for a sophisticated left-wing critique of Western society, all the more devastating because it issues . . . from a seemingly authentic Third World source."[13]

D'Souza questioned whether "Rigoberta's socialist and Marxist vocabulary sound typical of a Guatemalan peasant," and indeed, aspects of the book seemed more than a little contrived. This woman from a Central American peasant village promoted virtually every pet cause advocated in the faculty lounge. Menchu explains, for instance, that her people teach children that they "must never steal or abuse the natural world, or show disrespect for any living thing."[14] Homosexual rights, a hot-button issue on Western campuses, are another part of Menchu's message: "Our people don't differentiate between people who are homosexual and people who aren't; that only happens when we go out of our community. We don't have the rejection of homosexuality that the *ladinos* [European descendants] do."[15] Christianity, she says, "kept our people dormant while others took advantage of our passivity," but liberation theology set them straight.[16] And of course, Menchu and her fellow peasants align themselves with Karl Marx's economic doctrine: "We began to understand that the root of all of our problems was exploitation. That there were rich and poor and that the rich exploited the poor—our sweat, our labor. That's how they got richer and richer."[17] This, of course, was all music to the ears of countless professors.

Whatever questions critics might have had about the quality of the book or its politicized nature, those concerns were soon eclipsed by entirely new questions about the veracity of the Nobel Prize winner. Critics no longer wondered whether her description of her experiences was representative of other Central American peasants' experiences. Now they were asking if it was representative of her own.

OPPRESSORS OR OPPRESSED?

In 1980, Rigoberta Menchu did something that scores of fellow Guatemalans had already done: She fled to Mexico. This common occurrence was followed in the coming years by a chain of very atypical experiences. She went to Nicaragua, the bulwark of Communism in Central America at that time, where the Sandinistas treated her royally. "When I arrived in Nicaragua," she reported in a later book, "the place was bubbling with solidarity. The Nicaraguan Committee for Solidarity with Peoples organized a press conference for me."[18] She began to tell her story. Later, she traveled to Europe, where she met Arturo Taracena, an upper-class Marxist revolutionary who, like Menchu, had fled Guatemala. Taracena, who was studying in France at the time, was the Guerrilla Army of the Poor's local representative. Taracena convinced Menchu to embark on the book project, according to Menchu.[19] He introduced her to Elisabeth Burgos-Debray, a Marxist scholar whose husband, Regis Debray, was the chief exponent of Che Guevara's theory of peasant warfare. It was into Burgos-Debray's tape recorder that Menchu told her story. The words she spoke were then transcribed and published in book form.

At some point during the journey that began in Guatemala and concluded in Paris, Menchu's real-life experiences were divorced from her professed autobiography. Whether it was the Nicaraguans, Taracena, Burgos-Debray, or Menchu herself who was the catalyst for this change, we may never know. The shrouded origin of the lie is not for want of plausible suspects. Many stood to gain (and did) from such a story. Ultimately, even under the most generous of theoretical circumstances, Menchu is at least guilty of perpetuating a hoax.

At the core of *I, Rigoberta Menchu* is her family's struggle against racist oppression from wealthy *ladino* landowners. In Menchu's telling, her parents were "forced to leave the town because some *ladino* families came to settle there. They weren't exactly evicted but the *ladinos* just gradually took over. . . . The rich are always like that. When people owe them money they take a bit of land or some of their belongings and slowly end up with everything. That's what happened to my parents."[20] When Menchu's father had the temerity to fight his wealthy white oppressors, according to *I, Rigoberta Menchu*, he was thrown in jail and kept there because of political corruption. "When they put my father in jail, the landowners gave large amounts of money to the judge there," she explained.[21] Her father, she says, had waged a twenty-two-year "heroic struggle against the landowners who wanted to take our land and our neighbours' land." The "big landowners" appeared "when our small bit of land began yielding harvests and our people had a large area under cultivation," she maintains.[22]

What really happened is dramatically different from the story Menchu crafted. The unanimous recollection of those interviewed by David Stoll show that the Menchus' problems were with other Mayans, not with *ladinos*. Court records support that contention, demonstrating that over a seventeen-year period, eighteen of the nineteen petitions filed by the Menchus and their allies were directed toward other indigenous landowners. Other Mayan families also filed complaints against the Menchus. At one point, as a result of a land feud, a group of fellow peasants beat the Menchu family patriarch. There is no record of him as a political prisoner, but it seems that other peasants pressured authorities to jail him at one point.[23] "Unfortunately," Stoll observes, "a heroic view of peasants blinds us to the possibility that they consider their main problem to be one another. . . . [I]nstead of resisting the state, peasants are using it against other members of their own social class."[24]

It is highly unlikely that Menchu somehow mistakenly believed the dispute was with *ladinos*. Her father's primary antagonists were his wife's uncles and their sons. The mayor of Menchu's village in the early 1970s, at the time of the land dispute, confirmed to the *New York Times* in 1998 that the feud did not involve rich Europeans. "No," he said, "it was a family quarrel that went on for years and years." He continued, "I wanted peace but none of us could get them to negotiate a settlement."[25] Members of Rigoberta's own family seconded the mayor's account. "The Tums were our enemies," the Nobel Prize winner's half-sister remembered about her interfamilial adversaries. "They were always cutting the barbed wire on our fences, and they would send their animals into my late father's fields to eat our corn so that we would not have enough to eat."[26]

"To include the conflict with [other Indians] would bring up the internecine disputes that absorb so much of the political energy of subordinate groups," notes David Stoll. "It would contradict the vision of virtuous peasants rising up against their true class enemies. How more appropriate, then, to attribute all the boundary problems to ladino planters."[27]

INVENTING REALITY

David Stoll has revealed that Rigoberta Menchu invented far more than conflicts with greedy European landowners. The hero of her narrative is her father, Vicente Menchu, and at every turn, *I, Rigoberta Menchu* distorts details of his life to justify the Marxist worldview. She portrays him as having been conscripted into the military as a young man, but Stoll writes that "according to a member of Vicente's family, he joined the army as a volunteer. An elder recalled that after his first year and a half of duty, he liked the army well enough to reenlist."[28] She also claims that her father rejected Western missionaries' attempts to improve local farming techniques, saying, "Indians reject the chemical fertilizers they tried to teach us about."[29] Yet by all accounts Vicente Menchu was an enthusiastic participant in the Peace Corps and other programs that aided farmers.[30] In *I, Rigoberta Menchu*, Vicente is radicalized and helps build the foundation of the Committee for Campesino Unity (CUC), a revolutionary group seeking to overthrow the government. Stoll rejects this claim. "If there is a single CUC publication that claims Vicente as a member, let alone a founder, I have yet to find it," he states.[31]

Rigoberta implies that her father was an innocent killed by the army because of his participation in a political demonstration. What really occurred is that Vicente Menchu joined a mob of peasants and guerrillas who stormed the Spanish Embassy, taking prisoners and brandishing homemade explosives. In the ensuing confrontation, a fire broke out that consumed the rebels and their hostages, killing thirty-six people. While no one is sure how the fire started, credible evidence suggests that it spread because one of the guerrillas lobbed a Molotov cocktail at the Guatemalan police.[32]

The murder of twelve-year-old Petrocinio, as described by his sister Rigoberta, is something worthy of Dante's *Inferno* or a Wes Craven horror flick. Petrocinio's troubles supposedly began on September 9, 1979, when the army kidnapped him. Petrocinio is kicked and beaten. His sister remarked that "he didn't look like a person any more." Soldiers "even forced stones into his eyes." Parts of Petrocinio's flesh are burned, and his fingernails and toenails are removed, as are the soles of his feet. His testicles are tied to a stationary object and he is forced to run. He is thrown naked into a well full of corpses and is forced to stay there overnight. The skin on Petrocinio's head and part of his face is peeled off. His tongue is mutilated. Finally, the evil anti-Communists pour gasoline on Rigoberta's brother and his comrades. They are set ablaze. The diabolical anti-Communists, of course, roar with laughter at this final act of depravity. Begging for mercy from the accused Communists goes ignored. Rigoberta concludes, "[F]or me, it's a reality I can't forget."[33] The impression on many naïve undergraduates was unforgettable as well, and the story served as a tool to generate hatred against anti-Communism.

The ordeal of Rigoberta's younger sibling, however, never happened. Although her brother Petrocinio did die during Guatemala's civil war, David Stoll has revealed that his death did not resemble anything described within the pages of *I, Rigoberta Menchu*. Stoll writes, "When I brought up Rigoberta's story of prisoners being burned alive in the plaza of Chajul, all I harvested were quizzical looks."[34]

Unbiased readers might see the villains in Rigoberta Menchu's story as clichés straight out of central casting. Yet academics swallowed them whole, perhaps viewing these evil caricatures as the embodiment of what they always envisioned anticommunists to be. Even in the face of massive evidence contradicting her story, Menchu defiantly stuck by her account. "My truth is that my brother Petrocinio was burned alive," she told a gathering of reporters in Mexico City. "Show me the mass grave where he is buried. If someone will give me his body, I will change my view."[35] She later conceded, however, that she hadn't witnessed her brother's death, despite what she had previously maintained.[36]

Another brother, Nicolas, who dies of starvation in *I, Rigoberta Menchu*, is actually alive and well. Nicolas, she proclaims in the book, was "crying, crying, crying," with a "belly [that] was swollen from malnutrition."[37] Rigoberta blames his death on the exploitative economic system under which her family lived. But Nicolas was found in Guatemala, confused as to why his sister would say he was dead. Rigoberta Menchu, confronted with the fact that her brother was alive, suddenly said that she had another brother named Nicolas who had died in the manner she described.[38] Family members denied that this other "brother" ever existed.[39]

A LITERATE ILLITERATE

Equally dubious are Rigoberta Menchu's claims to have been an illiterate peasant toiling in the fields by day and organizing workers by night. In *I, Rigoberta Menchu*, the future Nobel laureate quotes her father as saying, "If I put you in a school, they'll make you forget your class, they'll turn you into a *ladino*."[40] In the second paragraph of the book, Menchu makes clear her credentials as someone who was illiterate for most of her life: "I must say before I start that I never went to school, and so I find speaking Spanish very difficult. I didn't have the chance to move outside my world and only learned Spanish three years ago. It's difficult when you learn just by listening, without any books."[41]

As it turns out, during the period she purports to have been laboring as a migrant worker active in the revolutionary movement, Menchu was actually attending a prestigious boarding school run by the Catholic Church. "I interviewed six women who studied with Rigoberta," Stoll reports, "plus three others who had heard stories about her." All agreed that Menchu attended a Catholic school.[42] The *New York Times* interviewed four nuns who taught at a school she attended, the Belgian-Guatemalan Institute, in Guatemala City.[43] Additional testimony came from members of Rigoberta's family. "Her way of talking was no longer that of ours," remembered a brother of her visits home from school. "She admonished us to speak correctly."[44]

Faced with this new evidence, Menchu claimed that she had learned to read and write in Spanish at the Belgian-Guatemalan Institute and at another school that she received a scholarship to attend. She declared, however, that she had been a maid, not a student, at the Guatemala City Institute. "It was not work that I was ashamed of," she said of her job. Although no one seemed to dispute that Menchu had done some work as a maid at the school, the universal account from students and teachers was that she had been a pupil as well. The nuns the *New York Times* interviewed even remembered Menchu as an extremely intelligent student.[45]

But why would Rigoberta Menchu lie about this seemingly trivial matter regarding her educational background? Perhaps because within the Marxist circles she traveled in, it was no trivial matter. Menchu certainly would have been correct to see the currency that comes with fitting into multiple categories of oppression. Being a Marxist woman and an Indian in war-torn Central America gave her a platform; exaggerating her poverty and falsely claiming illiteracy guaranteed that people would listen. Whatever this instance of dishonesty says about Menchu, it speaks volumes about the intellectuals she sought to impress—a group that sees illiteracy as a virtue.

A FAMILY AFFAIR

As the fighting over her memoir subsided, Rigoberta Menchu continued to display a tendency to invent wild tales and to portray herself as a victim. In the mid-1990s, a child relative of the Menchus was kidnapped while the Nobel Prize winner was attending a family wedding. The kidnappers, knowing of Menchu's newfound wealth, demanded money in return for the boy. Refusing to supply a ransom, Menchu lashed out at the Guatemalan army and government. She accused them of orchestrating the kidnapping. The real perpetrators were much closer to home. A week after his disappearance, the boy was mysteriously "returned" to his parents. In the days that followed, the parents' story unraveled. They finally admitted that they had kidnapped their own son in an attempt to extort money from their wealthy relative.

When Menchu's wild accusations were disproven, her enemies had a field day. The president of Guatemala quipped that the kidnapping was a family, not an army, affair. Red-faced with embarrassment, Menchu snapped back by calling him a "racist."[46] She would not let the unfortunate occurrence die. She contended that the incident had been "a wicked plot" assisted by a media "slur campaign" intended to "destroy me."[47] Her relatives were involved, she allowed, but the masterminds of the maleficent deed were her antagonists in the military. Who exactly in the military did this, she did not know. Nor did she offer anything to substantiate her claim. "The people who planned this simulated kidnapping are still free and we don't know who they are," she alleged.[48]

BLAMING THE MESSENGER

Menchu's reaction to David Stoll's revelations about her book was perhaps predictable—"Racism!" "Whites have been writing our history for five hundred years, and no white anthropologist is going to tell me what I experienced in my own flesh," she declared.[49] She also claimed that Elisabeth Burgos-Debray, the woman who edited her story, reworked it for maximum effect. Alas, Burgos-Debray possessed the tapes proving Menchu wrong.[50]

A news conference that Menchu convened in Mexico City in 1999 to try to refute the charges actually dealt a further blow to her credibility. The *New York Times* described her as "elusive" when she was pressed for specifics. Menchu told journalists that it was not becoming of her to "enter into little details" regarding the controversy surrounding her book. Instead she charged her accusers with harboring racist attitudes. "If anyone thinks I'm going to say I'm sorry because I was born Maya and am an ignorant Indian, they're wrong," she declared. This puzzling *non sequitur* disappointed admirers hoping she would disprove the allegations against her. She added that she had "a right to my own memories."[51]

"I didn't find anything in these reports that changes the fact that my people are dead," Menchu said. "And that is my truth."[52]

An organization founded by the former peasant was equally vague in her defense. Without addressing any of the charges specifically, the Rigoberta Menchu Tum Foundation condemned those who questioned Menchu's version of events. It labeled the charges of "dubious seriousness" and even accused Menchu's detractors of believing that they had "the right to lie with impunity." Despite its claims that the Nobel Prize winner did not fabricate anything, the organization's public statement asserted that Menchu "had a right to assume as her own personal story the atrocities that her people lived through."[53] The translation from the foundation's Newspeak is that Rigoberta Menchu did lie, and since her lies served a good cause she should be applauded for doing so.

The foundation's press release avowed:

Just when the commemorations of the 500th Anniversary appeared to have left behind the arrogance and the superiority complexes of those who have, until now, written history since the conquest, now we see how some people celebrate with unconcealed enthusiasm the appearance of these new chroniclers who attempt to return to their place—the same old place—those who had the audacity to add to the Official Story that which it was lacking: the vision of the conquered. And they do so protected by the presumably scientific rigor conferred upon them by the fact that they speak in the name of the North American academy.[54]

Yet the real racism could be found among those who had lowered the bar for Menchu because she came from a nonwhite culture outside the First World.

It is perhaps understandable that an orphaned twenty-something peasant engulfed in a civil war would concoct a story to gain sympathy for the combatants that she saw as on the side of the angels. Wartime propaganda is far from unusual. What is perhaps unforgivable is that the story would be promoted—without inspection—by so many whose vocation is to search out the truth.

Even David Stoll found excuses for those who championed Menchu's tale. "Given the need to arouse international opinion, it is hard to fault Elisabeth [Burgos-Debray] for publishing as soon as she could."[55] But is it the role of scholars to "arouse international opinion," or to propound what is true? Stoll contended that Menchu's invention of reality was understandable because she was in an "emergency situation." He maintained, "It's completely fair to call her on the accuracy of her statements, but on the other hand let's recognize that she was describing a real situation even if she was personalizing the story in the way that anybody telling a life story tends to simplify what happened."[56] Yet the Guatemalan author's cover-to-cover lying, as Stoll knew all too well, was hardly just a case of someone merely attempting to "simplify" what really occurred.

Even after the revelations about Menchu, many scholars and intellectual leaders have continued to treat *I, Rigoberta Menchu* as if nothing has changed. The committee that awards the Nobel Peace Prize dismissed calls to revoke Menchu's prize. "All autobiographies embellish to a greater or lesser extent," insisted Geir Lundestad, director of the Norwegian Nobel Institute and the permanent secretary of the Norwegian Nobel Committee.[57]

More troubling, many professors continued to assign the book in their courses, not caring about the reams of evidence indicating that the book is a fraud. Professor Timothy Brook of Stanford conveyed the prevailing view to the *Stanford Review*: "Authenticity and reliability are problems in all texts, [so] this controversy does not inauthenticate Menchu's book." Brook added that he was thinking about bumping the book from secondary to required reading in his course.[58]

"The controversy hasn't really changed my mind or made me think differently about Menchu at all," proclaimed Professor Ann Jones of Smith College. "I don't respect the Stoll book at all," she added. The professor of comparative literature, who required students to read Menchu's book in classes she taught but didn't include Stoll's critique, noted, "Our idea of eyewitness reporting may not at all correspond to the experience of somebody living" in Guatemala. She concluded that "there are ways of acquiring information that don't involve being there on the spot."[59]

"I don't think that any piece of written material is objective," opined Professor Marjorie Becker of the University of Southern California. "Scientists don't believe in objectivity. I don't think anything is God. But I do think that torture happened in Guatemala." Becker, who required *I, Rigoberta Menchu* in her freshman honors course "Race Matters: From Malinche to Cornel West," excluded readings critical of Menchu from the class. "We don't read Stoll's book," Becker affirmed. "I am somewhat suspicious of his scholarly credentials." Regarding Menchu's book, the historian added, "I'll be teaching it again."[60]

Boston College professor Deborah Levenson-Estrada maintained that Stoll's work "doesn't at all [make me] think that she's not describing Guatemalan reality. She is—completely." Levenson-Estrada, who encountered Menchu while doing activist work in Central America during the 1980s, had taught *I, Rigoberta Menchu* for years and said she would continue to do so in the future. "Not everything that she said happened, happened to her," she pointed out. "But it did happen to someone."[61]

University of California–Davis history professor Charles Walker thought that Stoll's standard for Menchu was too rigorous. "I don't know too many people who can hold up to the sort of analyses that Stoll carried out," he asserted. The historian added, "His argument that . . . Rigoberta has to be unblemished is ridiculous."[62]

Yale historian Greg Grandin and journalist Francisco Goldman likened Menchu's fabrications to Abraham Lincoln playing up his log cabin background. They wrote, "[I]t is no great surprise that political leaders rearrange events in their lives for political reasons. In his presidential campaign, Abraham Lincoln presented himself as a backwoods hayseed even though he was an accomplished legislator and lawyer."[63]

An ad hoc survey conducted by a reporter for the *Chronicle of Higher Education* found similar results, with most professors insisting that they would continue to assign the book without apologies. "We have a higher standard of truth for poor people like Rigoberta Menchu," complained a professor at Western Michigan University who continued to assign the book. Professor Margorie Agosin of Wellesley told the publication that she didn't care whether Menchu told the truth and would still use the book in class. "I think Rigoberta Menchu has been used by the Right to negate the very important space that multiculturalism is providing in academia," she complained.[64]

Stoll said that critics who shielded students from his work were "afraid to let their students debate the issues that obviously need to be debated." He added, "To this mentality, anybody who would criticize Rigoberta's story is by definition reactionary. I would expect that most of them have not read my book or only read it in anger and haste."[65]

Not all professors shunned Stoll's revelations. Though continuing to require their students to read *I, Rigoberta Menchu*, some professors did so in the context of Stoll's research. "I think it's a book that should be taught," maintained Professor Nina Scott of the University of Massachusetts–Amherst regarding *I, Rigoberta Menchu*. "I've taught this book for many, many years and I know how it impacts on students and how much they really love it." The professor of Spanish reported that she had been instrumental in hosting Menchu as a campus speaker in 1985, but that she was disturbed by the charges against the Nobel Prize winner. After the firestorm surrounding Menchu, Scott said, "I had [the students] read [*I, Rigoberta Menchu*] without telling them anything about the controversy to begin with because I didn't want to spoil it for them." Professor Scott then had her students read from Menchu's critics. The exercise spawned some "very personal turmoil" for students who "had committed to her," she confessed, but it also generated "some of the most interesting undergraduate papers I've ever gotten." Although Scott didn't question Stoll's research, she defended Menchu by insisting, "She comes from an oral tradition and a storytelling tradition where it's perfectly okay to incorporate things that have happened to other people and tell them as though they had happened to you."[66]

Ohio State comparative literature instructor Rick Livingston's syllabus included *I, Rigoberta Menchu* during the spring 2000 semester, but he didn't get to it because the class traveled at a slower pace than expected. He admitted, "I'm quite likely to go on teaching it in the future." Like Scott, he said he would do so in conjunction with an exploration of Stoll's thesis. *I, Rigoberta Menchu*, he claimed, "has a very powerful historical value and even an anthropological value." The book "still seems to me worth teaching and an extraordinarily interesting work," Livingston concluded.[67]

Scott's and Livingston's intellectual honesty—their willingness to include divergent points of view—relative to many of their colleagues was in some ways admirable. Why they would waste students' time by teaching a proven hoax, however, was puzzling. After all, what they were requiring their students to read was not a novel that sought social change in the tradition of *The Grapes of Wrath* or *The Jungle*. It was a book classified as nonfiction.

Rigoberta Menchu twisted and distorted for political ends the very real suffering she endured during the Guatemalan civil war. Had Menchu supported the Guatemalan government or rejected Marxism, her story would never have seen the light of day. Her book was published not because she represented a large portion of the Guatemalan populace. (She didn't; they rejected her views via the ballot box and through a long war.) It was published because she was a nonwhite, peasant spokesman for the ideas of elite academia. Stoll writes:

> Certainly Rigoberta was a representative of her people, but hiding behind that was a more partisan role, as a representative of the revolutionary movement, and hiding behind that was an even more unsettling possibility: that she represented the audiences whose assumptions about indigenas she mirrored so effectively. I believe this is why it was so indecent of me to question her claims. Exposing problems in Rigoberta's story was to expose how supporters have subliminally used it to clothe their own contradictions, in a Durkheimian case of society worshiping itself. Here was an indigena who represented the unknowable other, yet she talked a language of protest with which the Western left could identify. She protected revolutionary sympathizers from the knowledge that the revolutionary movement was a bloody failure. Her iconic status concealed a costly political agenda that by the time her story was becoming known, had more appeal in universities than among the people she was supposed to represent.[68]

Menchu's supporters find virtue in her mendacity because her falsehoods supposedly served a good cause. But if a cause is just, why does it need lies to generate a following? Experience dictates that noble causes do not need lies to gain acceptance. Bad ones do.

Menchu's cause was bad. While a long list of sins can be ascribed to opponents of Communism, these transgressions don't even begin to compare with the atrocities piled up by Communists. Menchu lied because the facts have never shown Communists to be on the side of justice. The side she cast her lot with was responsible for the murder of 100 million people during the twentieth century, in places as diverse as Beijing, Havana, and Tiranë. In Guatemala, the Communists Menchu supported attempted to impose their will on their fellow countrymen, who overwhelmingly did not see things their way. They declared that peasants who disagreed with Marxism suffered from false consciousness and shot many of them. Menchu's cartoon guerrillas don't kill anyone. Soldiers they capture are gently educated about their misdeeds and let go. By contrast, she depicts the opponents of Communism as butchers with imaginations for terror worthy of the Marquis de Sade. This is an inversion of reality to rival *Alice in Wonderland.*

Lies rarely promote good. They spread ignorance. Rather than serving as an educational tool, Menchu's book instead clouds whatever understanding its readers had about Central America. That colleges and universities, which aim to eradicate ignorance, value a text whose main purpose is to obscure the truth reveals a great deal about the state of education.

Just as what Menchu pushes in her book is literary snake oil, the ideology, masked as an academic genre, that promotes her book is a fraud. "Multiculturalism" is mostly used as a euphemism. Rather than gazing at all societies, it fixates on the West. It aims to expose racism, sexism, homophobia, and other forms of oppression—but only in Western civilization. On the rare occasion that multiculturalism looks outside the city walls, it presents a Disneyland version of other cultures—sterilized, reflexively positive, and superficial. By those who issue the harshest condemnations of America, we are told to refrain from passing judgment on foreign cultural practices. It's in bad taste to bring up North African female genital mutilation, human sacrifice among the Aztecs, Chinese foot binding, Polynesian cannibalism, Middle Eastern "honor killings," and other horrible practices past and present. Instead of showing cultures as they are, ideologues present them as they want them to be. Thus, each culture is merely a carbon copy of the next, all embracing socialism, sexual libertinism, and other faddish pursuits endorsed by multiculturalists. *I, Rigoberta Menchu* is rare among texts valued by multiculturalists in that it is set outside the United States, Canada, and Europe. Yet Menchu's fictionalized memoir is consistent with other works in the field because it tells us very little about voices within other cultures but quite a lot about certain voices within our own.

"Rigoberta is a legitimate Mayan voice," David Stoll permits. "So are all the young Mayas who want to move to Los Angeles or Houston. So is the man with a large family who owns three worn-out acres and wants me to buy him a chain saw so he can cut down the last forest more quickly. Any of these people can be picked out to make misleading generalizations about Mayas. But I doubt that the man who wants the chain saw will be invited to multicultural universities anytime soon. Until he [is], books like *I, Rigoberta Menchu* will be exalted because they tell many academics what they want to hear."[69]

In the bizarre world of intellectuals it is David Stoll the whistleblower, and not Rigoberta Menchu the liar, who elicits condemnation.

"HISTORY ITSELF AS A POLITICAL ACT"

The Three Stooges of Anti-Americanism

*The fact that so many hypotheses are necessary to reconcile a theory
with the facts should persuade one to abandon the theory itself.*

—RAYMOND ARON,
The Opium of the Intellectuals

"IT'S AN AMERICAN FLAG WITH A SWASTIKA ON IT," REMARKED
Cynthia Orr, describing her sign protesting war in Iraq. "It says 'Bush's
America.' I believe what Bush is doing currently is becoming a fascist dictator." Orr traveled more than five hundred miles to join tens of thousands of like-minded citizens on March 15, 2003, in Washington, D.C.
"The war crimes that America has done over there [in Afghanistan] are
just incomprehensible," the Ohio activist continued. "They packed people into trucks with no air and no water and let them slowly suffocate.
The people who died on 9/11 mostly died instantaneously. There's a big
difference in those kinds of deaths."[1]

"I think that what happened in Afghanistan was just as illegal and just
as destructive as the bombing of the World Trade Center," declared
David Werier, who, along with 100,000 others, protested U.S. policy on
the streets of New York City a month prior to the D.C. event that Ms.
Orr attended. The Ithaca, New York, activist, who believed the U.S.
threatened the rest of the world, said of the war in Iraq, "of course it's
about oil." He also supported a group called the United Neighbors,
which was trying to inspect America's weapons of mass destruction. "We
don't even know—it's so hard to believe the propaganda that's coming out
of the government—even who really did the [9/11] bombing," he main-

tained. "I know that there were some people who did it . . . and that's about it. I wouldn't even say it was Osama bin Laden."[2]

"I was not surprised by the events of 9/11," demonstrator Chris King remarked at a chilly Washington, D.C., march on January 18, 2003. "It's like I've been waiting for years for something like that to happen because I knew that the people of the world were starting to pull away from capitalism." The Vermont activist contended that 9/11 "was allowed to happen." "I saw 9/11 as the Reichstag," he maintained. "I'll compare it to what Cassius did to Spartacus back in Rome. I'll compare it to the *Lusitania*, to the *Maine*. I'll do it, every single time."[3]

The hundreds of thousands who gathered on the Mall in Washington, D.C., in midtown Manhattan, in downtown San Francisco, and in other cities around the world in the eighteen months between 9/11 and game day in Iraq largely concurred with these sentiments. Marchers chanted such mantras as "George Bush, corporate whore / We don't want your oily war." They took part in colorful street theater. A twelve-foot-tall Uncle Sam on stilts sported a Pinocchio nose as he paraded through the crowd on the Mall. Inflammatory placards exclaimed, "Get the Terrorists Out of the White House," "USA Is #1 Terrorist," and "We Support Our Troops When They Shoot Their Officers."[4]

"In comparison to what's happening over there [in Afghanistan]," a University of Connecticut student alleged, "[9/11] is like just one drop in the bucket."[5] Another protestor assessed the blame for 9/11: "Oh, God, I think it really comes back to us. The roosters come home to nest."[6] "Knew in advance?" shouted a Rhode Island man through a megaphone. "[George W. Bush] funded them. He created al Qaeda. He has been a longtime business associate of bin Laden."[7] A twenty-something activist declared that the rest of the world "should view us as they viewed the Germans and the Nazis."[8]

Where do these Internet-savvy, MTV-generation activists get their ideas? The primary source is a surprising trio of elderly writers who have collectively logged in more than 235 years on planet Earth. The young radicals may confuse Sgt. Pepper for a war hero, or Frank Sinatra for a character on *The Sopranos*, but their rhetoric shows that they do know Howard Zinn, Noam Chomsky, and Gore Vidal.

HOWARD ZINN

Who is the most influential historian among young people? Filmmaker Ken Burns? Could it be the Democrats' court historian, Arthur Schlesinger Jr.? Biographer David McCullough? How about the late Stephen Ambrose, whose triumphant view of American history brought alive such colorful characters as Meriwether Lewis, Crazy Horse, and George Custer?

Though an argument exists for any one of these men (even those who lack the proper academic credentials), a strong case could also be made for a decidedly less establishmentarian figure: Howard Zinn. For readers who prefer their history to be an accurate retelling of the past rather than marching orders for the present, Zinn's writings disappoint. While every historian has his biases, Zinn makes no effort to overcome his. What most historians consider vice—politically motivated inaccuracies, long-winded rants, convenient omissions, the substitution of partisanship for objectivity—Zinn transforms into virtue.

"Objectivity is impossible," the pop historian once remarked, "and it is also undesirable. That is, if it were possible it would be undesirable, because if you have any kind of a social aim, if you think history should serve society in some way; should serve the progress of the human race; should serve justice in some way, then it requires that you make your selection on the basis of what you think will advance causes of humanity."[9]

History serving "a social aim," rather than a detached chronicling of the past, is what we get in *A People's History of the United States.* Despite, or perhaps because of, the author's radical agenda, Zinn's 1980 tome has sold in huge numbers and continues to sell. A revised and updated edition came out in 2003, and an illustrated offshoot focusing on America's role in the world is set for 2006 release.

What accounts for the massive sales figures? *A People's History of the United States* has been the beneficiary of fawning celebrities and zealous professors.

Zinn has discussed politics with Pearl Jam's Eddie Vedder and was on Rage Against the Machine's reading list (note: beware of rock bands that issue reading lists).[10] In *Good Will Hunting,* Matt Damon's Will Hunting tells his psychiatrist that *A People's History of the United States* will "knock you on your ass."[11] At one point Damon and costar Ben Affleck, who grew up near Zinn outside of Harvard Square, reportedly were producing a miniseries based on their neighbor's magnum opus.[12] Zinn repaid the actors' youthful infatuation by including them in an inconsequential paragraph in the book's 2003 edition.[13]

Courses at the University of Colorado–Boulder, UMass–Amherst, Penn State, and Indiana University are among dozens nationwide that assign the book. It is so popular that it can be found on class syllabi in such fields as economics, political science, literature, and women's studies, in addition to its more understandable inclusion in history. A random check of Amazon.com's "popular in" section revealed that the book ranked #7 at Emory University, #4 at the University of New Mexico, and #9 at Brown University. In fact, sixteen of the forty locations listed in *A People's History*'s "popular in" section were academic institutions, with the remainder of the list dominated by college towns like Binghamton, New York; State College, Pennsylvania; East Lansing, Michigan; and Athens, Georgia.[14] It is reasonable to wonder, when one looks at these facts, whether most of the million or so copies sold have been done so via coercion—that is, college professors and high school teachers requiring the book. One academic believed the book so crucial to the development of young minds that his course syllabus decreed, "This is an advanced class and all students should have read Howard Zinn's *A People's History of the United States* before the first day of class, to give us a common background to begin the class."[15]

And what "common background" might that be?

Through Zinn's looking glass, Maoist China, site of history's bloodiest state-sponsored killings, transforms into "the closest thing, in the long history of that ancient country, to a people's government, independent of outside control."[16] The authoritarian Nicaraguan Sandinistas were "welcomed" by their own people, while the opposition Contras, who backed the candidate who triumphed when free elections were finally held, were a "terrorist group" that didn't appear to command the backing of any Nicaraguans.[17] Admitting some human rights abuses, Zinn writes that Castro's Cuba holds "no bloody record of suppression."[18]

The 2003 updated edition is plagued with more inaccuracies and poor judgment. The added sections on the Clinton years, the 2000 election, and 9/11 bear little resemblance to the reality his readers have lived through:

- In an effort to bolster his arguments against putting criminals in jail, aggressive law enforcement tactics, and the President Clinton–

endorsed crime bill, Zinn contends that in spite of all this, "violent crime continues to increase."[19] It doesn't. As with much of Zinn's rhetoric, if you believe the opposite of what he says in this instance, you would be correct. According to a Department of Justice report issued in 2003, the violent crime rate has been halved since 1993.[20]

- According to Zinn, it was Mumia Abu-Jamal's "race and radicalism," as well as his "persistent criticism of the Philadelphia police," that landed him on death row in the early 1980s.[21] Nothing about Abu-Jamal's gun being found at the scene; nothing about the testimony of numerous witnesses pointing to him as the triggerman; nothing about additional witnesses reporting a confession by Abu-Jamal—it was Abu-Jamal's dissenting voice that caused a jury of twelve to unanimously sentence him to death.[22]

- Predictably, Zinn draws a moral equivalence between America and the 9/11 terrorists. He writes, "It seemed that the United States was reacting to the horrors perpetrated by the terrorists against innocent people in New York by killing other innocent people in Afghanistan." Scare quotes adorn words and phrases Zinn dislikes, such as Bush's "war on terrorism" or post-9/11 "patriotism."[23]

Readers of *A People's History of the United States* learn very little about history. They do learn quite a bit about Howard Zinn. In fact, the book is perhaps best thought of as a massive Rorschach test, with the author's familiar reaction to every major event in American history proving that his is a captive mind long closed by ideology.

Theory First, Facts Second

If you've read Marx, there's no reason to read Howard Zinn. The activist professor relies on Marx's single-bullet theory of history ("The history of all hitherto existing societies is the history of class struggle") to explain all of American history.[24] Economics determines everything. Why study history when theory has all the answers?

Thumb through *A People's History of the United States* and you find greed motivating every major event. According to Zinn, the thirteen colonies' separation from Great Britain, the Civil War, and both world wars—to name but a few examples—all stem from base motives involving rich men seeking to get richer at the expense of other men.

Zinn's projection of Marxist theory onto historical reality begins with Columbus. According to Zinn, the seafaring Italian and those who followed him to the New World ventured for one reason: profit.[25] "Behind the English invasion of North America, behind their massacre of Indians, their deception, their brutality, was that special powerful drive born in civilizations based on private property," maintains the octogenarian scribe.[26]

A materialist interpretation continues with the Founding. *A People's History* informs that "important people in the English colonies made a discovery that would prove enormously useful for the next two hundred years. They found that by creating a nation, a symbol, a legal unity called the United States, they could take over land, profits, and political power from the favorites of the British Empire. In the process, they could hold back a number of potential rebellions and create a consensus of popular support for the rule of a new, privileged leadership."[27]

Zinn sarcastically lauds the "genius" of the Founding Fathers for crafting the "most effective system of national control" in recent memory.[28] He portrays the American Founding as a diabolically creative way to ensure oppression, rather than the spark that lit the fire of freedom and self-government throughout much of the world. If the Founders wanted a society they could direct, why didn't they put forth a dictatorship or a monarchy resembling most other governments at the time? Why go through the trouble of devising a constitution guaranteeing rights, political freedoms, jury trials, and checks on power? Zinn doesn't explain, contending that these freedoms and rights are merely a façade designed to prevent class revolution.

Zinn paints antebellum America as a uniquely cruel slaveholding society subjugating man for profit. Curiously, the war that ultimately results in slavery's demise is portrayed as a conflict of oppression too. Zinn writes that it was "money and profit, not the movement against slavery, that was uppermost in the priorities of the men who ran the country."[29] Rather than welcoming emancipation, as one might expect, Zinn casts a cynical eye toward it. "Class consciousness was overwhelmed during the Civil War," the author laments, placing a decidedly negative spin on the central event in American history.[30] America is in a lose-lose situation. The same thing, according to Zinn, caused both slavery and emancipation: greed. Whether the United States tolerates or eradicates slavery, its nefarious motives remain the same. Zinn's jaundiced eye fails to see the real

issues surrounding the Civil War. Instead, he believes the chief significance of the grisly conflict to be that it allegedly served as a distraction
from the impending socialist revolution.

By the time the reader reaches World War I, Zinn begins to sound like
a broken record. Of the Great War he writes, "American capitalism
needed international rivalry—and periodic war—to create an artificial
community of interest between rich and poor, supplanting the genuine
community of interest among the poor that showed itself in sporadic
movements."[31] Yet another diversion to delay the revolution!

"A People's War?" is Zinn's chapter on the war in which he served his
country. Zinn suggests that America, not Japan, was to blame for Pearl
Harbor, because it provoked the Empire of the Sun. The fight against fascism was all an illusion. While Nazi Germany and Imperial Japan may
have been America's enemies, Uncle Sam's real goal was empire. Regarding America's neutrality in the Spanish Civil War, Zinn asks if it was "the
logical policy of a government whose main interest was not stopping Fascism but advancing the imperial interests of the United States? For those
interests, in the thirties, an anti-Soviet policy seemed best. Later, when
Japan and Germany threatened U.S. world interests, a pro-Soviet, anti-
Nazi policy became preferable."[32] Reality is inverted. It's not the Soviet
Union that went from being anti-Nazi to pro-Nazi to anti-Nazi. Zinn
projects the Soviet Union's schizophrenic policies onto America. While
he awkwardly excuses the Hitler-Stalin Pact, he all but proclaims a Hitler-
Roosevelt Pact.

The reader learns that the Second World War was really about—surprise!—money. "Quietly, behind the headlines in battles and bombings,"
Zinn writes, "American diplomats and businessmen worked hard to make
sure that when the war ended, American economic power would be second to none in the world. United States business would penetrate areas
that up to this time had been dominated by England. . . . [T]he United
States intended to push England aside and move in."[33] Yet this didn't happen. The British Empire expired, but no American Empire took its place.
Despite defeating Japan and helping to vanquish Germany, America
rebuilt these countries. They are now America's chief economic rivals, not
its colonies.

The profit motive certainly is central to numerous major events in
American history. The discovery of gold at Sutter's Fort in 1848, for
example, undeniably stands as the primary reason—alongside the favorable outcome of the Mexican War—for the subsequent population explo-

sion in California.[34] The Gold Rush is one of several historical occurrences that conform to Zinn's overall thesis. Even a broken clock is right twice a day. For every major figure or event whose catalyst was economic interest, scores were sparked by unrelated concerns.

To question Zinn's method of analysis is not to say that economics does not influence events. It is to say that one-size-fits-all explanations of history are bound to be wrong more than they are right. History is too complicated to find a perfect fit within any single theory.

Uncooperative Facts

When fact and theory clash, the ideologue chooses theory. To the true believer, ideology is truth. Time and again, *A People's History of the United States* opts to mold the facts to fit theory, leaving the reader to wonder what "people" Zinn is referring to in the book's title. Dishonest people? Left-wing people? Delusional people?

Zinn claims that the wealthiest man in early America was George Washington.[35] He wasn't, but it makes for a good Marxist story—the richest man awarded the run of the government. In fact, Washington owed substantial debts to British moneylenders in the late 1760s and early 1770s. He was chronically cash-poor, and he actually had to borrow money to travel to New York on his election to the presidency. Washington certainly rose to accumulate great wealth; his last will and testament estimates his accumulated fortune at $530,000. Clearly, however, men of greater means roamed America during his lifetime.[36]

Zinn also ignores many complicating facts regarding the 1930s case of the Scottsboro Boys, a group of young black men in Alabama who were tried for allegedly raping two white women. Zinn applauds the Communist Party for becoming "associated with the defense of these young black men imprisoned" through "southern injustice."[37] Perhaps the party had become "associated" with the defense of the Scottsboro Boys, but the Communists merely used the embattled youngsters. Historian Richard Gid Powers notes that of the $250,000 the Communists raised for the Scottsboro Boys' defense, they put up a scant $12,000 for two appeals.[38] At the time, a black columnist quoted a candid Communist Party official stating, "[W]e don't give a damn about the Scottsboro boys. If they burn it doesn't make any difference. We are only interested in one thing, how we can use the Scottsboro case to bring the Communist movement to the people and win them over to Communism."[39] One might see an analogous situation in Zinn's view of history: He is interested in the past only when it serves socialist ideals.

"Unemployment grew in the Reagan years," Zinn claims.[40] Statistics show otherwise. Reagan inherited an unemployment rate of 7.5 percent. By his last month in office, the rate had declined to 5.4 percent. Had the Reagan presidency ended in 1982, when unemployment rates exceeded 10 percent, Zinn would have a point. But for the remainder of Reagan's presidency, unemployment declined precipitously.[41] While Zinn teaches history and not mathematics, one needn't be a math whiz to figure out that 5.4 percent is less than 7.5 percent. Despite unleashing an economy that created nearly 20 million new jobs during his tenure, Reagan continues to be smeared by historians—and it's not hard to see why. Reagan's free-market polices were anathema to Marxists like Zinn. Upset at the pleasant way things turned out—Reagan's policies unleashed an economy that grew continuously from late 1982 until mid-1990—historians prefer to rewrite history.[42]

By now one might be thinking: On what evidence does Zinn base his varied proclamations? One can only guess. Despite its scholarly pretensions, *A People's History of the United States* contains not a single source citation. While a student in Professor Zinn's classes at Boston University or Spelman College might have received an F for turning in a paper without documentation, Zinn's footnote-free book is standard reading in scores of college courses.

Every author makes mistakes. Zinn, it seems, would make fewer of them if he used his mind rather than his ideology to do his thinking.

Sins of Omission

More striking than Zinn's inaccuracies—intentional and otherwise—is what he leaves out.

Washington's Farewell Address, Lincoln's Gettysburg Address, Reagan's speech at the Brandenburg Gate—all fail to merit a mention. Nowhere do we learn that Americans were first in flight, first to fly solo across the Atlantic, and first to walk on the moon. Alexander Graham Bell, Jonas Salk, and the Wright Brothers are entirely absent. Instead, the reader is treated to the exploits of Speckled Snake, Joan Baez, and the Berrigan brothers. While Zinn highlights immigrants who went into professions like ditch-digging and prostitution, he excludes success stories like Alexander Hamilton, John Jacob Astor, and Louis B. Mayer. Valley Forge rates a single fleeting reference, while D-Day's Normandy invasion, Gettysburg, and other important military battles are left out. In their place, we get several pages on the My Lai massacre and colorful descriptions of U.S. bombs falling on hotels, air-raid shelters, and markets during 1991's Gulf War.

How do students learn about U.S. history with all these omissions? They don't.

"A Biased Account"

Zinn utters the most honest words of *A People's History of the United States* in the conclusion of the book's 1995 edition, when he concedes that his work is "a biased account." "I am not troubled by that," he adds, "because the mountain of history books under which we all stand leans so heavily in the other direction—so tremblingly respectful of states and statesmen and so disrespectful, by inattention, to people's movements—that we need some counterforce to avoid being crushed into submission."[43] Two wrongs, he seems to be saying, make a right.

"I wanted my writing of history and my teaching of history to be a part of social struggle," Zinn candidly remarked in an interview conducted long after the release of *A People's History of the United States*. "I wanted to be a part of history and not just a recorder and teacher of history. So that kind of attitude towards history, history itself as a political act, has always informed my writing and my teaching."[44] Indeed it has.

NOAM CHOMSKY

After Matt Damon's Will Hunting informs his psychiatrist of his admiration for Howard Zinn, the psychiatrist, played by Robin Williams, intones that Noam Chomsky is great too.[45] Occupying classrooms on opposing banks of the Charles River, the left-wing icons share more than a mention in a movie. In 1967, the professors enlisted in Norman Mailer's "armies of the night" demonstrating outside the Pentagon—deemed by Chomsky "the most hideous institution on this earth"—with Chomsky finding himself in a jail cell by the end of the protest. In 1971, both men again traveled to Washington, D.C., this time to block traffic to demonstrate their contempt for the Vietnam War. In the 1980s, Boston police arrested Zinn and Chomsky after they participated in a takeover of a federal building in the city to object to the Reagan administration's Central American policies.[46] This passion for public agitation has added credibility to both men among the activist Left.

"Chomsky ranks with Marx, Shakespeare, and the Bible as one of the ten most quoted sources in the humanities—and is the only writer among them still alive," the U.K.'s *Guardian* points out.[47] One biographer asserts, "Chomsky is one of this century's most important figures, and has been described as one who will be for future generations what Galileo, Descartes, Newton, Mozart, or Picasso have been for ours."[48] "In a saner world," another admirer believes, "his tireless efforts to promote justice would have long since won him the Nobel Peace Prize."[49]

Noam Chomsky gained fame as a linguist by theorizing that certain principles of language are biologically ingrained within humans. Like others studied in this book, Chomsky grew tired of his chosen field. He wandered. With Harvard Square a mile or so from his office, and the 1960s in full throttle, it is no wonder that he found a second home in politics. Supporters touted his brilliance within linguistics as if this automatically made him a brilliant analyst of international politics. It didn't. His prognostications revealed a knave. Among radicals, Chomsky's political writings have transformed the Philadelphia-born linguist into a hero, leaving several distinct imprints on the contemporary Left.

Chomsky's first legacy to the Left is a reflexive anti-Americanism that assigns blame to the United States for just about any disliked occurrence, no matter how tenuous the link. "So when people talk about Israeli atrocities or Turkish atrocities," advises the Massachusetts Institute of Technology professor, "they should be saying U.S. atrocities, because that is where it is coming from."[50] To this end, his writings refer to "U.S.-backed massacres in El Salvador," "Clinton-backed Turkish terror," and "a U.S.-backed Chinese invasion."[51] There is no El Salvadoran, Turkish, or Chinese responsibility, only American responsibility. It matters little if the conflicts he invokes involve no U.S. military support. If we trade with or provide aid to nations pursuing policies Chomsky objects to, then he blames America. Since the United States trades with just about every nation, and gives aid to about 140 countries, Chomsky's methodology ensures that America can be held responsible for the policies of almost any nation. On the rare occasion that America has withheld aid and restricted trade, such as with interbellum Iraq, Chomsky introduces a catchall clause, blaming America for *not* trading or giving aid and thus for causing any ensuing catastrophe.

Chomsky has bequeathed a second legacy: encouraging the Left to see every issue as a Manichaean moral struggle and to cast the opposing side as so diabolical as to exist outside the bounds of discourse. Calling the Vietnam War an "obscenity," he informed readers in the 1960s that "by accepting the presumption of legitimacy of debate on certain issues, one has already lost one's humanity."[52] The Left agreed, subsequently applying this maxim to affirmative action, free trade, sweatshops, and a host of issues demanding not righteous indignation but debate.

A third legacy inherited by the contemporary Left is the practice of attributing a moral equivalency between crimes committed by ideological allies and ideological enemies when large disparities in scale exist between the two. If an equivalent enemy crime doesn't exist, Chomsky invents one. For example, when he finally came to terms with the fact that the Chinese Communists did indeed liquidate their fellow countrymen, he dismissed their man-made famines as no different from deaths in India that, he said, were the result of that country's pursuit of a program of democratic capitalism. He contends that both instances "are ideological and institutional crimes, and capitalist democracy and its advocates are responsible for them, in whatever sense supporters of so-called Communism are responsible for the Chinese famine." Lest anyone accuse him of moral equivalence, he charges that the crimes of democratic capitalism "may be monstrously worse" than the crimes of Communism.[53] When denial is out of the question, he changes the subject. Bringing up Sandinista campaigns against Miskito Indians elicits a lecture on El Salvadoran death squads; a discussion of al Qaeda's 9/11 atrocities morphs into a condemnation of Clinton's bombing of a Sudanese medicine factory; invoking Pol Pot invites a long harangue about U.S. policy in Southeast Asia. Chomsky's body of work might best be seen as a massive *tu quoque*. Something like "So what? We've done worse" seems to be his stock reply to the atrocities of Islamists, Communists, and other enemies of the West.

Stemming from the first three legacies is a final one: twisting the truth to advance the cause. Allowing ideology rather than fact to serve as his guide, operating within an intellectual vacuum, and refusing to acknowledge the crimes of his ideological allies have led Chomsky to draw some ridiculous conclusions. For example, he has gushed over genocidal maniacs like the Khmer Rouge, predicted that the United States would visit a holocaust on Afghanistan, and imagined a postwar alliance between Uncle Sam and Nazi brownshirts. It is startling how many dumb ideas come from the brain of Noam Chomsky. Even more startling is how his ideas retain their power over the global Left.

Dumb Idea #1: The U.S.-Nazi Alliance

"We have to ask ourselves whether what is needed in the United States is dissent—or denazification," Chomsky wrote in the 1960s. "To me it seems that what is needed is a kind of denazification."[54] Since this time, the famous linguist has consistently made allusions to postwar America as a fascist regime. "I have often thought that if a rational Fascist dictatorship were to exist," Chomsky opined in the late 1970s, "then it would choose the American system."[55] In the 1980s he wrote, "By our standards, Hitler appears to have been rather sane."[56] In 1995 he warned, "Now we are moving to the state where you can really get the sense of potential fascism."[57] Eight years later he told a European interviewer that "the U.S. government is an extreme radical and nationalist group with some similarities to European Fascism."[58]

In the 1992 pamphlet *What Uncle Sam Really Wants*, Chomsky envisions an evil cabal of Nazis and State Department officials guiding international policy after World War II. Why the United States sacrificed hundreds of thousands of men to defeat the Nazis only to install them as the corulers of the world the tract leaves unexplained.

According to Chomsky, at war's end "the United States was picking up where the Nazis had left off."[59] Substitute "Soviet Union" for "United States" and this statement makes more sense. Mirroring Nazi imperial designs, the U.S.S.R. gobbled up Poland, Hungary, Czechoslovakia, Bulgaria, Albania, Romania, East Germany, Estonia, Latvia, and Lithuania in the years before, during, and after the war. What countries did the United States transform into imperialist outposts?

It is as if Chomsky suffers from a Tourette's syndrome of the typewriter, making absurd references to "the US-Nazi alliance" and "the postwar alliance between the US and the SS."[60] One senses that a good portion of Chomsky's readers who believe such things have the theme-music from *The Twilight Zone* running on a constant loop in their ears.

Chomsky blasts the United States for having supported internal movements to liberate Eastern Europe from Soviet totalitarianism. "These operations included a 'secret army' under US-Nazi auspices that sought to provide agents and military supplies to armies that had been established by and which were still operating inside the Soviet Union and Eastern Europe through the early 1950s."[61] This US-Nazi army is so "secret" that only Chomsky knows of it, and he has thus far kept the documentation of it to himself, lest his secret get out.

Dumb Idea #2: Denying Genocide

In 1977, Noam Chomsky and a cowriter lamented the "rewriting of history" to create the impression of the "sad results of Communist success and American failure. Well suited for these aims are tales of Communist atrocities, which not only prove the evils of communism but undermine the credibility of those who opposed the [Vietnam] war and might interfere with future crusades for freedom." They continued, "It is in this context that we must view the recent spate of newspaper reports, editorials and books on Cambodia, a part of the world not ordinarily of great concern to the press."[62] The piece, an apologia for the Khmer Rouge, deservedly haunts the MIT linguist to this day.

A decade after the embarrassing article appeared, Chomsky dishonestly maintained that he had always recognized the hideous nature of the Khmer Rouge. Along with the original piece's coauthor, Chomsky wrote in 1988, "Outside of marginal Maoist circles, there was virtually no doubt from early on that the Khmer Rouge regime under the emerging leader Pol Pot was responsible for gruesome atrocities."[63] His own paper trail tells a different story.

In the infamous review of three titles appearing in *The Nation*, Chomsky and his longtime collaborator, Edward Herman, lavish praise on a book denying the Cambodian genocide, and generally denigrate two other tomes that affirm the unprecedented mass killings. They describe the volume they fawn over as outlining "the destructive American impact on Cambodia and the success of the Cambodian revolutionaries in overcoming it, giving a very favorable picture of their programs and policies, based on a wide range of sources." Shortly thereafter, they condemn the *Wall Street Journal*, "which dismissed contemptuously the very idea that the Khmer Rouge could play a constructive role."[64] Chomsky mocks the notion that the Khmer Rouge forcibly relocated its subjects, compares Cambodia to postwar France, where anarchic conditions rather than official planning resulted in massacres and crimes, and quotes a Catholic priest denying government persecution of his flock (though one credible estimate posits that Pol Pot exterminated 48.6 percent of Cambodian Catholics).[65]

"[H]ighly qualified specialists who have studied the full range of evidence available," the duo assures readers, "concluded that executions have numbered at most in the thousands; that these were localized in areas of limited Khmer Rouge influence and unusual peasant discontent, where brutal revenge killings were aggravated by the threat of starvation resulting from the American destruction and killing."[66] Chomsky and Herman regarded the belief that a million or more Cambodians had been killed by their genocidal overlords as a joke. Of one such estimate *The Nation* review alleges, "The figure bears a suggestive similarity to the prediction by U.S. officials at the [Vietnam] war's end that a million would die in the next year."[67]

"The 'slaughter' by the Khmer Rouge," the article deduces, "is a [Robert] Moss–*New York Times* creation."[68]

One only wishes it were true.

"We all lived in an enormous concentration camp," remembers one Cambodian.[69] Pol Pot forced the entire nation, as if they constituted a massive sports team, to adopt an all-black uniform. The government forcibly evacuated the cities, including hospitals, in its disastrous attempt to transform the nation into an agricultural machine. The Communists killed people wearing glasses, on the grounds that spectacles represented either vanity or intellectualism. Pol Pot, the Khmer Rouge's "Brother Number 1," abolished crying, praying, and schools, forced Muslims to eat pork, used human beings for fertilizer, and routinely executed the handicapped as malingerers and shirkers. Probably more than a million Cambodians perished between 1975 and 1979 as a result of the Khmer Rouge. According to estimates, between one of seven and one of four Cambodians died under Pol Pot's brief reign.[70]

Dumb Idea #3: Cubans Enjoy a Higher Standard of Living Than Americans

In a Reagan-era essay, Chomsky cites an Overseas Development Council study that, he says, shows the quality of life in Cuba to be equal to that in the United States. Not satisfied with the inclusion of this bit of propaganda, Chomsky adds that Cuba is "actually better than the United States if we consider its more egalitarian character, thus with lower infant mortality rates than Chicago and far lower rates than the Navajo reservation."[71] Undoubtedly, Chomsky's scholarship on this matter provides the answer to the much-puzzled-over question of why so many Miamians risk their lives in rafts to escape the United States for Castro's paradise. It unravels the mystery of American baseball players slipping past their overseers to play ball in Cuba. Cases of alienated critics of the state making the Cuban best-seller lists, while facing jail sentences and firing squads in the United States, now seem easier to understand too.

While Castro has long claimed comparable rates of infant mortality, life expectancy, employment, and literacy between Cuba and the United States, difficulties present themselves in verifying this information. Since Castro remains the source of much of the statistics, believing them depends largely on one's view of Castro. Even figures of per capita annual income—around $1,500 by most accounts, making Cuba the second poorest country in the Western Hemisphere—remain sketchy. Still, there are objective facts about both countries that might serve as a basis of comparison.

Entirely absent from Cuba are rights many Americans take for granted: freedom of speech, religion, assembly, and the press; elections and voting; the right to bear arms; trial by jury; private ownership of property; and the freedom to travel and emigrate. Cubans are not free to leave their island prison. In 1994, for instance, seven thousand people died attempting to escape Communism's last foothold in Latin America.[72] Castro bans strikes and independent unions. "The union must not be used for the wrong purposes," a party mouthpiece noted after destroying Cuba's last remaining union.[73] For a brief period, Castro rounded up homosexuals and placed them in reeducation camps. He quarantined AIDS sufferers for many years. Not much has changed in Castro's criminal justice system since nearly twenty thousand gathered in the Palace of Sports in 1959 and literally delivered a death sentence to a partisan of Batista via a thumbs-down verdict, loosely imitating ancient Rome.[74] Forty-four years later, Castro executed three men just nine days after they hijacked a ferry (resulting in no injuries) in a failed attempt to flee to the United States.[75] Before taking power, Castro promised to hold elections, but after the revolution he famously remarked, "Elections? What for?"[76] He did make a superficial bow to democracy in 2002 that proved farcical. A few days after launching a petition drive calling for socialism to be a permanent part of the Cuban state, the government claimed that 99 percent of the population had signed it. The national assembly then voted to make it a crime for lawmakers to alter the socialistic system.[77] These abuses are among the reasons that Fidel Castro stands alone among heads of state in the Americas in banning Amnesty International and Human Rights Watch.[78]

Does it seem as though the quality of life in Cuba is better than the quality of life in the United States?

Clearly, Chomsky is a sophist who overlooks crimes committed by Cuban officials that he would loudly decry if committed by American officials.

Dumb Idea #4: U.S. Bombs Killed Tens of Thousands of Sudanese

The 9/11 attacks, Chomsky rationalizes in his slim book on the subject, were nothing compared with President Clinton's 1998 bombing in Sudan, which resulted in probably "tens of thousands of immediate Sudanese victims."[79] He approvingly cites analyses suggesting that, in proportion to the two nations' populations, the attack on Sudan would be as if bin Laden had killed more than 100,000 Americans.[80] In truth, the bombing of the Sudanese medicine factory, however foolish, resulted in just a handful of casualties.[81] The medicinal crisis that Chomsky claimed had engulfed the country following the bombing simply didn't take place. No humanitarian organization reported any sort of widespread catastrophe after the air raid. There is no proof whatsoever of ten deaths, let alone tens of thousands of deaths, resulting from the bombing-induced medicine shortages that Chomsky imagines. As Australian scholar Keith Windschuttle noted regarding Chomsky's invented body count, "That this could have happened without any of the aid organizations noticing or complaining is simply unbelievable."[82]

On what basis does Chomsky make his fantastic claim? In a 2002 interview with Salon.com he cited "estimates made by the German Embassy in Sudan and Human Rights Watch."[83] One of his sources, Human Rights Watch, not only denies that it had ever made such a claim but also notes that it never even investigated the matter. "In fact," the group's communications director told Salon.com, "Human Rights Watch has conducted no research into civilian deaths as the result of U.S. bombing in Sudan and would not make such an assessment without a careful and thorough research mission on the ground."[84] Chomsky's other source turns out not to be "the German Embassy" but Werner Daum, Germany's ambassador to the Sudan during the bombing. Daum, who noted that a death count was "difficult to assess," never conducted an investigation into the matter, but after he left his diplomatic post he did offer what he termed a "reasonable guess" that tens of thousands of lives were lost because of the attack.[85]

There you have it. Chomsky's sources for his grandstanding claim include a single, notoriously anti-American former ambassador's guess and a reputable organization that has repudiated Chomsky's citation of it. By these scholarly methods, you could prove just about anything.

Dumb Idea #5: The War on Terrorism Would Kill Millions of Afghanis

In the wake of 9/11, Chomsky issued a number of proclamations that not only seem preposterous upon reflection but seemed preposterous at the time as well. "At this point," Chomsky told a foreign radio interviewer just twelve days after 9/11, "we are considering the possibility of a war that may destroy much of human society."[86] As usual, within his statement the master linguist provided a lot of ready-made excuses in case he was mistaken—"considering," "possibility," "may"—but even the suggestion of pending worldwide doom was ridiculous. The professor initially cast doubt on the idea that Osama bin Laden engineered the attacks. While he acknowledged "the prima facie plausibility of the charge," he claimed that "the documentation is surprisingly thin."[87] Had bin Laden not boasted of his crime in a released tape, it is likely that Chomsky would still claim to be unsatisfied by the evidence.[88]

Incredibly, Chomsky maintained that "everyone was in favor of the overthrow of the Taliban, except the US government."[89] Incredible because the U.S. government overthrew the Taliban, whereas "everyone" else failed or didn't try.

No post-9/11 assertion proved as ridiculous as the Cambridge sage's off-base prediction that the U.S. bombing in Afghanistan would result in a South Asian holocaust. The month following 9/11, Chomsky proclaimed that the United States and its allies were "in the midst of apparently trying to murder 3 or 4 million people."[90] While real examples of slaughter by the millions in Cambodia and China failed to arouse Chomsky's indignation, imaginary ones sent him into a frenzy.

In a pattern that has grown familiar, Chomsky shuffled to blame the victim in the aftermath of 9/11. Lest the world show too much sympathy for America, he quickly tried to change the subject. After the obligatory denunciation of the 9/11 terror, Chomsky always seemed to qualify his disapproval with a "but." The terrorist attacks were terrible, *but* what about Nicaragua? Sudan? Indonesia? America wasn't the victim of 9/11, this mindset held, but its villain. "The US has already demanded that Pakistan terminate the food and other supplies that are keeping at least some of the starving and suffering people of Afghanistan alive," the professor announced. "If that demand is implemented, unknown numbers of people who have not the remotest connection to terrorism will die, possibly millions. Let me repeat: the US has demanded that Pakistan kill possibly millions of people who are themselves victims of the Taliban."[91] The United States issued no such demand. It asked Pakistan to seal its borders to lessen al Qaeda's chances of escape. Not doing so would have probably sealed the fate of "unknown numbers of people." Doing so saved lives.

In print, on the airwaves, and at lectures, Chomsky repeated his unfounded warnings of a U.S.-engineered holocaust. When his cries failed to arouse the masses, he lashed out at them too. He fulminated, "There was no reaction in the United States or in Europe to my knowledge to the demand to impose massive starvation on millions of people."[92]

The massive starvation Chomsky foresaw failed to materialize. Neither millions, nor thousands, nor hundreds of Afghanis died of starvation. The United States left a greater tonnage of food in Afghanistan than bombs. The U.S. military used a higher percentage of precision-guided aerial munitions than had been used in any previous conflict. As a result, civilian casualties were remarkably scarce. At the low end, the Associated Press counted Afghani civilian deaths at 500 to 600. At the high end, a University of New Hampshire economist estimated a civilian death toll of 3,100 to 3,800.[93] Somewhere between lies the truth. While one civilian death is one civilian death too many, all wars have costs. The costs of the Afghanistan phase of the war on terrorism included several hundred to several thousand—not several million, as Chomsky predicted—dead civilians.

Had the international Left wanted to alleviate suffering within Afghanistan, it had plenty of opportunities to do so over the more than twenty years of war that preceded the U.S.-led military campaign. In the five years of fighting that resulted in the Taliban's rise to power, 50,000 civilians died within Kabul. By contrast, the Taliban's ouster witnessed a mere 70 civilian deaths in Afghanistan's capital city.[94] Chomsky greeted the very real humanitarian crisis of the 1990s that led to extremist tyranny with virtual silence. He met the potential crisis that led to freedom with soapboxing and righteous indignation. The conflicting reactions raise a troubling question: Does Chomsky care about civilian casualties, or does he care about civilian casualties only when they serve propagandistic ends?

A week after allied military operations began in Afghanistan, Chomsky declared, "Looks like what's happening is some sort of silent genocide."[95] So silent, in fact, that someone forgot to tell its victims—girls permitted to attend school, young men knowing peace for the first time, homosexuals no longer facing execution by concrete walls toppled upon them, and women freely roaming about sans masks.

The Responsibility of Intellectuals

"It is the responsibility of intellectuals to speak the truth and to expose lies," Chomsky wrote with unintentional irony in 1966. "This, at least, may seem enough of a truism to pass without comment."[96] Maybe so, but because Noam Chomsky uttered these words they demand comment.

If we were dealing with some 1960s burnout, Chomsky's delusions might be easy to laugh at. But we're not. He is a tenured professor at one of the world's most prestigious institutions. He is a best-selling author many times over. He is the intellectual avatar of the global Left. And according to one study of the humanities, the number of scholarly citations of his work makes him the most sourced person on the planet. Chomsky's dishonesty is troubling. The intellectual class's veneration of Chomsky is more troubling.

In an Orwellian manner, Chomsky's followers deem him a latter-day Orwell. Other figures, both historic and literary, come to mind more readily—Baron von Münchhausen, Bill Clinton, Joe Isuzu, Pinocchio.

GORE VIDAL

In casting the 1995 film *With Honors*, producers presented movie star Joe Pesci with a list of prospects for the role of an elitist professor. "Why do we always have to get an English asshole for this sort of part when we have one of our own?" the diminutive Italian-American asked.[97] They cast Gore Vidal.

Rather than jumping into politics from some unrelated profession as Chomsky and so many others have done, Vidal gravitated from politics to literature—and back to politics again in life's curtain call. Grandson of Oklahoma senator Thomas Gore, Eugene Luther Vidal Jr. became so obsessed with the pursuit of politics that he lopped off part of his name and rechristened himself "Gore Vidal" to capitalize on his maternal grandfather's name. Twice in life he called on the people to usher him into

Congress, but according to his 1999 biography, he has failed to vote in any election since 1964.[98] His ballot box inactivity hasn't prevented him from complaining about how the rest of us vote.

While serving a stint in the army during World War II (a stint in which the pulling of strings kept him out of harm's way), Vidal began to churn out novel after novel. His third effort, *The City and the Pillar*, put his name on the best-seller lists, where it would appear with great frequency over the next six decades. *Myra Breckenridge*, *Burr*, *1876*, *Lincoln*, and other successes followed. Readers came to expect historical fiction or racy sexuality from his books. They often got both.

Broadway would stage six productions based on his work, two of which involved characters based on Richard Nixon. The first, *The Best Man*, was wildly successful. The second, *An Evening with Richard Nixon*, was dreadful. The *New York Times* headlined their review "Evening with Richard Nixon Is for Radical Liberals." After two weeks, the producers spared future audiences by canceling its run. Stung, the playwright blamed the bad reviews on a conspiracy. Others found more ominous signs in the public's rejection of the production. One friend's consoling missive to him read, "[T]his was not just the death of a play, but a condemnation of the American people."[99]

Vidal dabbled in movies and television as well. For hit films that didn't credit him as a writer, like *Ben Hur*, he claimed credit. For panned movies that did credit him, like the disastrous *Caligula*, he denied any meaningful involvement.[100]

Sometime in the 1960s, despite his prolific body of written work, Vidal became famous for being famous. Hanging out with Jack Kennedy, getting invited to glitzy parties, and chatting in our living rooms with Jack Paar and Johnny Carson, the pedigreed novelist traveled in fashionable circles. His life among the in-crowd was not without friction. He participated in public feuds with the likes of Bobby Kennedy, Norman Mailer, Truman Capote, William F. Buckley, Anaïs Nin, and even his own mother. It is difficult to think of anyone else hated by such a diverse array of people.

Vidal harbored seething contempt for Robert Kennedy. The nation's sixty-fourth attorney general reciprocated. Vidal verbally accosted the president's kid brother at a White House party, attacked him in print, and campaigned for his Republican opponent when the carpetbagging Bay State pol ran for the U.S. Senate in New York. When officials denied him a seat at President Kennedy's funeral (how dare they!) or when the

IRS audited him the next year (he had claimed a Jaguar automobile as a tax write-off), the spurned author imagined the dark hand of Bobby Kennedy.[101]

Vidal's feud with William F. Buckley is the stuff of legend. When ABC News paired them to give opposing commentary at the 1968 Democratic National Convention, the duo's contempt for each other was palpable. After Buckley labeled the demonstrators in the streets of Chicago as provocateurs in the style of neo-Nazis marching through Jewish communities (as had recently occurred in nearby Skokie), his on-air nemesis responded, "As far as I'm concerned, the only pro- or crypto-Nazi I can think of is yourself." All hell broke loose. "Now, listen, you queer," the usually gracious conservative responded. "Stop calling me a crypto-Nazi or I'll sock you in your goddamn face and you'll stay plastered."[102] Live television had never been so live.

After Vidal compared Norman Mailer to Charles Manson, the pugnacious Mailer head-butted him prior to a 1971 appearance on *The Dick Cavett Show*.[103] Six years later, Mailer tossed the contents of his drink on Vidal and then hurled the empty glass at his face for good measure. When Vidal's longtime companion, Howard Austen, volunteered to fight Mailer in Vidal's stead, Mailer replied, "My fourteen-year-old son could take you."[104]

In 1995, Vidal attempted to settle scores in his memoirs. *Palimpsest* reads as a bound scandal sheet, with Vidal's unseemly hatred for his mother fueling many distasteful passages. Vidal divulges, for instance, his theory of how his mother overcame his stepfather's erectile dysfunction to become pregnant with his half-brother and half-sister. "I *think* she inserted—with a spoon?—what she called 'the bugs' in order to create my demi-siblings."[105] Vidal exposes readers to his gratuitous claim that Jackie Kennedy demonstrated to his half-sister how to douche after sex, how his father had three testicles, and that a future president of Colombia "was the first boy in our class to have pubic hair."[106] Some things are better left unsaid.

In the spirit of Rousseau and St. Augustine, the novelist reserves *Palimpsest's* most scandalous entries for himself. Vidal regales the reader with descriptive tales from his underground lifestyle, which may have even aroused the interest of Alfred Kinsey when the fledgling writer confessed his sexual history to the famous researcher in 1948.[107] He boasts of sharing "boys" in Italy with Tennessee Williams and gossips of unmanning Jack Kerouac in a drunken encounter.[108] "I calculated, at twenty-five, that I had had more than a thousand sexual encounters," this Wilt Chamberlain of the ascot set contends.[109] But not all dates went well. In Seattle, a pickup went disastrously wrong when a merchant mariner attempted to rape Vidal anally, a scene the memoirist describes in graphic detail.[110] Despite the risks, Vidal finds "a beauty and fulfillment in sex with strangers that one seldom enjoys with people one knows."[111]

Some of these anonymous hookups hinged on an economic transaction. By his own admission, Vidal has frequently played the part of "john" and, on at least one occasion, that of "hustler" too.[112] "So from the age of thirty on, a man or woman was, for my purposes, already a corpse—not that I ever had much on my mind when it came to sex with men," states Vidal. "In my anonymous encounters, I was what used to be called trade. I did nothing—deliberately, at least—to please the other. When I became too old for these attentions from the young, I paid, gladly, thus relieving myself of having to please anyone in any way."[113]

If thirty is too old, what ages did he go for? "Naturally, like most men, I am attracted to adolescent males," he declares.[114] Later in *Palimpsest* he reiterates his preference for "boys" to "men," which he claims is "a universal taste."[115] Like Kinsey, Vidal seems to project his own desires onto the rest of society. Implicit in Vidal's claim that the "universal taste" is for "boys" is the self-congratulatory argument that he is the only one honest or brave enough to admit it. Years earlier he attempted to jazz up his degenerate predilections with an academic defense. He proclaimed, "[P]ederasty among the non-neurotics is by no means a negative act. It is not the result of a delayed emotional development nor is it a substitute for heterosexual relationships; a man is a pederast not out of hatred or a fear of women but out of a natural love for men which is traditional, affirmative and, in the best sense, respectable."[116]

In spite (one hopes!) of Vidal's bathhouse exploits and professed desires for adolescent boys, Hollywood couples Paul Newman and Joanne Woodward and Susan Sarandon and Tim Robbins both named the literary giant as a godfather to their children.[117]

The Self-Hating American

America rejects Gore Vidal's lifestyle. Gore Vidal, in turn, rejects America.

Shades of the bitter America-phobe of later life could be gleaned as early as the 1950s. "[I]f ever there was a people ripe for dictatorship it is the American people today," Vidal hysterically wrote in his first article for

The Nation. "Should a home-grown Hitler appear, whose voice amongst the public orders would be raised against him in derision?"[118] *The Nation* published this rant, it should be noted, at a time when the president of the United States was the man primarily responsible for defeating the Nazis in Western Europe. Soon Vidal would be casually throwing about terms such as *empire* and *fascism* when discussing the United States. Amid bitter denunciations of his homeland during the Vietnam War, he sought to settle abroad permanently. "I'm sometimes in Ireland and therefore in London in my quest for *any* nationality other than this mark of Cain I bear with the rest of my unlucky countrymen," he wrote an acquaintance during the Nixon presidency.[119] What Alec Baldwin threatened in the 2000 election cycle, Gore Vidal actually carried out a generation earlier. Vidal left America, publicly citing Richard Nixon and Vietnam. While policy played a role in his departure, his primary policy objection was something less fashionable than his stated reasons. The political exile was more accurately a tax refugee.[120] Until recently, Vidal, along with his late companion, whom he met in a Manhattan bathhouse more than fifty years ago, lived in self-imposed exile in Italy.

Approaching eighty, the onetime *enfant terrible* of American letters hasn't produced many novels, plays, or filmscripts lately. But he has reemerged as an energized polemicist critical of post-9/11 America. He does not share Zinn's old-school Marxism, nor does he follow an obscure socialist sect, as Chomsky does. While he yields to no man in his reliability in excoriating America, he is remiss in making the stock genuflections to leftist issues that normally accompany such sentiments. Within the leftist milieu, he takes contrarian positions on Abraham Lincoln, foreign aid, and government funding for the arts. He expresses a kind of admiration for America's Founding Fathers. This has even won him enthusiasts on the political Right.[121] Lifestyle conflicts, general leftist sensibilities, and adopted Continental snobbery all influence Vidal's negative view of the United States, but it is just as important to recognize that his is an anti-Americanism that stems from disappointment in the unfulfilled possibilities of the American Founding. Specifically, the departure from Washington's consul in his Farewell Address to avoid foreign wars has enraged this senator's grandson. "I hate the American Empire," he maintains, "and I love the old republic."[122]

Oklahoma City and 9/11

Vidal's twenty-first-century offerings *Perpetual War for Perpetual Peace: How We Got to Be So Hated* and *Dreaming War: Blood for Oil and the Cheney-Bush Junta* seek to unveil America as a money-hungry empire through a series of essays devoted to such subjects as 9/11, Timothy McVeigh, the Cold War, and World War II.

The opening pages of *Dreaming War* hold, "[W]e still don't know by whom we were struck that Tuesday, or for what true purpose."[123] Actually, we do know who struck us on 9/11—al Qaeda. The man behind the attacks, Osama bin Laden, has admitted his role in the nefarious deed. Even if he hadn't, a mountain of evidence points to his guilt. If Vidal's statement weren't foolish enough, later in the book he contradicts it. First Vidal claims that we do not know why we were hit. Then, as if he hadn't even read his own book, he informs the reader why we were attacked: "We had planned to occupy Afghanistan in October, and Osama, or whoever it was who hit us in September, launched a preemptive strike."[124] Vidal refrained from offering any substantiation for this would-be bombshell, perhaps saving it for a future volume.

Despite an abundance of proof, Vidal dismisses the idea that the terrorists have been correctly fingered. Without any evidence, on the other hand, he shows no sign of wavering in his belief that President Bush knew of the attacks in advance. George W. Bush "allowed the American people to go unwarned about an imminent attack upon two of our cities in anticipation of a planned strike by the United States against the Taliban in Afghanistan."[125]

Why would George Bush let this happen?

For oil, stupid! This, of course, is the hackneyed answer the anti-American Left uses to explain just about every U.S. military action. Even a country like Afghanistan, which lacks the rich oil reserves of many of its neighbors, is somehow linked to the West's unquenchable thirst for black gold. Making claims later prominently echoed in Michael Moore's *Fahrenheit 9/11*, Vidal writes, "[T]he conquest of Afghanistan had nothing to do with Osama. He was simply a pretext for replacing the Taliban with a relatively stable government that would allow Union Oil of California to lay its pipeline for the profit of, among others, the Cheney-Bush junta."[126] The oil crusade would not stop with Afghanistan, according to Vidal. The campaign in Afghanistan was probably a dress rehearsal for America's "next giant step, which is to conquer Eurasia."[127]

Vidal paints the Oklahoma City Bombing, like 9/11, as an act of terrorism that the U.S. government allowed to occur. "Evidence," he writes in *Perpetual War for Perpetual Peace*, "is overwhelming that there was a plot involving militia types and government infiltrators—who knows?—as prime movers to create panic in order to get Clinton to sign that infamous Anti-Terrorism Act."[128] Vidal declines to share this "overwhelming" evidence with the reader.

As was the case with his flip-flopping over why America was struck on 9/11, Vidal alternates his view on Tim McVeigh's involvement in killing 168 people in Oklahoma City. Like Osama, McVeigh was "provoked" by the U.S. government. The Gulf War veteran "told us at eloquent length" why he bombed the Murrah Building, Vidal says, "but our rulers and their media preferred to depict him as a sadistic, crazed monster—not a good person like the rest of us—who had done it just for kicks."[129] Did our "rulers" and "their media" merely *portray* McVeigh as a bad guy, or was he really a bad guy no matter what government officials and journalists said? If a murderer of 168 people is not a bad person, who, exactly, earns that distinction in Vidal's judgment?

Vidal then seems to contradict himself, suggesting that the man who "eloquently" confessed his reasons for exploding a Ryder truck didn't really blow up said truck. "Many an 'expert' and many an expert believe that McVeigh neither built nor detonated the bomb that blew up a large part of the Murrah Federal Building on April 19, 1995."[130] Vidal then makes clear that he agrees with both the experts and the "experts." The fact that McVeigh "concocted a fairly complex bomb,"* loaded it onto a truck, and detonated it without killing himself or provoking suspicion "all

---

*Like Vidal, I am no explosives expert. My limited experience in blowing things up does make me skeptical of claims that the bomb (a) couldn't cause the destruction it did and (b) was too complex for McVeigh to construct. As a Marine Reservist in the summer of 1995, I participated in a one-day demolition course in Twenty-nine Palms, California. At its conclusion, the major conducting the demolition package amused himself by staging a finale explosion featuring two hundred pounds of ammonium nitrate, some diesel fuel, and a small amount of other munitions. The potent recipe closely resembled McVeigh's formula. Rather than "fairly complex," creating such a bomb is so simple that a child could do it. The ensuing blast unleashed a rain of earth and shrapnel several hundred feet from its origin. It sent the shell of a World War II–era tank several stories into the sky. If a bomb a fraction of the size of McVeigh's released such a massive and frightening force, it seems clear to me that McVeigh's concoction could have inflicted the destruction it wrought on the Murrah Building.

defied reason."[131] It didn't, but what Vidal seems to be saying is: Let's pretend that it did.

Fact or Fiction?

In this novelist's foray outside of the world of fiction, make-believe is readily injected into polemical arguments. Every few pages contain some brazen lie or another:

- Vidal bizarrely claims that the military gets more than half the federal government's annual revenues.[132] The Department of Defense's piece of the 2004 budget is actually 17 percent, with its percent of revenues slightly higher.[133]

- *Dreaming War* maintains that America gives "the lowest in foreign aid among developed countries," adding that Israel receives most of this aid.[134] The United States actually gives a larger amount in foreign aid than any country in the world. The 2003 federal budget allotted $16 billion to its foreign operations budget. This amount did not include funds for debt forgiveness, the International Monetary Fund, and other related programs. While Israel received more aid than any other nation in 2003, it did not receive anything close to most of our foreign aid budget, which *Dreaming War* alleges.[135]

- The Bush administration, *Perpetual War for Perpetual Peace* contends, "has casually torn up most of the treaties to which civilized nations subscribe—like the Kyoto Accords or the nuclear missile agreement with Russia."[136] The nuclear agreement he speaks of wasn't with "Russia" but with the Soviet Union—a country that no longer exists. Nor did most "civilized nations" participate in the treaty; it was an agreement between two countries. President Bush, like President Clinton before him, didn't sign the Kyoto Accords. Neither man has "torn up" the document. It appears extremely unlikely that the Senate will ever ratify the treaty, meaning that probably no president will get the chance to approve or reject it.

- Vidal says that during the past half-century median household income had been slashed by 7 percent.[137] No U.S. economic statistics indicate anything remotely close to a 7 percent decline in median household incomes over the previous fifty years, or any fifty-year period for that matter.

Vidal's attempts at history are likewise the stuff of fiction. America gave Japan "no alternative but war" prior to Pearl Harbor. Elsewhere he claims that "the A-bombs were dropped *after* Japan was ready to surrender," ignoring the obvious fact that the Empire of the Sun refused to surrender until *after* Nagasaki.[138] The postwar Soviet Union gets a pass from Vidal too. "We started to renege on our agreements with Stalin," Vidal claims. "Stalin went ape at this betrayal."[139] Up is down. Good is evil. Day is night.

Vidal claims that fellow America-hater Noam Chomsky is "largely blacked out by U.S. media."[140] Reality begs to differ. As reported in his book *Public Intellectuals*, Richard Posner found 1,300 media mentions of Noam Chomsky between 1995 and 2000. A sample of the media mentions suggested that nearly 90 percent of the references had to do with his political activism, rather than his scholarly work in the field of linguistics. While Chomsky had fewer than half the media references of Vidal himself, the MIT professor had more mentions than Thomas Sowell, Samuel Huntington, Richard Pipes, and other intellectuals who hold a decidedly different view of the world.[141] Who's really being blacked out?

Other Vidalisms are equally perplexing. He labels *The New Republic* a "far-right" magazine, while Supreme Court Justice John Paul Stevens, who usually can be counted on to vote with the liberal wing of the bench, is deemed a "conservative."[142] For Vidal, words have little to do with their real meanings.

Gore Vidal is reflexively anti-American. Because he always assumes the worst about the country whose uniform he once wore, he's prone to error. One need not look far to find examples of the author molding the facts to suit his theories. Since there is a large audience of Americans willing to believe lies about their country, Vidal will always have admirers who parrot his rants, like the Iraq war protestors of 2003.

Vidal can still turn a phrase, and the general idea that America would be better off if it didn't involve itself in the affairs of nonbelligerent foreign nations is a good one. Nevertheless, a vague understanding of a good idea and artsy prose don't make up for wild theories and uninhibited use of falsehood. Clever writing doesn't redeem sloppy thinking.

CAPTIVES OF IDEOLOGY

Like death and taxes, you can count on Howard Zinn, Noam Chomsky, and Gore Vidal. No matter the issue, you can count on the triumvirate to fall back on a programmed response that blames America. As has been shown, allowing theory to preordain one's view of the facts is a practice fraught with danger. Time and again, these three stooges of anti-Americanism have embarrassed themselves by remaining captives of ideology.

America renounces socialism and atheism. Thus, Zinn, Chomsky, and Vidal renounce America. Discrediting their country means vindicating their ideology. Their motives are pretty simple.

The antiwar protestors we met at the chapter's outset are a clear sign of this trio's extraordinary influence. And those impressionable young people don't stand alone in mimicking the rhetoric of Zinn, Chomsky, and Vidal. Protestors of all ages taking to the streets to demonstrate against the U.S. government have followed their anti-American talking points.

Toting a sign reading "Bush Is the Real Terrorist," a convert to Islam marched along the Mall in Washington to protest American military action in Iraq. On this cold January day in 2003, the New Jersey woman declared, "When it comes down to it, it's all for oil and global domination." She suspected that many in the U.S. government knew about the 9/11 attacks in advance. "Another thing about 9/11—the United States is like a stuck-up little bitch. They just do and take all of what they please. I mean, 9/11 was terrible, but it was the first terrorist attack on this country. It's like, 'Oh, no! Somebody broke the United States' nail, now the whole earth is going to blow up.'"[143]

Two months later, at another D.C. protest march, an angry New Jersey teacher remarked, "And where do we get the moral high ground to tell anybody what kind of weapons to have? We, who are the only nation to have used weapons of mass destruction, against civilian populations no less, in Hiroshima and Nagasaki three days later. What kind of a nation does this? We are unrivaled in brutality and hypocrisy." The teacher found the history imparted bothersome as well. "What passes for history in our high schools is nothing but propaganda," he observed. "It's the glorification of American culture, and it's bullshit."[144]

"We would be for the defeat of the U.S. war," noted Abram Megrete, the leader of a group of New York activists that converged on the nation's capital on the eve of the Iraq war. "We are for the defense of Iraq. It is in the interest of working people in the United States that the same government which is trying to intimidate and silence them be defeated in this war."[145]

"The United States is the biggest devil," a masked anarchist explained at a postwar hate-fest in Washington, D.C. "We're in the belly of the beast right here." The man believed that former president George H. W. Bush met with the Taliban in prewar Afghanistan to force the regime to build an oil pipeline for Western capitalists and that the U.S. government had foreknowledge of 9/11. "They knew. Someone knew."[146]

On the streets of Manhattan, a seasoned protestor asked, "Who was responsible for 9/11? American imperialism and George Bush in particular. The Bush family and the bin Laden family have long, long economic ties. They're co-investors in the Carlyle Group."[147]

"The first casualty when war comes is truth," Senator Hiram Johnson once remarked.[148] The antiwar activists who gathered around the country in 2003, inspired by a trio of literary cranks, prove the rectitude of the senator's remarks. As we shall see in the next chapter, Johnson's aphorism also applies to the proponents of war.

"A TRUTH THAT LESSER MORTALS FAILED TO GRASP"

How Ideologues Hijacked U.S. Foreign Policy

If you want war, nourish a doctrine. Doctrines are the most frightful tyrants to which men are ever subject, because doctrines get inside of a man's own reason and betray him against himself.

—WILLIAM GRAHAM SUMNER

DESPITE BROAD *CULTURAL* INFLUENCE, ZINN, VIDAL, CHOMSKY, AND their marching followers have scant *political* influence. Whether we choose to believe or disbelieve the blame-America-first crowd's more outrageous statements, such as that the White House allowed 9/11 to happen or that President Bush went to war to hoard the world's oil supply, national policy does not hinge on such fabricated claims. But what happens when those *in power* look to their ideology, and not the facts, to guide them? The consequences, as we've learned since March 19, 2003, can be deadly.

For more than a decade, a group of hawkish Republicans urged U.S. presidents to topple Saddam Hussein. With the election of George W. Bush, many of these armchair generals found themselves in positions of power, particularly within the Department of Defense. These hawks saw the 9/11 attacks as an opportunity to attack their longtime nemesis and start to remake the Middle East in America's image. Almost immediately after the attacks, Secretary of Defense Donald Rumsfeld, his deputy Paul Wolfowitz, and other administration figures called for the United States to go after Iraq.[1] At the time, the president sided with Secretary of State Colin Powell, who argued that al Qaeda stood as the more dangerous and immediate threat. Knowing that the American people are traditionally leery of foreign wars, the advocates of attacking Iraq knew that simply showing Saddam Hussein as an evil dictator would not be enough to generate support for their project. So they looked for reasons to attack Iraq, and not surprisingly, they found them.

Citing connections to al Qaeda, an attempt by Saddam Hussein to purchase uranium from Niger, and stockpiles of chemical and biological weapons, the war party within the administration convinced the president, the Congress, and the American people to invade Iraq. The administration launched an offensive that dwarfed the amount of time, money, and troops expended to fight al Qaeda in Afghanistan. The war proved successful in a matter of weeks. The peace proved far more problematic. Many more Americans died in the long months after Bush declared victory than in the war itself. Moreover, as the postwar occupation dragged on, the long-term prospects for a democratic Iraq seemed unlikely. Equally troublesome was that most of the central arguments for going to war in the first place began to appear fraudulent.

WEAPONS OF MASS DELUSION

"The British Government has learned that Saddam Hussein recently sought significant quantities of uranium from Africa," President Bush announced in his 2003 State of the Union address.[2] Other administration figures parroted this line, including National Security Adviser Condoleezza Rice, Vice President Richard Cheney, White House spokesman Ari Fleischer, and for a time even Secretary of State Colin Powell.[3]

As it turned out, the uranium story was a hoax. Ten months prior to making the claim, the White House had been warned that the documents purporting to show this were fraudulent. Among others, former ambassador Joe Wilson labeled the claims "bogus and unrealistic" following an eight-day fact-finding mission to Niger in March 2002.[4] "We investigated every single intelligence claim that was provided alleging Iraq was pursuing nuclear weapons and did not find any evidence of the revival of a nuclear weapons program," an International Atomic Energy Agency spokesperson stated.[5] Greg Thielmann, an official with the State Department at the time, later admitted, "A whole lot of things told us that the report was bogus."[6]

By confusing the geographic proximity of Saddam Hussein and Osama bin Laden for ideological proximity, the Bush administration crudely insinuated a tie between the Iraqi dictator and 9/11. Consider the vice president's statements on this matter:

- In late 2001, Cheney told NBC's Tim Russert that "it's been pretty well confirmed that [al Qaeda terrorist Mohammed Atta] did go to Prague and he did meet with a senior official of the Iraqi intelligence service in Czechoslovakia last April, several months before the [9/11] attack."[7]

- Nearly a year after 9/11 he remarked, "We have reporting that places [Atta] in Prague with a senior Iraqi intelligence officer a few months before the attacks on the World Trade Center."[8]

- A year after that, Cheney again reiterated this claim to Russert, this time with a qualifier: "With respect to 9/11 . . . the Czechs alleged that Mohammed Atta, the lead attacker, met in Prague with a senior Iraqi intelligence official five months before the attack, but we've never been able to develop anymore of that yet, either in terms of confirming it or discrediting it."[9]

Investigations by Congress, the Central Intelligence Agency (CIA), and the Federal Bureau of Investigation (FBI) found nothing to validate this charge. The FBI and the CIA believed that Atta remained in Virginia Beach at the time of the phantom Prague meeting. "We ran down literally hundreds of thousands of leads and checked every record we could get our hands on, from flight reservations to car rentals to bank accounts," the director of the FBI explained in April 2002.[10] The search yielded nothing. The Iraqi intelligence agent who supposedly met with Atta not surprisingly denied the claim as well. Even the Czechs, the sole source of the claim, backed off. A month after his government authoritatively issued the claim, Czech Republic president Vaclav Havel said there was a "70 percent" chance that the Atta-Iraq clandestine meeting took place. In 2002, however, Havel privately admitted to the Bush administration that no evidence existed to confirm the rendezvous. The Czech Republic's source, it turned out, was an Arab student who occasionally served as an informant for the country's intelligence.[11]

Is this the kind of evidence to go to war over?

The main argument for war focused on stockpiles of chemical and biological weapons that Hussein allegedly kept hidden. Right around the time that the Defense Intelligence Agency concluded, "There is no reliable information on whether Iraq is producing and stockpiling chemical weapons," the defense secretary reported to Congress that Iraq had "amassed large, clandestine stockpiles of chemical weapons, including VX, sarin, cyclosarin and mustard gas."[12] To generate support, the White House conjured up ghastly images in the minds of Americans of chemical weapons being used on them. "Imagine those 19 hijackers with other weapons and other plans—this time armed by Saddam Hussein," the president said in his 2003 State of the Union address. "It would take one vial, one canister, one crate slipped into this country to bring a day of horror like none we have ever known."[13] But the United Nations inspectors couldn't find such weapons leading up to war, or in the many months they spent searching Iraq after the American victory.

The inability of weapons inspectors to find evidence of biological or chemical weapons did not raise doubt among the true believers but rather served as proof that Hussein was expert at hiding things. The search for Iraq's weapons of mass destruction began to resemble Monty Python's quest for the Holy Grail. Just give the inspectors some time, officials assured us, they'll find the weapons. Theories abounded as to why WMD hadn't been found, including that Hussein's own lackeys had lied to him about having them and that Iraq had hidden the weapons in Syria.[14] This latter theory was quite convenient for hawks pushing to invade Syria following the Iraq adventure. Administration officials seemed to entertain every idea except the possibility that they had been wrong. While chemical or biological weapons may very well turn up someday—after all, Hussein gassed internal and external enemies during the 1980s—the salient fact remains that Saddam Hussein didn't use chemical or biological weapons when a superpower invaded his country. If he didn't use these weapons in this instance, what plausible scenario exists in which he would have used them against the United States?

That the Bush administration more readily believed British and Czech intelligence than the CIA and the FBI demonstrates the extent to which it grasped at straws. Numerous high-profile administration figures first decided to wage war on Iraq, and then constructed reasons to support their decision. They put the cart before the horse.

"What we have here is advocacy, not intelligence work," observed Patrick Lang, a former intelligence analyst on Iraq.[15] A senior military officer complained to *Time*, "They were inclined to see and interpret evidence a particular way to support a very deeply held conviction."[16] Former Reagan hand Lawrence Korb maintained, "They came in with a world view, and they looked for things to fit into it."[17]

Why the colossal misinterpretation of intelligence? Why the rush to invade a foreign nation that posed no threat to the United States? Why the lack of hesitation in pawning off on the public dubious intelligence as pure truth?

A partial answer to these questions, writers in such publications as the *New York Times, Le Monde, Der Spiegel,* and *Asia Times* have suggested, is found in an unlikely place: the books and essays of Leo Strauss, a deceased University of Chicago professor who had a great deal to say about Plato, Maimonides, and Machiavelli, but next to nothing to say about the United States, the Middle East, foreign policy, and modern warfare.

THE INTELLECTUAL GODFATHER

Today, Leo Strauss (1899–1973) is perhaps the most talked about but least read intellectual. He is generally hated not for anything he said or did, but for who his students, or his students' students, are. Deputy Secretary of Defense Paul Wolfowitz; the director of the Pentagon's Office of Special Plans, Abram Shulsky; and Undersecretary of Defense for Intelligence Stephen Cambone are the most prominent government officials fingered as Straussians. Followers of the mysterious academic among the intellectual class include Lincoln scholar Harry Jaffa, Harvard professor Harvey Mansfield, neoconservative founding father Irving Kristol and his ubiquitous son William, and Professor Allan Bloom, the late author of *The Closing of the American Mind.* As the *New York Times* noted in May 2003, the neoconservative admirers of Strauss "have penetrated the culture at nearly every level—from the halls of academia to the halls of the Pentagon."[18]

It's easy to see the appeal of Leo Strauss to conservatives. A scholar of long-forgotten works, he helped rejuvenate interest in the Great Books. Strauss implored readers to remember the West's philosophical tradition and defended the West from contemporaneous threats. In *The City and Man*, he wrote, "[T]he destruction of the West would not necessarily prove that the West is in a crisis: the West could go down in honor, certain of its purpose. The crisis of the West consists in the West's having become uncertain of its purpose."[19] The threat to the West in Strauss's lifetime came exclusively from Western ideologies. A Jewish émigré from Nazi Germany, Strauss condemned the inability of much of the scholarly community to pass judgment on regimes. He'd have none of that, plainly labeling the governments of Hitler and Stalin tyrannies. In *On Tyranny* he noted the great failure of the intellectuals of his time: "[W]hen we were brought face to face with tyranny—with a kind of tyranny that surpassed the boldest imagination of the most powerful thinkers of the past—our political science failed to recognize it."[20] He lashed out against intellectual fashions, particularly historicism, social scientist Max Weber's distinction between statements of fact and of value, and relativism. The last of these he saw as self-refuting. If truth is relative, what makes relativism true? If Strauss privately scoffed at the idea of God, his belief in the necessity of religion for the good of the regime nevertheless gained him the admiration of some religious conservatives.

Amherst College professor Hadley Arkes encountered Strauss in the early 1960s as "a legend to be fathomed." Upon arriving at the University of Chicago, Arkes noticed that his unimposing professor attracted "students of all ages, with people in their fifties, with a handful of Catholic priests, along with the expected crowd of smart, aggressive Jewish students in their twenties."[21] Buried beneath oversized glasses and a tweed jacket was a charismatic gentleman capable of resurrecting the dormant philosophies of the ancients. Teacher-student relationships proved exceptionally close. "The specialness, if not exclusivity, of the Strauss circle was not lost upon spouses who sensed that they could no longer share the most important things with their husbands," student George Anastaplo recalled.[22]

Left-out wives were not the only ones who failed to appreciate fully the tight-knit subculture. One scholar remembers at Chicago "a clique of Straussians who thought they knew a truth that lesser mortals failed to grasp and condescended according." The academic recalls opining to one of Strauss's students, "A man who attracts disciples seems to me a bad man—stunting independent growth among his pupils by inviting them to surrender their own judgment to his superior insight."[23] Some find the Straussians cultish. Political science professor Shadia Drury writes that Strauss's large following "tended to have the attributes of a cult—its secrecy and faith in the authority of Strauss and of ancient philosophers he supposedly followed."[24] One follower partly concedes this fault and admits, "Straussians talk in a kind of code to one another."[25]

The Straussians seem more Masonic Lodge gathering than Raelian mass meeting, though. They maintain an insider language, practice a form of Straussian nepotism, and genuflect to their great guru, but allow for intramural debate and a plethora of political opinions. If they have a secret handshake, they've done a good job of keeping it a secret.

Part defense mechanism against a hostile academy, part consequence of an ideology that lauds esotericism, their surreptitiousness is what is so off-putting to outsiders. Professor Drury explains, "The ridicule of the Straussians in the academy is connected to their unquestioning devotion to a set of ideas that they cannot or will not defend except to those who are already convinced. It is therefore not the case that they are simply being persecuted for thinking differently, it is for disseminating their views in a manner that is destructive of intellectual life itself. For they do not want their ideas discussed openly or even known to anyone outside the charmed circle of initiates."[26] The furtiveness often masks deception, further infuriating critics. Strauss publicly lauded religion as he privately embraced atheism, for example, and his popular evangelist Allan Bloom preached family values but practiced anonymous sex until stopped by AIDS. What's good for the goose, it seems, is not good for the gander.

Critics also regard Strauss as a foe of democratic governance. His deliberately elliptical writing style certainly betrays an elitist contempt for the masses. But did his distrust of democracy go beyond that? Shadia Drury contends that "Strauss abhorred liberal democracy."[27] Like charges that the Straussians constitute a cult, this criticism is not altogether accurate, but it does contain more than a grain of truth. At best, Strauss could muster two cheers for democracy. He famously remarked that the American Republic stood on "low but solid ground."[28] When one was faced with alternatives like Hitler and Stalin, democracy would do just fine.

The seminal event of Strauss's life was the rise and fall of Nazism. It shaped his hatred of tyranny, as well as his skepticism of democracy. The Weimar Republic's inability to smother Hitlerism in its crib made a skeptic out of Strauss, as did favorable electoral outcomes for the Nazis. Likewise, Hitler's unimpeded invasions of neighboring countries instilled a belief that tyrannies must be stopped. As evidenced by the activist approach to foreign policy trumpeted by present-day Straussians, Strauss passed this trait on to his progeny. His tempered support of democracy seems in some respects to have been a recessive gene. Like Strauss, the acolytes find an aristocratic republicanism suitable to themselves, but their stated enthusiasm for democracy beyond America's borders seems an evangelical passion.

Rather than a sign of minding others' business when you should be tending to your own, Strauss regards the pursuit of empire as not only a universal impulse among states but proof of health in nations, as well.[29] Yet if just a few nations actually carried out this aim "pursued by all societies," then the world would be constantly at war—not exactly a "healthy" environment for any people, even the victors.[30] Though he described "empire" as one half of "mankind's great objects," Strauss's relevance to U.S. foreign policy has little to do with this aim—unless one accepts the dubious proposition that the Bush administration craves perpetual war or dreams of empire, à la ancient Rome or Victorian England.[31] Rather, Strauss's influence has more to do with his embrace of the "noble lie"— which permeates the professor's entire corpus—and his much-ridiculed method of textual interpretation.

PERSECUTION AND THE ART OF WRITING

Like Colonel Jessup in *A Few Good Men*, Leo Strauss thinks that you can't handle the truth. Like Darth Vader in *Star Wars*, he believes in empire. And like John Nash in *A Beautiful Mind*, he scours texts for encrypted messages that aren't there.

Persecution and the Art of Writing, Strauss's 1952 manifesto claiming to uncover the secret of how philosophers write, stands as the professor's most important book. While non-Straussians may applaud ideas in *What Is Political Philosophy?* or *The City and Man*, acceptance of the tenets of *Persecution and the Art of Writing* (a less-read book) generally indicates whether one properly falls under the label "Straussian."

The book conveys a very simple idea: Persecution compels philosophers to write in a coded language that only other great thinkers can decrypt. These elliptical writings contain one theme understood by the vulgar (the exoteric theme), and another, real message understood by the elect (the esoteric theme). Several of *Persecution and the Art of Writing*'s main points seem uncontroversial. From Socrates to Jesus to Galileo to Solzhenitsyn to Salman Rushdie, persecution remains a constant for thinkers voicing subversive thoughts in restrictive societies. While these men faced their persecutors without tempering their public utterances, it's not a stretch to believe that some philosophers attempt to avoid trouble by carefully shielding their real views from their would-be persecutors. What seems preposterous is Strauss's contention that a virtual "who's who" of philosophy—Plato, Spinoza, Machiavelli, Hobbes, Locke, and more—adopted this method of writing. Approaching a Kabbalistic or intentionally obscure writer from a Straussian perspective may help the reader comprehend the text, but approaching the great philosophers in such a manner will only deepen the reader's ignorance.

Persecution and the Art of Writing insists that past scholars have entirely misinterpreted philosophy's greatest works. Strauss—thank God!—is here to shine light on the darkness. You see, when we thought Plato, Machiavelli, Hobbes, and others were saying one thing, Strauss reveals in his body of work that they were saying something else entirely. How does the professor come to his unique take on leading philosophers? Through a special method of reading, which embraces a form of numerology, places added importance on a book's first and last words, and assumes that many great philosophers intentionally deceive readers.

The primary device Strauss uses to deconstruct texts involves scouring an author's works in search of ambiguities, contradictions, and even what he refers to as "meaningful silences." Strauss's general rule holds that if an author repeatedly expresses a view, but then on one occasion says something vaguely suggesting a divergent view, one should take the second view as the author's true view. The careful reader, the theory goes, will pick up on the contradiction and realize the author's true intention; the vulgar reader, on the other hand, will be oblivious to it. By these methods, the author supposedly gets his message out to the right people while ensuring his safety from the unwashed masses. Strauss claims, "[A]ll ambiguities occurring in good books are [due], not to chance or carelessness, but to deliberate choice, to the author's wish to indicate a grave question."[32] Regarding Spinoza's *Theologico-Political Treatise*, "in case of a contradiction, the statement most opposed to what Spinoza considered the vulgar view has to be regarded as expressing his serious view; nay, that even a necessary implication of a heterodox character has to take precedence over a contradictory statement that is never explicitly contradicted by Spinoza."[33] In other words, when overt contradictions fail to arise, search for something that might merely imply a thought that goes against the societal grain. Strauss advises: "one is at liberty, and even under the obligation, to disregard Spinoza's own indications."[34]

If it's all right to disregard what Spinoza says, what's to stop Strauss's readers from viewing *Persecution and the Art of Writing* as an ironical work intended to ridicule childishly imaginative interpretations? At least in this case, Strauss makes his meaning quite explicit, making a Straussian interpretation of his own argument unnecessary:

Persecution, then, gives rise to a peculiar technique of writing, and therewith to a peculiar type of literature, in which the truth about all crucial things is presented exclusively between the lines. That literature is addressed, not to all readers, but to trustworthy and intelligent readers only. It has all the advantages of private communication without having its greatest disadvantage—that it reaches only the writer's acquaintances. It has all the advantages of public communication without having its greatest disadvantage—capital punishment for the author. But how can a man perform the miracle of speaking in a publication to a minority, while being silent to the majority of his readers? The fact which makes this literature possible can be expressed in the axiom that thoughtless men are careless readers, and that only thoughtful men are careful readers. Therefore an author who wishes to address only thoughtful men has but to write in such a way that only a very careful reader can detect the meaning of his book. But, it will be objected, there may be clever men, careful readers, who are not trustworthy, and who, after having found the author out, would denounce him to the authorities. As a matter of fact, this literature would be impossible if the Socratic dictum that virtue is knowledge, and therefore that thoughtful men as such are trustworthy and not cruel, were entirely wrong.[35]

This argument depends on wishful thinking. The paragraph contains two major problems. First, "virtue" isn't "knowledge," and "thoughtful men" can indeed be untrustworthy and cruel. Stating that *intelligent* readers will stumble upon what Strauss believes is the author's intended truth is a way of begging the question. This circular logic dictates that only readers who employ Strauss's methods are intelligent. If you don't find what Strauss wants you to find, you lack intelligence. Second, what exists "between the lines"? The answer: blank space. It's the reader, rather than the writer, who fills in this empty space. In Strauss's system, readers cease being readers and become sleuths, code-breakers, and forensic scientists. Writers, meanwhile, cease to determine the meaning of the words they write. Those embracing this formula have stirred up untold mischief. Their students become ignorant and stay that way until they break out of Strauss's mental straitjacket.

When we learn that by "persecution" Strauss means anything from capital punishment to "social ostracism," it becomes clear that he intends his theory to cover not just the truly persecuted but any writer.[36] His catch-all definition of persecution applies as easily to a critic of Stalin writing in Leningrad in 1938 as to an opponent of gambling living in Las Vegas in 2004. Is it honest to apply the term *persecution* to both of these very different cases?

Strauss's tarot-card philosophy employs other peculiar methods. He places particular importance on where in a text an author features a passage. For instance, Strauss might deduce that the chapter that appears in the center of a book is where the author is trying to make his real point. Some numbers, such as seven and thirteen, alert Strauss to a text's hidden meaning. A paragraph, subhead, or chapter count adding up to a designated number, or that number's factor or multiple, indicates special meaning for Strauss, even when the text's author leaves no evidence that he devised any sort of code-laden numeric scheme.

"The *Prince* consists of 26 chapters," writes Strauss on Machiavelli. "Twenty-six is the numerical value of the letters of the sacred name of God in Hebrew, of the Tetragrammaton. But did Machiavelli know this? I do not know. Twenty-six equals 2 times 13. Thirteen is now and for quite sometime has been considered an unlucky number, but in former times it was also and even primarily considered a lucky number. So 'twice 13' might mean both good luck and bad luck, and hence altogether: luck *fortuna.*"[37]

This borders perilously close to insanity. What evidence is there that Machiavelli paid any attention to the precise number of chapters in *The Prince*, let alone included that many chapters to deliver an encrypted message about luck or God?

Something similarly bizarre is at work in Strauss's discovery of coded meanings in the first and last words authors use. His discussion in *Natural Right and History* of John Locke provides a glimpse of this strange mind at work. Strauss points to a chapter in Locke's treatises on government that "happens to be the only chapter of the entire *Treatises* which opens with the word 'God.' It happens to be followed by the only chapter of the entire *Treatises* which opens with the word 'Men.'" He continues, noting a sign he observed in Locke's *Essay Concerning Human Understanding:* "It so happens that there is also only one chapter in the *Essay* which opens with the word 'God' and which is followed by the only chapter of the *Essay* whose first word is 'Man.'"[38] From Strauss's grassy knoll, he divines that these chapters' opening words provide the key to understanding the true meaning of the text. Through the opening and closing words written in these chapters, Strauss deduces that Locke is covertly undermining

Christian teaching. As with a lot of what Strauss says, the thing that jumps out at the reader is not necessarily his conclusion, but how he got from point A to point B.

THE RIGHT'S DECONSTRUCTIONISTS

And it is this way of getting from point A to point B that leads Straussians astray. If you base your interpretations on word games, numerology, and meaningful silences, you're going to be wrong a lot more than you're right. In his interpretation of famous philosophers, Strauss is wrong quite a bit:

- "Strauss turns upside down the meaning of the *Republic*," maintains noted scholar of classical philosophy M. F. Burnyeat.[39] Examples abound. Strauss repeatedly and incorrectly contends that Plato's favored definition of justice entails "helping one's friends and hurting one's enemies."[40] Readers get the impression that Strauss views *The Republic* as Plato's ironical argument *against* utopia, rather than the Greek's vision of a good regime. He mocks the idea that Socrates generally spoke for Plato, at times queerly seeing Thrasymachus and Polemarchus as the author's true spokesmen.[41] "It's not through literary insensitivity that readers of the Platonic dialogues, from Aristotle onward, have taken Socrates to be Plato's spokesman," Burnyeat observes.[42]

- "Of all of Strauss's brilliant and imaginative textual analysis of Machiavelli," author Ted McAllister writes, "the most intriguing and debatable is his reconstruction of the Florentine's religious beliefs. No other subject requires that Strauss rest so much of his argument upon Machiavelli's silence. Similarly, Strauss's position requires that Machiavelli shift the meaning of key words two or even three times." According to McAllister, Strauss's Machiavelli believes neither in Christ nor in the gods of Greece and Rome, but in an Averroist conception of religion.[43]

- "Locke cannot have recognized any law of nature in the proper sense of the term," Strauss writes. "This conclusion stands in shocking contrast to what is generally thought to be his doctrine."[44] It sure does. The Declaration of Independence practically plagiarizes Locke when enumerating man's God-given rights. Did Jefferson miss something?

No, as usual, Strauss's case rests on discoveries of self-contradictions, "ambiguous language," and reading "between the lines."[45] Locke's "inconsistencies," he contends, "are so obvious that they cannot have escaped the notice of a man of his rank and his sobriety."[46] Locke goes so far to cover his tracks, according to Strauss, that he quotes only thinkers in the natural law tradition while referencing none of the thinkers in opposition, with whom he secretly agrees.[47]

Strauss sets up a false dichotomy of ancients (good) and moderns (bad). When the philosophers don't fit into their chronologically assigned categories, Strauss usually adjusts their philosophies to fit accordingly.

Now that Strauss has been dead for more than three decades, his followers have begun to partake in a cottage industry of applying Straussian readings to Strauss's own writings. Since Strauss lived his saying that "one writes as one reads," this is not without reason.[48] But why did a man protected by the freedoms offered in the United States write like this? Even a friendly scholar remarked, "[O]ne wonders what persecution Strauss faced in such a liberal and tolerant society."[49] Another has conceded, "[I]t is hard to attribute his style to any fear for his own welfare."[50] To write in a hermetic style is to invite attention and spawn debate, which is perhaps the point. Like the village oracle whose enigmatic pronouncements leave the commoners guessing, Strauss ensures that he will be a continual subject of debate—academic and otherwise—by deliberately writing in a confusing manner.

If his elliptical style has fostered some peculiar interpretations of Strauss from opposing scholars, it is equally to blame for the bizarre readings offered by his admirers. In searching for "clues" that "Strauss provides the reader" in "How To Begin To Study *The Guide of the Perplexed*," an essay on the philosopher Maimonides, Steven Lenzner points out that "two 'To's surround 'Begin'" in the title. Because they are capitalized, Lenzner, who teaches politics at Harvard, states, the "To"s really mean "two" and thus guide the reader to go first to the truth contained in Chapter 2 of Maimonides' book.[51] Whatever one thinks of this interpretation, one can't help but see it as an indictment of Strauss. Either one believes that Strauss wrote in this nutty-professor style, which makes him a major-league screwball, or one sees that Strauss has inspired followers to read texts in this outlandish manner.

"I submit in all seriousness that surrender of the critical intellect is the price of initiation into the world of Leo Strauss's ideas," M. F. Burnyeat stated in his famous piece in the *New York Review of Books*.[52] Burnyeat's keen observation is why the public should be concerned about Straussians occupying high office.

STRAUSSIANS IN HIGH PLACES

In many ways, the uproar that arose in the wake of the Iraq war regarding Leo Strauss resembled the tale of the boy who cried wolf. Political liberals had chronically invoked the boogeyman of Strauss over the years. To these liberals, Strauss was the puppeteer pulling the strings of right-of-center politicians from Ronald Reagan to Newt Gingrich to Bob Dole to George W. Bush. During the 1980s, *Newsweek* reported that Strauss enjoyed "a powerful but little-publicized influence within the Reagan administration."[53] In the pages of the *New York Times*, Richard Bernstein recognized Strauss as "a sort of intellectual godfather to the Contract With America."[54] During the 1996 presidential election, *Time* deemed Strauss "perhaps one of the most influential men in American politics."[55] Scores of media outlets issued ominous warnings about Strauss after George W. Bush became president.

The specter of the long-dead Strauss influencing national policy proves too convenient an image not only for many liberals but for some Straussians as well. Both camps cart out prominent figures, who may have taken a class taught by a Straussian or expressed admiration for one of Strauss's books, to demonstrate the deceased intellectual's influence. Clarence Thomas, William Bennett, Newt Gingrich, and other important figures suddenly became Straussians. From the crypt, the émigré professor's tentacles seemed to control not only the entire conservative movement but the reins of government as well.

Or at least that is what many of Strauss's media and academic critics would have us believe. Reality is not so dramatic. If the idea of a mystical professor posthumously directing the U.S. government is too fantastical for serious people to believe, shouldn't it be alarming enough that a few of his gentleman followers have been well placed within the American foreign policy apparatus? Why all the exaggerations when the truth is disturbing enough?

Knowing what we know about the strange ideas of Leo Strauss, we need to ask a few questions. Is it comforting that a Straussian has been in charge of interpreting intelligence at the Department of Defense? Are Americans safer because a Straussian serving in the number-two position at the Defense Department has helped determine whether America is at peace or war? Have prominent Straussians advising the commander in chief made him more enlightened or more confused? Can we trust them to be straightforward with the president and the American people?

Leaders deceiving the public to pursue unpopular policies, particularly wars, predate the Straussians. So far as we know, not even the *New York Times* blames Strauss for the Gulf of Tonkin incident or the munitions covertly transported by the *Lusitania*. So the executive branch's shenanigans prefacing the Iraq War not only had historical precedent but also involved an awful lot of people who had never heard of Leo Strauss. But it seems that a nation decreases the chances of deception by government if it keeps individuals out of power who believe that deceiving the people is a noble calling.

By a Straussian reading of intelligence, U.S. officials imagined an Iraqi nuclear weapons program that in reality hardly existed; they dreamed Iraqi complicity in 9/11 even as they minimized the role of Saudis; they saw a reincarnated Hitler poised to attack and not a toothless tiger kept in check by a decade of isolation; they glimpsed stockpiles of chemical and biological weapons that apparently were so well hidden that even the Iraqis couldn't find them when the globe's lone superpower invaded; and they imagined a country ripe to be a mini-America in the Middle East rather than America's West Bank. We may never know if they gleaned this information from meaningful silences, numerology, or some equally absurd method. We know only that they drew conclusions not warranted by the facts.

"HUMAN WEEDS"

The *Real* Foundations of
the Abortion-Rights Movement

*I think it is agreed by all parties that this prodigious number of children
in the arms, or on the backs, or at the heels of their mothers, and frequently
of their fathers, is in the present deplorable state of the kingdom a very great
additional grievance. . . . I propose to provide for them in such a manner
as instead of being a charge upon their parents or the parish, or wanting food
and raiment for the rest of their lives, they shall on the contrary contribute
to the feeding, and partly to the clothing, of many thousands.*

—JONATHAN SWIFT,
A Modest Proposal

"MY BODY, MY CHOICE," THE FAMILIAR REFRAIN GOES. THE BABY
growing within the mother, abortion-rights leaders claim, is actually part
of the pregnant woman's body. The mental gymnastics exerted to maintain this position requires the belief that a woman can have two distinct
sets of DNA, incompatible blood types, and both male and female genital organs. "My Body, My Choice" is almost too silly an argument to con-
template, but it makes for a pithy bumper sticker.

Another belief holds that what pregnant women carry is neither a baby
nor human life. When life begins, abortion-rights activists assert, is a
great mystery unsolved by modern science. If the content of the womb is
not a human life, what is it? Is it a monkey? Is it an emu? Is it a goat?
When they refer to the unborn child at all, abortion-rights proponents
typically refer to the baby as a fetus—a word that almost never appears in
discussion when women intend to bring life into the world. Can you recall
an expecting sister, mother, or wife saying, "Come here and feel the *fetus*

kicking"? Or how about, "Check out this sonogram picture of my *fetus*"? It is only within the abortion debate that sanitized terms such as *fetus* substitute for universal terms such as *baby*.

The 1973 *Roe v. Wade* case legalizing abortion throughout the United States embraced a similar form of dishonesty. Finding a right to privacy that the Founding Fathers apparently forgot to include in the Constitution, the Supreme Court then decided that from this "right" to privacy—perhaps inscribed in invisible ink—it followed that women had a right to abortion in just about any instance. A century prior to *Roe*, the legal code of almost every state carried strict prohibitions on abortion. By the time the Court decided *Roe*, the laws of all fifty states restricted abortion in ways contrary to *Roe*. Did every state misinterpret the Constitution? Yes, the court audaciously responded. By *making* law, seven unelected judges arrogated the legislative function from Congress, thereby undermining democracy.

To make rancid food edible, chefs douse it with spices. To make horrible things palatable to the public, it's necessary to dress them up in euphemism. Thus, in the feminist lexicon, an abortion becomes a "medical miscarriage," an abortuary a "women's clinic," and an abortionist a "reproductive health provider." The truth about abortion is too gruesome. Its backers know this, and their assault on language is a tacit admission of it.

The matron saint of the abortion-rights movement, fittingly, was a world-class liar. The activists of today, we shall see, merely follow in the footsteps of the woman who guided the movement out of its nascent stage. As part of their mission to codify their moral outlook, these contemporary activists do not merely employ euphemism to describe their agenda. They also must overlook, and at times cover up, the sinister ideas and policies that their matriarch endorsed, as well as the disgraceful personality traits she exhibited. Apart from its obvious victims, the abortion movement's more understated casualty is truth.

THE SANGER OF HISTORY VS. THE SANGER OF REALITY

Chroniclers of Margaret Sanger's life need not travel far on her near eighty-eight-year time line to encounter examples of the birth-control crusader deliberately clouding the facts. Born Margaret Higgins on September 14, 1879, in Corning, New York, Sanger appropriated a younger sibling's birth date as her own and maintained throughout her life that she was four years younger than her actual age. She went so far to foster this seemingly trivial piece of fiction that when depositing her papers at Smith College she altered her mother's inscriptions on a family Bible that included the names and dates of birth for the Higgins children. Scholars researching her life later discovered the crude forgery.[1] Such minor fibs would give way to lies of a greater magnitude.

The middle sibling of the eleven surviving children of Anne and Michael Higgins, Margaret inherited the radicalism of her father, who preached socialism. The parishioners of the Higginses' local Catholic church viewed the family patriarch as a heretic. In contrast to her husband, Anne Higgins was a devotee of the Church, which, in times of trouble, came to the aid of her hungry family.

Margaret was working-class, Irish, and female and so had few options in turn-of-the-century America. She decided to study nursing. While practicing her trade as an apprentice in Manhattan, she met William Sanger, a fellow socialist. They married within six months. The Sangers grew increasingly involved in the radical politics of the day, with Margaret helping to organize laborers for the International Workers of the World, more popularly known as the "Wobblies." By 1913, she had drawn the ire of the authorities for publishing articles in the *New York Call* promoting contraception. The government banned the articles. When a similar fate befell her writings after she launched her own newspaper, *The Woman Rebel*, she was thrust into the national spotlight. In subsequent years, she would be arrested for civil disobedience while fighting for birth control. In 1916, she opened the first birth-control clinic in America in Brooklyn. The next year she launched *The Birth Control Review*, a publication aimed at expanding popular support for birth control. Today, she is perhaps best known as the founder of Planned Parenthood.

Like the life of Rigoberta Menchu, the story of Margaret Sanger has undergone a fictionalized rewrite. The mythic Sanger that emerges is a progressive heroine. The real-life Sanger embraced tenets of Nazism, terrorism—and abortion for any reason at any time. It should come as no shock that the progenitor of the mythologized view of Margaret Sanger was Sanger herself. "Margaret Sanger was a natural storyteller who stressed vivid impressions, not chronology," notes biographer Emily Taft Douglas. Douglas affirms that Sanger left out large portions of her own story, and that "[m]ost of these omissions were deliberate. As the leader of a cause widely thought to be obscene, if not subversive, she simply avoided some items which might have helped her enemies."[2] Yet as we shall see, it wasn't just Sanger who was guilty of deliberate omissions. Court historians, including Douglas, have presented an account of the life and ideas of Margaret Sanger at great variance with reality.

THE WOMAN REBEL

In 1914, Margaret Sanger launched *The Woman Rebel.* "Why The Woman Rebel?" a headline in the inaugural issue asked. "Because," the newspaper's founder answered, "I believe that woman was enslaved by the world machine, by sex conventions, by motherhood and its present necessary child-rearing, by wage slavery, by middle-class morality, by customs, laws and superstitions."[3] Rebel women, the publication announced, claim the right "to be lazy," "to be an unmarried mother," "to destroy," "to create," "to love," and "to live."[4]

The infant journal was not well received. The *Pittsburgh Sun* labeled it "a mass of dirty slush," adding, "The whole thing is nauseating."[5] Even in corners where Sanger might have expected to find praise, criticism abounded. Sanger had committed "that most unfeminine of errors, the tendency to cry out when a quiet and contained utterance is indispensable," contended Max Eastman in the radical *Masses.*[6]

Sanger found her most vehement critic not in the press but in the government. Anthony Comstock, a puritanical codger who had inspired the 1873 antiobscenity laws bearing his name, immediately took notice of *The Woman Rebel.* The Comstock laws forbade the distribution of lewd or obscene material—including birth-control devices—so when Sanger sent copies of her publication's March issue through the mail, postal authorities confiscated roughly half of all copies of the allegedly lewd newspaper. The release of the July issue of *The Woman Rebel* raised the legal stakes of the Sanger-Comstock battle, particularly because an article in that issue criticized Comstock himself.[7] Sanger was hit with numerous indictments.

Although the charges probably would have been revoked if she had apologized or promised not to break the law again, Sanger would have none of it. On principle, she refused to plea-bargain. Additionally, she correctly believed that her defiance would bring media attention to the causes she championed. In the fall of 1914, Sanger fled to Europe via Canada. She left behind a sickly daughter, two young sons, and a husband soon to be arrested for selling one of her pamphlets. Her exile was unnecessary; it was all part of the political theater she so excelled at. After Sanger returned to America in 1915, the elderly Comstock and Sanger's frail daughter both died. Any enthusiasm to try the case died with them. The government dropped the charges.

As so often happens in cases of censorship in a free society, the attempts to suppress Sanger's voice only amplified it. Sympathizers viewed her as a martyr. The ordeal catapulted her into the public eye, where she remained for decades to come.

Sanger, the fiery propagandist, was largely responsible for popularizing this martyr image. When facing government charges, she had claimed that she was being prosecuted for detailing scientific information regarding contraception. Yet *The Woman Rebel* had not done this. Sanger's publication advocated birth control, but it did not inform its readers how to engage in the practice. Not one of the dozens of articles that appeared in the newspaper's short history bothered to instruct readers on methods of contraception. While Sanger was certainly guilty of shrill prose, hyperbole, sloppy grammar, and numerous other literary offenses, *The Woman Rebel* did not, despite Comstock's accusations, contain lewd, vile, and obscene material—even by the standards of 1914. Had *The Woman Rebel* flouted the law by offering birth-control instruction, Comstock probably would have gone into an even greater frenzy.

No, the most serious charge against Margaret Sanger had nothing to do with birth control. Rather, it involved *The Woman Rebel's* irresponsible endorsement of a botched assassination plot against John D. Rockefeller Jr., the dauphin of Standard Oil (who, ironically, became one of Sanger's most generous benefactors a decade later).[8] In May 1914, a group of aspiring revolutionaries hatched a plot to kill Rockefeller and the other fat cats attending his annual Independence Day picnic at the famous family's Pocantico Hills estate in Westchester County, New York. Fortunately for the picnic-goers, the radical terrorists' dynamite bomb detonated while its creators were still constructing it, killing the would-be mass murderers in a Harlem tenement house.

Sanger used the July issue of *The Woman Rebel* to pay homage to the fallen terrorists, who, like Sanger, were Wobblies. The front page was silent on the matter of birth control, but it passionately advocated assassination, bombings, and even the overthrow of the U.S. government. The paper also spewed venom at John D. Rockefeller Jr. The wealthy heir had drawn the upstart publication's ire for sitting on the board of the Colorado Fuel and Iron Company, whose feud with striking workers had resulted in more than a dozen deaths during 1914's Ludlow Massacre.

The monthly's lead article, anonymously penned by Sanger, screamed off the pages:

Even if dynamite were to serve no other purpose than to call forth the spirit of revolutionary solidarity and loyalty, it would prove its great value. For this expression of solidarity and loyalty and of complete defiance to the morality of the masters, in a time of distress and defeat and death, is the most certain sign of that strength and courage which are the first essentials of victory. On July 4th, three revolutionists, Caron, Berg, and Hanson, were killed by the explosion of dynamite—sacrificed because of their willingness to risk their life for their convictions. This tragedy created a wonderful spirit of loyalty and solidarity among their comrades. It ought to have awakened the same spirit among all those who advocate the overthrow of the present system—at least among the agitators and leaders who urge direct and revolutionary tactics against the master class.[9]

The words were the mutterings of a lunatic. It is not hard to understand why hagiographers would seek to airbrush out of the official picture this disturbing aspect of the seminal event in Sanger's life.*

"It is time to learn to accept and exult in every act of revolt against oppression, to encourage and create in ourselves that spirit of rebellion which shall lead us to understand and look at the social situation without flinching or quavering or running for cover when any crisis arises," she decreed. "Not until we do create this spirit will the revolutionists ever be feared or even respected in America."[10]

Another article, titled "A Defense of Assassination," called for the murder of Rockefeller. "It is generally agreed that lower forms of life must give place to higher types," Robert A. Thorpe's article began. Although it never mentioned the second-generation tycoon's name, the

---

*Had it not been for Sanger's grandson, what was written within the pages of *The Woman Rebel* might have been lost to history. The remaining copies of the publication were mysteriously stolen from the New York Public Library. Sanger's grandson, thankfully, had made Xerox copies of the seven issues of the publication. Today, they can be read by anyone through New York University's Margaret Sanger Papers Project.

article exhibited the subtlety of a sledgehammer. It was quite clear whom the author was speaking of when he remarked, "[U]nless it can be shown that there is room enough on earth for both savage and civilized, the savage must go."[11] This was the article the authorities specifically cited when they charged *The Woman Rebel* with inciting terrorism.

Facts got in the way of a good story. In *Margaret Sanger: Pioneer of Birth Control*, Lawrence Lader and Milton Meltzer do not mention that Sanger endorsed terrorism. Instead they focus on the prudery of the Comstock laws. If Sanger pled guilty to the charges, they write, "she would be saying birth control was only some other form of obscenity or pornography." Her fight, they say, was to "demonstrate how degrading this law was that kept women in bondage."[12] Similarly, in *Margaret Sanger: Pioneer of the Future*, Emily Taft Douglas goes into excruciating detail about the intricacies of "Comstockery" but is altogether silent about the charge that Sanger used her publication to incite assassination.[13]

It strains credulity to believe that these writers are simply guilty of an oversight. Both cite passages from *The Woman Rebel* and quote from selected portions of the indictment handed down against Sanger. Yet both carefully exclude the crackpot rhetoric that Sanger is clearly guilty of, and the legal charge of inciting murder, to make her more palatable to modern audiences. The omission of *The Woman Rebel*'s front-page extremism and the legal charges that it brought raise serious questions about scholarly ethics. Were the exclusions simply mistakes, or were they intentional?

This would not be the first time Sanger and her academic votaries sanitized portions of her life story.

"THE PERPETUATION OF QUACKERY"

Upon her self-imposed exile, Margaret Sanger lamented, "United States—what stupidity controls thy destiny—to drive from your shores those who can contribute to the happiness of its down trodden people. Who can enlighten the ignorant—& help to raise the standards of knowledge."[14]

Starting with Sanger herself, partisans of the movement to separate sex from responsibility have written a script depicting their opponents as grunting Neanderthals while casting themselves as the deliverers of humanity from ignorance. History is rarely as simple as a screenplay.

Sanger certainly didn't lack zeal in her crusade to prevent unwanted pregnancy. She saw neglected children and burnt-out parents, and she wanted to fix things. But did she help fix matters? This is the crucial question. As fanaticism is apt to do, Sanger's zeal blinded her to the reality that her actions occasionally worked against her desired purposes.

The law curtailing her from disseminating sexual information, Sanger alleged, "caused the perpetuation of quackery. It has created the fake and the quack who benefits by its existence."[15] More than anyone else, Margaret Sanger herself proved the validity of this assertion. As she cloaked her instruction in the guise of enlightenment, progress, and science, she spread ignorance. Passion for birth control did not translate into wisdom about birth control.

Sanger probably refrained from using *The Woman Rebel* to spread medical instruction regarding contraception not because she feared the authorities, but because—like her readers—she was ignorant on the subject. As she ventured deeper into activism on the issue, she felt compelled to provide instruction. The booklet *Family Limitation*, released in the fall of 1914, represents her first large-scale foray from the role of propagandist to that of educator. She was not particularly effective at teaching others how to prevent the arrival of unwanted children. In the booklet, she advises those worried about pregnancy to take "five or ten grains of quinine," the malarial medicine, before going to bed. While its reliability in impeding conception is questionable, quinine in large quantities can cause uterine paralysis and act as a poison.[16] Elsewhere in *Family Limitation*, she offers other quack remedies. "A very good laxative (though it is a patent medicine) is Beecham Pills. Two of these taken night and morning, four days before menstruation, will give a good cleansing of the bowels, and assist with the menstrual flow."[17] Thus, if only one takes laxatives to eject excrement from the body, then pregnancy will not occur! Sanger does not seem to realize that once conception occurs, no number of trips to the bathroom will undo matters.

Expectedly, pupils of Sanger's sex education received rude awakenings—normally in the form of human trophies commemorating nights of passion. Angry letters followed. "I am pregnant," wrote a despondent follower, "and that rubber cap I used has irritated the growth and caused it to swell and become inflamed, also that I must have an operation which won't come under two hundred dollars." The prolific woman continued, "Anyway, I really hope that the [American Birth Control League] will some day get the right thing to help people like me, something that realy & truly will prevent unwanted children."[18] That day would come, but in spite of, not because of, Margaret Sanger.

UPROOTING "HUMAN WEEDS"

During the 1920s and '30s, a mass movement gained traction for the furtherance of "race betterment." Its charismatic leader called for putting millions of people in concentration camps. Those the movement deemed subhuman would be sterilized to protect future generations from the corruption of the gene pool. The campaign would give special attention to racial minorities.

These ideas evoke images of an angry man sporting a Charlie Chaplin mustache, a bad haircut, and a blood-red armband. Yet it was an attractive woman donning the latest fashions, rather than the Hun dictator parading around in a ludicrous military costume, who specifically promoted these ideas. The movement occurred in America, not Nazi Germany. The leader was Margaret Sanger, not Adolf Hitler.

Idealism run amok fueled the international eugenics movement. Herbert Spencer, an early eugenics backer, declared that "all imperfection must disappear."[19] Like Communism, eugenics—creating the well born, the biologically pure, the master race—is a utopian delusion. God had created a flawed world. Man would make things perfect. The hominid god, however, proved an unworthy successor to the biblical God. The road to Eden always detours to Hell. The detours on the path to Immaculate Man led to the gas chamber, the concentration camp, and the operating table. Human perfection, an unattainable goal, relied on euthanasia, segregation, sterilization, and abortion to achieve its dream of the *ubermensch*. Margaret Sanger rejected putting the unfit to sleep, but she promoted aborting, sterilizing, and segregating them. She did this to make the world perfect. The pursuit of the loftiest goals condones the employment of the basest methods.

Like playing the role of god, racism is an exercise in narcissism. The eugenicist's ideal man always seemed to resemble the eugenicist—fair haired, light complexioned, and Nordic. People who looked like Margaret Sanger needn't worry about the state coming after them for polluting the gene pool.

Thankfully, Sanger's vision of work camps for the "unfit" never came to fruition—at least in the United States. Still, in the first half of the twentieth century, state governments sterilized upwards of sixty thousand Americans. More than half the states sterilized citizens, with Virginia, California, and Kansas leading the way.[20] What Indiana introduced to the world in 1907, European governments soon adopted. Prideful of standing on the cutting edge of "progress," Sweden, Norway, Finland, Denmark, and, of course, Nazi Germany introduced compulsory sterilization laws to disastrous results. In all instances, the laws disproportionately targeted women and minorities.[21] While sterilization doesn't seem high on its agenda these days, the birth-control movement's focus on keeping minority populations from growing has outlived Sanger. Today, about a third of all abortions performed in the United States are on unborn African-American children, with predominantly black areas like Washington, D.C., witnessing more abortions than live births.[22]

Incredibly, Margaret Sanger's hagiographers, and her most devoted followers in the abortion-rights movement, deny and gloss over the eugenicist nature of her program. But Sanger herself trumpeted her belief in the birth-control aspect of eugenics.

In accepting an award in 1937, Sanger proclaimed that blocking the procreation of undesirables "makes possible the spread of scientific knowledge of the elements of sound breeding. It makes possible the creation of a new race; a new generation brought into this world consciously conceived. It makes possible the breeding out of human weeds—the defective and criminal classes—[and] the breeding in of the clean, strong and fit instruments to carry on the torch of human destiny."[23] Earlier in the speech she claimed to be speaking on behalf of those "too inarticulate to speak for themselves."[24] Had these "human weeds" the ability to put together a coherent thought, it's not too difficult to imagine how they might have responded!

Sanger actively promoted eugenics, which she saw as an integral part of the birth-control philosophy. She embraced forced sterilization and other means of suppressing the birth rate of "dysgenic" groups, although she parted company with eugenicists regarding their encouragement of procreation from parents with ideal genes. As editor of *The Birth Control Review*, she devoted a special issue to eugenics and commissioned a steady stream of articles by the country's leading eugenicists.[25] Her own articles, particularly ones like "The Eugenic Value of Birth Control" and "Birth Control and Racial Betterment," were the best representation of her enthusiasm for eugenics.[26] On at least one occasion, in the spot on the front cover reserved for the publication's motto, the editors placed the phrase "To create a race of thoroughbreds."[27] Sanger even suggested that *The Birth Control Review* might merge with the journal *Eugenics*.[28]

In 1932, Sanger put together what she labeled "A Plan for World Peace." In the April edition of *The Birth Control Review*, she published the summary of her program, which she had made public in an address in New York City that January. In the first sentence, she called for the implementation of President Woodrow Wilson's Fourteen Points. In the remainder of her remarks, she focused on eugenics as the key to addressing the problem of international conflict. Judging by Sanger's words alone, the speech was one of the most shocking and despicable ever delivered on American soil. Yet historians have ignored the speech's contents for more than seven decades.

Sanger exhorted the U.S. Congress to set up a "Parliament of Population." Its first objective would be "to raise the level and increase the general intelligence of population." Its fourth objective called for "a stern and rigid policy of sterilization and segregation to that grade of population whose progeny is already tainted, or whose inheritance is such that objectionable traits may be transmitted to offspring." Some "dysgenic groups in our population," she permitted, would be given "their choice of segregation or sterilization."[29] The plan took an even uglier turn with its final point, which called on the government to "apportion farm lands and homestead for these segregated persons where they would be taught to work under competent instructors for the period of their entire lives." She outlined how she would achieve this last goal:

> The first step would thus be to control the intake and output of morons, mental defectives, epileptics.
>
> The second step would be to take an inventory of the secondary group such as illiterates, paupers, unemployables, criminals, prostitutes, dope-fiends; classify them in special departments under government medical protection, and segregate them on farms and open spaces as long as necessary for the strengthening and development of moral conduct.
>
> Having corralled this enormous part of our population and placed it on a basis of health instead of punishment, it is safe to say that fifteen or twenty millions of our population would then be organized into soldiers of defense—defending the unborn against their own disabilities.[30]

This Mother of All Concentration Camps would have housed roughly one out of every seven Americans. Somehow, all six Sanger biographies examined for this chapter failed to include her insane plan for Nazism in America.[31]

THE UNFIT

Who were the "human weeds" whom Sanger sought to uproot?

She maintained that "the aboriginal Australian" was "the lowest known species of the human family, just a step higher than the chimpanzee in brain development."[32] "The Jewish people and Italian families," she testified before New York's legislature, "who are filling the insane asylums, who are filling the hospitals and filling our feeble-minded institutions, these are the ones the tax payers have to pay for the upkeep of, and they are increasing the budget of the State, the enormous expense of the State is increasing because of the multiplication of the unfit in this country and in the State."[33] Sanger's associates included a number of racists who no doubt salivated over the prospect of eliminating black population growth.[34] Sanger, who in at least one letter used the word "nigger" in referring to a black man, even spoke at a 1926 Ku Klux Klan rally in the Northeast.[35] Despite all this, one historian writes: "Sanger was no racist."[36]

Sanger took a peculiar interest in ensuring that sterilization programs and birth-control clinics focused on blacks. In 1943, for instance, Sanger complained to a Planned Parenthood director that she was not being informed about the progress of the group's "negro programme." She was particularly offended because she credited herself with being "mainly responsible for arousing interest in the negro programme" and for raising money to support it.[37] In addition to opening up clinics in predominantly black areas such as Harlem, Sanger's program recruited prominent African-Americans, including W.E.B. Du Bois and Adam Clayton Powell, to create the appearance that blacks themselves were behind the movement to limit black procreation. Writing in the publication Sanger founded, Du Bois declared that "the mass of ignorant Negroes still breed carelessly and disastrously," adding that black opponents of birth control "must learn that among human races and groups, as among vegetables, quality and not mere quantity really counts."[38] Dr. Dorothy Boulding Ferebee, an African-American physician, told a Birth Control Federation of America gathering in 1942, "Those of us who believe that the benefits of Family Planning, as a vital key to the elimination of human waste, must reach all groups of the population, also believe that a double effort must be made to extend this program as a public health measure to Negroes whose need is proportionately greater than other groups."[39] White segregationists certainly concurred. Sterilization laws were quite popular in the South (one of several regions where the coercive practices were widespread) during the first half of the twentieth century. Dixieland states that sterilized "human waste" in these years included Virginia, North Carolina, South Carolina, Mississippi, and Georgia. It is the height of naïveté to believe that Sanger was unaware that unenlightened government bodies in these states were far more likely to deem blacks "unfit" to procreate.

"We do not want the word to go out that we want to exterminate the Negro population and the minister is the man who can straighten that idea out if it ever occurs to any of their more rebellious members," Sanger wrote in 1939 to Dr. Clarence Gamble, the Procter & Gamble heir, who served as the Birth Control Federation of America's Southern regional director.[40] Did Sanger intend to "exterminate" blacks? Probably not. In fact, with this letter she was actually trying to combat the notion that she sought to exterminate blacks; she wanted to enlist clergy to prevent misinformation about the program from spreading. Ironically, in her attempts to curtail the propaganda of her adversaries, she handed them a brickbat to beat her with. To this day, abortion opponents seize on the comment to suggest a deliberate plan of genocide against African-Americans. This is a stretch. Regardless of intent, the effect of her program was nefarious enough—to suppress the black population.

Racism is the belief in the inherent superiority or inferiority of individuals based on their genetic membership in certain racial groups. Typically it is associated with the unenlightened and the ignorant—hence the images of goose-stepping brownshirts or tobacco-stained rednecks. For many years, however, the educated and the elites were the greatest exponents of bigotry, giving the mindset intellectual airs. Margaret Sanger, a racist under even the strictest definition of the word, fit this latter category of bigot.

IRRELIGIOUS FANATIC

For decades, Sanger served as the leading hater of Catholics in America. The Church's opposition to eugenics, concentration camps, and abortion, as well as its charitable endeavors, put it at odds with Sanger's ideology. "My own position is that the Catholic doctrine is illogical, not in accord with science, and definitely against social welfare and race improvement," she wrote in 1932. "Assuming that God does want an increasing number of worshipers of the Catholic faith, does he also want an increasing number of feeble-minded, insane, criminal, and diseased worshipers?"[41]

From the outset of the campaign for sterilization and birth control, the Church stood athwart it. A week before Christmas in 1921, Archbishop Patrick Joseph Hayes of New York noted that "the Christ-Child did not stay His own entrance into this mortal life because His mother was poor, roofless and without a provision for the morrow." The archbishop added that although "the moral, mental or physical deformity of parents, may appear to human eyes hideous, misshapen, a blot on civilized society, we must not lose sight of this Christian thought that under and within such visible malformation there lives an immortal soul to be saved and glorified."[42]

That the Church viewed the mentally retarded, physically handicapped, diseased, and deformed as equals before the eyes of God struck Sanger as anathema to the dictates of the Brave New World she saw emerging around her. Why couldn't Rome just change with the times? It is Sanger's position, however, that today seems a relic of an ugly time.

Sanger compared the Catholic Church to the Ku Klux Klan and Communist dictatorships and attempted to portray the Church as the only institution opposing her agenda. When Jews, Protestants, or even Hindus spoke out against her—Gandhi publicly condemned her agenda when she traveled to India—Sanger declined to invoke their religions as the cause of the dispute. Catholics who opposed her, on the other hand, did so only because Rome controlled them. Catholics, Sanger claimed, were incapable of being good citizens because devotion to their Church conflicted with their allegiance to their country. Committed worshipers of other faiths whose religious beliefs conflicted with the birth-control agenda were somehow immune from these same assertions regarding their patriotism.

Confronted with "the growing insidious power of the Roman Catholic Church, I shudder for the future," she wrote to Rabbi Sidney Goldstein, a prominent New York supporter.[43] Writing of a meeting with the famous Lady Astor, Sanger reassured a colleague, "She is Anti-Catholic thank God. So she & I were one on many things."[44] After delivering a Catholic-bashing address, segregationist congressman Graham Barden received a congratulatory note from Sanger, who wrote, "I especially liked your comparison of Communistic lackeys and the Roman Catholics who are subject to the Vatican. They are exactly the same, and it was a splendid retort and a courageous one indeed." She closed her letter by labeling Catholics "black moles" who were "invading our buildings of democracy."[45]

The Birth Control Review acted as the main organ transmitting Sanger's anti-Catholic hatred in her prime years. As the Catholic New York governor Al Smith geared up for his run for the White House in 1928, a *Review* editorial warned of the "tyrannical intolerance and usurpation of power exercised by office-holders born and bred in the Roman Catholic faith."[46] An earlier editorial, from 1924, insisted:

> Our experience of the last ten years of constant fighting has been that of all the reactionary groups in the country the Roman Catholic Church is the most politically pernicious and menacing to any progressive movement. We know nothing of the Ku Klux Klan. We have covered the United States from the Atlantic to the Pacific and the Klan has neither fought us, nor stood by us. . . . Whenever there has been a group attack on Birth Control on the platform or in the press, it has been instigated or organized by Roman Catholics.[47]

More than a decade later, Sanger repeated this slur. Without mentioning Catholics by name, it was clear just whom she referred to when she asked local affiliates of a national women's club to affirm a resolution that declared:

> The organized bigotry of a minority group stands in the way. Not in isolated cases, but persistently and in all parts of the country, a group which gives its first allegiance to its Church rather than to our country, holds the rest of us back. . . . [Committed Catholics] should isolate themselves. They have no place in community life. . . . Freed from the tyranny of this minority group, we can march steadily forward toward a healthier and more intelligent state.[48]

Sanger quietly voted for socialist Norman Thomas in presidential elections for most of her adult life. On just two conspicuous occasions, she spoke out during contests for the White House: 1928 and 1960, the only presidential elections in her lifetime in which a Catholic carried the nomination of a major party. Sanger vehemently and publicly denounced Democrats Al Smith and John F. Kennedy, even promising that if the American people elected the Catholic senator from Massachusetts she would leave the country. She didn't. Uncharacteristically, she voted for the Republican candidate in both elections.[49]

During the presidency of Franklin Roosevelt, she fumed when his administration sent an emissary to the Vatican. "What depresses me more than the economic situation," she wrote during the waning years of the Great Depression, "is the rise of the power of the Catholics in the Dem. party. Priests having tea at the WH."[50]

Ironically, Sanger's hatred of Catholics was so great that it nearly side-tracked the development of the birth-control pill. John Rock, a Harvard medical researcher, was developing innovative methods to both boost and curtail fertility. Since the doctor was Catholic, Sanger initially tried to derail any project that involved him.[51] Despite her efforts, Rock moved forward and was an integral part of the development of the first birth-control pill. Had Sanger had her way, the Pill's arrival probably would have been delayed.

Sanger behaved strangely for one who publicly depicted religion as antiquated and unenlightened. She baptized her three offspring in the Episcopal Church over the objections of her children's father, an atheist. She frequently consulted psychics, mediums, and other clairvoyants, describing one as "a very wise seer." She even claimed to have communicated with her deceased daughter through a medium.[52] Clearly, her aversion to superstition was selective.

Margaret Sanger was definitely a fervent practitioner of that most "progressive" of all bigotries, anti-Catholicism. Others caught issuing similarly intolerant condemnations of individuals based on their religion, or ethnicity, have incurred the wrath of unforgiving historians. Whether as a result of what she stood for or because of whom she attacked, Sanger has been given a dispensation.

CHARITY FOR ME, BUT NOT FOR THEE

When it served her purposes, Sanger was clearly not averse to telling bald-faced lies. A case in point: The Planned Parenthood founder publicly condemned abortion but privately helped provide it. During the course of her life, abortion was a practice championed by fringe groups. To proclaim support for the procedure was to issue a self-imposed death sentence against one's public credibility. To reassure a skeptical public that abortion was not her aim, Sanger frequently denounced it. For example, in 1932 she wrote in *The Nation* that abortion "is an alternative that I cannot too strongly condemn. Although abortion may be resorted to in order to save the life of the mother, the practice of it merely for limitation of offspring is dangerous and vicious. I bring up the subject here only because some ill-informed persons have the notion that when we speak of birth control we include abortion as a method. We certainly do not."[53] At the very time subscribers of *The Nation* read this article, Sanger was directing her employees at birth-control clinics to refer pregnant women to underground abortionists. Sanger even raised money so that these women would not have to pay for the procedure.[54]

Another seeming contradiction was Sanger's harsh condemnation of charity as a cruelty, while her every endeavor and very existence depended on the generosity of others. Her impoverished upbringing, her second marriage to the wealthy cuckold Noah Slee, and her subsidized activism all provided ample proof of cognitive dissonance on this point. The feminist propagandist's hypocritical Darwinism was on display on the front cover of *The Birth Control Review*'s December 1927 number, which issued a "Christmas Appeal": "Give No More Doles to Charity."[55] Exceptions, of course, were made for gifts to Margaret Sanger's organization, which freely accepted just about any donation.

While government spending on ostensibly charitable endeavors has always been a point of debate, Sanger's opposition to private charity is fairly unusual. "My criticism," her book *The Pivot of Civilization* argued, "is not directed at the 'failure' of philanthropy, but rather at its success."[56] She pointed to "dangers inherent in the very idea of humanitarianism and altruism," which have "produced their full harvest of human waste."[57] The budding author personified the Dickensian caricature of elitist mean-spiritedness. A classic illustration of this is her counsel to overflowing households. Without Swift's satiric intentions, Sanger immodestly proposed: "The most merciful thing that the large family does to one of its infant members is to kill it."[58]

Though Sanger is portrayed as a founding mother of modern feminism, many of her policy prescriptions regarding charity quite clearly hurt women. *The Pivot of Civilization*, for instance, called for closing maternity centers that catered to poor women. The author conceded that the centers reduced infant mortality and made the experience of giving birth less dangerous and painful. The problem was that by doing this, the centers worked against eugenics. Making the birthing process easier for poor women would not discourage further reproduction. As she put it, giving government money to maternity centers "would facilitate the function of maternity among the very classes in which the absolute necessity is to discourage it."[59] It would, therefore, contribute to a "very definite deterioration in the human stock."[60] That Sanger held such ideas suggests that her feminist admirers are either ignorant of her beliefs or hiding their own.

SELF-ENRICHMENT

American history is replete with examples of individuals sacrificing personal interests for causes that they saw as benefiting the common good. Robert Morris, the richest man in colonial America, bankrolled the American Revolution to his great personal detriment. He died penniless. Robert E. Lee sacrificed a U.S. Army commission and his ancestral estate to fight for what he saw as a just cause. Rather than spend his life in upper-middle-class comfort, Martin Luther King suffered government harassment, beatings, and jail. He eventually paid the ultimate sacrifice so that others could be treated with the dignity and respect denied to him.

Self-abnegation is the very opposite of what was at the heart of Margaret Sanger's activism. She sought to change society not for its benefit but for her own personal gratification. It was self-enrichment, not sacrifice.

Sanger's personal sexual morals were akin to those of a call girl. She was a serial adulterer. Among the scores who shared her bed were some of the most famous men of her time, including novelist H. G. Wells and sex researcher Havelock Ellis. As she cheated on her husband of the moment with not-so-secret lovers, she cheated on these paramours with still other beaus. These encounters, biographer Ellen Chesler suggests, were limited neither to members of the opposite sex nor to two participants.[61] It was quite accommodating, then, that she called for the separation of sex from any responsibilities that stemmed from it.

Chesler labels Sanger "strangely indifferent to the responsibilities of mothering," while biographer Madeline Gray notes that she "barely noticed what was happening to her children. She declared she was seized with a mysterious 'nervous malady' whenever she had to take care of them."[62] Sanger refused to do housework, ignored her daughter's regressive polio-induced leg ailment, and never bothered to say goodbye to her children when she fled the country in 1914. After realizing he risked losing Margaret, husband Bill Sanger acceded to her demands to be emancipated from motherhood. He wrote to her, "I know you're right that you must be relieved from the family care."[63] His acquiescence was unneeded, for she had long since abdicated her responsibilities as a mother, eventually, determining that motherhood was a drag and abandoning her children.

Her ten-year-old son Grant, who was shipped away to boarding school, pathetically wrote to her, "It is getting near Spring. The birds are coming from the South. I know you are very busy or you would come see me." Weeks later he wrote, "Am I coming home Easter? Write and tell me so, please." Prior to Thanksgiving he once again plaintively cried out for her affection: "Now you put down in your engagement book, Nov. 28, Go down to see Grant." She never went.[64]

Sanger's other son, Stuart, recalled years later that he once walked twenty miles to greet his mother at a train station to discover that she had never boarded the train. She neglected to wire him that she wouldn't be coming.[65]

Most significant, of course, was what happened to her daughter, Peggy. Always precarious, Peggy's health deteriorated after her mother absconded to Europe during her *Woman Rebel* days. Peggy died soon after her mother returned. Grant put the blame for this tragedy on Margaret Sanger's abandonment and neglect.[66]

Should it surprise us that the woman who sought to separate sex from its consequences did just that in her private life by abandoning her children?

Her utopian scheme offered the Faustian bargain of more sex with fewer children. Those in want of common sense went along. Realists scoffed. Margaret Sanger at once advocated smaller families and more of the only practice that creates larger families. The predictable result was a world with more abortions, illegitimate children, and sexually transmitted disease. The sex-without-consequences message of Margaret Sanger resulted in dire consequences for those who fell for it.

DEATH AND REBIRTH

Margaret Sanger died a bitter woman. With the passage of World War II—which Sanger opposed even after Pearl Harbor—many of her views were no longer suitable for airing in polite company. The horror of the Nazi atrocities did nothing to temper her perspective. As she grew older, the requests for interviews, speeches, and articles diminished, but her appetite for attention didn't. While birth-control groups were content

with awarding her honorary titles, they were hesitant to give her any platform, however small, to speak. On the occasions that she did emerge from
her desert hermitage in Arizona, she gave the leadership of the movement
that she started all the more reason to keep her locked away in the attic.
In 1950, she was awarded the Lasker Prize for medicine. Too sick to
attend the dinner ceremony, she sent her son Grant and instructed him to
read her prepared remarks. Calling for government pensions for "unfit"
couples who agreed to be sterilized, her speech horrified the tuxedo-and-
diamond-necklace set in attendance.[67] Her 1957 interview with Mike
Wallace broadcast her anti-Catholic venom to a nationwide television
audience.[68] Alcoholic and addicted to the painkiller Demerol, she spent
her last years feeling abandoned and ignored by her former comrades.
She died on September 6, 1966. Her Tucson funeral was sparsely
attended.

Today, Margaret Sanger is viewed as a noble icon.

"Margaret Sanger was a big hero," one participant in 2004's March for
Women's Lives volunteered. "Margaret Sanger was a trailblazing woman.
She was pro-birth control, and she went around New York City in the
slums . . . helping women, giving them birth control, and explaining it."[69]
Not quite, but that's the mythology in a nutshell. "Margaret Sanger is a
very controversial figure because a lot of people did a lot to discredit her
and associate her with some pretty dangerous right-wing causes," noted
another marcher who pointed to Sanger as a hero. "But history has
proved that none of them were accurate."[70]

A poll of readers of the National Organization for Women's official
newspaper ranked her as one of the five most admired "sheroes" of history, along with Eleanor Roosevelt, Susan B. Anthony, Harriet Tubman,
and Sojourner Truth.[71] *Time* magazine named Sanger one of the hundred
most important people of the twentieth century, offering a lionizing tribute penned by Gloria Steinem.[72] Planned Parenthood annually bestows a
Margaret Sanger Award on a person the organization wishes to honor.
Past recipients include Martin Luther King, Lyndon Johnson, Katharine
Hepburn, and Ann Landers. Sanger's posthumous makeover replaced all
the ugliness and hate with a seraphic figure deserving of secular canonization, St. Margaret of Tucson.

To advance this chimera requires a generous amount of both self-
delusion and active concealment. Sanger's disingenuous followers learned
at the foot of a master deceiver. From white lies, like manufacturing a
more youthful birth date, to more consequential ones, like publicly con-

demning abortion as murder while privately procuring it for clients, Sanger had a long history of dishonesty in the service of herself and her cause. Lies might have been the most venial of her offenses. She publicly promoted assassination and terrorism. She made little effort to hide her contempt for minorities, the poor, the disabled, Catholics, and other groups she deemed "unfit." Most troubling were her selfish nonsolutions to poverty, racism, and other social ills—her advocacy of sterilization to prevent "human weeds," concentration camps so that she didn't have to see people of "inferior stock," and abortion to rid the world of extra mouths to feed.

The true believers have bowdlerized their heroine's personal history. They haven't exaggerated the Planned Parenthood founder's historical weight. Planned Parenthood's latest annual report lists revenue of three-quarters of a billion dollars, with the largest benefactor, the taxpayer, exceeding the generosity of the rest of its contributors combined. More than 21,000 employees and volunteers run the organization and its 866 centers in all fifty states.[73] The organization has come a long way since 1916, when its founder, armed with a fifty-dollar contribution and a rag-tag staff, opened America's first birth-control clinic in Brooklyn, New York.[74] Moreover, Sanger's impact transcends borders. The International Planned Parenthood Federation, which sprang from Sanger's initial creation, lists affiliates in 180 countries, boasts funding from more than twenty governments, and receives "Category I consultative status" from the United Nations.[75] Most significant, the organizations she helped spawn have performed millions of abortions throughout the world with the imprimatur of the state.

No doubt, Sanger played a key role in shaping her own image. But her present-day admirers perpetuate the myth to uphold her as a feminist trailblazer, instead of an anti-Catholic bigot who advocated concentration camps and forced sterilization. Sanger was a self-described propagandist and fanatic. Her lies, then, are almost to be expected. Her contemporary cheerleaders include journalists and historians whose professional creed venerates truth above all else. What's their excuse?

"ABSOLUTELY SEGREGATE THE RACES"

How a Racial Separatist Became a
Civil Rights Icon

*Men who set too much store by their dogmas and who will
not allow themselves to be guided by the give-and-take between ideas
and experience are likely to suffer defeat in one way, if not another.*

—DANIEL BOORSTIN,
The Americans: The Colonial Experience

"ONE EVER FEELS HIS TWONESS—AN AMERICAN, A NEGRO; TWO
souls, two thoughts, two unreconciled strivings; two warring ideals in one
dark body, whose dogged strength alone keeps it from being torn asun-
der."[1] When W.E.B. Du Bois penned these words more than a century
ago, he was referring to the struggle of individual African-Americans to
come to terms with both the *African* and the *American*, their race and their
nation. One might just as easily project the idea upon the collective. Two
competing strains of thought have also warred for the soul of black
America.

The first vision finds the ideals of America appealing but bemoans the
failure of the nation to fulfill its promise to *all* its citizens. Proponents of
this view have included segments of the Abolitionist Movement, the
Southern Christian Leadership Conference, and the National Association
for the Advancement of Colored People (NAACP). They looked at documents like the Declaration of Independence, or at America's boast as the
land of opportunity, and demanded a stop to the national hypocrisy.
Blacks wanted in on the American Dream. Present-day examples of this
philosophy in action include cable television mogul Robert Johnson,

rapper/clothing entrepreneur Sean "P. Diddy" Combs, and Oprah Winfrey, the world's first black woman billionaire.

The second outlook sees America as so repugnant that it urges blacks and other minorities to circle the wagons and separate from the inherently evil society that surrounds them. Advocates of this position have included the Pan-Africa Movement, the Nation of Islam, and the Black Panthers. Present reminders of this attitude include hostility to cross-racial adoptions; separate standards for minorities in hiring and admissions; excluding nonblacks from teaching black history; black-only dormitory floors, graduation ceremonies, and student clubs; calls for jury nullification on racial grounds; and demands for slavery reparations from nonslaveholders to nonslaves.

The paradox we find ourselves in today is that as more African-Americans actualize the dream within the integrationist paradigm, voices backing the separatist paradigm grow louder. The phenomenon seems confined neither to blacks nor to the United States, as increased opportunity for immigrants and other minorities in many Western nations has been met by reluctance to integrate within the larger culture.

When we think about the first group desiring greater inclusion, we think of Martin Luther King Jr. When we think of the second group desiring further exclusion, we don't immediately think of W.E.B. Du Bois, but we should.

AIRBRUSHING HISTORY

W.E.B. Du Bois famously quipped, "I would have been hailed with approval if I had died at 50. At 75 my death was practically requested."[2] The Bay State intellectual had never made so keen an observation. Born in 1868 in Great Barrington, Massachusetts, William Edward Burghardt Du Bois traveled far over the course of his ninety-five-year life—quite literally, as he died half a world away in western Africa. Yet his journey was more than physical; it was also intellectual.

In 1895, Du Bois became the first African American to earn a doctorate from Harvard. Eight years later he famously predicted in *The Souls of Black Folk* that the problem of the twentieth century would be the problem of the color line. In 1905, the rising black aristocrat gave birth to the Niagara Movement by organizing the first of five gatherings that sought an alternative to the prevailing accommodationist solutions to black disempowerment. In 1910, he helped found the NAACP and became its director of research. His ongoing intellectual give-and-take with Booker T. Washington during the first decade of the twentieth century ranks as one of the great running debates in American history. These were years of great promise.

Unfortunately, a deluge of embarrassing blunders followed. It is difficult to think of any major issue during the last half of Du Bois's life on which he didn't stand on the wrong side. From his endorsements of segregation to his arguments for sterilization and state ownership of children to his unmitigated enthusiasm for Stalin to his naïve interpretations of life in Hitler's Germany and Imperial Japan, Du Bois had a penchant for backing the wrong horse. On some occasions, he simply got caught up in the intellectual fashions of his time. Other instances can't be explained away so easily.

Du Bois was a man of contrasts and contradictions, to say the least. He was a crusader for black civil rights, but became a standard-bearer for racial separatism. He was both an elitist who called for a "talented tenth" of black Americans and an enthusiastic proponent of Communism late in life. He was both a stuffy moralist and a serial adulterer. Although a careful pedagogue, he wrote in a style that degenerated into ideological rants.

Du Bois is now regarded alongside Martin Luther King, Medgar Evers, and Rosa Parks as a civil rights hero. Harvard has named an institute in his honor; Penn, a dormitory; and the University of Massachusetts–Amherst, a twenty-six-story library (the world's tallest). PBS has broadcast several laudatory documentaries on his life. David Levering Lewis has won not one but two Pulitzer Prizes for his admiring biographies of Du Bois. The U.S. Post Office paid homage to the cultured professor by placing his stately visage on a postage stamp.

In many ways, Du Bois's story parallels that of Margaret Sanger, of whom he was a great supporter. Just as Sanger's extant admirers do with their heroine's life story, Du Bois's followers airbrush out of the "official" narrative the unpleasant aspects of his near-century-long existence. Du Bois was far from the great champion of civil rights he is considered today.

THE SEGREGATIONIST

Only the seventh African-American admitted to Harvard and the first black to earn a postgraduate degree from America's oldest college, Du Bois quickly became one of the leading black intellectuals in the United

States. Following his ambitious but nevertheless flawed doctoral dissertation, *The Suppression of the African Slave Trade*—its estimate of tens of millions of slaves exported from Africa to the New World dramatically overcounted; the accepted figure is under 10 million—the new doctor of philosophy compiled an exhaustive sociological survey, *The Philadelphia Negro.*[3] In 1903 he released his magnum opus, *The Souls of Black Folk*, a collection of essays exploring the duality of being both black and American. Little that Du Bois produced after that contributed anything of scholarly value. Anticipating later trends among celebrity academics, Du Bois alternated the rest of his long earthly sojourn between serving political causes and writing numerous autobiographies.

As he raised his profile, Du Bois began an internecine dispute with Tuskegee University founder Booker T. Washington. The Alabama-based Washington, the undisputed leader of black Americans at the start of the twentieth century, sought race improvement by working within the system and, perhaps most upsetting to his Harvard-educated foe, stressed vocational learning to get ahead. The upstart Du Bois did the unthinkable by challenging the ideas of Washington and his Tuskegee Machine. The Northerner wanted absolute justice, not incremental victories. Rather than low-paying jobs for workers trained for industry, Du Bois called for a "talented tenth" of educated blacks to lead the race out of its low position.

Despite occasional sniping between Du Bois and Washington, the debate sparked a number of advances, including the establishment of the NAACP. Du Bois's rivalries with fellow black leaders would not always be so cordial, however. By the time of Washington's death in 1915, Du Bois was the preeminent statesman of black Americans, a station that he jealously guarded. Thus he clashed bitterly with fellow black leader Marcus Garvey in the early 1920s.

The conflict between Du Bois and Garvey was largely personality-driven. The two men had similar philosophies, as they both emphasized black nationalism and Pan-Africanism. Yet each saw the other as a threat to his leadership within the race. Moreover, the middle-aged Du Bois couldn't have been more different temperamentally from the Universal Negro Improvement Association's founder. Whereas Du Bois was a surly patrician whose pedantic style was off-putting to the masses, Garvey was a charismatic immigrant who, duded-up in elaborate costumes, won over working-class blacks like himself.

Garvey's supporters in the United Negro Improvement Association elected the New Yorker by way of Jamaica the "Provisional President of Africa." Du Bois's rival led massive rallies in Northern urban centers to call for black self-segregation in America and an independent black colony in Africa for Africans of the diaspora. When Garvey's Black Star Line actually purchased a ship, the *Yarmouth*, to carry out his plans of returning blacks to Africa, he transformed from a street-corner demagogue into the leader of one of the first mass movements of blacks in American history.

Du Bois engineered a sub-rosa campaign against the Jamaican-born demagogue. He warned Secretary of State Charles Evans Hughes of Garvey's potential for mischief. He quietly instigated a public letter by Liberia's president undercutting the popular perception that Africans welcomed the endeavors of the "Negro Moses." He began a whisper campaign among the "talented tenth" against Garvey's plan to return blacks to Africa. Publicly, he raised questions about the finances of Garvey's Black Star Line.[4]

Garvey fought back, charging that Du Bois "likes to dance with white people and dine with them and sometimes sleep with them, because from his way of seeing things all that is black is ugly, and all that is white is beautiful."[5] In response, Du Bois called Garvey a "traitor" and a "lunatic."[6] Garvey's attacks escalated. For the first time, Du Bois began to be booed and heckled by members of his own race. Though Garvey would be jailed for mail fraud and eventually deported, Du Bois had suffered some lasting damage from his conflict with the Jamaican. Some resented his role in bringing down another black leader.

By this point, Du Bois's racialist views had become more strident. Earlier he may have been merely guilty of failing to rise above his age when he wrote that in one county in Georgia, "The Jew is the heir of the slave-baron."[7] His description of his lineage in the autobiographical *Darkwater* as "a flood of Negro blood, a strain of French, a bit of Dutch, but, thank God! no 'Anglo-Saxon,'" or his confession that during his younger days he "cordially despised the poor Irish and South Germans" (immigrants that he saw as drunks and slobs), similarly shrieks in the sensitive ears of the modern listener.[8] But his rhetoric hardly differs from the harsh language used by Woodrow Wilson, Theodore Roosevelt, and other noteworthy men of the age. What is significant is that as the years progressed, Du Bois's racial views didn't. In 1920, as the editor of the NAACP journal *The*

Crisis, he made his first of many public calls for segregation. If democracy and fairness for blacks were not an option, "Absolutely segregate the races and sections of the world," Du Bois told his shocked subscribers.[9] By 1933 he was calling for a plan that "will involve increased segregation and perhaps migration. It will be pounced upon and aided and encouraged by every 'nigger-hater' in the land."[10] Two wrongs, Du Bois seemed to argue, do make a right: "I fight Segregation with Segregation."[11]

This was an odd argument to make in the prime literary organ of an association dedicated to *ending* segregation. The NAACP's board members let their editor know this. It didn't help matters when NAACP leaders learned that segregationists were quoting Du Bois to justify preventing blacks from benefiting from New Deal relief programs.[12] The organization wanted him to stop his calls for voluntary separatism, but the stubborn editor refused. Once again, Du Bois was brawling with his fellow black leaders, in this case with top officials in the organization he had helped found. When NAACP secretary Walter White and his assistant Roy Wilkens opposed his plan for black separatism, Du Bois conducted a vicious campaign against the pair. "Walter White is white," the normally highbrow Harvard man said of the NAACP leader. "He has more white companions and friends than colored. He goes where he will in New York City and naturally meets no Color Line, for the simple and sufficient reason that he isn't 'colored.'"[13] The dispute over separatism finally drove Du Bois to resign from the NAACP, effective July 1, 1934, and to give up his role as editor of *The Crisis*, a position he had held since the publication's inception in 1910.

It is worth noting that many of Du Bois's present-day admirers are often the first to call for the excommunication of historical figures from the pantheon of heroes when it is discovered that they were guilty of offending twenty-first-century sensibilities. Du Bois, however, gets a pass.

After splitting from the NAACP, Du Bois would only become more extreme, caustic, and belligerent. Even Martin Luther King, who emerged as the most prominent black leader in Du Bois's final decade, did not escape criticism. The cranky intellectual blasted King for rejecting violence when confronted with violence. The older leader complained that King was reckless to call for boycotts that had cost blacks jobs without a plan to offset the economic losses.[14] He contrasted what he saw as King's naïveté with his own realism: "I do not pretend to 'love' white people. I think that as a race they are the most selfish of any on earth."[15]

Walter White, Roy Wilkens, and Martin Luther King saw the path of black achievement linked with integration. During the second half of his life, Du Bois increasingly advocated the opposite course of action: racial separatism. That the methods of White, Wilkens, and King were vindicated by *Brown v. Board of Education*, the lunch-counter strikes, and Rosa Parks is hardly necessary to point out. Strikingly, Du Bois is today held aloft beside these men as a civil rights icon.

W.E.B. Du Bois was not the forerunner of Martin Luther King. He was the mirror image of the white racists he claimed to be fighting against. The true inheritors of his legacy were leaders like Malcolm X and Louis Farrakhan, who echoed his hateful rhetoric without the academic accent.

HEAVEN ON EARTH

Racial separatism was not the only cause to which W.E.B. Du Bois devoted himself. Like many other so-called progressives, Du Bois took up the utopian enterprise of creating a paradise on earth through Communism. The true believers would do anything to further this cause. Within the borders of the Soviet Union, many killed to achieve heaven on earth. Outside the U.S.S.R., men like Du Bois lied in pursuit of this goal.

Nearly every ideal that Du Bois and other progressives publicly extolled, Communists in practice attacked. The first action of the Soviet Cheka secret police, for instance, was to break up a strike in Petrograd.[16] Shortly thereafter, *Pravda* announced, "The best place for strikers, those yellow noxious parasites, is the concentration camp!"[17] A better place for organized laborers, Lenin thought, was the bottom of the Volga River, where thousands were sent with stones tied around their necks.[18] Campaigns of government-enforced ethnic hatred resulted in the deaths of millions by starvation in the Ukraine. The Soviet Union used capital punishment more than nearly any nation in history. "Every intellectual must have his own file" was Lenin's view of freedom of expression. "They must be controlled, closely watched and divided up, and those who are ready to support the Soviet regime and demonstrate this by their actions and their words should be considered for promotion."[19]

Some progressives viewed these and other transgressions against their ideals as a bargain trade-off for the end result of a centrally planned socialist society. Others deluded themselves into believing that the totalitarianism of the Communists was the product of capitalist propaganda.

However they rationalized their deception, almost to a man progressives making the trek to the Soviet Union returned to their respective homelands with tales of heaven on earth. W.E.B. Du Bois was one of these men.

In 1911, Du Bois joined the Socialist Party. Despite his membership in Eugene Debs's political organization, he retained a pragmatic outlook and chose not to waste his vote on the third party. He welcomed the news of the Bolsheviks' triumph in 1917, but it would be many years before he became fully converted. In 1926, during his first trip to the Soviet Union, arranged and funded by a trio he suspected of being Communist agents, he declared allegiance to Bolshevism.[20] By 1933 he was publicly describing Karl Marx as a "colossal genius" and ranking *Das Kapital* alongside the Bible in importance.[21] Within a few years, any remnant of intellectual independence departed him. He parroted the Moscow line for the remainder of his years. By 1961, he engaged in the formality of joining the Communist Party of the United States. "Communism," he wrote to party chairman Gus Hall, "is the only way of human life." "Capitalism," on the other hand, "cannot reform itself; it is doomed to self-destruction." He predicted, "In the end Communism will triumph. I want to help bring that day."[22]

That day never came. What did come were plenty of opportunities for the misguided professor to be shaken out of his myopic vision of Communism. One such case was the Hitler-Stalin pact of August 1939. Prior to Hitler's declaration of war on the United States, Du Bois denounced Britain's fight against Nazi Germany as an imperialist crusade. His tune changed dramatically when the Nazis turned on the Communists in June of 1941, and he suddenly displayed a curious fervor for war.[23] The murder of Lovett Fort-Whiteman also failed to shake his faith. The most prominent African-American Communist of the 1920s and '30s, Fort-Whiteman on several occasions attempted to bring Du Bois into the Communist fold. In the 1930s Fort-Whiteman moved to Moscow, where paranoid Stalinists accused him of being a Trotskyite. In 1936, he disappeared. After the fall of the Iron Curtain, documents revealed that the unfortunate Communist, an American citizen, had died in 1939 in a Stalinist gulag, his teeth kicked in. His disappearance evoked no protest from Du Bois or any of his ideological soul mates.[24]

By 1948, Du Bois was so active in support of the Communists that the U.S. government indicted him for failing to register as an agent of a foreign government. His Peace Information Agency, the government alleged, was a front for Soviet Communists to propagandize in the United

States. No official link was ever established between the Peace Information Agency and the Soviet Union (although there is little dispute that the agency merely parroted the party line), and the government dropped the case. For nearly a decade thereafter, the State Department imposed an international travel ban on the elderly Marxist.

Still, Du Bois traveled extensively throughout the Communist world over the course of his long life. He made four visits to the Soviet Union and two to China, as well as trips to Romania, Czechoslovakia, and East Germany. He attained private audiences with Mao Zedong and Nikita Khrushchev. His travels behind the Iron Curtain, coupled with his comprehensive reading of Marx and Engels, exclude the possibility of mere ignorance of the true nature of Communism. What is so damning is that he knew the truth and yet chose to conceal it.

Du Bois eulogized Stalin, for instance, as a "great" and "courageous" man, "attacked and slandered as few men of power have been."[25] In Mao's China, site of the state-induced deaths of more than 60 million people, Du Bois beheld "a sense of human nature free of its most hurtful and terrible meanness and of a people full of joy and faith and marching on in a unison unexampled in Holland, Belgium, Britain, and France; and simply inconceivable in the United States."[26] The suppression of religion behind the Iron Curtain was the "the greatest gift of the Russian Revolution to the modern world." In the posthumously published English version of his final autobiography, he wrote:

> Many folk follow religious ceremonies and services; and allow their children to learn fairy tales and so-called religious truth, which in time the children come to recognize as conventional lies told by their parents and teachers for the children's good. One can hardly exaggerate the moral disaster of this custom. We have to thank the Soviet Union for the courage to stop it.[27]

Although accolades escaped Du Bois in his homeland during this period, other nations honored him. In 1959, for example, the Soviet Union awarded him the Lenin Peace Prize and China celebrated a national holiday in his honor.[28] Decades before American schools recognized him, Moscow State University, Czechoslovakia's Charles University, and East Germany's Humboldt University bestowed honorary degrees on the aging intellectual.[29] Socialist Ghana held a state-sponsored funeral to pay respects to the country's most famous immigrant.[30]

Historian Daniel Boorstin reminds us that "illusions die hard, and the brighter they are the longer they take adying."[31] No illusion burned as brightly as Communism's promise of earthly deliverance. It took more than seventy years of reality to extinguish this illusion, yet it still flickers. For Du Bois, the fire never went out.

FRIENDS IN LOW PLACES

Just as Soviet propagandists were able to cozy up to Du Bois and use him to disseminate their lies, Imperial Japanese agents found in him a worthy pawn. "Enough can be gleaned from the spotty record of correspondence and Justice Department files," biographer David Levering Lewis reveals regarding the Japanese agent who directed the academician's travels to the Orient, "to deduce that Hikida [Yasuichi] was the point man for Japan's low-budget operation to influence black American public opinion."[32] Du Bois was his most prized dupe.

People of color ruled the Empire of the Sun, Du Bois reasoned, so how could it do wrong? When he delivered this message in China, his audience, already having experienced the Japanese takeover of Manchuria, was aghast.[33] The color of their oppressors mattered little to them. "Why is it that you hate Japan more than Europe when you have suffered more from England, France, and Germany than from Japan?" he asked his incredulous hosts.[34] Du Bois was incapable of grasping the notion that people could inflict great indignities upon other people of the same racial background. Nor could he comprehend how anyone other than whites could be guilty of cruelty on a grand scale. His simplistic explanation for the hostility between East Asia's two great powers was China's "submission to white aggression and Japanese resistance" to it.[35] In 1937, Du Bois penned a ridiculous article contending that the Japanese seizure of Manchuria actually benefited the Chinese.[36] So absurd were his claims that *China Weekly Review* alleged that Hirohito's government was paying him for his services.[37]

The benefit of hindsight did little to alter his jaundiced perspective. After the cessation of hostilities he declared, "Every American Negro has been unhappy over the war with Japan because it is a war between nations of different colors, between Europe and Asia. And because we cannot help but believe that the fundamental impulse back of this war was, on the one hand, the century-old determination of Europe to dominate the yellow peoples for the benefit of the white; and on the other hand, the resentment of Asiatics at being considered and treated as inferior to Europeans."[38] Even the admiring Lewis concedes, "Du Bois would shave the edges of responsible opinion repeatedly when writing about the Japanese."[39]

The NAACP founding father's writings on Japan's wartime ally were similarly unscholarly. "In a desire to be objective, as well as from awe, some of Du Bois's readings of National Socialism ran from equivocal to complimentary," Lewis admits.[40] Conspicuous among these is an item entitled "The German Case Against Jews," printed in 1937. While condemning the Third Reich's anti-Semitism, Du Bois at times sought to excuse it. The reaction against the Jews "is a reasoned prejudice" based on "economic fear," he claimed.[41] In the piece, Du Bois simply repeated the base slurs he heard uttered against the Jews on his trip to Germany: The Jews control the stock exchange, the legal profession, business, and so on.[42]

Hitler's Germany, Du Bois told readers of the *Pittsburgh Courier* in a series of letters, was prosperous, orderly, efficient, and at peace: "[T]hey have a nation at work, after a nightmare of unemployment; and the results of this work are shown not simply by private profits, but by houses for the poor; new roads; an end of strikes and labor troubles; widespread industrial and unemployment insurance; the guarding of public and private health; great celebrations, organizations for old and young, new songs, new ideals, a new state, a new race."[43] These rosy conditions were the result of socialism, Du Bois insisted.

Like Churchill, Du Bois saw Nazism and Communism as two sides of the same coin. Unlike Churchill, he welcomed the advent of both. "Germany today is, next to Russia, the greatest exemplar of Marxian socialism in the world," he proclaimed in 1936. He compiled a list showing readers the remarkable similarities between Nazi Germany and the Soviet Union; in some areas, he said, the two nations were nearly identical. So it was with great confusion that Du Bois discussed Hitler's "unreasonable bitterness" toward Bolshevism.[44]

Needless to say, Du Bois's enthusiasm for aspects of Nazism, no matter how qualified and tempered, is an inconvenience for his votaries. If revealed, it besmirches not only Du Bois, but those who promote him as well. It also uproots the myth that the two ideologies are polar opposites. Communism and Nazism were not bitter enemies. They were bitter rivals. This reciprocal enmity is popularly mistaken for evidence that the two occupy opposing positions on the ideological spectrum. In reality, the hostility between Communism and Nazism is analogous to the competition between Coke and Pepsi, two virtually indistinguishable products vying for the allegiance of the same target audience. Overlooking such glaring clues as the Third Reich's red flag and the fact that Nazi serves as an abbreviation for National *Socialist*, partisans of left-wing ideas portray Nazism as antithetical to Communism. Du Bois knew better.

ANTI-AMERICAN PROPAGANDIST

Germany, Japan, and the Soviet Union held in common a hatred for the United States—a feeling shared by Du Bois. Du Bois's reflexive anti-Americanism blinded him to the fact that people of color were not the only oppressed, and that white people were not the only oppressors. Preoccupied with color in the same way as some of the Southern whites he held in contempt, he willingly overlooked the sins committed by nations that stood against America. Any enemy of America was a friend of his.

Wittingly and unwittingly, Du Bois served as a propagandist for America's most despicable enemies. He offered that race relations in Nazi Germany were a vast improvement on race relations in his homeland. After more than five months in the Third Reich, he declared, "It would have been impossible for me to have spent a similarly long time in any part of the United States, without some, if not frequent cases of personal insult or discrimination. I cannot record a single instance here."[45] For a long time Du Bois seemed oblivious to the hyperracism of Imperial Japan, the same nation that inflicted a 27 percent death rate on white prisoners of war but a marginal one against fellow Asian POWs.[46] He gullibly proclaimed that racial discrimination was virtually nonexistent in the Soviet Union because it was outlawed.[47] Du Bois would have his listeners believe that only in the United States, and other predominantly white countries that rejected socialism, did racism abound.

As with any good propagandist, deceit was a staple of his trade. The Korean War, he maintained, erupted after *North* Korea was attacked.[48] The "sinister" Winston Churchill was the "chief leader . . . toward death and destruction of human civilization."[49] Conversely, "there is no statesman speaking who is the equal of Molotov," he noted of the U.S.S.R.'s foreign minister.[50] Though the Soviet Union eventually gobbled up Eastern Europe, he found that nation's intentions during World War II to have been benevolent. The Allies, he suggested, went to war to prevent Germany and Japan from engulfing colonies they had designs on.[51]

As Du Bois grew older, his anti-Americanism grew more passionate. In 1952, he declared that America was the "the greatest warmonger of all history."[52] The next year he asserted that outgoing president Harry Truman "ranks with Adolf Hitler as one of the greatest killers of our day."[53] In 1954, he insisted that "few nations fear the Soviet Union; all fear the United States."[54] Many began to question his sanity. By the accounts of those close to him, however, his mind retained its sharpness until the very end.

In a final act of hatred for his native country, Du Bois renounced his American citizenship. He spent his final two years in Kwame Nkrumah's Ghana.[55] Although as a nonagenarian he could not have expected to live much longer, his retreat away from the capitalist world ironically hastened his demise. Botched medical treatment in Ghana sparked an infection of his prostate, for which he sought treatment in Romania. Surgery in Romania proved unsuccessful. At this point, Du Bois opted for practical necessity over ideological solidarity and sought treatment in the free world.[56] The toll on his health had been too great, however, and within a year he was dead.

As fate would have it, the death of black America's most renowned separatist and reviler of the United States coincided with the apex of the philosophy he had derided as destined for failure. As the Christian minister Martin Luther King told a crowd of 250,000 on the Mall in Washington, D.C., about his dream, a Ghanaian witch doctor presided over the atheist Du Bois's funeral. The juxtaposition of events in August 1963 made it clear which path to equality was triumphant.

"FREEDOM, JUSTICE, PEACE AND RACIAL EQUALITY"

W.E.B. Du Bois still casts a long shadow. Although he essentially abandoned scholarly pursuits early in his career to focus on convincing a mass audience to support his political causes, his central legacy is in the world of higher education. In fact, he anticipated a major academic trend by decades. At its best, Du Bois's scholarship uncovered a history of African people that had been obscured. At its worst, it counteracted oversights of black accomplishment with exaggerations of it. Alexander Hamilton was probably part black, he suggested to readers, and the Sphinx at Giza was black.[57] "Black Africa," he wrote, "had been a revered example to ancient Greece and the recognized contender with imperial Rome."[58] According to Du Bois, most of the inhabitants of ancient Egypt were black, the Industrial Age began as a result of black labor, and both world wars were waged over control of African colonies.[59] This scholarship failed to exert much influence in his lifetime, but a generation after his death such revisionism came into vogue in the writings of Molefi Kete Asante, Martin Bernal, Ivan Van Sertima, and a host of other tenured Afrocentrists. The bad history that Du Bois put forward was a dress rehearsal for the Afrocentric classroom of the future.

Yet Afrocentrism is just a fraction of the patrimony he left the modern academy. Du Bois is a progenitor of the multiculturalism that pervades today's college campuses. This multiculturalism is strangely indifferent to foreign cultures, but it is preoccupied with the negative aspects, both real and imagined, of our own culture. Du Bois's anti-Americanism and Marxism certainly focused on the failings of our society while ignoring the flaws in other cultures. Multiculturalism, too, often is a euphemism for what Du Bois advocated: racial separatism. He even hinted that only blacks could properly teach the history, sociology, literature, or philosophy of blacks, an argument that by now has become common. He also employed a tactic that some academics today use to stifle any debate: He sometimes alleged that African-Americans who disagreed with him were in fact whites in disguise. All of this makes Du Bois a fitting hero for multiculturalists.

Princeton history professor Sean Wilentz has noted that "on campus and off, Du Bois and his writings have become so respectable that they are almost impossible to avoid."[60] Indeed, the Library of America has published several of Du Bois's titles, and professors compel countless undergraduates to read his work.

Du Bois posthumously won the endorsement of the academic in-crowd. His absurd characterizations of life behind the Iron Curtain, rather than damaging his standing in the academic community, enhanced it. It is therefore unsurprising to discover that those who found it so easy to forgive Du Bois's dishonesty also disregard the truth when it suits their interests.

In 1996, when UMass–Amherst named its library after Du Bois, Chancellor David Scott justified the decision by saying that the sometime advocate of racial separatism "worked tirelessly to end racial discrimination."[61] Likewise, the institution's president at the time, Michael Hooker, lauded the angry Stalinist's "ceaseless efforts on behalf of freedom, justice, peace and racial equality."[62] David Levering Lewis regards the subject of his two-volume biography as the "premier architect of the civil rights movement."[63]

Du Bois was none of these things. He was a bitter Communist whose embrace of two of history's most prolific murderers—Mao and Stalin—is a disgrace. He became the black mirror image of George Wallace, Theodore Bilbo, and John Rankin by promoting separatism. He was not a scholar but a propagandist who sacrificed honest scholarship in favor of anything that furthered his ideology. His hatred of America was so great that he compared Nazi Germany and Imperial Japan favorably with the United States. In the end, he even took the extreme step of renouncing his U.S. citizenship. How anyone would characterize him as a friend of "freedom, justice, peace and racial equality" is perplexing, to say the least.

The attempt to make Du Bois into something he was not is an acknowledgment that his real views are unpalatable to mainstream audiences. It also suggests that those distorting his record embrace his repulsive views yet recognize the need to link him to popular causes that he had nothing to do with.

The followers of W.E.B. Du Bois paid homage to him during his life by parroting his hateful rhetoric on a variety of issues. It is an appropriate tribute that after his death they would adopt another of his methods—lying—to win for him a place of honor in America. No doubt this proud recipient of the Lenin Peace Prize rolls in his grave over the current tributes from the one country he so passionately hated.

"FORGERY BY TYPEWRITER"

A Half-Century of Leftist Delusions

Alger went to jail for all our sins.

— DIANA TRILLING

IMAGINE IF AMERICANS FOUND OUT FOLLOWING 9/11 THAT OSAMA bin Laden had placed several hundred agents within the U.S. government. What if we learned that these agents had stolen blueprints for a nuclear bomb, infiltrated the occupation government in Iraq, and discovered the formula to print currency? How might the American people react to learning that these terrorist agents occupied positions in the Departments of State and Treasury, the CIA, and the White House itself?

The scenario seems too ridiculous to comprehend. Yet halfway through the twentieth century, America, as well as other Western nations, faced a situation quite similar to this. It wasn't radical Islamists who established a beachhead in Washington, London, Ottawa, and points beyond, but Communist turncoats. Dubbed a decade of fear, hysteria, and paranoia, the period immediately following World War II is better thought of as the Age of Delusion, when American liberals mistook Communists for other liberals, compared very real subversives to imaginary witches, and dismissed charges of espionage as the product of conspiracy-minded right-wingers. A fitting symbol for the Age of Delusion is Alger Hiss.

Like W.E.B. Du Bois, Alger Hiss was more deluder than deluded. Moscow controlled legions of Western intellectuals like Du Bois. Far more precious were its platoons of government officials. Alger Hiss was a star enlistee in this latter unit. Substantial evidence emerged that this high-level U.S. government official was in fact a Communist agent who passed state secrets to the Soviet Union and influenced policy to aid Stalin's regime. He nevertheless maintained his innocence to the grave. To many, his claims of a frame-up seemed laughable in the face of the mountains of evidence against him, but somehow Hiss inspired armies of loyal defenders. These were the deluded. Unflinchingly committed to the idea of Hiss's innocence, they ignored the truth.

When it comes to Alger Hiss, the delusion has continued for more than half a century. More important than the small delusion of their hero's innocence is the larger delusion that the charge he stood accused of—serving as a Communist agent in the land of the free—was never really a crime anyhow.

HE SAID, HE SAID

Days after Hitler and Stalin entered into an alliance to carve up Europe, Whittaker Chambers walked into an FBI office and began to tell his fantastic story. It would take almost a decade for the rest of the world to listen.

Chambers alleged that there was a massive conspiracy of Communists working for the aims of the Soviet Union within the U.S. government. He knew this, he explained, because he had served this conspiracy. Chambers named names. One of the men he accused was Alger Hiss, a rising star in the State Department. Chambers told his story to Assistant Secretary of State Adolph Berle. Conflicting stories report that Berle either sat on the information for more than a year or relayed it to President Franklin Roosevelt (who allegedly laughed it off as the product of an imaginative crank).[1]

Although the ex-Communist repeated his charges to the FBI and State Department investigators, no action was taken. The Soviet Union, after all, was our ally in the fight against Hitler. Then, after Franklin Roosevelt died and World War II ended, the Cold War began. Officials began to listen to people like Chambers.

Shortly after World War II ended, Igor Gouzenko, a Russian code clerk at the Soviet embassy in Ottawa, defected. Among the many pieces of information he gave Canadian authorities was that an assistant to the U.S. secretary of state was a Soviet agent. Canadian and American authorities both deduced that the unnamed figure that he described bore a striking resemblance to Alger Hiss. That same fall Elizabeth Bentley, a former courier for a Soviet espionage apparatus, told the FBI about a vast network of Communist spies in government that included Treasury official Harry Dexter White, who later served as the head of the International Monetary Fund, and Lauchlin Currie, a former top aide to Roosevelt. She also recalled a story about how years earlier a member of her network, Charles Kramer, informed her that Alger Hiss had lured away one of her contacts, Harold Glasser, to become part of his network. Bentley's and Gouzenko's warnings about Hiss, who stayed in government through 1946, went unheeded.

Then in the summer of 1948, Bentley was called to testify before the House Committee on Un-American Activities. She retold her story about Hiss. On August 2, Whittaker Chambers was called before the committee to substantiate Bentley's allegations. If the rather average-looking Bentley failed to live up to expectations after the tabloids dubbed her "the blonde spy-queen," Chambers unraveled a story so remarkable that he upstaged the woman whose account he was merely supposed to corroborate. The most explosive of his charges was that Alger Hiss, the intelligent young New Dealer who some believed might one day be secretary of state, was a secret Communist.

Alger Hiss, as his supporters frequently pointed out, was a graduate of Harvard Law School who had clerked for Supreme Court Justice Oliver Wendell Holmes. He was an aide to Roosevelt at Bretton Woods, Dumbarton Oaks, and Yalta, and in 1945 he served as secretary-general of the conference at which the United Nations was founded. After more than a decade of public service, Hiss was appointed president of the Carnegie Endowment for International Peace, whose board included Dwight Eisenhower and John Foster Dulles. Supreme Court Justices Felix Frankfurter and Stanley Reed, Governor Adlai Stevenson of Illinois, and Secretary of State Dean Acheson all vouched for Hiss's character. Working in positions of responsibility in all three branches of government, Alger Hiss was a paragon of establishment respectability.

Whittaker Chambers, who had become a senior editor at *Time* magazine since his departure from the Soviet underground, was not armed with such a brilliant pedigree. As one of Hiss's lawyers alleged, Chambers was "a confirmed liar," "a blasphemer," the author of "a filthy, despicable play about Jesus Christ," and an enthusiast of "atheism," "lies," and "stealing."[2] Indeed, Chambers at one time or another had been all of those things. A defense witness who met Hiss's antagonist in the 1930s remembered Chambers as looking "as if he had slept on a park bench the night before. His clothes were old, unpressed and rather dirty. His linen was not clean. He would never look me in the eyes, but kept glancing suspiciously around the restaurant."[3] On top of all this, the Hiss defense team alleged, Chambers was mentally ill and a homosexual, and had dirty teeth. Whereas Hiss was slim, sleek, and handsome, Chambers was fat and unkempt and appeared as though he hadn't slept in days.

Hiss, in effect, argued that his links to presidents, Supreme Court justices, senators, and college presidents rendered the charges against him false. In other words, it was innocence by association. At the same time, Hiss and his legal team tried to defame Chambers. "Surely we intend to smear Chambers," Hiss lawyer Harold Rosenwald candidly admitted. "I have no objection to such smearing and hope that it will be very thoroughly and effectively done."[4] Fastening Hiss to respected public figures and Chambers to despicable practices had no relevance to the questions at hand: Was Hiss a Communist? Did he supply the Soviet Union with government secrets? Did he steer policy to favor the Soviets at the expense of America? The strategy Hiss used is by now a familiar one: Tarnish the reputation of the accuser, associate the accused with pious men and noble causes, and at all costs avoid any discussion of the merits of the charges.

Unfortunately for Hiss, the accusations were so serious that a discussion of the facts was inevitable.

BOKHARA RUGS, PROTHONOTARY WARBLERS, AND A FORD ROADSTER

Hiss initially denied ever having known Chambers. But Chambers certainly seemed to have known Hiss. He detailed the interior of Hiss's homes, described the avid birdwatcher's excitement at glimpsing a rare prothonotary warbler (a bird Hiss confirmed spotting), and even purchased his farm a year after the Hisses had made a deposit on the very same property. Edith Murray, a maid for the "Cantwells" (one of numerous fictitious surnames the Chamberses used) from the fall of 1934 until the spring of 1936, reported meeting Priscilla Hiss at least four times and Alger Hiss once.[5] As the evidence piled up suggesting a friendship between the two men, Hiss's staunch denials of knowing the portly intellectual tested the credulity of his defenders.

Upon examining Chambers in front of members of the House Committee on Un-American Activities in 1948, Hiss declared that he did, after all, know his accuser—not as "Karl," Chambers's underground name, but as "George Crosley." House investigators found it suspicious that Hiss, who had claimed not to know Chambers after viewing pictures of him, now conceded that he had shared a home with him and even claimed that he had given him a car during the Great Depression. Hiss maintained that "Crosley" was a deadbeat journalist who had sought information from him and ended up siphoning off money and rent from him, in addition to the car. Chambers, a man of many names, denied ever going by the name "George Crosley." When members of the committee asked Hiss to produce three people who knew Chambers by that name, one person he identified was dead and the two others did not know the ex-Communist as "Crosley."[6] Only the Hisses testified to knowing Chambers by the name "Crosley."

Chambers, meanwhile, contradicted the claim that Hiss had given him a car in 1935. As the House committee learned, Hiss was trying to obscure the embarrassing truth that he had really given it to a Communist organizer. House investigators unearthed records from the Cherner Motor Company from July 23, 1936, showing that Hiss signed over his 1929 Ford Roadster to the company. On the very same day that Hiss gave Cherner Motor his car, the dealership sold the car to a William Rosen for the nominal fee of $25. Rosen, as he later admitted to investigators, was a Communist. So was the man who undersigned the transaction, Baltimore lawyer Benjamin Bialeck. The owner of the company affirmed that taking a car without payment and then selling it for a small fee that day seemed "very unusual."[7] The signature on the "very unusual" transfer was, by the accused's own admission, that of Alger Hiss.[8] Once again, Hiss's version of events was proven false. He did not give the car to Whittaker Chambers.

Chambers supplied more evidence of Hiss's connection to the Communist underground. He revealed that in late 1936 his spymaster, Boris Bykov, gave him several hundred dollars and instructed him to purchase four Bokhara rugs imported from the Soviet Union. The rugs were to be given as rewards to his most important government contacts: the Railroad Retirement Board's Abraham George Silverman, the Treasury Department's Harry Dexter White, and the State Department's Julian Wadleigh and Alger Hiss. All four men claimed either not to know Chambers or not to know him very well, but it became quite clear that Chambers was telling the truth about his past connections to them. Receipts and shipping records corroborated his story: Chambers gave Bykov's money to a friend in New York, Meyer Schapiro, who purchased the four Bokhara rugs and shipped them to Silverman in Washington.[9] Chambers also held that after the rugs had been delivered to Washington in 1937, he personally presented Hiss with his rug.[10]

Wadleigh, who by 1948 had admitted his role in domestic subversion, conceded that he had received a Bokhara rug from Chambers for his service to the Soviet Union. But others were not as forthright. Silverman admitted receiving the rugs and giving one to Harry Dexter White, but he claimed that Chambers had given him two Bokharas to repay part of a debt he owed. Like Silverman, Hiss acknowledged receiving a rug from Chambers but alleged that it had been given to him as repayment for past debts. As if to show that he had nothing to hide, Hiss claimed that he had displayed the rug in his home continuously since its arrival. That claim, too, proved false. Hiss's maid testified that her boss had kept the rug locked in a closet for more than a year, and records showed that Hiss paid to have the Bokhara kept in storage in 1937 and 1938.[11] Hiss's possession of the rug not only linked him to his fellow Marylander, it linked him to Chambers after 1936—the date that Hiss definitively set as his last meeting with "George Crosley."

Amid the back and forth of testimony, the Harvard Law School graduate challenged his antagonist to repeat his charges in a forum that did not offer him immunity from libel suits, as a House committee did. Chambers repeated his charges on *Meet the Press* on August 27, 1948. After a month's delay, Hiss sued Chambers for libel.

Just as Hiss upped the ante, Chambers met him and raised the stakes. Chambers revised his position, now claiming that Hiss was not only working for the policy objectives of the Soviet Union but had pilfered top-secret documents for the Communist superpower as well. Later, explaining why he had not initially mentioned Hiss's espionage in his testimony, Chambers wrote, "I did not wish to harm, more than was unavoidable, those whom I must testify against, of whose lives in the years since I had left them I knew next to nothing, many of whom might no longer be Communists."[12] Yet with his back against the wall, Chambers reversed himself, in the process revealing that he had lied to the committee when he denied Hiss's involvement in espionage.

While the facts of the case certainly weren't helpful to Hiss, his reactions to the questions of House investigators were disastrous. Chambers agreed without hesitation to take a lie detector test. Hiss declined. The accuser answered the committee's questions in a straightforward manner, while the accused prefaced 198 of his assertions by stating, "To the best of my knowledge . . ."[13] Hiss testified surrounded by lawyers; Chambers, alone. After initially denying that he had known Chambers, that copies of top-secret memos were in his handwriting, and that he had signed over his Ford to Cherner Motor, Hiss backtracked. In contrast, the only information that Chambers withheld stood to damage his antagonist, not himself. He admitted facts against his own interest and risked incriminating himself.

A freshman congressman on the House Committee on Un-American Activities, Richard Nixon, began to smell a rat.

DUMBWAITERS AND PUMPKINS

In 1937, after twelve years of serving the Communist Party—first in the open party as an organizer and editor of both the *Daily Worker* and *New Masses*, and then in the underground as a courier for the Soviet espionage apparatus—Whittaker Chambers ceased believing in Communism. The next year, he broke from the Communist Party underground. "By any hard-headed estimate, the world I was leaving looked like the world of life and of the future," Chambers later observed. "The world I was returning to seemed, by contrast, a graveyard."[14]

As Whittaker Chambers prepared to defect, he decided to retain possession of the U.S. government documents his contacts had turned over to him. Much like Monica Lewinsky's blue dress, the secret papers served as an insurance policy. In 1938 he traveled to the home of his wife's nephew, Nathan Levine, in Brooklyn and placed the incriminating papers in the shaft of a dumbwaiter in Levine's bathroom. For ten years they sat.

On Sunday, November 14, 1948, Chambers wired Levine to tell him that he would be meeting him in Brooklyn. Levine, whose parents now occupied his house, took Chambers to where he had left the documents. The two old friends opened up the dumbwaiter, not knowing if it still contained what had been placed in it a decade earlier. An envelope wrapped in elastic bands and dust emerged. It contained sixty-five typed sheets of paper, five rolls of microfilm, and numerous sheets of handwritten notes.[15] Two days later, after some hesitation, Chambers brought the contents of Levine's dumbwaiter—minus the microfilm—before the grand jury. The dynamics of the case, which up until this point had been one man's word against another's, were forever altered.

The sixty-five documents he brought forward were typed copies or summaries of seventy-one confidential U.S. government reports and memos. Sixty-eight of the original seventy-one documents were traced as having traveled through Alger Hiss's office. Three experts hired by Hiss's defense team affirmed what *Time* magazine's experts and the FBI's investigators had already concluded: Hiss's Woodstock typewriter had produced all but one of the documents Chambers had brought forward as evidence. By comparing the purloined documents with letters typed by Hiss's wife, Priscilla, both the FBI and Hiss's own experts concluded that Mrs. Hiss had typed these copies.[16] Yet Hiss responded to the allegations at his trial by proclaiming, "Until the day I die, I shall wonder how Whittaker Chambers got into my house to use my typewriter." The courtroom, including the jury, erupted with laughter at this peculiar statement.[17]

The handwritten pages introduced as evidence were verbatim duplicates and summaries of government reports, three of which pertained to military matters and a fourth to a diplomatic crisis in which the Soviet government held against her will an American woman married to a Russian. Handwriting experts attested, and Hiss eventually conceded, that Alger Hiss himself had written the nine pages of notes.[18]

Less than a month after extracting his packet from Arthur Levine's dumbwaiter, Chambers once again "used against the Communist Party exactly the conspiratorial methods which it had taught me to use against others."[19] On December 2, 1948, Chambers traveled to his farm in Westminster, Maryland, with two House investigators to reveal a last piece of evidence. He took the investigators to his pumpkin patch, reached into a hollowed-out pumpkin, and pulled out five rolls of microfilm.

Although much of the microfilm was unreadable, the information that could be read was incriminating. Like the papers he had turned over a few weeks before, the microfilm contained both original, and typed copies of, government documents that had passed through the State Department's Trade Agreements Division, in which Hiss had worked. There was, however, one major difference between the two document handovers. The first took place before a grand jury and because of its secrecy did nothing to change public opinion on the case. Chambers gave the "Pumpkin Papers," on the other hand, to the House Committee on Un-American Activities, which, for reasons both noble and ignoble, made the revelation public. Chambers's cloak-and-dagger theatrics escalated interest in a case that already seemed to contain more than its fair share of intrigue.

Central to the mythology built around the Hiss case is the idea that the documents Chambers produced were by no means secret government papers. In *Alger Hiss: The True Story*, author John Chabot Smith main-

tains, "As spy papers, these clearly weren't much; not worth risking anyone's neck for," while in *The Unfinished Story of Alger Hiss* Fred Cook
holds that a "significant point in connection with the memos is that none
dealt with vital secrets."[20] A few items produced by Chambers do not
seem to be all that crucial. Chambers, however, brought forward a massive amount of material, not just a few inconsequential items. As historian
Allen Weinstein notes in his book on the case, *Perjury*, "The contents of
the stolen State Department documents cannot be considered peripheral
or unimportant—certainly not to professional diplomats at the time—
when viewed in the context of major issues then dominating world affairs:
the Sino-Japanese War, the German takeover of Austria, the Spanish Civil
War, possible German aggression in Czechoslovakia, Japanese threats to
American interests in Asia, the response of other major powers in Europe
and Asia toward the Soviet Union."[21] Moreover, Stalin could have
matched documents that Hiss pilfered against American encrypted cables
to crack the U.S. code.

What was Alger Hiss doing when he manually transcribed documents
that were routed through his office? How did Whittaker Chambers, an
admitted courier for the Soviet spy apparatus, get hold of the documents
after they were in Hiss's possession? Why did these transcriptions contain
sensitive information? Does it seem possible that a man who shared a
home with another man for months and gave him several large "loans"
would not recognize that man? The answers to these questions did not
bode well for Hiss.

If the Pumpkin Papers weren't convincing enough, several other witnesses came forward to corroborate Chambers's charges. Hede Massing,
known in her spying days as Hede Gompertz, testified to knowing Alger
Hiss as an agent of the Soviet Union. Julian Wadleigh, the State Department official who had passed on secret documents to Soviet courier
Whittaker Chambers during the 1930s, confessed in 1948 that Chambers's charges against him were true. Esther Chambers swore to her husband's activities and her family's relationship to the Hisses. In 1952,
Nathanial Weyl, an Agricultural Adjustment Administration colleague of
Hiss's during the New Deal, came forward to report that Hiss was a fellow Communist. Despite the various individuals who joined Chambers in
accusing Hiss of covert Communist activities, the controversy continued
to be portrayed as a "he said, he said" ordeal. "Only Whittaker Chambers
said things about Hiss which Hiss denied, and which nobody could corroborate—except Chambers's wife," claims John Chabot Smith.[22] Clearly,

it wasn't just the word of Whittaker Chambers against Alger Hiss; it was the word of several people against Hiss.

TWO TRIALS

The startling turn of events brought on by the revelation of the documents Chambers had kept hidden for more than a decade changed the case dramatically. The libel suit that Hiss had filed against Chambers was dead in the water. Public opinion, which had been largely split, shifted to Chambers. The Truman administration, perhaps smarting from the political damage Chambers had inflicted, initially sought to indict Chambers for perjury. Since Chambers had lied when he initially claimed that Hiss had not engaged in espionage activities, there is little doubt that legally such a charge would have been on solid ground. The Pumpkin Papers, however, made it politically untenable for the Justice Department to pursue Chambers while it ignored Hiss. On December 15, 1948, a federal grand jury indicted Alger Hiss.

The statute of limitations had run out on the charge of espionage, so Hiss was indicted on two counts of perjury. One charge pertained to his claim that he did not know Chambers after 1936, the other to his denial of handing documents over to Chambers.

The first Hiss trial began on May 4, 1949. Judge Stanley Kaufmann, lambasted for bias throughout the trial, excluded crucial prosecution witnesses Hede Massing, who had identified the defendant as a coconspirator in the Soviet underground, and William Rosen, the Communist organizer who had received Hiss's old Ford. With eight votes for conviction and four for acquittal, the jury stood deadlocked, and the trial ended on July 8.

The second trial launched on November 17, 1949. In addition to a new judge and jury, Hiss got a new lawyer. Rosen and Massing got to testify during the new trial, and the jury also heard from defense psychiatric experts—experts who had never examined their subject—who deemed the prosecution's chief witness, Chambers, a pathological liar. On January 21, 1950, a jury convicted Alger Hiss on two counts of perjury. Ostensibly, the conviction was for perjury; in reality, everyone knew that his real crime was espionage.

VENONA AND THE SOVIET ARCHIVES

After serving forty-four months of a five-year sentence, Alger Hiss was released from prison on November 27, 1954. A few days later, Joseph McCarthy was condemned by his colleagues in the Senate. The intensity with which anti-Communists sought out subversives in government quickly subsided because of both their past effectiveness and their declining fervor. A decade later, academics would look back on the postwar years as the "Red Scare," with Alger Hiss as its chief martyr. With President Nixon's fall from grace, his former antagonist began to be viewed in a new light. The government restored Hiss's pension, the Massachusetts bar reinstated him, and the *New York Times* published an op-ed by him. By 1976, an informal poll of prominent thinkers split down the middle on the question of Hiss's guilt or innocence.[23]

If the lessening of Cold War tensions in the 1960s and '70s was a benefit to Alger Hiss, its end in the early 1990s harmed him greatly.

In 1995, the U.S. National Security Agency (NSA) declassified its Venona program, which had intercepted Soviet spy cables during the Roosevelt-Truman era. Although it intercepted more than 100,000 Soviet transmissions, the NSA managed to decipher about 2,900 messages, many of which remain only partially translated. Since it intercepted messages during a limited time period, didn't intercept every message, and translated only about 2 percent of the messages it did intercept, Venona could provide only a glimpse into the inner workings of the Communist conspiracy. This peephole did show that at least 349 residents of the United States were involved with the Soviet spying apparatus and that a sizable number of these people worked for the federal government.[24] It also reconfirmed that one of Moscow's most valuable men in Washington was Alger Hiss.

A Venona intercept dated March 30, 1945, discusses a Soviet spy codenamed ALES, whom the NSA determined was "[p]robably Alger Hiss."[25] The message reports that "ALES has been working with the NEIGHBORS [Soviet military intelligence] continuously since 1935" and notes, "For some years past he has been the leader of a small group . . . for the most part consisting of his relations." The missive mentioned ALES's role in providing military, and not "BANK [State Department]," intelligence. Finally, it revealed, "After the Yalta Conference, when he had gone on to Moscow," ALES was awarded medals by the Soviet government.[26] Like

ALES, Alger Hiss worked in the State Department, went to the Yalta Conference, and traveled to Moscow at the conclusion of the historic summit along with three other men: Secretary of State Edward Stettinius, Stettinius's aide Wilder Foote, and Office of European Affairs director Freeman Matthews. Of the four, only Hiss had any allegations of spying lodged against him. Chambers alleged that Hiss began espionage activities in 1935 and was an agent of the GRU (Soviet military intelligence) rather than the NKVD, and that among his partners in treason were his brother Donald and his wife, Priscilla. If ALES and Alger Hiss seem to have a lot in common, it is because they are the same person.

In addition to Hiss, those Whittaker Chambers accused of espionage who appear in the intercepted Venona spy cables include John Apt, Frank Coe, Laurence Duggan, Charles Kramer, Victor Perlo, Abraham George Silverman, Harold Glasser, and Harry Dexter White.[27] Kramer, Perlo, and Glasser also appear in the limited number of files the Russians released after the collapse of the Soviet Union. So, too, do others Chambers named as espionage agents, including Ondra Emery, Marion Bachrach, J. Peters, Max Bedacht, and Phillip Rosenbliett.[28] The grand total of individuals Chambers accused of espionage who have since admitted the rectitude of his charges, or whom the Russians themselves have confirmed as Soviet agents, exceeds twenty.

Amazingly, Hiss partisans now claim that Venona *vindicates* their hero. Alger Hiss, John Lowenthal writes in *Intelligence and National Security*, "would have been pleased but not surprised to learn that Venona documents, released in the year of his death but too late for his comprehension, provide further confirmation of his innocence."[29] Lowenthal employs tortured logic to make this point. For example, he contends that the Venona intercept in question cannot be about Hiss, since it is dated 1945 and Chambers detailed Hiss's espionage only up until 1938; if Hiss indeed were a spy, Lowenthal argues, he would have had to have stopped in 1938.[30] Because we know Chambers ceased betraying his country at that time, it doesn't follow that Hiss did too. Since Chambers was unable to detail the inner workings of the Soviet underground after his departure from it, Lowenthal assumes it simply didn't exist—at least with Hiss as a member—after this point. "Nor is it believable," he adds, "that Soviet officials would have agreed in 1945, as they did agree, to the appointment of Hiss as secretary-general of the United Nations organizing conference in San Francisco if he was then one of their spies, given the diplomatic costs to the Soviet Union if he were to have been unmasked."[31] On the contrary, it was to the Soviets' advantage to have one of their agents guiding the founding of the United Nations—so much so that the Russians themselves, and not the Americans, suggested Hiss for the post.[32]

In addition to Venona, a series of documents retrieved from the archives of former Soviet bloc countries confirms the New Dealer's role in domestic subversion. In one memorandum sent to Moscow in 1936, Hede Gompertz expresses her concern about how Hiss attempted to recruit for his GRU apparatus Noel Field, who already reported to the NKVD: "Alger let him know that he was a Communist, that he was connected with an organization working for the Soviet Union and that he knew [Field] also had connections but he was afraid they were not solid enough, and probably, his knowledge was being used in a wrong way."[33] Gompertz's boss, the Russian station chief, then complains, "The result has been that, in fact, [Field] and Hiss have been openly identified to [Laurence Duggan]," another agent working within the government.[34] In a separate cable from a few weeks later, the station chief regretfully discusses Gompertz's meeting with Hiss: "As we understand, this occurred after our instruction that [Hiss] was 'the neighbors' man' [working with military intelligence], and that one should leave him alone."[35] This series of dispatches identically matches Gompertz's midcentury description of her interactions with Hiss in the 1930s.[36]

As shown by Czechoslovakian and Hungarian archived material, the object of Hiss's ill-advised attempts at recruitment would confirm his suitor's role in espionage. Noel Field, who defected behind the Iron Curtain, confessed to Hungarian interrogators—interrogators who believed Field to be a spy for the United States!—that he was a Soviet spy. Field reported to his captors that Alger Hiss, who had once recommended him for a State Department job in the Philippines, was one of his associates.[37] Since his confession came under duress during a time when Stalinist paranoia was devouring committed Communists like Field, skeptics balk at the confession's significance. If viewed apart from the corroborating material, the Field statements might rightly be taken with a grain of salt. But because his words mirror the testimony of Hede Gompertz, as well as statements by Soviet spymaster Iskhak Akhmerov uncovered after the fall of the Soviet Union, Field's disclosure carries some weight.

Other documents outline Moscow's reaction to Chambers's damaging 1948 testimony. One Soviet intelligence officer wired a proposal to frame Chambers as a Nazi:

As "Karl" [Chambers's primary underground pseudonym while a Soviet agent] is of German origin [and] lived and studied for some time in Berlin, [we could] "find" in German archives "Karl's" file from which it would become clear that he is a German agent who by Gestapo instructions was carrying out espionage work in the U.S. and penetrated into the American Communist Party. If we claim it in our press and publish some "documents" which could be produced at home, the effect of this will be very great. This information will be snatched not only by foreign Communist parties but by the progressive press in all countries, and, as a result, positions of the Committee on Un-American Activities, the grand jury [then considering testimony from Hiss, Chambers, and others on the matter] and other organs will be strongly undermined.[38]

Moscow rejected the plan not because it doubted that Western progressives would buy it but because the story might reflect poorly on Hiss, White, and other agents accused of involvement with Chambers. These agents, it was conjectured, might then cooperate with U.S. officials because their Soviet bosses had sold them down the river by portraying them as collaborators with the "Nazi" Chambers.[39]

DISTORTING THE RECORD

Upon Alger Hiss's death in 1996, news items broadcast on NBC's and ABC's nightly news, and printed by the Associated Press, Reuters, and the *Washington Post*, mentioned nothing of Venona but bizarrely claimed that the convicted perjurer had been exonerated in the last years of his life. "He protested his innocence until the very end," Peter Jennings, for instance, reported on ABC's *World News Tonight*, "and last year we reported that Russian President Boris Yeltsin said that KGB files had supported Mr. Hiss's claim."[40] President Yeltsin had never said anything like that.

Why would Peter Jennings and so many of his colleagues utter such baseless claims? In 1992, General Dmitri Volkogonov, a historian of the Soviet Union's intelligence apparatus, announced that there were no records of Hiss spying for the Soviet Union within the defunct nation's KGB archives. "I carefully studied many documents from the archives of the intelligence services of the USSR as well as various information provided for me by the archive staff," Volkogonov wrote. "On the basis of a very careful analysis of all the information available, I can inform you that Alger Hiss was never an agent of the intelligence services of the Soviet Union."[41] The announcement, Victor Navasky later bragged in the *Nation* magazine, "achieved page-one status across the country."[42]

An elderly Hiss labeled the general's assertions as the "final verdict" on the matter. Using words that came back to haunt the Hiss camp, the former State Department official proclaimed, "I can't imagine a more authoritative source than the files of the old Soviet Union."[43]

Shortly after issuing his proclamation, Volkogonov conceded that he had sent his letter at the request of Hiss's lawyer, John Lowenthal. "His attorney, Lowenthal, pushed me hard to say things of which I was not fully convinced," the Soviet general revealed.[44] Volkogonov admitted that he had not reviewed even a tiny fraction of the archived material and added that much of the material had been destroyed in the wake of Stalin's death. Informed that Hiss was accused of spying for the GRU, Russian military intelligence, and not the NKVD, the predecessor to the KGB, Volkogonov affirmed that even if a thorough search of the KGB archives had been done, it might not be relevant to this case. Peter Jennings, Tom Brokaw, and numerous other journalists issued retractions.[45] Ironically, as Western reporters announced the complete dearth of material about Alger Hiss in the Soviet archives, two historians uncovered numerous documents in the former KGB headquarters that once again confirmed the espionage activities of Hiss and Chambers. While false information that seems to help Hiss's case receives "page-one status," Soviet intelligence and intercepted Venona cables demonstrating his guilt are ignored.

Popular histories have further contributed to the confusion. What these works lack in facts, they attempt to make up for in conspiracy theories, psychoanalysis, and Alice-in-Wonderland portrayals of incriminating evidence as proof of innocence. These three major themes in the literature on the subject grant its progenitors the ability to make their form of analysis produce any conclusion they desire. The smear campaign Whittaker Chambers documented in his best-selling 1952 autobiography has continued for decades. "No depravity was too bizarre to 'explain' Chambers' motives for calling Hiss a Communist," he observed. "No hypothesis was too preposterous, no speculation too fantastic, to 'explain' how all those State Department documents came to be copied on Hiss's Woodstock typewriter. Only the truth became too preposterous to entertain."[46]

A common theme throughout pro-Hiss books is that the overwhelming evidence linking Hiss to espionage activities actually vindicates him, since no spy would be so foolish as to put himself in so many compromising positions. "Does anyone seriously doubt that, in ten years, Hiss couldn't have found a better way to dispose of the typewriter if he knew it to be an instrument of guilt?" asks Fred Cook in *The Unfinished Story of Alger Hiss*.[47] Nearly every pro-Hiss author remarks that if Hiss really were a spy, he would never have so closely associated himself with another spy, Chambers, by living with him and giving him various gifts. "A man would have to be a near idiot," Cook argues, "to entrust to others hand-written notes that, if discovered, would be damning proof of treason."[48] John Chabot Smith wonders, "Whoever heard of a spy carefully putting his initials on a stolen document before it was microfilmed, so that it could easily be traced to him if it fell into the wrong hands?"[49] By this tortured line of reasoning, every proof of guilt is really proof of innocence. It's as if a child stealing a candy bar were to be believed when he pleaded that the chocolate smeared all over his face actually vindicated him.

Another pro-Hiss book has tried to use psychoanalysis to prove that Chambers was a liar and explain his motives, much as Hiss's defense employed two psychiatrists to smear the accuser as a disturbed liar. In *Friendship and Fratricide*, Dr. Meyer Zeligs claims special insight into Chambers's personality by interpreting in a Freudian manner not only his poems and writings but, bizarrely, the books that he translated too. Among other things, Zeligs deduces that Chambers was sexually attracted to his brother Richard, willed Richard's suicide so he could be his mother's only son, and used Alger Hiss to relive his relationship with his late sibling.[50] How Chambers willed Richard's death when he saved him from previous suicide attempts goes unexplained. As he allegedly did to his brother Richard, Whittaker Chambers would have to destroy Alger Hiss if he were to reenact Richard's demise. Zeligs also reports that Whittaker Chambers was merely reenacting a book he had translated from German to English when he supposedly destroyed Richard Chambers and Hiss. Hiss's defense psychiatrists had similarly discovered parallels between this book, *Class Reunion*, and the Hiss-Chambers case. "There appears a banana stuffed with poison which may have furnished the explanation for the pumpkin stuffed with poisonous evidence in the form of microfilm" was how one psychiatrist tenuously connected fiction with fact.[51] Yet there seem to be few parallels between the book and the case, and Richard's death occurred before Chambers had read the book. Zeligs explains even Chambers's late-in-life return to college through psychoanalysis: "In this symbolic return Chambers . . . made restitution for his brother's ill-fated college career."[52] Finally, the psychoanalyst reports that when Chambers saw his own son John reach age twenty-five—Whittaker's own age when his brother committed suicide—the elder Chambers felt at ease to kill himself. It's an interesting theory, but it ignores a simple fact: Whittaker Chambers died of heart failure.[53]

As preposterous as Zeligs's psychobabble are the plentiful conspiracy theories trumpeted by Hiss partisans. Fred Cook, for instance, wonders, "Must [Chambers] have had, perhaps on several levels, official collaborators in the perfection of his story and the completion of his deed?"[54] One such theory parroted in the cottage industry of books on the subject is that the Woodstock typewriter that linked the defendant with the incriminating typed documents was a fake constructed by nefarious forces. Another wild hypothesis is that conspirators could obtain top-secret documents "by pinching them out of one of those wire baskets on a Monday morning when a messenger left his handcart briefly unguarded," or perhaps the messenger would give them away for "a small tip."[55] What about the handwritten copies Hiss penned? "The four handwritten notes were evidently picked out of a wastebasket, which could have been done by anyone who wanted to," one theorist offers.[56] Who stood behind these odious schemes? There are practically as many answers as there are conspiracy theories. The FBI, the KGB, the House Committee on Un–American Activities, Richard Nixon, Nazis, Trotskyists, and the Communist Party have been among those accused of manufacturing the plot against Hiss.[57] Like most conspiracies, they exist only in the minds of their theorists.

However ridiculous these authors' ideas are, one must remember that they wrote their books before Venona and the release of Soviet bloc documents. The thinking of Hiss's defenders prior to the fall of Communism, it could theoretically be argued, was based on ignorance and not dishonesty. Today, one can no longer offer as generous an assessment.

Entrusted with passing on the truth to the rising generation, higher education does the opposite. During his life, Alger Hiss garnered speaking invitations at such institutions as Harvard, Cornell, Princeton, and Columbia. In death he is memorialized by academia as the chief martyr of a midcentury "witch-hunt." New York's Bard College boasts an Alger Hiss Professor of Social Studies.[58] New York University has launched a website, funded in part by the *Nation* and administered by a Hiss confidant, aimed at vindicating Hiss.

The NYU website, titled "The Alger Hiss Story: Search for Truth," is particularly absurd in that its aim is the opposite of its stated goal. The site's time line on the case relies solely on Hiss's version of events. It claims that Chambers delivered the now-famous rug to Hiss as a repayment of a loan, not as a gift from the Soviet Union, that Hiss knew Chambers only as "George Crosley," and that the Hiss-Chambers relationship ended not because Chambers escaped the Soviet underground but because he refused to repay supposed loans from Hiss. Of greater significance than the fibs included are the facts excluded. Amazingly, the time line does not even mention the testimony of other former Communists, such as Nathaniel Weyl, detailing Hiss's work as a Soviet spy. The NSA's 1995 declassification of Soviet spy cables that identified Hiss as a spy against his own country and the documents released by the Russian government are completely absent from the time line as well. The former documents are mentioned on the site only in a manner suggesting that they vindicate the web page's subject. The latter documents are not mentioned at all, but General Volkogonov's letter—minus its author's disavowal of it—is.[59] The whole endeavor is an exercise in dishonesty.

These and other defenders of Alger Hiss are true believers. And true believers let nothing stand in the way of their faith. If facts interfere, they brush those facts aside or twist them to conform to their skewed vision of the world. Or like the creators of the NYU website, they simply pretend that inconvenient facts don't exist.

The evidence proving the veracity of the charges against Hiss is so overwhelming that many of his longtime defenders now acknowledge his guilt—sort of. As one anti-anticommunist historian put it, spies like Hiss merely "did not subscribe to traditional forms of patriotism."[60] Those who once reflexively shouted "witch-hunt" or "McCarthyism" at any accusation of Communism are today the first to dismiss the significance of the crimes committed by Cold War–era Communists after their guilt has been established. In grudgingly acknowledging what most have known for decades, these Hiss partisans still act as if the truth does not matter. One is left to wonder whether the anti-anticommunists ever thought accused Communists were innocent in the first place, or if they just argued their innocence because they believed the crimes of the accused were not crimes at all.

But they were crimes. "The American people, through the Constitution and under laws enacted by the Congress, invested in Presidents Roosevelt and Truman authority to share or not share the nation's secrets with our allies," scholars John Earl Haynes and Harvey Klehr note. "They did not invest that authority in Harry White, Theodore Hall, Alger Hiss or Lauchlin Currie. These men never went before American voters to ask for this authority or to account for their actions, but arrogated to themselves the right to give secrets to a foreign power. They betrayed the American people and the Constitution. Moreover, not one of them had the courage to admit what he had done and accept the consequences. Why admire and apologize for them?"[61]

"I am confident," Alger Hiss remarked after being found guilty, "that in the future the full facts of how Whittaker Chambers was able to carry out forgery by typewriter will be disclosed."[62] The full facts did come out. They did not reveal a plot to conduct "forgery by typewriter" by Whittaker Chambers, Richard Nixon, or J. Edgar Hoover. The facts uncovered from the files of intelligence agencies in both the United States and the Soviet Union confirm the rectitude of the allegations that Whittaker Chambers and others levied against Hiss. In the face of this, Hiss partisans demand new facts.

"IT'S TOTALLY RATIONAL"

The Gospel According to John Galt

*All active mass movements strive, therefore, to interpose a fact-proof
screen between the faithful and the realities of the world. They do this
by claiming that the ultimate and absolute truth is already embodied in
their doctrine and that there is no truth nor certitude outside it.
The facts on which the true believer bases his conclusions must not be
derived from his experience or observation but from holy writ.*

—ERIC HOFFER,
The True Believer

IN HIS 1971 LOW-BUDGET COMEDY *BANANAS*, WOODY ALLEN PLAYS A
bohemian Manhattanite feigning interest in radical politics to impress a
girl. Allen's character, Fielding Mellish, finds himself caught up in a
banana republic revolution in San Marcos, a fictional country in Latin
America. Esposito, the Castroish revolutionary Mellish follows, appears
as a noble leader who selflessly seeks to bring freedom to his people.
When Vargas, the military dictator, mistakenly sends for reinforcements
from the UJA—the United Jewish Appeal—instead of the CIA, Esposito
leads the rebels to victory. But as Esposito delivers his inaugural address
to the people, it is clear to Fielding Mellish and his cohorts that something has gone terribly wrong.

"Hear me!" Esposito imperiously declares. "I am your new president!
From this day on, the official language of San Marcos . . . will be Swedish.

"Silence!

"In addition to that, all citizens will be required to change their underwear every half hour. Underwear will be worn on the outside, so we can

check. Furthermore, all children under sixteen years old are now . . . sixteen years old."[1]

For the Objectivist followers of Ayn Rand, there would be many underwear-will-be-worn-on-the-outside moments.

Drawn to a philosophy that worshiped fact and reason, Objectivists would be taken by a charismatic leader into a web of insanity and unreason. By erasing excommunicated Randians, holding kangaroo courts, pretending the Soviets had staged *Sputnik*, swearing off family members, and adopting conformity in aesthetic predilections, Objectivists had become what they denounced. The coda for the organized Objectivist mass movement would be played when Rand demanded that her followers denounce her second-in-command for reasons she refused to divulge. Ironically, followers of a creed of selfishness were asked to sacrifice their own judgment in favor of blind faith in the judgment of one woman. Many did.

FROM ST. PETERSBURG TO HOLLYWOOD

With nearly 30 million books sold, Ayn Rand (1905–1982) is one of the most widely read authors of the past century. Based on the unfriendly response of critics and the infrequency of her name on college syllabi, one would never guess her enormous popularity. An early 1990s survey conducted by the Library of Congress and the Book of the Month Club found that save for the Bible, *Atlas Shrugged* was the most influential book among respondents.[2] Clearly, readers had launched a full-scale rebellion against critics and academics.

Hollywood legend Clark Gable is said to have erupted in a temper tantrum upon discovering that Warner Brothers, and not MGM, the studio that had him under contract, had purchased the rights to Rand's book *The Fountainhead*. MGM offered the rival studio nine times what it had paid for the rights, but Warner Brothers ultimately made the movie based on the Russian immigrant's novel and screenplay. The 1948 film starred Gary Cooper as Howard Roark.[3] In addition to several productions of her plays and a few movies based on her novels, Rand was the subject of the Oscar-nominated 1997 documentary *Ayn Rand: A Sense of Life*. Her novels are popular among businessmen. In the wake of the Enron scandal, many under-siege entrepreneurs supposedly found reinforcement for their beliefs in Rand, and corporate leaders of Burger King once encouraged company executives to read her work.[4] Some even credit her writings with helping to launch a political party. "Without Ayn Rand," attests Libertarian Party founder David Nolan, "the libertarian movement would not exist."[5] Individuals of diverse backgrounds credit Rand with influencing their lives, including tennis great Billie Jean King, *Sweet Pickles* author Jacquelyn Reinach, and rock drummer Neil Peart of Rush. By far the most influential of her followers is Alan Greenspan, longtime chairman of the Federal Reserve. Today, Greenspan appears as the archetypal Washington establishment figure. Earlier in life, as a member of the Randian "Collective," he was an active participant in the purges, star-chamber trials, and cultlike behavior that characterized Rand's inner circle.

Ayn Rand's philosophy, Objectivism, maintains that truth is attainable through reason, that rational self-interest should guide all human action, and that capitalism is the only moral system to govern man's interaction with man. Force and faith—"Attila" and "the Witch Doctor"—are its enemies.

Newcomers to the ideology are often shocked at the debased position that compassion, sacrifice, and altruism occupy within Objectivism. "Altruism holds that man has no right to exist for his own sake, that service to others is the only justification of his existence, and that *self-sacrifice* is his highest moral duty, virtue, and value," Rand wrote. "Capitalism and altruism are incompatible; they are philosophical opposites; they cannot co-exist in the same man or in the same society."[6] Just as the hostility to altruism catches those being introduced to Objectivism off-guard, the exalted status selfishness holds within Objectivism tends to surprise too. Rand declared, "The basic *social* principle of the Objectivist ethics is that just as life is an end in itself, so every living human being is an end in himself, not the means to the ends or the welfare of others—and, therefore, that man must live for his own sake, neither sacrificing himself to others nor sacrificing others to himself."[7]

If her ideas didn't shock Objectivist neophytes, her eccentric look did. A physical manifestation of the stereotypical stocky Russian female, Rand had darting, oversized dark eyes, a Dutch-boy haircut locked in a 1920s time warp, and eclectic accessories—including an elongated cigarette holder and a dollar-sign-capped walking stick—that made her stand out like a sore thumb. The tall, Aryan, rock-faced heroes that peopled her novels bore no physical resemblance to their creator. Their attitudinal and ideological similarities, however, were uncanny.

Born Alice Rosenbaum in St. Petersburg, Russia, Ayn Rand allegedly named herself by taking her first name from a male Finnish writer and her last from the Remington-Rand typewriter she used. As Ayn (rhymes with *line)* approached her twenty-first birthday, she begged her mother to send her to the United States. Emigration from the Soviet Union following the October Revolution was difficult, but the young woman's mother made the requisite sacrifices and found a way to satisfy her daughter's demand. On the eve of her departure, a fellow Russian implored, "If they ask you, in America—tell them that Russia is a huge cemetery, and that we are all dying slowly."[8] She told them in her 1936 novel *We the Living*. Few listened, at least at first. Just as the Roosevelt administration ignored Whittaker Chambers's charges against Alger Hiss, the American publishing industry didn't care to hear Rand's story of life in Soviet Russia, especially during the so-called Red Decade of the 1930s. The book was rejected by scores of publishers. MacMillan finally released a small press run, destroying the printing plates of a book that sold several million copies when it was rereleased in the more amenable climate of the late 1950s.[9]

In many ways, Rand personifies the classic American immigrant success story. This young Russian woman who could barely speak let alone write English became one of America's most widely read novelists. Along the way, she ironically enjoyed the charity of her cousins in Chicago and, later, the philanthropy of various kind souls in Hollywood eager to aid a struggling writer.[10] In the late 1920s, Rand embarked upon stints at various studios, including RKO and MGM, mostly poring over boring scripts rather than writing. Her 1929 marriage to Frank O'Connor, a strikingly handsome bit actor, would soften the coming harshness of life as a starving artist in Depression-era America. It would also solve a more immediate concern: citizenship. "Ours was a shotgun wedding," O'Connor joked, "with Uncle Sam holding the shotgun."[11] Rand's growing success as a studio writer and playwright, but not yet as a novelist, granted her modest financial success as the 1930s came to a close. Her breakthrough finally came with the release of her third novel, *The Fountainhead*, in 1943. It took her nearly fifteen years, but her follow-up, *Atlas Shrugged*, surpassed her earlier smash in terms of both sales and quality.

With the release of *Atlas Shrugged* in 1957, Ayn Rand was no longer a mere novelist. She was the leader of a burgeoning movement known as Objectivism.

THE NOVEL AS SCRIPTURE

The themes of Rand's four novels—*We the Living, Anthem, The Fountainhead,* and *Atlas Shrugged*—are identical. Each depicts the rational individual rebelling against an irrational world. As far as the philosophy of her novels goes, to read one is to read them all.

Her characters, too, are depressingly repetitive. Isn't *Atlas Shrugged*'s Hank Rearden just a male version of Dagny Taggart? All seem to be atheistic, workaholic, childless smokers who lack a sense of humor. Write about what you know, fledgling writers are often advised. Rand evidently took this maxim to heart. Rand's heroic leading men and women, we are supposed to believe, are without contradictions or flaws. This doesn't ring true to reality. In a certain sense, comic book heroes like the Hulk and Superman are more believable than the deiform John Galt and droidlike Howard Roark. It's easy to suspend disbelief for superpowers, ghastly monsters, or alien invasions, but for readers to believe that human nature has somehow been repealed is asking a bit much.

Take, for instance, Hank Rearden, whose Rearden Metal threatens to put his competitors out of business and make life better for consumers. Clearly, the reader of *Atlas Shrugged* is supposed to like Rearden. Yet the steel tycoon's robotic nature makes him hard to like. It is a task even to identify with him as a fellow person. "If his family called him heartless," *Atlas Shrugged* informs, "it was true."[12] An exchange with his mother, after his deadbeat family falls on hard times, typifies Rearden's icy personality:

> "Oh God, Henry, can't you see? All we want is only to know that you . . . that you feel some concern for us."
> "I don't feel it. Do you wish me to fake it?"
> "But that's what I'm begging you for—to *feel* it!"
> "On what ground?"
> "Ground?"
> "In exchange for what?"[13]

Rearden's love for Dagny Taggart is similarly soulless. "I love you," he proclaims. "As the same value, as the same expression, with the same pride and the same meaning as I love my work, my mills, my Metal, my hours at a desk, at a furnace, in a laboratory, in an ore mine, as I love my ability to work, as I love the act of sight and knowledge, as I love the action of my mind when it solves a chemical equation or grasps a sunrise, as I love the things I've made and the things I've felt, as *my* product, as *my* choice, as a shape of *my* world, as my best mirror, as the wife I've never had, as that which makes all the rest of it possible: as my power to live."[14]

Is the reader supposed to crack up laughing, or really believe that any woman would go for this? *Wuthering Heights*, it isn't.

If her heroes exude absolute perfection, her villains are absolute buffoons. Ellsworth Toohey's newspaper column "One Small Voice" in *The Fountainhead* typifies this clownish outlook. "A man braver than his brothers insults them by implication," his readers learn. "Let us aspire to no virtue which cannot be shared." "We are all brothers under the skin—and I, for one, would be willing to skin humanity to prove it," proclaims Toohey.[15] Rand's liberals are caricatures of real liberals, but perhaps she can't help it if many real liberals are themselves cartoonish.

Despite the flaws, Ayn Rand is read for good reason. The premise of *Atlas Shrugged*, for instance, is ingenious: What if the creative minds of the world went on strike? The idea alone is worth the cover price. No reader of Ayn Rand is going to get cheated by stream-of-consciousness nonsense; every paragraph, every sentence, every word has been labored over by an author who took her craft seriously. If her books were propaganda dressed up as novels (and they were), at least they were propaganda offsetting much of the rest of the propaganda in literature. The type of critic who would undoubtedly fawn over books like *The Jungle*, *Looking Backward*, or *The Crucible* was suddenly aghast that Rand would use the genre of fiction to radicalize an unsuspecting readership. Of most importance, her books entertain.

Taken as a novel, *Atlas Shrugged* is worth reading. As scripture, it falls short. And scripture is how *Atlas Shrugged* is viewed by Rand's followers, with *The Fountainhead*, *Anthem*, and *We the Living* seen as something akin to holy texts of lesser value.

AYN RAND, HIGH PRIESTESS

Rand rejected the God of Abraham, Isaac, and Jacob, but embraced the god of Dagny, Ragnar, and Francisco. Clearly, John Galt's creator intends him to be seen as a Christ-like figure. Galt's Gulch is heaven on Earth, and only the people who accept the principles of Objectivism gain admittance. Working a simple job, Galt and his disciples spread a revolutionary doctrine that promises to save humanity—or more accurately, those humans they deem worth saving. "Who is he to go against the whole world, against everything ever said for centuries and centuries?" James Taggart angrily wonders.[16] For spreading the good news through his pirate broadcast, John Galt becomes the target of the authorities. Galt's crucifixion comes by way of the torture device within the mysterious government military site "Project F." But like Christ, Galt cannot be stopped by his persecutors. Objectivism's Star of David, its cross, its crescent is the dollar sign. Dagny Taggart draws it in red lipstick on the base of a statue of her ancestral hero, Nathaniel Taggart. It appears on the cigarettes made in Galt's Gulch. John Galt traces the symbol in the dirt to bring the story to an end. It is the Objectivist holy sign.

If John Galt is a god, what does this make his creator? Among the true believers, Rand was a god. "You could almost look at her as a more advanced species of humanity than the normal person," one admirer said. Another professed, "The achievement of Ayn Rand may be compared to a skyscraper built in the midst of . . . mud-thatched huts."[17] Upset that someone had poked fun at Rand, one Objectivist curtly retorted, "[Y]ou wouldn't mock God."[18] Through Ayn's statements *and* example, her flock believed in the perfectibility of man. As we shall see, they set themselves up for a letdown.

If Objectivists see Rand as godlike, how does this make them any different from Catholics, Orthodox Jews, and others they ridicule for believing? Imitation is the sincerest form of flattery. Randians celebrate the anniversary of Rand's famous Ford Hall lectures as Objectivist Easter, cull *Atlas Shrugged* instead of the Bible for children's names, and substitute Objectivist psychoanalysis for confession. Whereas Christ's close disciples are known as the apostles, Rand's circle was known as the Collective. Excommunication awaited members of the Collective, and even mere students of Objectivism, who strayed from the party line. To avoid such a fate, Randians pore over her books like monks over the Bible. "Between the ages of fourteen and eighteen, I read and reread *The Fountainhead* almost continuously with the dedication and passion of a student of the Talmud," writes Nathaniel Branden, who became Rand's right-hand man. One passage he reread more than one hundred times, he says.[19] Author Jeff Walker tells the story of how Rand's designated intellectual heir, Leonard Peikoff, boasted of having read *The Fountainhead* sixty times but admitted that he did not fully understand its message regarding independence until the sixty-first reading.[20]

Objectivists have even held Randian weddings. At one such event in New York, a passage from the Objectivist holy book—*Atlas Shrugged*—was read and the couple pledged their loyalty to Ayn Rand.[21] Since Objectivism could rationally determine what singles belong together, leading Randians would play the role of cupid. When these unnatural unions ter-

minated, the Chuck Woolery–*Love Connection* figure would inevitably
pronounce that a hidden irrationality existed in one or perhaps both of
the parties.22 After all, there was nothing irrational about the scientific
manner in which they were brought together. Randians proved that they
could play homewrecker better than they played matchmaker. Among the
reasons that Nathaniel Branden banished anarcho-libertarian Murray
Rothbard from the circle was that Rothbard had married a Christian and
refused to leave her when she didn't succumb to anti-God audiotapes and
essays put out by the Objectivists.23

"C'MON GET HAPPY"

If Rigoberta Menchu and other relativists made the mistake of consign-
ing truth to their pile of outmoded concepts, Ayn Rand regularly confused her own subjective views with truth. Rather than being polar
opposites, relativists and Objectivists occupy opposite sides of the same
coin. Both commit offenses against truth: One denies it, the other con-
flates opinion with it.

"[I]t can be rationally proved," Rand held, "that the works of Victor
Hugo are *objectively* of immeasurably greater value than true-confession
magazines."24 No, it can't. No, something like this cannot be *objectively*
proven. What Randians considered "objective" were in fact personal
tastes—that is, Ayn Rand's eclectic tastes. Watching *Charlie's Angels*,
admiring the acting of Gary Cooper or Marlene Dietrich, taking up tap
dancing, reading the hard-boiled detective fiction of Mickey Spillane, or
praising the utilitarianism in modern architecture could all be proof of
some inner virtue. Conversely, appreciating art that Rand disliked became
a basis for damnation. Shakespeare, Beethoven, Rembrandt, and Van
Gogh, according to Rand, were mediocrities. Admiring their product
reflected a warped "sense of life." Objectivism was more like Subjectivism.

Just as evangelicals ask, "What would Jesus do?," Objectivists asked,
"What would Ayn do?" Out-of-step Randians either got their tastes in
order or found a new leader to follow. Longtime apostle Barbara Branden
explains: "[I]f a friend did not respond as she did, she left no doubt that
she considered that person morally and psychologically reprehensible.
One evening, a friend remarked that he enjoyed the music of Richard
Strauss. When he left at the end of the evening, Ayn said, in a reaction
becoming increasingly typical, 'Now I understand why he and I can never
be real soul mates. The distance in our sense of life is too great.'"25

"One must never fail to pronounce moral judgment," Rand stressed to her followers.[26] Unfortunately for her close friends, she went to embarrassing lengths to practice what she preached. "Attending any event with Ayn," Barbara Branden recalls, "was usually a traumatic experience: she rarely went to a movie, a play, a ballet, an opera, and when she did so she would announce her judgments in a clearly audible voice—and her judgments usually were negative. 'They must understand what immoral trash they're seeing,' she would insist when friends begged her not to disturb the audience. There was nothing her friends could do but wish they could hide under their seats until the ordeal was over."[27]

Rand's own peculiar affinities begged for sufferance. Tolerance for Objectivists whose artistic preferences departed from Rand's was not forthcoming from their guru. What is significant is not that Rand's own likings strike us as peculiar (whose tastes seem totally normal?), but that she was quick to condemn those who didn't share her quirky predilections. What, really, are we to make of a lover of the Partridge Family song "C'mon Get Happy" lecturing connoisseurs of Beethoven about the irrationality of their musical choices?

RANDROIDS

Strangely, a philosophy exalting individualism bred clones of its founder. Smoking became obligatory. WWAD? After all, hadn't *Atlas Shrugged* taught, "When a man thinks, there is a spot of fire alive in his mind—and it's proper that he should have the burning point of a cigarette as his one expression"?[28] Facial hair, frowned upon by the leader, became verboten. "A man wears a moustache or a beard," Rand declared, "because he wants to hide behind it; there's something he wants to conceal, not just a physical defect, but a spiritual defect; I would never trust such a man."[29] Objectivism had an insider language aping Rand's jargon. *A is A*, *sense of life*, *blank out*, *qua*, and *whim worshiper* were among the terms and phrases separating true Objectivists from the heathen. For some, speaking the *lingua franca* was not enough. One had to sound like Rand too. WWAD? Numerous Randians affected phony Russian accents—a spectacle leaving an indelible imprint on the memory of anyone witnessing it.

Randians enforced this culture of conformity by monitoring, denouncing, and snitching on their coreligionists. The Objectivist movement resembled a giant Communist Party cell of the 1950s, minus the FBI agents. If Objectivists didn't possess traits of paranoia and intolerance prior to joining, they could certainly pick them up by imitating their leader. Rand usually relied on question-and-answer periods at lectures—especially during the Q&A periods at other Objectivists' lectures—to tear into members of her flock. Margit von Mises, wife of economist Ludwig von Mises, expressed years after attending an Objectivist lecture that she was "shocked at Ayn Rand's behavior. . . . Someone asked her a question, and she answered in such a rude, disagreeable way that I couldn't understand how anyone could take it. She just killed the questioner with her reply. You can do indescribable harm to people that way."[30]

Nathaniel Branden recalls another such incident:

> Once, a man with a thick Hungarian accent began his question, "In his speech, Galt contends that . . ." He never got any further because Ayn exploded. "Galt does not *contend*," she shouted. "If you have read *Atlas Shrugged*, if you profess to be an admirer of mine, then you should know that Galt does not 'strive,' 'debate,' 'argue,' or 'contend.'" The man looked stricken. He pleaded, "But Miss Rand, all I meant was . . ." Ayn thundered back at him, "If you wish to speak to me, first learn to remember to whom and about what you are speaking!"[31]

Branden notes that the man never returned to the meetings. "I can still see the expression of hurt and shock on his face."[32]

"BAD PREMISES"

Bayou populist Huey Long once remarked that if fascism ever came to America, it would come by calling itself antifascism. Something akin to this is at work with regard to Objectivism. *Objectivism* the word bespeaks a detached, fact-based rationalism. Objectivism the philosophy too often reflects the biases of an interested party.

One event that challenged the validity of Rand's theory was the Soviet Union's launch of a satellite into space in the fall of 1957. The nation that most closely resembled the dystopias presented in Rand's novels couldn't possibly have accomplished such a mammoth achievement. Thus, the naturalized American dismissed *Sputnik* as an elaborate fraud. If Objectivism were true, then *Sputnik* was necessarily false. And so, within her circle, it became false—at least for a little while.[33]

With the exception of *Anthem*'s Equality 7–2521, just about all of Rand's major fictional heroes and heroines—Dagny Taggart, Howard Roark, Leo Kovalensky, John Galt, Hank Rearden—smoked. Rand herself was something of a human chimney, smoking two packs of Tareytons every day for several decades. When she came down with lung cancer in the final decade of her life, her fetishization of smoking as an objectively virtuous activity initially overcame common sense. Her doctor pled with her to stop. "But *why?*" Rand asked. "And don't tell me about statistics; I've explained why statistics aren't proof. You have to give me a *rational* explanation. *Why* should I stop smoking?"[34] Apparently, astronomically higher rates of lung cancer for smokers vis-à-vis nonsmokers failed to register as proof.[35] Nathaniel Branden remembers that she claimed statistics linking smoking to cancer "were put out by people trying to destroy free enterprise and the cigarette industry. She would not accept *any* evidence that smoking was bad for you."[36]

If smoking didn't cause cancer, what did? According to Barbara Branden, Rand "tended to think that cancer, as well as many other illnesses, was the result of what she termed 'bad premises'—that is, of philosophical-psychological errors and evasions carried to their final dead end in the form of physical destruction." Yet even this Objectivist explanation for disease became an intellectual conundrum for Rand. "How could she have had a malignancy, when she had no bad premises?"[37]

Sometimes, though, even Rand recognized problems with her ideas. After the initial press run of her 1936 novel *We the Living*, she made a substantial alteration to hide some rather ugly sentiments. In the original version of the book, the character Andrei intones, "[W]e can't sacrifice millions for the sake of the few." In response, the novel's heroine, Kira, proclaims:

> You can! You must. When those few are the best. Deny the best its right to the top—and you have no best left. What are your masses but mud to be ground underfoot, fuel to be burned for those who deserve it? What is the people but *millions of puny, shriveled, helpless souls* that have no thoughts of their own, no dreams of their own, no will of their own, who eat and sleep and chew helplessly the words others put into their mildewed brains? And for those you would sacrifice the few who know life, who are life? I loathe your ideals because I know no worse injustice than justice for all.

Because men are not born equal and I don't see why one should want to make them equal. And because I loathe most of them.[38]

The bowdlerized version omits Kira's fantasy of liquidating the masses, sanitizes much of the harsh language, and tones down the rhetoric concerning equality and justice.[39]

Perhaps the most antireason aspect of Objectivism is its insecure avoidance of ideas that challenge its fundamental principles. "You know what my policy is?" asked Rand. "I don't deal with those who disagree."[40] Not having the argument is certainly one way of ensuring that you never lose the argument. Her disdain for ideas that differed from her own was so great that, according to one author, she reviewed books and movies that she did not read or view.[41] From the grave, Rand apparently bequeathed this quirk to her intellectual heirs. "I certainly do not recommend this book," Leonard Peikoff said of Barbara Branden's biography of Rand, crucially adding, "I have not read it and do not intend to do so."[42] WWAD?

RAND ON RAND

When writers attempt to buttress their point, they often cite statistics, rely on studies, or quote authorities in the field. When Ayn Rand sought to bolster her arguments, she quoted Ayn Rand.

"The key to understanding the encyclical's social theories," Rand wrote on a papal letter, "is contained in a statement of John Galt."[43] She once told a University of Wisconsin audience, "Since I am to speak on the Objectivist Ethics, I shall begin by quoting its best representative—John Galt, in *Atlas Shrugged*."[44] (Did the undergraduates in Madison even realize that the Mr. Galt she quoted was as real as Cinderella or Mickey Mouse?) Rand even quoted her fictional enemies in order to refute their points. "To help you untangle this, I can only quote Ellsworth Toohey in *The Fountainhead*," she wrote in a collection of articles.[45]

Her book *The Virtue of Selfishness* is peppered with such self-references. While she quoted from or referred readers to her own work more than a dozen times, she never quoted another individual—with the exception of her chief acolyte, Nathaniel Branden—in an approving manner. She did cite the Declaration of Independence, the Bill of Rights, and the *New York Times*, but that is it. Her other works of nonfiction follow a similar pattern.

Repeatedly quoting oneself, or one's fictional alter egos, is highly unusual. Why did Rand do it? There are several contributing explanations:

1. For Rand and her followers, it was important that Rand be thought of as the sole originator of her ideas. With the exception of Aristotle, she owed a philosophical debt to no one.[46] "That someone might be influenced by his or her teachers is a rather uncontroversial thesis," writes Rand scholar Chris Sciabarra. "Yet when placed within the context of Rand scholarship, this thesis has been criticized by some who believe that mere consideration of Rand's possible predecessors constitutes an assault on her originality."[47]

2. While debate occurred within Objectivist circles regarding whether Nathaniel Branden or Aristotle occupied the position of second greatest philosopher, it was clear to Objectivists that Rand was the greatest thinker in human history. If Rand was the giant she claimed, wouldn't it be beneath her to defer to the words of lesser men?

3. Ayn Rand was too smart for her own good. If you think you know it all, learning is a waste of time. Rand possessed incredible brilliance but lacked any passion for reading. Nathaniel Branden remarks that Rand "was not a conscientious scholar of the history of philosophy. Far from it; in the eighteen years of our relationship, I cannot recall a single book on philosophy that she read from cover to cover. She skimmed."[48] His ex-wife, Barbara, concurs: "She was never a voracious reader, and as the years passed she read less and less."[49] Why did she need to know facts when her philosophy already supplied her with all the answers? Murray Rothbard observed, "[M]any ex-cultists remain imbued with the Randian belief that every individual is armed with the means of spinning out all truths *a priori* from his own head—hence there is felt to be no need to learn the concrete facts about the real world, either about contemporary history or the laws of the social sciences. Armed with axiomatic first principles, many ex-Randians see no need of learning very much else."[50]

4. Quoting herself was an exercise in egoism in action. For the woman who proclaimed "the virtue of selfishness," what more audacious celebration of the self could there be than to act as if no other great thinkers existed and to refer her readers to her writings alone?

5. Her philosophy came out better when interacting with fictional straw men and perfect demigods than it did with real-life individuals. Real

people scoffed at the idea of putting her theories into practice. But John Galt didn't. Neither did Kira Argounova, Howard Roark, or Francisco d'Anconia. In response to an otherwise positive review that labeled *Atlas Shrugged* an allegory, Rand angrily declared, "My characters are *not* symbols."[51] If they weren't symbols, what were they? As Rand became increasingly detached from the outside world, the world she created inside her head became a more dominant part of her existence. "I thought that for all the years of writing the novel [*Atlas Shrugged*]," Nathaniel Branden remembers, "Ayn had lived with Dagny, Rearden, Francisco, and Galt as her daily companions."[52]

Randians operate in a closed environment. This circular philosophy ensures that conclusions conform to Objectivism. It's telling that Rand condemned potential allies peddling competing ideas in harsher terms than she used to condemn ideological enemies pushing opposing ideas.[53] Note, too, the mantra of not giving sanction to the enemy by reading their works. A weak philosophy can withstand neither criticism nor exposure to outside ideas. With debate shunned, nonapproved books ignored, and adherents expected to read and reread *Atlas Shrugged* and *The Fountainhead*, all roads lead to Ayn Rand.

SEX, LIES, AND OBJECTIVISM

What if readers of *Atlas Shrugged* and *The Fountainhead* could be organized into a society of like-minded individuals? Nathaniel Branden set out to do this in the late 1950s. With a skeptical Rand's authorization, he began by offering courses on Objectivism in Manhattan. To Rand's surprise, the lectures elicited an overwhelming response. The courses spread like wildfire. Rand, though comfortable with her confidant Branden acting as her mouthpiece, was apprehensive about letting others speak on behalf of Objectivism. Thus, instead of finding local surrogates, Branden mainly conducted the lectures through audiotapes as they grew in popularity. Though it might be difficult to envision rooms packed with people eager to listen to a machine, this is exactly what happened. Thousands enrolled in the classes by the mid-1960s, with such exotic locations as a Polaris submarine beneath the Atlantic Ocean and an Arctic Circle outpost in Greenland hosting courses.[54]

The 1960s were Objectivism's golden age. Rand gave nationally televised interviews with Mike Wallace and Johnny Carson, delivered speeches to business and campus groups, and began delving into nonfiction writing. By 1968, the newsletter *The Objectivist* had more than twenty thousand subscribers. Objectivist clubs began appearing. The vortex of this universe was the Nathaniel Branden Institute (NBI), an educational organization designed to propagate Ayn's ideas, which ultimately set up shop in the Empire State Building. NBI's headquarters hosted lectures, monthly dances, theatrical performances, films, even a fashion show. If Objectivists viewed Rand as an ephemeral god living on a Mount Olympus six stories above Thirty-fourth Street, they saw Nathaniel Branden as her earthly vicar spreading the gospel to the elect.

Unbeknownst to all but the two couples involved, Nathaniel Branden and Ayn Rand embarked on a fourteen-year affair in 1954. At the advent of the romance, the paramours met twice weekly in Rand's apartment. If Frank hadn't yet departed, Nathaniel's arrival would mean temporary exile for the washed-up actor from his own home. Branden would then have sex with O'Connor's wife in O'Connor's bed. Today, Branden acknowledges his behavior as "barbaric."[55]

Initially, Rand and Branden promised their meetings would be purely platonic. That changed within a short time, which left Rand scrambling to justify the affair. There was the twenty-five-year age gap, the adultery, and the abuse of the mentoring relationship. Yet Rand sought moral approval for the seedy affair from the two victimized parties: Barbara Branden and Frank O'Connor. "But it is the logic of who we are that led us to this," she told the left-out twosome. "It's completely rational that Nathan and I should feel as we do toward each other. It's totally rational, given our premises, that our feelings would include the sexual."[56] Rand's domineering personality and sophist's wisdom ensured that she received their sanction.

They had initially told their spouses that the relationship wouldn't evolve into a sexual one, and now that it had, they had to lie to their fellow Objectivists. "But, of course, *lie* was a word we never used," remembers Nathaniel Branden. "We didn't have to. We had a philosophical explanation for everything."[57]

The bizarre situation accelerated Frank's drinking, transforming him into a full-fledged alcoholic. Rand, who could never see the real Frank through the mythic Frank she created, denied his drinking. Years later, when numerous liquor bottles were found in Frank's painting studio after his death, Rand defensively claimed that her husband had merely used the bottles for mixing paints.[58]

Frank O'Connor was but one casualty of the affair. Barbara Branden began suffering panic attacks. During a particularly vicious attack, Mrs. Branden felt compelled to do something she had never done before: phone her husband during one of his semiweekly "meetings" with Rand. The temperamental writer erupted in a fury. "How dare you!" Rand intoned. "Do you think *only* of yourself? Am I *completely* invisible to you? *I* don't ask anyone for help! There's your whole problem in the fact that you called—if you *want* something, that's all you know or care about! Don't dare to dream of coming here!"[59]

No one came out of the affair unscathed. This was especially true of Ayn Rand.

Over a period of months in 1968, the truth trickled in to Objectivism's high priestess. As Rand had aged, the physical relationship with Branden cooled. The affair had become more platonic. When she tried to resume her sexual relationship with Nathaniel Branden, the aging author's swain resisted. Soon Nathaniel informed her that he wanted out of the relationship. Later, Rand learned that he had been cheating on her since 1964 with a stunningly beautiful actress many years her junior. Finally, Barbara Branden came clean that she had known of Nathaniel's new romance for several years without telling Rand. The champion of reason exploded in an insane rage. Think Glenn Close in *Fatal Attraction*.

"You bastard, you bastard!" Rand repeated upon hearing the truth of his other relationship. "You nothing! You fraud! You contemptible swine!" Nathaniel Branden recalls an unstable Rand leaping and shouting, "I don't want to be alone in the same room with you! I want Barbara here! I want Barbara to know about this obscenity!" Rand then called the divorced Mrs. Branden and ordered, "Come down at once and see what this monster has done!"[60] For Rand, nothing seemed amiss in enlisting the woman whose marriage she had broken up to partake in a ritual condemnation of her former husband for the sin of cheating on his longtime mistress.

The bitter abuse persisted for several weeks. "You have no right to casual friendships, no right to vacations, no right to sex with some inferior woman! Did you imagine that I would consent to be left on the scrap heap? Is that what you imagined? Is it?" Rand rhetorically asked her former beau.[61]

Finally, the day of reckoning had arrived. The man who had issued the expulsion order to so many Objectivists now faced excommunication himself—social life, friendships, a life's work all down the drain. Robes-pierre's turn at the guillotine had come.

"Get that bastard down here!" Rand commanded. On August 23, 1968, Nathaniel Branden made the lonely elevator ride down fourteen floors to Rand's apartment. "What a loathsome creature you are!" she lec-tured. Amid abusive comments, such as calling him a "Peter Keating"* and wishing him impotence, the sixty-three-year-old woman scorned smacked Branden several times. "You have rejected *me? You* have dared to reject *me?*"[62] It was done. Ayn Rand had excommunicated Nathaniel Branden. For the Objectivists, it was as if Jesus had expelled St. Peter, or Alabama had fired Bear Bryant. While the public never stopped reading Rand's fiction, the movement she spawned never fully recovered.

AFTERMATH

The leader of a movement that stressed reason and independent thought threatened to expel followers who refused to denounce Nathaniel Bran-den at her command. No explanation, just Rand's whim, was given for the ceremonial denunciation. But she made quite clear that she had banished her onetime protégé. Rand removed his name from the dedication of *Atlas Shrugged*, and in a 1970 addendum to several of her nonfiction books, she rather gratuitously informed readers, "P.S. Nathaniel Branden is no longer associated with me, with my philosophy or with *The Objec-tivist.*"[63] Privately she sought vengeance wherever possible. Rand vowed to stop the publication of Nathaniel Branden's book, which she had labeled a "work of genius" before the split.[64] She failed to get the literary agency she employed to drop him as a client, but the book company that had contracted to publish Branden's book did drop the author on a pre-text.[65] Some actually believed that Rand wanted Nathaniel dead, and at least one student of Objectivism wondered aloud whether it would be eth-ically right to kill Nathaniel Branden.[66]

Not unlike other internecine conflicts, the Branden-Rand split of the late 1960s pitted doctor against patient, teacher against student, and sib-ling against sibling—literally. Objectivist psychologists who refused to

---

*Architect Peter Keating is the villainous parasite in *The Fountainhead* who lacks original-ity and pilfers ideas from others.

take the loyalty oath lost clients.[67] Instructors leading Objectivist courses enjoined students to sign contracts that forbade contact with the Brandens and banned students from buying any future books by either of them.[68] For almost a decade, two of Nathaniel Branden's sisters shunned their brother.[69] To this day, Leonard Peikoff, Barbara Branden's cousin and Rand's designated heir, refuses to speak with Mrs. Branden.[70] Long-time friends treated the Brandens as nonpersons. Barbara Branden's stockbroker sent her a terse missive informing her that he would no longer manage her money.[71]

The result of the loyalty oaths, trials, excommunications, and purges was somewhat predictable. Objectivists maintaining independence and self-respect refused to go along with the hysteria. Rand tossed them out of the movement, and along with them went all of Objectivism's free minds. Weak-minded followers remained. This guaranteed that the official movement would be composed of easily led danglers unable to think outside of the narrow constraints Rand put in place.

In the decades since, Rand's devoted followers have done whatever they can to portray their leader as a godlike being. Like Stalin airbrushing Trotsky out of revolution-era photographs, Randians have erased from their official history the Brandens and other *personae non gratae*. In tapes of Rand lectures from the 1950s that are marketed today, an overdub of a narrator overwhelms the voices of Nathaniel and Barbara Branden.[72] The documentary *Ayn Rand: A Sense of Life* totally glosses over the nasty conclusion to the covert Rand-Branden romantic relationship, with Leonard Peikoff feigning ignorance by saying that "one thing or another precipitated the break."[73]

It isn't just ex-friends that Rand's groupies have erased. When her own words seemed incongruent with her public philosophy, they were tossed down the memory hole. In a single passage from a posthumously published Rand journal entry, Chris Sciabarra discovered a half dozen alterations—four of importance—from the original. Most significant, Rand's estate erased a reference to Old Right author Albert Jay Nock from the original.[74]

"CRAZY"

Social movements that embrace the cult of personality become writ-large reflections of the object of their veneration. This doomed Objectivism.

Modeling oneself after an unstable and abusive woman is tragic. A mass movement imitating such a person is dangerous.

In *Bananas*, Woody Allen's Fielding Mellish and his silver-screen comrades depose their leader Esposito when they hear his demands that the citizens of San Marcos speak Swedish and wear their underwear on the outside of their pants. When Ayn Rand made her underwear-on-the-outside demands, her followers further indulged her. In the end, Objectivism taught not the submission of all else to the self, but the submission of the self to Ayn Rand. What phenobarbital and vodka was to Heaven's Gate, and poisoned Kool-Aid was to the People's Temple, Ayn Rand's rationalizing egomania was to Objectivism.

Onetime friend Edith Ephron, who saw Rand as a "manipulative," "repressed" woman suffering from "very complicated paranoia," perhaps provided Rand's most fitting epitaph: "There is no way to communicate how crazy she was."[75]

"COMFORTABLE CONCENTRATION CAMP"

Feminism's Fitting Matriarch

I am woman, hear me roar.

—HELEN REDDY

"SOME MEN BELIEVE THAT WOMEN ARE IRRATIONAL, ILLOGICAL, incompetent, emotion-driven and unreliable," Ayn Rand wrote in the 1970s. "Women's Lib sets out to disprove it by the spectacle of sloppy, bedraggled, unfocused females stomping down the streets and chanting brief slogans, over and over again, with the stuporous monotony of a jungle ritual and the sulkiness of a badly spoiled child."[1]

Rand proved an enigmatic figure to many feminists. A fiercely independent woman, Rand chose career over children, tenaciously supported a right to abortion, and left us with some of the most unforgettable heroines in the history of literature. Yet Rand scathingly mocked feminists. In one such barb, she remarked, "Women's Lib screams protests against the policy of regarding women as 'sex objects'—through speakers who, too obviously, are in no such danger."[2]

Some postulate that Rand herself was a feminist of a sort. She demanded equality under the law for women and the same political freedoms as men, but not much else. Perhaps one could say that Rand was a practitioner of individualist feminism. The activists she mocked, on the other hand, might be labeled followers of collectivist feminism, which demands preferences based on sex, tax-funded abortions, statutory prohibitions against all-male private clubs, and other favorable treatment from the state. One feminism looks to government for empowerment. The other looks for government to get out of the way.

A member of this former group of feminists—who experienced her movement's heyday at roughly the same time as Objectivism's golden age—ironically saw the treatise on womanhood that she authored receive a favorable review from Ayn Rand's newsletter.[3] Betty Friedan's 1963 book, *The Feminine Mystique*, is often credited with launching the modern feminist movement in America. Claiming that too many women lived unfulfilling lives trapped as housewives, the forty-something writer called for women to seek opportunities outside the home. The book's revolutionary potential was immediately obvious to many. Paraphrasing Marx, one excited reader humorously wrote to Friedan, "To arms, sisters! You have nothing to lose but your vacuum cleaners."[4] Millions of women would buy the book.

Friedan presented herself as a typical stay-at-home mom of that era. She was anything but that. Far from being simply a wife and mother, she was a longtime political activist who, as her husband later admitted, took little interest in the family's home life. Yet the image of the put-upon homemaker was critical to the success of *The Feminine Mystique* and ultimately to the success of the modern feminist movement.

So what if it wasn't true? It served the cause.

Friedan would stretch the truth in other ways to further her agenda. Too many journalists and historians accepted her stories at face value. Little wonder, then, that Betty Friedan became such an admired activist for women's rights. She helped found the National Organization for Women (NOW) and served as its first president. She was instrumental in the creation of the National Association for the Repeal of Abortion Laws (NARAL), the National Women's Political Caucus, and numerous other groups promoting liberal stances on women's issues. During the 1970s, she spearheaded the failed effort to codify the Equal Rights Amendment. Her outspokenness earned her audiences with Indira Gandhi, the shah of Iran, Golda Meir, United Nations Secretary-General Kurt Waldheim, and Pope Paul VI. Harvard, Yale, Northwestern, Cornell, New York University, the University of Southern California, Temple, and numerous other schools have hired her to teach.

Betty Friedan is the mother of modern feminism, even if she sometimes disagrees with the positions her offspring have adopted. Once extreme, many of her ideas have become mainstream. Her effectiveness has pushed the perimeters of debate farther left, allowing her progeny to take positions even more radical than she dared, or cared, to take.

FRIEDAN'S SELF-PORTRAIT VS. REALITY

The Feminine Mystique gave a name to what Betty Friedan characterized as the problem that had no name. The problem that she spoke of was the lack of meaning in the average postwar woman's life. The mystique pushed women to conform to a conception of femininity that robbed them of any purpose outside the home. Besides home, husband, and children, what fulfillment could women find in their lives? Friedan hinted that these problems were the result of a conspiracy. Since "so few have any purpose in life other than to be a wife and mother, somebody, something pretty powerful must be at work."[5] Those to blame for the advance of the mystique, the author argued, included Sigmund Freud, women's magazines, advertising executives who created the consumer culture, anthropologist Margaret Mead, and women's education geared toward married life. "In a sense that is not as far-fetched as it sounds," the manifesto screamed, "the women who 'adjust' as housewives, who grow up wanting to be 'just a housewife,' are in as much danger as the millions who walked to their own death in the concentration camps—and the millions more who refused to believe that the concentration camps existed."[6] Thus, she famously described the home as a "comfortable concentration camp."[7]

Central to the appeal of *The Feminine Mystique* was the idea that Friedan wrote from experience. American women bought the book in droves because the author presented herself as one of them. But the self-image Friedan painted was far different from her life's real history. More than three decades after she styled herself as a locked-up, middle-class everywoman, biographer Daniel Horowitz uncovered the truth about Friedan, showing that she had greatly embroidered her tale.

The mother of American feminism was not a child of Harvard Square or Greenwich Village, but of Peoria, Illinois. The young Bettye Goldstein (she would later drop the "e") grew up in Peoria, in a family of great wealth that afforded her a luxurious home life. According to Horowitz, "a maid cleaned the house, a nurse took care of the children when they were young, and on special occasions a man served as chauffeur and butler."[8]

She experienced some of the same benefits when she married Carl Friedan, an advertising executive who earned a large income. The Friedans vacationed in trendy spots, and she could afford to visit psychoanalysts at will. In 1957, the Friedans moved into not-so-Spartan living quarters overlooking the Hudson River. The mansion they inhabited was located in a relatively wealthy New York county and cost $25,000, which made it more expensive than 95 percent of the county's residences at that time. As Horowitz describes it, "The house had eleven rooms, three bathrooms, and many elegant details such as marble fireplaces, French doors, and arched windows. It stood on an acre of land overlooking the river; on the hill above the house was a large, spring-fed natural pool."[9] An Auschwitz on the Hudson her household was not.

A maid who worked three to four days a week usurped the traditional duties of homemaker. The parents of her children's playmates even ejected Friedan from their carpooling arrangement when they learned that she had sent their children to school in a taxi rather than drive them herself.[10] While the Friedans' children have grown to be successful people, Carl Friedan has acknowledged that his spouse "seldom was a wife and a mother."[11]

After Horowitz revealed these inconsistencies, Friedan feigned forthrightness by confirming his assertions in her own memoir, published in 2000. With a ho-hum manner, she suggested to readers that she had never kept her history hidden in the first place. She even added to the revision by revealing that she had "never baked a cake myself" or "learned to run a washer and dryer."[12] Yet she had by no means been aboveboard in *The Feminine Mystique*. Within the first dozen pages of the book, she reminded the reader of her credentials as a wife and mother three times.[13] "I married, had children, lived according to the feminine mystique as a suburban housewife," Friedan wrote, adding, "I could sense no purpose in my life, I could find no peace."[14]

One reason she had little time to devote to her family was that she was a longtime political activist who remained focused on her writing. Her work for radical causes had always been important to her, and she would not abandon that work to become a homemaker. After marrying Carl Friedan, she wrote full-time for Communist-controlled publications and later worked out of her home as a freelance writer.

Friedan was first exposed to Marxism in the 1930s at Smith College, the elite "Seven Sisters" school, which was then (as it is now) dominated by left-wing thinkers and activists. Guest lecturers, professors, required readings, and fellow students on the Northhampton, Massachusetts, campus all pushed her in the direction of near full acceptance of the Soviet line. While Friedan was at Smith, the school hosted lectures by Soviet propagandists Corliss Lamont and Anna Louise Strong, among many others. As a college student, the young Bettye Goldstein protested with the American Youth Congress (a Communist front) and wrote pacifist screeds in the school paper against American entry into World War II.[15] The campus atmosphere informed Friedan's ideology, and for more than a decade she served the cause of international Marxism in various capacities.

While pursuing a postgraduate degree at Berkeley, Friedan dated David Bohm, a Communist working under J. Robert Oppenheimer on the atomic bomb project. Her housemates were members of the Communist Party, and her writings reflected Moscow's influence. Friedan's FBI file—which biographer Daniel Horowitz labels "a document of problematic reliability but nonetheless one that has to be reckoned with"— claims that she tried to join the party formally while at Berkeley. According to Horowitz, "In 1944 an informant told the FBI that [Friedan] went to a party office in the East Bay area, announced that she was already a member of the [Young Communist League], and sought entrance into the party itself, as well as a job writing for its paper, *The People's World*." Friedan was refused entry, an FBI report said, and was told that she could serve the Soviet cause better from outside of the party.[16]

In 1943, Friedan began nine years of working as a labor journalist. Despite knowing little about the world she would be writing about—and coming from a privileged environment in which factories and strike lines did not play a part—she was hired because she had the "correct" outlook. That is, her employers knew she would follow the party line laid down in Moscow.

The publications she worked for—the *Federated Press* and the *UE News*—were ostensibly union publications, but in reality they were Communist fronts. The *Federated Press* was a wire news service founded at the 1919 Farmer-Labor Party convention by Socialist Party members, Wobblies, and other radicals. Friedan penned articles for the *Federated Press* on subjects ranging from the 1948 presidential campaign by Progressive Party candidate Henry Wallace to supposed government-corporate conspiracies to the opening of the Jefferson School of Social Science, a Communist Party center of indoctrination that she hailed as "a people's university for adults of all ages and all walks of life."[17] The *UE News*, meanwhile, was the official publication of the United Electrical, Radio, and Machine Workers of America. Horowitz cites two other historians who showed that this union was "the largest Communist-led institution of any kind in the United States" in the 1940s and was "the only effectively led large pro-Soviet affiliate" of the Congress of Industrial Organizations at the time.[18] Friedan's articles even appeared in the *Daily Worker*,

New Masses, and *Jewish Life: A Progressive Monthly*, a publication that whitewashed Stalin's anti-Semitism.[19]

Yet Friedan discussed none of this Communist activity in *The Feminine Mystique* or in subsequent years. Daniel Horowitz claims that fear of "McCarthyism" (some variation of Senator McCarthy's name curiously graces his book's pages several dozen times) prevented Friedan from telling the truth about her activities during the 1940s and '50s. But her biographer overlooks other possibilities. Perhaps Friedan lied about the time she spent within the Red fold because she recognized that she led a shameful life promoting an ideology that claimed millions of lives. Just as a former enthusiast for Nazism might attempt to shield his past views in pursuit of public approval, those who fawned over Mao, Stalin, and their B-list counterparts might try to obscure their past to gain mainstream acceptance.

Friedan might have had another, more practical reason to cover up her past associations with Communists. The more radical ideas preached within *The Feminine Mystique* had been advocated for years by her former comrades within the Communist Party. But as Friedan must have realized, no one took these proposals seriously coming from the political fringe. Friedan understood the efficacy of masquerading as something that she was not to transmit her opinions to a mainstream audience. Thus, Friedan manufactured a new persona designed to give her ideas an authenticity in the eyes of her readers. She traded honesty for utility.

Unfortunately, others took her at her word. "Once Friedan became famous," Horowitz observes, "journalists, authors of standard reference works, and historians simply repeated the narrative of her life offered in *The Feminine Mystique* and elsewhere."[20] Because those writing about Friedan so often sympathized with her views, they didn't bother to investigate her past. Horowitz himself questioned whether it was appropriate to make public the inconvenient information he discovered about a woman and a movement he admired. In his biography Horowitz writes, "I worried that I might be revealing elements of Friedan's past that conservatives could use to discredit not only Friedan but the entire women's movement."[21]

Friedan continues to guard her past carefully. She denies scholars permission to quote from her unpublished work and implies legal action if they do so. She refuses requests for interviews. Her complete papers are hidden from the public at Radcliffe College and will be kept under lock and key for decades. She denounces as tools of the Right those who criticize her for masking her past association with Communist groups—even those, like Daniel Horowitz, who celebrate and embrace her radical past.[22] To be sure, she almost certainly would have continued to perpetrate a false self-portrait had she not been called on her deception.

By the time Betty Friedan came clean about aspects of her past, doing so was largely irrelevant. She had long been hailed as a brave pioneer, and the feminist movement had been established for decades. The revelations about her past, both Horowitz's and her own, could not cause much damage. The deception had served its purpose.

LIES, DAMN LIES, AND STATISTICS

It wasn't just her own life that Friedan got wrong. As independent researcher Keith Reeve found in his study *Cheerless Fantasies*, "*The Feminine Mystique* is replete with mistakes, distortions and a range of other deficiencies."[23] Like many ideologically inspired writers, Friedan makes many unnecessary mistakes. She always seems to err in support of her philosophy. It's hard to find errors that, if mistaken for the truth, undermine her point.

Friedan misled readers when she claimed that "the birth rate continued to rise in the U.S. from 1950 to 1959."[24] It didn't. After the birth rate in 1957 matched the decade's highest yearly rate, it declined for the four straight years leading into Friedan's research for *The Feminine Mystique*.[25] Friedan's own source showed the decline in the birth rate, but she chose instead to make an unfounded claim that supported the notion that the baby boom continued unabated. "By the end of the fifties," she maintained, "the United States birthrate was overtaking India's."[26] It wasn't, and Friedan's source contained a warning against making such an interpretation.[27] Again, she chose to ignore the contradictory evidence.

Moreover, she noted a "drastic increase" in suicides of women over forty-five years of age in Bergen County, New Jersey, during the 1950s.[28] She failed to inform readers that this went against the general downward trend in female suicides, including those for older women, nationwide.[29] Telling readers the good news about declining female suicide rates might have undermined her point.

Friedan emphasized to readers that "*the proportion of women among college students has declined, year by year.*"[30] It is true that the GI Bill generated an influx of men into college in the postwar years, but the proportion of women vis-à-vis men enrolled in higher education increased, with some yearly deviations, in the 1950s.[31] The reality of more than two decades of female majorities among undergraduates has put to rest the ominous implications of Friedan's faulty statistics.[32]

BETTY FRIEDAN: ABUSED OR ABUSER?

In Friedan's 2000 autobiography, *Life So Far,* she charged her former husband, Carl Friedan, with being a wife beater. She recalled the first time: "I must have gotten sharper with Carl about his deals, when we were so far behind on our bills, or his not getting home for dinner. I seem to remember a sense of unspeakable horror, fear; I felt numb, until, one night, he hit me."[33] Friedan reported numerous other examples of her husband beating her over the course of more than a decade. "I was going to be permanently scarred, the doctors told me. The black eyes were getting serious."[34] Finally in 1969, questioning how she could "reconcile putting up with being knocked around by my husband while calling on women to rise up against their oppressors," she "summoned the courage to get a divorce." In her memoir she reported that "the violence between us had not stopped."[35]

Shortly after making the charge, Friedan explained that what she had written was not exactly true. The *New York Times* printed two corrections regarding the allegations against her divorced husband.[36] On *Good Morning America* she flirted with expressing regret at having made the allegations: "I almost wish I hadn't even written about it, because it's been sensationalized out of context. My husband was no wife-beater, and I was no passive victim of a wife-beater. We fought a lot, and he was bigger than me."[37] But by the time Friedan qualified her story it was too late. Thousands of copies of her book, numerous reviews, and the book's promotional material all repeated her original allegation. Perhaps the canard had been intended to give her an enhanced authenticity in the eyes of a new generation of feminists who value victimhood—just as her lies about her homemaker status a generation earlier had given her added currency then.

In response to Friedan's initial allegations against him, Carl Friedan recounted his own story of abuse at the hands of his wife. It was with "considerable reluctance" that he exposed "episodes of Betty Friedan's extreme irrational behavior," Mr. Friedan explained, but he had "no intention of going to my reward labeled a wife beater." Mr. Friedan charged the feminist pioneer with "uncontrollable hysteria and physical violence" during their marriage. Numerous people witnessed such incidents, he maintained.[38] He recounted one particular incident at a beach house he had rented in which, he claimed, Mrs. Friedan used a lamp to smash up the house in a fit of rage. Mr. Friedan absconded, leaving his wife to smash twenty-seven panes of glass, in the presence of guests. In another instance, Friedan's former husband said, she attacked him while he was driving on the highway, leaving him a bloody mess. Other scary moments, he reported, involved his wife approaching him in attack mode with kitchen knives and long slivers of glass from a mirror she had smashed.[39]

In Carl Friedan's opinion (perhaps an opinion many somewhat bitter divorced men have of their former mates), his wife was literally crazy. "In the mid-sixties one psychiatrist of hers, Dr. Dalmau, prescribed the drug Thorazine which she took for a week or two until she discovered it was widely used at that time to subdue hysterical mental patients," he recalled. "She stopped taking it, insulted that a doctor would consider her nuts."[40]

BIZARRE EXCUSES

Despite launching the modern women's liberation movement, Betty Friedan is now a pariah in some feminist circles. Like Trotsky, she helped launch a revolution that ultimately disowned her. Friedan's dissembling (a habit shared by many of her progeny) is certainly not the reason for the split. Nor is it that Friedan has moved to the Right, which she has not. Rather, the schism has resulted because Friedan has not migrated as far to the Left as the modern feminist movement has. Nowhere have feminists stretched the bounds of sane discourse more than in education. Consider a few examples of how farcical feminists have become:

- Equity in history demands equal representation of men and women in history books, accuracy be damned. Such guidelines have been codified in California. "Whenever an instructional material presents developments in history or current events, or achievements in art, science, or any other field, the contributions of women and men should be represented in approximately equal number," state guidelines demand.[41]

- Some professors reinterpret virtually anything according to feminist constructs. For example, University of Minnesota professor Susan McClary has said that Beethoven's music perpetuates rape. She claims that Beethoven's Ninth Symphony is "one of the most horrifying moments of music." The professor asserts that "the carefully prepared cadence is frustrated, damning up energy which finally explodes in the throttling, murderous rage of a rapist incapable of attaining release."[42]

- In literature, feminism imposes de facto quotas on the lists of authors read and in some cases requires changes in classic texts that campus Savonarolas deem insensitive. In one instance, Arizona State drama instructor Jared Sakren was denied tenure after refusing to change the text of Shakespeare's *The Taming of the Shrew*. While Shakespeare was labeled too offensive, the department offered "Betty the Yeti: An Eco-Fable."[43]

- *Women's Ways of Knowing* is the title of a book and of numerous college courses. It is also a growing philosophy, which states that logic and reasoning are men's ways of knowing, and feeling and intuition are women's ways of knowing. "Mind was male, nature was female," William Patterson College professor Paula Rothenberg contends, "and knowledge was created as an act of aggression."[44] This way of thinking has permeated feminist "science." The Dartmouth course "Ways of Knowing: Physics, Literature, Feminism" stressed "shifts from absolute to relative, certain to probable, dualistic to systematic, and static to dynamic," while offering a critique of "rational, binary, hierarchical, and patriarchal thinking."[45] The irony of so-called feminists parroting the same nonsense that misogynists uttered several decades ago has not been lost on older generations of feminists.

- Even architecture is not safe from the feminist critique. Speaking at a University of Massachusetts campus rally, Libbie Hubbard, a graduate student who calls herself Doctress Neutopia, counseled students to "take a look at the buildings around this campus. There's a penis in the center of campus. The library is a giant dick. We must tear it down and get back to the ovum. We have to start constructing buildings in the side of hills so that they look like vaginas."[46]

Today the author of *The Feminine Mystique* often angers the extremists who have taken over the movement. In her memoir she noted, "I didn't think then and still don't that the women's movement for equality was synonymous with lesbianism."[47] She added that she is a heterosexual "who loves the missionary position."[48] She also confessed that she had never had an abortion, writing, "Motherhood is a value to me, and even today abortion is not."[49] She divulged that she had always rejected the notion that "to be a liberated woman you had to make yourself ugly, to stop shaving under your arms, to stop wearing makeup or pretty dresses or any skirts at all."[50] Perhaps most offensive to the ears of contemporary activists was her quite candid proclamation that "I never felt as alive if I didn't have a man."[51]

As is the case with many mothers and daughters, Friedan and her twenty-first-century feminist offspring have much in common but just don't get along. Friedan, embarrassed by the excesses of the modern radical feminists, has often made bizarre excuses for them.

In *Life So Far* she acknowledged that lesbians had emerged as a dominant force within the women's movement by the early 1970s, but she did not blame extremists within the movement for pushing feminism outside the mainstream. Rather, she pointed the finger at secret agents. "The question was who was provoking the disruptions and pushing the lesbian agenda?" Naturally, she felt, it was *agents provocateurs*. "It was those agents, though the extent was never clear, who engineered much of the violence and shock tactics that would alienate the most radical of those anti-war, student and civil rights groups from mainstream America."[52]

Similarly, she conjured up images of a government plot playing a role in her resignation as president of NOW in 1970. When another woman had decided to run against her, Friedan had withdrawn her candidacy. She later raved in her memoir, "Who knows what role was played by the CIA and FBI agents?"[53] To derail feminism, she posited with an exaggerated sense of self-importance, the government needed to oust her.

The "black helicopter" excuses continued. Friedan did not hold the lesbians within the women's movement responsible for publicizing NOW leader Kate Millet's bisexuality in 1970. She offered an alternative version: "Again I suspected *agents provocateurs*."[54] How were radicals able to take over a 1974 NOW gathering in Houston? Was it a coincidence that she was at a conference in Iran at the time and was therefore unable to prevent the radical takeover? "I later came to think that the CIA had deliberately gotten me out of the country so that NOW could get taken over by *agents provocateurs*. That may be paranoid. But the takeover wouldn't have happened if I hadn't been in Iran."[55]

Predictably, she saw her enemies at work when radicals overran a second women's conference in Houston a few years later, at the height of the debate over the Equal Rights Amendment. Friedan believed that "some of the demonstrators in Houston were planted to weaken the authority and the effectiveness of this exploding massive force to transform society."[56] What did she base her belief upon? "I knew that one of the favorite tactics of the anti-ERA protagonists was to inflame the lesbian issue. . . . It cannot have been an accident that the lesbian issue arose stridently just as we needed maximum unity."[57] Friedan went so far as to blame an attack by a loose dog in a park as an intimidation tactic by her enemies.[58] Such a jaundiced view of events reveals a disturbing paranoia, egomania, and absence of sound logic.

MIXED LEGACY

Feminism has fundamentally reshaped society. Today, women have ample professional opportunities in government, science, the corporate world—even in such unlikely quarters as the military and professional sports. Yet not every change has been for the better. Rape, violence against women, unwanted pregnancy, spousal abandonment, and bearing the burden of raising children without the support of the men who spawned them have become common problems in our society. It would be unfair to blame feminism as the sole cause for this assortment of degrading trends, just as feminist exaggerations of the movement's positive impact have been self-servingly mistaken.

Women, not surprisingly, view the feminist legacy as a mixed bag. In a late 1990s *Time* magazine poll, for instance, only one-fifth of young women thought of themselves as feminists. More viewed feminism negatively (43 percent) than viewed it positively (32 percent).[59] The constituency that would seem to be feminism's natural amen corner—largely childless women at their most idealistic—delivered a Scotch verdict at best.

Part of the problem for feminists, it seems, is that many Americans wonder if feminism has outlived its need. Women long ago secured the right to vote and the same legal standing as men, but that is not all. Men now constitute a minority of college graduates.[60] For every woman incarcerated, there are about fourteen men in jail.[61] Women continue to outlive men, and of the ten leading causes of death, men outrank women in every category. Even after a century that saw more than 100 million men die in combat, governments still force men to fight and die. The vast majority of the homeless in this country are males, as are 60 percent of high school dropouts, 75 percent of alcoholics, two out of every three drug abusers, and 80 percent of all suicide cases.[62] Confronted with this reality, many simply view the notion of a special-interest group seeking to eradicate "oppression" against women as a relic of a bygone era.

Yet radical feminists march onward. While feminists may have some difficulty attracting followers among young women, they hold on to certain redoubts. The campuses, of course, remain a feminist stronghold. *Thelma and Louise, Fried Green Tomatoes, Mona Lisa Smile*, and other feminist pap that Hollywood feeds audiences are virtually never offset by movies offering a critical perspective of feminism. The news media regularly defer to feminist leaders as the voice of all women, with the feminist sensibilities of journalists coming through loud and clear in their reporting. A former White House correspondent for *Time*, for instance, revealed a confused feminism by saying of President Clinton during the Monica Lewinsky scandal, "I'd be happy to give him [oral sex] just to thank him for keeping abortion legal."[63] The remark certainly left some old-school feminists scratching their heads and thinking, "We *have* come a long way, baby."

FEMINISM'S MATRIARCH

Today, Friedan is a grandmotherly figure. Juxtaposed with the angry lesbians and out-to-lunch academics that people NOW gatherings, the *Feminine Mystique* author appears neither menacing nor uncongenial. Since she reigned over the feminist movement at a time when women made great strides in the workplace, education, and law, history may very well write a kind epitaph. May it also note that she butchered the facts, exhibited an unhealthy paranoia, and masqueraded as someone she was not.

Although she has at times been at odds with extremists within the movement she helped launch, Betty Friedan is the individual embodiment of modern feminism. For radical feminists the end clearly justifies the means. They applaud falsifying statistics, making untruthful allegations, and teaching a history that never occurred. Whether it's the media myth of domestic violence hitting its annual peak on Super Bowl Sunday or the discredited statistic that tens of thousands of American women die each year from anorexia (it's actually around a hundred), utility trumps honesty among feminists.[64] Who cares if the facts are jumbled on these little matters when the greater truth of feminism is advanced?

Likewise, when truth and ideology conflicted, the mother of the women's movement chose the latter. To make her message more appealing to the mainstream, Friedan falsely presented herself as a prototypical homemaker of the 1950s and early '60s, covering up her past involvement in Communism. Later, when victim chic became the rage, she propagated a dubious story of surviving a marriage to a wife beater. These days she has created a paranoid fantasy world where it is not feminists who are to blame for the excesses of feminism but the FBI, the CIA, and an assortment of imagined atavists and misogynists.

Betty Friedan has been exposed as a fraud. Modern feminists deserve such a matriarch.

"THEREFORE WE WILL BE INCOHERENT"

Postmodernism and the
Triumph of Ideology over Truth

*It is one of the most depressing aspects of the brilliant French culture that
opinions so fundamentally silly should command so much prestige.*

—John Bowle

OBJECTIVITY IS A FRAUD, FACTS ARE AN INVENTION, AND THE
world around us doesn't exist. Thus began physicist Alan Sokal's 1996
article in the academic journal *Social Text*.[1] Laced with obscurantist language, postmodernist insider jargon, and bold but illogical statements,
the piece seemed no different from numerous articles that had appeared
in the strangely esteemed journal. In one crucial way, Sokal's "Transgressing the Boundaries: Towards a Transformative Hermeneutics of
Quantum Gravity" did differ from all of *Social Text*'s previous articles: The
other pieces were deadly serious; Sokal's was a parody.

The hoax became the most famous article ever printed in *Social Text*.
Soon a phalanx of newspaper writers, talk-show hosts, and commentators
cited the affair as evidence that much of the academic world had
descended into an abyss of babble.

"Would a leading North American journal of cultural studies," Sokal
wondered, "publish an article liberally salted with nonsense if (a) it
sounded good and (b) it flattered the editors' ideological preconcep-
tions?"[2] By printing his article, the editors of *Social Text* answered in the
affirmative.

Sokal's article made a number of ludicrous claims. In opaque language,
he argued that the mathematical idea of equality owes much to modern
feminists. Quantum field theory, he further stated, validates Jacques

Lacan's psychoanalytic theories.[3] Sokal seemed to be saying that post-modernist assertions about science are just as valuable as the contributions of scientists themselves. Since the article's conclusion was politically correct, *Social Text*'s editors didn't bother to question its absurd suppositions. The stunt was particularly effective, Sokal astutely observed, because "the blow that can't be brushed off is the one that's self-inflicted."[4]

Sokal's parody struck many as hilarious, but not everyone appreciated his humor. The butts of the joke were particularly incensed. Postmodernist Stanley Fish, the executive director of *Social Text*'s publisher, Duke University Press, whined that "it is Alan Sokal, not his targets, who threatens to undermine the intellectual standards he vows to protect."[5]

The satire left others in a more somber mood for another reason. The intellectual vacuity Sokal so brilliantly exposed is hardly a fringe movement in intellectual circles. It is the dominant school of thought within literary criticism and is increasingly powerful elsewhere in the academy. Consider, for example, that Stanley Fish is one of the most famous academics in America, and that even after the Sokal affair the University of Illinois at Chicago chose him as its dean of arts and sciences. Postmodernism is hardly a laughing matter.

At stake in this debate is the concept of truth itself. By implication, the role of the intellectual, which traditionally has been to find the truth, is altered as well. What matters now is not truth but the political ramifications of scholarship. The intellectual that emerges is not a scholar but his antithesis: the ideologue. Truth is sacrificed at the altar of ideology.

DECONSTRUCTING DECONSTRUCTIONISM

Where did this school of thought come from? How did we get to the point at which Alan Sokal's gibberish could pass for serious scholarship?

Jacques Derrida, the man deemed "perhaps the world's most famous philosopher—if not the only famous philosopher" in the pages of the *New York Times*, is a nonentity in a great number of philosophy programs.[6] Derrida's popularity is most conspicuous in literary theory, but it is also found in architecture, feminism, music, painting, and politics. Like Marx, Derrida is immensely popular in scores of academic concentrations but is something of a pariah in his own.

He was born in colonial Algeria in 1930. He immigrated to France to study philosophy at the École Normale Supérieure in 1952 and began teaching at the Sorbonne in 1960. In 1965 he returned to the École Normale Supérieure and began a two-decade-long tenure there. By 1967 he would become a celebrity with the release of three books, and launch what has become known as deconstructionism.

Deconstructionism does to words what Freudian psychology does to people. It divorces terms from their surface definitions and purports to find deeper meanings by analyzing the surrounding text for other, subconscious messages. What matters is not so much what the author says but what the reader wants the author to say. As one of Derrida's academic admirers puts it, "[D]econstructive criticism aims to show that any text inevitably undermines its own claims to have a determinate meaning, and licenses the reader to produce his own meanings out of it by an activity of semantic 'freeplay.'"[7]

The same anarchic way deconstructionism instructs us to read texts is the way Derrida and his followers pen their own works. This creates obvious difficulties in trying to understand what Derrida and his imitators are attempting to say (or not say). Derrida's passages are criticized as intentionally vague and devoid of meaning. Relying on riddles and equating words with their antonyms, the texts confuse even the most careful of readers. "Therefore we will be incoherent," Derrida proudly announces in *Writing and Difference*, "but without systematically resigning ourselves to incoherence."[8] This statement sums up his style of writing, in that it's a meaningless riddle. The Frenchman's other writings follow this pattern. Derrida writes in *Of Grammatology*, for instance, about how something is "more or less close to pure language or pure nonlanguage."[9] In *Writing and Difference*, he remarks, "The independence of self consciousness becomes laughable at the moment when it liberates itself by enslaving itself."[10] What he means is anyone's guess, and perhaps that is his point. If you are arguing for a system of reading separated from the author's intent, what better way to make your point than to write nonsense and wait for the reader to explain what it is you said? The lack of coherence in Derrida's writing, admirer Alan Bass maintains, is a result of the inadequacy of translation to convey what he says. "The question arises—and it is a serious one—whether these essays can be read in a language other than French," Bass wonders.[11] The question is not serious at all. From *Candide* to *Les Misérables*, works translated from French have had few problems reaching English-speaking readers. Derrida's work, his apologists contend, somehow differs.

Derrida maintains that the relationship between the author and the reader is akin to that of master and slave. What he offers is liberation. In *Of Grammatology*, he celebrates that "the science of writing—*grammatology*—shows signs of liberation all over the world."[12] This emancipation is "the liberation of the signifier from its dependence or derivation with respect to the logos and the related concept of truth or the primary signified."[13] Words and their meanings, he is saying, should have a tenuous relationship. When they have a literal connection, linguistic slavery exists.

"Emancipation from this language must be attempted," he writes. "But not as an *attempt* at emancipation from it, for this is impossible unless we forget *our* history. Rather, as the dream of emancipation. Nor as emancipation from it, which would be meaningless and would deprive us of the light of meaning. Rather, as resistance to it, as far as is possible. In any event, we must not abandon ourselves to this language with the abandon which today characterizes the worst exhilaration of the most nuanced structural formalism."[14]

The system that Derrida seeks to replace is deficient because it is theological and totalitarian—with the author as the god or the supreme ruler, dictating meaning to readers. It is only right, he implies, that totalitarianism be overthrown and the god no longer be worshiped. Deconstruction is the method to achieve these supposedly laudable goals. Regarding theater, Derrida writes:

> The stage is theological for as long as its structure, following the entirety of tradition, comports the following elements: an author-creator who, absent and from afar, is armed with a text and keeps watch over, assembles, regulates the time or the meaning of representation, letting this latter *represent* him as concerns what is called the content of his thoughts, his intentions, his ideas. He lets representation represent him through representatives, directors or actors, enslaved interpreters who represent characters who, primarily through what they say, more or less directly represent the thought of the "creator." Interpretive slaves who faithfully execute the providential designs of the "master."[15]

For several decades, Derrida remained coy about his own politics, as well as the political ramifications of the school of thought he established. Theoretically, deconstruction is a politically neutral philosophy. It can serve the Left as well as the Right. To prove its practical utility to elements on the Right, one could point to readings of the U.S. Constitution that overlook the legislative approval necessary to embark upon warfare, or to the followers of Leo Strauss who impose "Straussian readings" upon various thinkers. These deviations aside, deconstructionism has been used almost exclusively by the academic Left since the late 1960s. Did Derrida, the father of deconstructionism, intend for his philosophy to be an ideological tool?

In the early 1990s, the Frenchman broke his longstanding silence on contemporary political questions. "My hope as a man of the left, is that certain elements of deconstruction will have served or—because the struggle continues, particularly in the United States—will serve to politicize or repoliticize the left with regard to positions which are not simply academic," he explained.[16] His statement confirmed what detached observers had known for years. Naturally, deconstructionism has expanded beyond literature. What does Derrida deconstruct? "Everything!" he explained. "I am critical of what I'm watching. I am trying to be vigilant. I deconstruct all the time."[17] Others do too. Deconstructionist architecture, Derrida said, is "a critique of everything that subordinated architecture to something else; use, beauty, or living. We have to refuse the hegemony of functionality, of the aesthetic, and of dwelling. It's a move to free architecture from all those external finalities, those extraneous goals."[18] If utility and beauty are "extraneous" to architecture, what then is the purpose of architecture? The answer is "no purpose." The French found this out the hard way in the 1980s when they built a public park on deconstructionist principles. Complete with a bridge that abruptly stops without going anywhere and a running track that crosses through a barroom, the monstrosity was a $200 million, taxpayer-funded reality check on deconstructionist architecture.[19]

Deconstructionism in music wreaks havoc on common sense as well. UCLA musicologist Susan McClary has tackled ludicrous questions, like whether Beethoven's Ninth is a rape symphony, or if Brahms musically attempts to undermine the patriarchy.[20] Regarding a musical composition for a theatrical production of *Jack and the Beanstalk*, she wrote, "The music depicting the beanstalk's erection and penetration is a highly venerable gesture—one that marks the heroic climax of many a tonal composition. A kind of pitch ceiling consolidates, against which melodic motives begin to push as though against a palpable obstacle. As the frustration mounts, the urgency of the motivic salvos increases; they move in shorter and shorter time spans, until they succeed finally in bursting through the barrier [the clouds] with a spasm of ejaculatory release."[21]

In literature, deconstruction has become a particularly popular tool of sexual libertines. Unable to abolish canonical works totally, activists have settled for retelling traditional novels, plays, and stories from nontraditional perspectives. Professor Laura Robinson of Canada's Royal Military College argued before a major academic conference that *Anne of Green Gables* is really a tale of teenage lesbian infatuation. "No matter how you want to argue it, [main characters such as] Leslie and Anne are undeniably erotically involved," she said. Robinson also claimed that Anne's relationship with another female character is "informed by sado-masochism." The professor maintained that others had not come to the same conclusion because evidence of lesbianism is "encoded" in the novel and its sequels. She was the only one, apparently, who had cracked the code. According to deconstructionism's perverse logic, the lack of evidence of lesbianism was in fact evidence of lesbianism. Excluding such evidence, said Robinson, was a way to "draw attention to what is excluded."[22]

Ironically, Derrida and his followers remain particularly sensitive to unflattering readings of his work. "Only by plucking them out of context for polemical purposes can his opponents ignore the meticulously argued character of Derrida's readings," Johns Hopkins professor Christopher Norris insists.[23] It seems the author's intent matters after all.

FOUCAULT AND POSTMODERNISM

Along with the deconstructionist Jacques Derrida, the other central figure in the rise of postmodernism was Michel Foucault, who was in fact one of Derrida's teachers. A more serious thinker than his student, Foucault focused his studies on society's institutions and conventions that suppressed deviancy—insane asylums, prisons, and sexual morality. Rather than merely reading about his interests, Foucault plunged headlong into them. He lived as an observer in mental institutions, studied prisons from the inside, and explored the dark side of human sexuality with great zeal. Of this latter pursuit he professed, "Sex is worth dying for."[24] His words would prove prophetic.

Although they share hostility toward values such as truth and logic, Derrida, Foucault, and others labeled as postmoderns do not have much else to unite their ideas. "Given the impossibility of imposing any logical order on ideas as dissimilar as these," author Mark Lilla notes, "postmodernism is long on attitude and short on argument. What appears to hold it together is the conviction that promoting these very different thinkers somehow contributes to a shared emancipatory political end, which remains conveniently ill-defined."[25]

With his trademark shaved skull, simple wire-rimmed glasses, and turtleneck sweater, Foucault became the physical embodiment of post-modernism. But it was his body of work (scholarly and activist) more than his cartoonish look that made him the intellectual movement's leading figure. During the 1970s, Foucault became the archetype of the Public Intellectual. Here, writing screeds supporting the Islamic Revolution in Iran; there, organizing petitions to release "political prisoner" Roger Knobelspiess. Only later would Foucault have to deal with the real-life consequences of his work. The revolution he supported brought about a society far more repressive than the one it replaced. The holdup man Knobelspiess, when released, went on a crime wave, robbing people at gunpoint and firing shots at two police officers. Foucault, his enemies joked, should have been awarded the "Knobel" prize for his work on the discredited case.[26]

At times, Foucault dropped the cloak of the intellectual altogether and donned the garb of the activist. On several occasions he brawled with police, by all accounts giving as good as he got. In early 1969, while teaching at France's Vincennes University, he joined a mob calling for democratized universities devoid of professiorial authority. Foucault and his fellow demonstrators retreated to a rooftop after the police arrived and hurled bricks at the cops below. The mob's "Down with the University" chants were put into action in the philosophy department that Foucault assembled at Vincennes. One professor he hired, Judith Miller, gleefully confessed to awarding course credit to strangers on the bus. Echoing Foucault, she denounced the university as a product of "capitalist society" and promised, "I will do my best to make sure it [the university] functions worse and worse."[27] The monster Foucault helped create came back to haunt him. A degree from Vincennes became meaningless, and the caliber of students who enrolled soon reflected this. Eventually, students began disrupting *his* classes. Frustrated, Foucault increasingly withdrew from intellectual life at the university.[28] Like the Frankfurt School leaders who endured death threats, office break-ins, and classroom invasions, he was no longer comfortable in the world that he had made.

Foucault's philosophy was Nietzschean. He questioned the very concept of truth. To the extent that it existed, truth was whatever the powerful decided it was. "We are subjected to the production of truth through power and we cannot exercise power except through the production of truth," he declared.[29] Since to him truth was arbitrary, it wasn't truth at all. Power, not justice or truth, was what mattered. "It is not to 'awaken consciousness' that we struggle," he frankly remarked in 1972, "but to sap power, to take power."[30] His followers learned that facts, and just about everything else, were socially constructed. Madness, abnormal sex, and criminality were not objective categories but rather social constructs. Empty the prisons, integrate the insane back into society, and abolish all sex laws, including prohibitions on rape and pedophilia—these were solutions he offered.[31] Such ideas became chic in intellectual circles in the 1970s, actually influencing public policy debates in a number of Western countries.

Unfortunately for Foucault, he practiced what he preached. An enthusiast of sadomasochism and a recreational drug user, he embraced what the mainstream rejected. "I hope I'll die of an overdose of pleasure of any kind," the Frenchman gleefully divulged.[32] He got his wish in 1984, when he died of AIDS. After he was infected with the disease, he recklessly visited gay bathhouses and sex clubs. He infected countless others.[33] His actions, intentional or not, were hardly incongruous with his nihilistic philosophy. Still sicker was the reaction from one of Foucault's sex partners, who alleged that he had contracted the lethal disease from the philosopher. "I die happy," he is said to have explained, "because I was infected by Michel Foucault."[34]

Foucault's sexual martyrdom inspired others to rebel against the mind at the urging of the body. The manner of his demise enhanced his reputation as the sage of a postmodern hedonism that added the dismissal of such concepts as logic, reasoning, and facts to its embrace of eros. In death, Foucault breathed life into postmodernism. Where there was one, thousands now stood. No longer the *raison d'être* of the intellectual, truth became an object of ridicule. "A simple criterion for science to qualify as postmodern is that it be free from any dependence on the concept of objective truth," an academic couple wrote.[35] Postmodernist Jean-Francois Lyotard held, "[T]he games of scientific language became the games of the rich in which whoever is wealthiest has the best chance of being right."[36] A postmodernist of a feminist bent argued, "I am suggesting that a feminist science practice admits political considerations as relevant constraints on reasoning."[37] Foucault's heirs firmly planted their victory flag on the academic world.

AN UGLY PAST

As its name implies, postmodernism rejects modernity. Specifically, it rejects the Enlightenment, which is seen as the catalyst for the modern age. Hence comes the term *postmodern*. Like the Frankfurt School, postmodernists reject Enlightenment values such as truth, rationality, reason, objectivity, and the scientific method. What they seek to replace these values with is unclear. Unlike the Frankfurt School, postmodernists don't uniformly embrace Marx. They find their roots in decidedly less fashionable sources. Friedrich Nietzsche, the philosopher crudely adopted by the Nazis, was Foucault's prime influence. Jacques Derrida traced his intellectual lineage to Martin Heidegger, an actual Nazi who supported Hitler through the duration of the Third Reich.

Another of Derrida's mentors was Paul de Man. The Belgian-born de Man immigrated to the United States in the postwar years and eventually became deconstructionism's evangelist in America from his sanctuary at Yale University. Whereas Derrida bickered publicly with his former professor Foucault, he showed exceptional loyalty to the elder de Man.

A few years after his death in 1984, de Man was revealed to have written for pro-Nazi propaganda newspapers during World War II in occupied Belgium. His writings expressed awe at the current "revolution"—that is, Hitler's foreign conquests. The world, he claimed, was entering "a mystical age." Some of his articles were blatantly anti-Semitic. In one piece, the future Yale professor offered "a solution to the Jewish problem." The best that can be said for his plan of deporting the sons and daughters of Israel to an isolated island colony is that it was more humane than the brutal actions that the Nazis would soon carry out. He seemed interested mainly in the effect that his proposal would have on the literary life of the West. He wrote of how his plan would ensure that "Western intellectuals" could continue to "safeguard themselves from Jewish influence," which he called "degenerate and decadent." Deporting Jews, he assured readers, "would not entail, for the life of the literary West, deplorable consequences," for Europe would lose only "a few personalities of mediocre value."[38] De Man's concern for the effect a twentieth-century pogrom would have on literature seems exceptionally callous in light of the horrific fate of millions of European Jews in those dark years.

While Derrida delivered an obligatory condemnation of the offending passages once they were revealed, he simultaneously attempted to absolve his late friend of responsibility for them. "Who will ever know how this text was written and published?" he asked. "Who can exclude what happens so often in newspapers, and especially during that period and in those conditions, when editors can always intervene at the last moment?"[39] Perhaps knowing that this line of reasoning was not very persuasive, Derrida attempted to use deconstruction to whitewash his mentor's sins. What seems like anti-Semitism to the rest of us was merely "rhetorical play" to Derrida. Paul de Man, Derrida explained, adopted the tactics of the "nonconforming smuggler"—one who appears to be part of the system but is really undermining it.[40] "It was as if his articles were denouncing the neighboring articles," Derrida strangely announced.[41] Deconstruction had again proved its utility to an agenda. As one observer put it, Derrida's response to the controversy fostered an impression that "deconstruction means you never have to say you're sorry."[42]

In the wake of the controversy, critics wondered if there was more to postmodernism's Nazi connection than Paul de Man's youthful anti-Semitic rants for a pro-Nazi rag. With an omnipresent nihilism, and with Heidegger and Nietzsche as driving influences, postmodern thinking bears many striking resemblances to Nazism. What matters in both ideologies is not the rectitude of one's position but the power behind it. This makes both "isms" dangerous and wrong. It does not necessarily follow, however, that the postmodernists view themselves as the intellectual heirs of the Nazis or harbor the same nefarious intentions as their fellow nihilists in the Third Reich. Ideological similarities between Nazism and postmodernism are nevertheless undeniable.

THE TRUTH HURTS

It's not hard to imagine postmodernism as a giant parody of academic excess, not unlike the hoax that Alan Sokal foisted on the cognoscenti. Alas, postmodernism is very real. If postmodernism were a parody, it might be something we could all laugh at. Since it is a major strain of thought among scholars, it is a source of despair rather than humor.

Despite having been dead for years, Michel Foucault was revealed by a 2001 study to have been cited more times in scholarly journals during the last five years of the twentieth century than any other public intellectual. Foucault's 13,238 citations were nearly double the number of scholarly references of his nearest competitor. To put things in perspective, Foucault had more citations than Milton Friedman, Jean-Paul Sartre, Claude Lévi-Strauss, John Maynard Keynes, Hannah Arendt, Gunnar

Myrdal, and Martha Nussbaum *combined*. Derrida ranked fourth on the list. Stanley Fish, Roland Barthes, and numerous other postmodernists were liberally sprinkled among the top one hundred public intellectuals.[43]

We end where we began. Like the Critical Theory of the Frankfurt School, postmodernism seeks to institutionalize dishonesty as a legitimate school of thought. The idea of truth as the ultimate goal of the intellectual is discarded. In its place, scholars are asked to pursue political objectives— so long as those political objectives are the "correct" ones. Postmodernism is not fringe within the community of scholars. It is central. This tells us a great deal about the life of the mind today. Peruse any university course catalogue, and you find names like Foucault, Derrida, and Barthes. Scour the footnotes of scholarly books and journals and a similar story unfolds. With the primacy of philosophies—postmodernism, Critical Theory, and even the right-leaning Straussianism—that exalt dishonesty in the service of supposedly noble causes, is it at all surprising that liars like Alfred Kinsey, Rigoberta Menchu, Alger Hiss, and Margaret Sanger have achieved a venerated status among the intellectuals?

"A TERRIBLE THING TO WASTE"

Use no way as a way.

—BRUCE LEE

IN THE LATE 1970S, FARMERS BEGAN NOTICING STRANGE GEO-
metric patterns appearing in their fields. These so-called crop circles first
grabbed attention in England and later popped up in Canada, India, and
scores of other places on the map. The phenomenon soon took on a life of
its own. Crop circles inspired sightseeing tours, clubs, websites, scientific
studies, and a blockbuster Hollywood production, *Signs.* The huge designs
were too complex to be the work of mere humans, enthusiasts reasoned;
obviously, extraterrestrial beings were trying to tell us something.

In 1990, two Englishmen, Doug Bower and Dave Chorley, admitted
to a reporter that they launched the hoax in 1978 and had made more
than a thousand crop circles since. To add credence to their claims, they
allowed a reporter to tag along as they created one of their glyphs. Using
a string attached to a pole to outline the initial perimeter, the duo then
pressed the grain into the ground with a board. The clever reporter then
invited a prominent crop-circle "expert" to assess Bower and Chorley's
creation.[1]

"No human being could have done this," Patrick Delgado observed.
"These crops are laid down in these sensational patterns by an energy that
remains unexplained and is of a high level of intelligence."[2]

The mysterious "energy" that fuels the crop circles turns out to be
alcohol. Bored yahoos of all races and nations—usually drunk, deprived
of sleep, and without the aid of sunlight—imitated the original pranksters

and created the intricate patterns, which researchers of the "unexplained" have deemed the work of superintelligent aliens. Less the result of mysterious cosmic forces than of last call, the circles became a celebrated hoax on a par with the Loch Ness Monster, Big Foot, and the Alien Autopsy.

Self-described "cerealogists" cried foul. Perhaps some of the circles were man-made hoaxes, they allowed, but many remained clouded in mystery. "Hoaxers have sought to deceive, confuse, and muddy research waters, in the same way that computer virus writers seek attention and attempt to destroy data," one website declared of the late-night rural merrymakers.[3]

The true believers target those who've disproved the crop-circle myth. "Any divergence from what they say, they will smear your name on the Internet, in publications," explained skeptic Peter Sorensen. "I've been called a CIA agent. It's absolutely nuts."[4] In the early 1990s, writer Matt Ridley set out to create crop circles in the north of England and "found that I could make a sophisticated pattern with very neat edges in less than an hour." After Ridley went public with his find, he recalled, believers in a less earthly explanation for the phenomenon depicted him as part of a government cover-up, intimating that he was an agent of the British intelligence agency MI5.[5]

John Lundberg has taken the crop-circle fad into the high-tech age. The Circlemakers founder uses computers to plan his designs, some nearly as large as two football fields. His group has anonymously created dozens of crop circles and even offers how-to manuals on its website. Believers in otherworldly phenomena single out the London artist for abuse. "I'm a heretic," Lundberg explains. "I'm attacking their belief system."[6]

Colin Andrews, a researcher of crop circles, laments, "I wish John and his band of merry men would just disappear."[7]

More than anything else, this is what the true believer wants: for his enemies to disappear. In the Soviet Union and Nazi Germany, true believers quite literally made their enemies vanish. Most of the time, the disappearing act is more figurative. True believers simply act as if their critics and their criticisms don't exist. Joiners circle the wagons around the group lie. As they do, it becomes harder to breach the enclosure with the truth.

IDEOLOGICAL DELUSIONS, PARANORMAL DELUSIONS

Crop-circle believers and intellectual morons have a lot in common.

Joiners don't want the truth. They want their collective delusion to continue. Ignoring legitimate criticism, enveloping oneself in an echo chamber filled with other pod people, and dehumanizing the opposition all further this end. The joiner presents his cause, be it saving the planet through environmentalism or spreading the word that another world is communicating to us through crop circles, as the one that will change all of history. He is blindly devoted to the idea. Evidence to the contrary fails to dissuade; rather, it proves the skill and massiveness of the conspiracy out to discredit his faith. Joiners insulate themselves from Doubting Thomases by practicing intellectual snobbery—refusing to debate, invoking the authority of science, speaking an insider language unintelligible to the uninitiated, and so forth. Joiners don't think. They follow. There is safety in numbers.

One startling difference does exist between intellectual morons and the crop-circle crowd: public respectability. Society ridicules alien abductees, time travelers, crystal healers, and other assorted cranks. We find intellectual morons on the theater marquee, running academic departments, occupying best-seller lists, and lining their pockets from the largesse of wealthy philanthropists. Consider some of the outlandish claims of the intellectual morons, and the accolades, awards, and attention that nevertheless follow them:

- Noam Chomsky was an apologist for the Khmer Rouge, compared Cuba favorably with the United States, predicted U.S.-administered genocide in Afghanistan, and imagined a victorious America collaborating with the defeated Nazis to rule the postwar world. By some accounts, he is the world's most cited scholar, with the vast majority of these citations having nothing to do with his work in linguistics.

- Rigoberta Menchu fabricated her life story to serve a cause. In return, Western intellectuals sympathetic to that cause made her life story a staple of the college curriculum. The Norwegian Nobel Committee awarded her its Peace Prize.

- Alfred Kinsey sought to mainstream his perversions by falsely portraying his fellow countrymen as a pack of degenerates. He stacked his surveys with homosexuals, sex offenders, pimps, and prostitutes. He took pedophiles at their word that their "partners" enjoyed sex. Indiana University houses an institute named for him, Twentieth Century Fox produced a biopic about the "scientist," and academic journals continue to cite him more than any other sex researcher.

- The only way to save the planet, Paul Ehrlich contends, is to adopt an extreme environmentalist program. Ehrlich predicted doomsday and, when it failed to come, predicted doomsday again and again. Despite his lackluster record as a prophet, Ehrlich has appeared dozens of times on national television shows like *The Tonight Show* and *Today*, received the most prestigious environmental prizes, and sold millions of copies of a discredited book that professors still require students to read.

When it's politically convenient, people will advance nutcases and even nuttier causes. Such myths as the shadow people, Roswell's alien crash site, and leprechauns satisfy no ideological desire, so they are believed only by the very strange. Du Bois's tales of Soviet utopia, Ehrlich's pending environmental apocalypse, and Vidal's vision of the U.S. government lurking in the shadows behind the two greatest acts of terrorism on U.S. soil bolster various agendas. Thus, those unwilling to believe ridiculous hoaxes regarding the paranormal find themselves promoting similarly absurd myths that propel their ideological desires.

Is Rigoberta Menchu's fabricated biography any less a lie than, say, tales of the yeti? Aren't current partisans of Alger Hiss cut off from reality in a manner similar to New Age cultists? Can't we acknowledge that biographers who omit Margaret Sanger's hosannas to concentration camps are in denial, just as the Trekkies are who believe their favorite television show is real? All lies may not be equal, but all lies *are* lies. For some reason, when deception serves a political cause, society seems to bestow an unearned respectability on it.

If their causes are just, then why do intellectual morons have to resort to dishonesty to realize their goals? Plato spoke of "noble lies" told to the people to serve the common good. These "noble lies," however, are a rare, if not nonexistent, creature. Far more common are ignoble lies—falsehoods employed to generate enthusiasm for despicable programs. From forced sterilization to pedophilia to infanticide to totalitarianism, the causes championed by the subjects of this book are more often than not evil rather than just wrong. In a democratic society, a well-informed public, not a confused one, is the best arbiter of which paths are desirable and which ones should be avoided. The popularity of misleading the public demonstrates the lack of confidence many elites have not only in the masses but in their own programs as well.

The means by which they confuse are many. The ideologue will always shift his principles to fit his circumstances. He will impugn motives—"racist!" "sexist!" "homophobe!" he shouts—and use straw men to shift the focus from the accused to accuser. When a critic's argument undermines the ideologue's falsehoods, he will invoke authority, declare that the majority of experts agree with him, and challenge the credentials of the one raising questions. Censorship and intimidation can sometimes be used to shield the public from particularly threatening information. In desperate situations, when confronted with an unflattering fact, the ideologue declares that "there is no truth," a sophist's canard that equates two inherently unequal concepts—truth and falsehood—and attacks not merely the opposing argument but the whole idea of truth itself.

"Faith is a wondrous thing," Arthur Koestler noted; "it is not only capable of moving mountains, but also of making you believe that a herring is a race horse."[8] For some, faith transforms science fiction into science fact. For intellectual morons, faith transforms socialist hellholes into Eden, man-hating animal-rights activists into humanitarians, and censorship into tolerance.

Bad ideas, politically inspired falsehoods, one-size-fits-all systems, and other products of the intellectual morons are unfortunate constants in the world of ideas. As long as there are ideologies, there will be fanatics who delude themselves and others, believe the ends justify the means, and smother adversarial ideas.

There are safeguards we can take, however, to diminish the influence of the intellectual morons. Exposing ideological falsehoods not only has an immediate positive effect, but it also tends to inoculate would-be dupes against succumbing to future lies: They become aware of their own gullibility as well as the ideologue's penchant for dishonesty. Striving for debate, free inquiry, openness, honesty, tolerance, and diversity in intellectual settings will help create conditions that cultivate thinking rather than programming. Finally, it is important to step outside ourselves and dispose of our ideological prejudices when evaluating information. We are all against lies when they undermine our preferences. Opposing falsehood when it aids our allies and interests is the real test of a commitment to truth. Aristotle famously observed that his loyalty to truth outweighed even his loyalty to Plato. The philosopher remarked, "For though we love both the truth and our friends, piety requires us to honor the truth first."[9]

BAD IDEAS, BAD CONSEQUENCES

Social philosopher Eric Hoffer once observed, "There is hardly an atrocity committed in the twentieth century that was not foreshadowed or even advocated by some noble man of words in the nineteenth."[10] Indeed, long before the October Revolution, Karl Marx laid out the blueprint for the ideology that consumed 100 million lives. Likewise, Hitler's racialism was hardly a novel concept that he devised. The seeds of his murderous reign were planted long before he rose to power.

Ideas have consequences. This was demonstrated when the theories and views of the previous era came of age—sometimes disastrously—during the twentieth century. One needn't possess clairvoyant powers to deduce that bad things will happen if the ignoble lies of our age are further ingrained as "truths" within society.

Lincoln was fond of asking, "If you call a dog's tail a leg, how many legs does a dog have?" "Five," his audience would invariably respond. The correct answer, he would point out, is four. Calling a tail a leg does not make it a leg. Calling lies truth doesn't make them truth.

In the ongoing culture war, the standard of truth was long ago discarded in favor of ideology. If the search for truth is to replace ideological utility as the intellectual's *raison d'être*, then ignoble lies need to be exposed far and wide. Every propagandist's habit of calling his lies truth is a tacit acknowledgment that the public abhors naked falsehood. Sunlight is the solution. The truth is still a standard that deserves to be held high.

When you refuse to think, someone else will determine your thoughts for you. Joiners look for their ideas from gurus and the systems that they lay down. Rather than bringing them closer to truth, as joiners seem to believe, gurus and systems act as an intellectual ball and chain. They stifle the thought of many otherwise brilliant people. The intellectual moron is one who is gifted but who squanders his talent by relying on ideology to assign him his beliefs. As the old slogan of the United Negro College Fund says, "A mind is a terrible thing to waste."

When confronted with new information, the joiner's immediate concern is, "Will it serve my cause?" We would all be better off if we approached untested assertions by instead asking ourselves, "Is it true?"

Notes

Introduction: "The True Believer"

1. Al Gore, *Earth in the Balance: Ecology and the Human Spirit* (Boston: Houghton Mifflin, 1992), p. 325.

2. Rob Jennings, "Laci Peterson Case Tied to Roe Debate," DailyRecord.com, April 20, 2003, available at www.dailyrecord.com/news/03/04/20news3-laci.htm, accessed on April 20, 2003. Lisa De Pasquale, "Feminists Have 'No Comment' as One Family Mourns This Mother's Day," CNSNews.com, May 9, 2003, available at www.cblpolicyinstitute.org/petersoncase.htm, accessed on January 5, 2004.

3. Scores of marchers I interviewed agreed with these sentiments. Those specifically cited follow. Author interview of Edward Lopez at protest of Bush administration's foreign policy in Washington, D.C., on March 15, 2003. Author interview of marcher who refused to give his name at a protest of Bush administration's foreign policy held in New York City on February 15, 2003. Author interview of Reesa Rosenberg at protest of Bush administration's foreign policy in Washington, D.C., on January 18, 2003.

4. Peter Singer, *Animal Liberation: New Revised Edition* (New York: Avon Books, 1991). Peter Singer, "Heavy Petting," www.nerve.com/Opinions/Singer/heavy Petting/main.asp, accessed on March 14, 2001. For a discussion of PETA president Ingrid Newkirk's defense of Singer's stance on bestiality ("daring and honest"), see Debra J. Saunders, "One Man's Animal Husbandry," *San Francisco Chronicle*, March 20, 2001, p. 21.

5. For a discussion of "the issue is not the issue," see Terry H. Anderson, *The Movement and the Sixties: Protest in America from Greensboro to Wounded Knee* (New York: Oxford University Press, 1995), p. 201.

6. Eric Hoffer, *The Ordeal of Change* (Cutchogue, NY: Buccaneer Books, 1976), p. 97.

7. Raymond Aron, *The Opium of the Intellectuals* (New Brunswick, NJ: Transaction, 2002), p. 89.

8. C. S. Lewis, *Mere Christianity* (Glasgow: Fount, 1997), p. 23.

9. Quoted in "Rosie O'Donnell," www.virtualology.com/virtualmuseumof history/hallofrhetoric/epideicticartiste/ROSIEODONNELL.ORG/, accessed on January 8, 2004.

10. John Lott, "When It Comes to Firearms, Do as I Say, Not as I Do," *Los Angeles Times*, June 11, 2000, p. 11.

11. Rich Connell and Robert J. Lopez, "Huffington Paid Little Income Tax," *Los Angeles Times*, August 14, 2003, p. 1.

12. Quoted in "Michael Moore Fires Back at Salon," Salon.com, July 3, 1997, available at www.salon.com/july97/moore970703, accessed on July 22, 2004. Daniel Radosh, "Moore Is Less," Salon.com, June 6, 1997, available at www.salon.com/june97/media/media970606, accessed on July 22, 2004. Quoted in Matt Labash, "Michael Moore, One-Trick Pony," *Weekly Standard*, June 8, 1998, available at www.weeklystandard.com/Utilities/printer_preview.asp?idArticle=4285&R=9F1220, accessed on July 22, 2004.

13. Barbra Streisand, "Stewards of the Earth," *Tikkun*, January/February 2000, p. 51.

14.   "Stars Are Two-Faced on SUVs," *New York Post*, January 13, 2003, p. 10. Matt Drudge, "Streisand Bought Eight Hundred Shares of Cheney's Halliburton," DrudgeReport.com, October 3, 2002, available at www.drudgereport.com/strei5. htm, accessed on January 8, 2004. Art Moore, "High-Living Celebs Tie SUV Owners to Terror," WorldNetDaily.com, January 10, 2003, available at www.worldnetdaily.com/news/article.asp?ARTICLE_ID=30412, accessed on January 7, 2004.

15.   Kenneth R. Weiss, "Judge Rejects Streisand Privacy Suit," *Los Angeles Times*, December 4, 2003, p. B1.

16.   Stephen Spender in *The God That Failed*, Richard Crossman, ed. (New York: Books for Libraries Press, 1972), p. 253.

17.   Eric Hoffer, *The True Believer: Thoughts on the Nature of Mass Movements* (New York: Perennial Classics, 2002), p. 79.

18.   Hoffer, *The True Believer*, p. 156.

19.   Plato, *Phaedrus* 275b (Stephanus number).

Chapter 1: "Fiction Calls the Facts by Their Name"

1.   Quoted in Daniel J. Flynn, "Free Speech Torched at Cornell—Again," *Campus Report*, January 1998, p. 1.

2.   Tracey Lomrantz, "Smeaton Calls Removal of Flag a Mistake," *The Brown and White*, September 17, 2001, p. 1.

3.   "Insensitive Sensitivity Training," *Campus Report*, May 2000, p. 4.

4.   Herbert Marcuse, "Repressive Tolerance," in Robert Paul Wolff, Barrington Moore Jr., and Herbert Marcuse, *A Critique of Pure Tolerance* (Boston: Beacon Press, 1970), p. 109.

5.   Speech: William Lind, "The Origins of Political Correctness," Accuracy in Academia Summer Conference, George Washington University, Washington, D.C., July 10, 1998.

6.   Martin Jay, *The Dialectical Imagination: A History of the Frankfurt School and the Institute of Social Research—1923–1949* (Berkeley: University of California Press, 1973), p. xii.

7.   Robert M. Young in Herbert Marcuse, *Negations: Essays in Critical Theory* (London: Free Association Books, 1988), p. viii.

8.   Rolf Wiggershaus, *The Frankfurt School: Its History, Theories, and Political Significance*, trans. Michael Robertson (Cambridge, MA: The MIT Press, 1995), pp. 127–128.

9.   Wiggershaus, *The Frankfurt School*, pp. 434, 654.

10.   Wiggershaus, *The Frankfurt School*, p. 249.

11.   Wiggershaus, *The Frankfurt School*, pp. 47, 66–67, 95–96, 237, 538.

12.   Wiggershaus, *The Frankfurt School*, pp. 397, 479.

13.   Jay, *The Dialectical Imagination*, pp. 13, 170–171.

14.   Jay, *The Dialectical Imagination*, p. 4; Wiggershaus, *The Frankfurt School*, pp. 78, 80.

15.   Jay, *The Dialectical Imagination*, p. 171.

16.   Quoted in Wiggershaus, *The Frankfurt School*, p. 162.

17.   Quoted in Wiggershaus, *The Frankfurt School*, p. 391.

18.   For a brief discussion of the ordeal of Karl Wittfogel, see Jay, *The Dialectical Imagination*, pp. 284–285.

19. T. W. Adorno, Else Frenkel-Brunswik, Daniel J. Levinson, and R. Nevitt Sanford, *The Authoritarian Personality* (New York: Harper and Brothers, 1950), p. 142.

20. Adorno et al., *The Authoritarian Personality*, p. 254. The statement that found a multiplicity of uses read: "The businessman and the manufacturer are much more important to society than the artist and the professor."

21. Wiggershaus, *The Frankfurt School*, p. 420.

22. Herbert Marcuse, *An Essay on Liberation* (Boston: Beacon Press, 1971), p. 36.

23. Marcuse, "Repressive Tolerance," in Wolff, et al., *A Critique of Pure Tolerance*, p. 117.

24. Herbert Marcuse, *Counterrevolution and Revolt* (Boston: Beacon Press, 1972), pp. 80–81.

25. Marcuse, *Counterrevolution and Revolt*, p. 16.

26. Jay, *The Dialectical Imagination*, p. xii.

27. Herbert Marcuse, *Eros and Civilization: A Philosophical Inquiry into Freud* (Boston: Beacon Press, 1966), p. 45.

28. Marcuse, *Eros and Civilization*, p. 201.

29. Marcuse, *Eros and Civilization*, p. 152.

30. Marcuse, *Eros and Civilization*, p. 152.

31. Marcuse, *Eros and Civilization*, p. 151.

32. Marcuse, *Eros and Civilization*, p. 274.

33. *Comedy and Tragedy: College Course Descriptions and What They Tell Us About Higher Education* (Herndon, VA: Young America's Foundation, 2003), p. 77. Eric Langborgh, "X-Rated Academia," *Campus Report*, March 2000, p. 1. "Spring Semester 2000: LGBT Related Courses," www.oberlin.edu/stuorg/LGBCC/spr2000.htm, accessed on March 2, 2004.

34. Herbert Marcuse, *One-Dimensional Man: Studies in the Ideology of Advanced Industrial Society* (Boston: Beacon Press, 1967), p. 62.

35. Marcuse, *One-Dimensional Man*, p. 123.

36. Marcuse, *One-Dimensional Man*, p. 147.

37. Marcuse, *One-Dimensional Man*, p. 168.

38. Marcuse, *One-Dimensional Man*, p. 158.

39. Marcuse, *An Essay on Liberation*, p. 86.

40. Marcuse, "Repressive Tolerance," in Wolff, et al., *A Critique of Pure Tolerance*, p. 119.

41. Marcuse, "Repressive Tolerance," in Wolff, et al., *A Critique of Pure Tolerance*, p. 106.

42. Marcuse, "Repressive Tolerance," in Wolff, et al., *A Critique of Pure Tolerance*, p. 119.

43. Marcuse, "Repressive Tolerance," in Wolff, et al., *A Critique of Pure Tolerance*, p. 109.

44. Marcuse, "Repressive Tolerance," in Wolff, et al., *A Critique of Pure Tolerance*, p. 101.

45. Marcuse, "Repressive Tolerance," in Wolff, et al., *A Critique of Pure Tolerance*, p. 111.

46. George Orwell, *Animal Farm* (New York: Signet Classic, 1997), p. 137.

47. Marcuse, "Repressive Tolerance," in Wolff, et al., *A Critique of Pure Tolerance*, p. 89.

48. Marcuse, *One-Dimensional Man*, p. 102.

49. Marcuse, *An Essay on Liberation*, p. 85.
50. Marcuse, *An Essay on Liberation*, p. 86.
51. Marcuse, *One-Dimensional Man*, p. 40.
52. Marcuse, *One-Dimensional Man*, p. 6.
53. Marcuse, *Counterrevolution and Revolt*, p. 29.
54. Marcuse, *Counterrevolution and Revolt*, pp. 5–6.
55. Marcuse, *One-Dimensional Man*, p. 256.
56. Marcuse, *Counterrevolution and Revolt*, p. 45.
57. Marcuse, *Counterrevolution and Revolt*, p. 45.
58. Marcuse, *Counterrevolution and Revolt*, p. 47.
59. Marcuse, *An Essay on Liberation*, p. 61.
60. Marcuse, *An Essay on Liberation*, p. 61.
61. Lydia Meuret, "The Slovenly Science: A Look at Women's Studies" (Herndon, VA: Clare Boothe Luce Policy Institute, 1996), p. 2.
62. This is based on the author's count of the number of courses listed in both fields within the course catalogues at the three universities.
63. Eds. Henry Abelove, Michele Aina Barale, and David Halperin, *The Lesbian and Gay Studies Reader* (New York: Routledge, 1993), p. xvi.
64. Wiggershaus, *The Frankfurt School*, pp. 626–632.
65. Quoted in Wiggershaus, *The Frankfurt School*, p. 633.
66. Jay, *The Dialectical Imagination*, pp. xii–xiii.
67. Quoted in Jay, *The Dialectical Imagination*, p. 279.
68. John Leo, "PC Standards Are Too One-Sided," New York *Daily News*, July 29, 2000, p. 21.
69. George Orwell, *1984* (New York: Signet Classic, 1983), p. 205.

Chapter 2: "Science!"

1. Will Durant and Ariel Durant, *Rousseau and Revolution* (New York: MJF Books, 1967), pp. 6, 8, 18.
2. Paul Johnson, *Intellectuals* (New York: Harper & Row, 1989), p. 60.
3. Quoted in Johnson, *Intellectuals*, p. 74.
4. "Kids Get Graphic Instruction in Homosexual Sex," www.massnews.com/past_issues/2005/5_May?maygsa.htm, accessed on October 13, 2003.
5. Gregory A. Freeman, "Bug Chasers: The Men Who Long To Be HIV+," *Rolling Stone*, February 6, 2003, pp. 45–48.
6. Laura Brown, "Transsexual Toilet Costs T $8G," *Boston Herald*, June 6, 2000, p. 1.
7. Katie Zernike, "At Nude Youth Camp, Skin Is Bare but Lust Is Verboten," *New York Times*, June 18, 2003, p. 18.
8. Quoted in Matt Smith, "Public Enema No. 2," SFWeekly.com, February 23, 2000, available at www.sfweekly.com/issues/2000-02-23/feature.html/1/index.html, accessed on October 13, 2003.
9. Quoted in Judith Reisman, "Exposing Pornography's Addictive, Destructive Effects," Human Events Online, December 16, 2003. Available at www.humaneventsonline.com/article.php?print-yea&id-2618, accessed on May 1, 2004.

10.   James H. Jones, *Alfred C. Kinsey: A Public/Private Life* (New York: W. W. Norton, 1997), p. 33.

11.   Jones, *Alfred C. Kinsey*, p. 32.

12.   Jones, *Alfred C. Kinsey*, pp. 153–154.

13.   Jones, *Alfred C. Kinsey*, p. 82.

14.   Jones, *Alfred C. Kinsey*, pp. 117–118.

15.   Jones, *Alfred C. Kinsey*, p. 139.

16.   Jones, *Alfred C. Kinsey*, p. 264.

17.   Jones, *Alfred C. Kinsey*, p. 155.

18.   Jones, *Alfred C. Kinsey*, p. 172.

19.   Jones, *Alfred C. Kinsey*, p. 174.

20.   Quoted in Jones, *Alfred C. Kinsey*, p. 281.

21.   Jones, *Alfred C. Kinsey*, p. 189.

22.   David Halberstam, *The Fifties* (New York: Villard Books, 1993), pp. 272–281.

23.   William O'Neill, *American High* (New York: The Free Press, 1986), pp. 45, 47.

24.   Paul Johnson, *A History of the American People* (New York: HarperCollins, 1998), p. 840.

25.   William Manchester, *The Glory and the Dream* (Boston: Little, Brown, 1974), pp. 477, 478.

26.   Jones, *Alfred C. Kinsey*, p. 533.

27.   Jones, *Alfred C. Kinsey*, p. 610.

28.   Jonathan Gathorne-Hardy, *Sex the Measure of All Things: A Life of Alfred C. Kinsey* (Bloomington, IN: Indiana University Press, 2000), pp. 336, 414.

29.   Jones, *Alfred C. Kinsey*, p. 739.

30.   Gathorne-Hardy, *Sex the Measure of All Things*, p. 415.

31.   Jones, *Alfred C. Kinsey*, p. 607.

32.   Jones, *Alfred C. Kinsey*, pp. 499, 608.

33.   Jones, *Alfred C. Kinsey*, p. 491.

34.   Jones, *Alfred C. Kinsey*, pp. 335, 532, 602.

35.   Jones, *Alfred C. Kinsey*, p. 397.

36.   Gathorne-Hardy, *Sex the Measure of All Things*, p. 124.

37.   Alfred Kinsey, Wardell Pomeroy, and Clyde Martin, *Sexual Behavior in the Human Male* (Philadelphia: W.B. Saunders, 1948), p. 550.

38.   Kinsey et al., *Sexual Behavior in the Human Male*, p. 597.

39.   Kinsey et al., *Sexual Behavior in the Human Male*, p. 585.

40.   Kinsey et al., *Sexual Behavior in the Human Male*, p. 623.

41.   Kinsey et al., *Sexual Behavior in the Human Male*, p. 670.

42.   Gathorne-Hardy, *Sex the Measure of All Things*, pp. 330, 130–131.

43.   Judith Reisman and Edward Eichel, *Kinsey, Sex and Fraud: The Indoctrination of a People* (Lafayette, LA: Huntington House, 1990), p. 27.

44.   Kinsey et al., *Sexual Behavior in the Human Male*, p. 544.

45.   Reisman and Eichel, *Kinsey, Sex and Fraud*, p. 27.

46.   Gathorne-Hardy, *Sex the Measure of All Things*, p. 258.

47.   For a look at the geographic distribution, see Kinsey et al., *Sexual Behavior in the Human Male*, p. 5.

48.   Reisman and Eichel, *Kinsey, Sex and Fraud*, p. 27.

49.   Jones, *Alfred C. Kinsey*, p. 387.

50.   Jones, *Alfred C. Kinsey*, p. 387.

51.   Gathorne-Hardy, *Sex the Measure of All Things*, p. 239.

52.   Kinsey et al., *Sexual Behavior in the Human Male*, p. 216.

53.   Gathorne-Hardy, *Sex the Measure of All Things*, p. 248.

54.   Gathorne-Hardy, *Sex the Measure of All Things*, p. 307.

55.   Gathorne-Hardy, *Sex the Measure of All Things*, p. 189.

56.   Reisman and Eichel, *Kinsey, Sex and Fraud*, p. 23; A. C. Kinsey, W. B. Pomeroy, C. E. Martin, P. H. Gebhard, *Sexual Behavior in the Human Female* (Philadelphia: W.B. Saunders, 1953), p. 21.

57.   See Judith Reisman, *Kinsey: Crimes & Consequences* (Arlington, VA: Institute for Media Education, 1998), p. 94; Reisman and Eichel, *Kinsey, Sex and Fraud*, p. 22.

58.   Reisman and Eichel, *Kinsey, Sex and Fraud*, p. 22.

59.   Reisman, *Kinsey: Crimes & Consequences*, p. 94.

60.   Reisman and Eichel, *Kinsey, Sex and Fraud*, pp. 22–24. Passage includes the authors' estimate that 25 percent of the male sample group Kinsey used for his book were inmates, and Kinsey Institute staffer John Gagnon's opinion that 900–1,000 of the males used for the survey were prisoners.

61.   Kinsey et al., *Sexual Behavior in the Human Female*, p. 286.

62.   Kinsey et al., *Sexual Behavior in the Human Female*, pp. 474–475.

63.   Kinsey et al., *Sexual Behavior in the Human Female*, p. 416.

64.   Kinsey et al., *Sexual Behavior in the Human Female*, pp. 505–507.

65.   Jones, *Alfred C. Kinsey*, p. 399.

66.   Kinsey et al., *Sexual Behavior in the Human Female*, p. 22.

67.   Kinsey et al., *Sexual Behavior in the Human Female*, pp. 21–22.

68.   Kinsey et al., *Sexual Behavior in the Human Female*, pp. 31–37.

69.   See charts on the prevalence within religious classifications of premarital sex (p. 305), extramarital affairs (pp. 424–425), and homosexuality (pp. 464–465) in *Sexual Behavior in the Human Female*.

70.   Kinsey et al., *Sexual Behavior in the Human Female*, p. 31.

71.   Kinsey et al., *Sexual Behavior in the Human Female*, p. 79.

72.   Kinsey et al., *Sexual Behavior in the Human Female*, p. 53.

73.   Kinsey et al., *Sexual Behavior in the Human Female*, p. 327.

74.   Gathorne-Hardy, *Sex the Measure of All Things*, p. 377.

75.   Kinsey et al., *Sexual Behavior in the Human Female*, pp. 410–411.

76.   Dr. Judith Reisman, "The Scientist as Contributing Agent to Child Sexual Abuse: A Preliminary Consideration of Possible Ethics Violations," 5th World Congress of Sexology, Jerusalem, Israel, July 23, 1981.

77.   Kinsey et al., *Sexual Behavior in the Human Male*, p. 161.

78.   Kinsey et al., *Sexual Behavior in the Human Male*, p. 180.

79.   Reisman, "The Scientist as Contributing Agent to Child Sexual Abuse."

80.   Kinsey et al., *Sexual Behavior in the Human Female*, p. 121.

81.   Kinsey et al., *Sexual Behavior in the Human Female*, p. 120.

82.   Kinsey et al., *Sexual Behavior in the Human Female*, p. 122.

83.   Kinsey et al., *Sexual Behavior in the Human Female*, pp. 121–122.

84.   Reisman, *Kinsey: Crimes and Consequences*, pp. 167, 170.

85.   Kinsey et al., *Sexual Behavior in the Human Male*, p. 177.

86.   *Secret History: Kinsey's Paedophiles*, Yorkshire Television, Channel 4 (October 8, 1998), Producer, Tim Tate.

87.   Reisman quote and information on Kinsey's adolescent sperm collection appear in E. Michael Jones, *Degenerate Moderns: Modernity as Rationalized Sexual Misbehavior* (San Francisco: Ignatius, 1993), p. 108.

88. *Kinsey's Paedophiles*, Tim Tate.

89. Judith Reisman, *Kinsey: Crimes and Consequences* (Institute for Media Education: Crestwood, Kentucky, 2000), p. 166 (2nd edition).

90. Quoted in Judith Reisman, *Kinsey: Crimes and Consequences* (Institute for Media Education: Crestwood, Kentucky, 1998), pp. 165–167.

91. Quoted in *Kinsey's Paedophiles*, Producer, Tim Tate.

92. Reisman, *Kinsey: Crimes and Consequences*, p. 162.

93. Phone interview of "Esther White" by author, August 2, 2000.

94. Information comes from my phone interview of White on August 2, 2000, as well as the documentary *Kinsey's Paedophiles*, Producer, Tim Tate.

95. Phone interview of Esther White by author, August 2, 2000.

96. Gathorne-Hardy discusses Kinsey's work with children in Columbus on pp. 208, 215, 227.

97. *Kinsey's Paedophiles*, Producer, Tim Tate.

98. Phone interview of Esther White by author, August 2, 2000.

99. Reisman, *Kinsey: Crimes and Consequences*, p. 41.

100. Gathorne-Hardy, *Sex the Measure of All Things*, p. 395.

101. Quoted in Gordon Muir, *Sex, Politics, and the End of Morality* (Raleigh: Pentland Press, 1998), p. 9.

102. Jones, *Alfred C. Kinsey*, p. 550.

103. Albert Deutch, "The Sex Habits of American Men," *Harper's Magazine*, December 1947, pp. 490, 493.

104. Joseph B. Wheelwright, "The Start of an Important Series on U.S. Sex Life," *The San Francisco Chronicle–This World*, January 18, 1948, p. 25.

105. Norman Reider, "Kinsey's Book Is Sound Research—But It Will Be Misused," *The San Francisco Chronicle–This World*, September 13, 1953, p. 15.

106. Jones, *Alfred C. Kinsey*, p. 545.

107. Jones, *Alfred C. Kinsey*, pp. 552–553.

108. Jones, *Alfred C. Kinsey*, p. 553.

109. Gathorne-Hardy, *Sex the Measure of All Things*, p. 274.

110. For examples of both, see Gathorne-Hardy pp. 275, 434.

111. Muir, *Sex, Politics, and the End of Morality*, p. 19.

112. Reisman, *Kinsey: Crimes and Consequences*, p. 81.

113. Muir, *Sex, Politics, and the End of Morality*, pp. 19–20.

114. Reisman, *Kinsey: Crimes & Consequences* (2nd edition, 2000), p. 205.

115. Reisman, *Kinsey: Crimes & Consequences* (2nd edition, 2000), p. 205.

116. Gerald Hannon, "Gay Youth and the Question of Consent," in *Lavender Culture*, eds. Allen Jay and Karla Young (New York: NYU Press, 1994), p. 359.

117. Hannon, "Gay Youth and the Question of Consent," in *Lavender Culture*, eds. Jay and Young, p. 364.

118. Hannon, "Gay Youth and the Question of Consent," in *Lavender Culture*, eds. Jay and Young, p. 362.

119. Hannon, "Gay Youth and the Question of Consent," in *Lavender Culture*, eds. Jay and Young, p. 358.

120. Gayle Rubin in "Thinking Sex: Notes for a Radical Theory of the Politics of Sexuality," in *The Lesbian and Gay Studies Reader*, eds. Henry Abelove, Michele Aina Barale, and David Halperin (New York: Routledge 1993), p. 7.

121.   Gayle Rubin in "Thinking Sex: Notes for a Radical Theory of the Politics of Sexuality," in *The Lesbian and Gay Studies Reader*, eds. Abelove et al., p. 15.

122.   Gayle Rubin "Thinking Sex: Notes for a Radical Theory of the Politics of Sexuality," in *The Lesbian and Gay Studies Reader*, eds. Abelove et al., p. 15.

123.   Michael Capel, "Pedophilia 101 at Cornell," *Campus Report*, October 1998, p. 1.

124.   Pat Califa, *Public Sex: The Culture of Radical Sex* (San Francisco: Cleis Press, 1994), p. 39.

125.   Califa, *Public Sex*, p. 39.

126.   Quoted in Gathorne-Hardy, *Sex the Measure of All Things*, p. 31.

127.   Kinsey et al., *Sexual Behavior in the Human Male*, pp. 21–34.

128.   For a discussion of the history of sex research, see Gathorne-Hardy, *Sex the Measure of All Things*, pp. 151–162; or Kinsey et al., *Sexual Behavior in the Human Male*, pp. 21–34, 617–622.

129.   Kinsey et al., *Sexual Behavior in the Human Male*, pp. 618–619, 621.

130.   "University of Chicago Study Disputes Myths About American Sexual Habits," Irving B. Harris Graduate School of Public Policy Studies (Contact: Joel Williams), October 13, 1994. Page was viewed on August 24, 2000. www.harrisschool.uchicago.edu/news/pressreleases/pr_american_sex_stdy.htm).

131.   Gathorne-Hardy, *Sex the Measure of All Things*, p. 286.

132.   The Kinsey Scale can be found on page 638 of the male report. The chapters on homosexuality are the longest of all chapters in both the male and female volumes. The male chapter on homosexuality runs from page 610 to 666. The chapter on female homosexuality runs from page 446 to 501.

Chapter 3: "Coercion in a Good Cause"

1.   Kristen Green and Joe Hughes, "Militant Group Suspected of Torching Condo Project," *San Diego Union-Tribune*, August 2, 2003, pp. 1. Pauline Repard, "Militants Say They Set $50 Million Condo Blaze," *San Diego Union-Tribune*, September 9, 2003, p. B1.

2.   "Animal Extremist/Ecoterror Crimes," www.furcommission.com/attack/, accessed on August 15, 2003.

3.   Bjorn Lomborg, *The Skeptical Environmentalist: Measuring the Real State of the World* (Cambridge, U.K.: Cambridge University Press, 2001), p. 193.

4.   Quoted in Walter Williams, "Average Americans vs. Environmentalists" (March 2003), www.gmu.edu/departments/economics/wew/articles/fee/average.html, accessed on September 1, 2003.

5.   Interview of Paul Watson, BiteBack #3, "Paul Watson: The Conservative Republican Pirate," http://directaction.info/#, accessed on May 16, 2004. Quoted in Thomas Ryan, "The Greens' Favorite Terrorist," FrontPageMagazine.com, May 4, 2004. Available at www.frontpagemag.com/Articles/Printable.asp?ID=13159, accessed on May 4, 2004.

6.   Quoted in "Sea Shepherd Conservation Society," www.activistcash.com/organization_overview.cfm/oid/347, accessed on May 16, 2004.

7.   Quoted in Walter Williams, "Average Americans vs. Environmentalists" (March 2003), www.gmu.edu/departments/economics/wew/articles/fee/average.html, accessed on September 1, 2003.

8.   Quoted in *The Environmentalists' Little Green Book* (Washington, DC: U.S. Chamber of Commerce, 2000), p. 30.

9.   Quoted in Lomborg, *The Skeptical Environmentalist*, p. 91.

10.   Quoted in John Tierney, "Betting on the Planet," *New York Times Magazine*, December 2, 1990, p. 54.

11.   Paul Ehrlich, *The Population Bomb* (New York: Ballantine Books, 1968), p. xi.

12.   Paul Ehrlich, *The Population Bomb*, revised edition (New York: Ballantine Books, 1978), p. xi.

13.   Ehrlich, *The Population Bomb*, rev. ed., p. 93.

14.   Ehrlich, *The Population Bomb*, rev. ed., p. 39.

15.   Ehrlich, *The Population Bomb*, rev. ed., p. 28.

16.   Ehrlich, *The Population Bomb*, rev. ed., p. 140.

17.   Ehrlich, *The Population Bomb*, rev. ed., p. 148.

18.   Ehrlich, *The Population Bomb*, rev. ed., p. 47.

19.   Ehrlich, *The Population Bomb*, rev. ed., p. 48.

20.   Ehrlich, *The Population Bomb*, rev. ed., p. 145.

21.   Ehrlich, *The Population Bomb*, rev. ed., p. 53.

22.   Ehrlich, *The Population Bomb*, rev. ed., p. 72.

23.   Ehrlich, *The Population Bomb*, rev. ed., p. 75.

24.   Ehrlich, *The Population Bomb*, rev. ed., p. 131.

25.   Ehrlich, *The Population Bomb*, rev. ed., p. 132.

26.   Ehrlich, *The Population Bomb*, rev. ed., p. 132.

27.   Ehrlich, *The Population Bomb*, rev. ed., pp. 132–133.

28.   Ehrlich, *The Population Bomb*, rev. ed., pp. 151–152.

29.   Ehrlich, *The Population Bomb*, rev. ed., p. 152.

30.   Quoted in Steve Otto, "Can You Predict the Future?" *Tampa Tribune*, November 30, 1999, Florida/Metro p. 1.

31.   Quoted in Roger Highfield, "A Billion People 'Could Starve to Death by 2010,'" *Daily Telegraph*, November 22, 1990, p. 4.

32.   Quoted in Jeff Jacoby, "Overpopulation?" *Boston Globe*, May 15, 1998, p. 19.

33.   Quoted in Bob MacDonald, "Boom Spells Doom," *Toronto Sun*, September 7, 1994, "My World" section, p. 27.

34.   Quoted in "A Doomsday Message That Won't Die," *Tampa Tribune*, November 23, 1999, p. 14.

35.   Lomborg, *The Skeptical Environmentalist*, pp. 249–251.

36.   Lomborg, *The Skeptical Environmentalist*, p. 111.

37.   "Latest Findings on National Air Quality: 2002 Status and Trends," Environmental Protection Agency, August 2003, available at www.epa.gov/airtrends/2002_airtrends_final.pdf, accessed on October 31, 2003.

38.   Lomborg, *The Skeptical Environmentalist*, p. 203.

39.   Lomborg, *The Skeptical Environmentalist*, p. 125.

40.   Lomborg, *The Skeptical Environmentalist*, p. xxi.

41.   Paul Ehrlich and Anne Ehrlich, *Betrayal of Science and Reason: How Anti-Environmental Rhetoric Threatens Our Future* (Washington, DC: Island Press, 1996), pp. 11–12.

42.   Ehrlich and Ehrlich, *Betrayal of Science and Reason*, p. 39.

43.   Ronald Bailey, *Ecoscam: False Prophets of Ecological Apocalypse* (New York: St. Martin's Press, 1993), p. 53.

44.   Quoted in Matt Ridley, "Beware of the Greens Who Cry Wolf," *Times* (London), March 25, 1995.

45.   Richard Tren and Roger Bate, "When Politics Kills: Malaria and the DDT Story" (Washington, DC: Competitive Enterprise Institute, 2000), p. 16.

46.   Joseph L. Bast, Peter J. Hill, and Richard C. Rue, *Eco-Sanity: A Common Sense Guide to Environmentalism* (Lanham, MD: Madison Books, 1994), p. 100.

47.   Lomborg, *The Skeptical Environmentalist*, pp. 178–180.

48.   Mark Shrope, "Successes in Fight to Save Ozone Layer Could Close Holes by 2050," *Nature*, December 7, 2000, p. 627.

49.   Michael Fumento, *Science Under Siege: Balancing Technology and the Environment* (New York: William Morrow, 1993), pp. 19–44.

50.   Quoted in Charles Petit, "Two Stanford Professors Offer to Bet Optimistic Economist," *San Francisco Chronicle*, May 18, 1995, p. 16.

51.   Michael Fumento, "Doomsayer Paul Ehrlich Strikes Out Again," *Investor's Business Daily*, December 16, 1997, p. 1.

Chapter 4: "Speciesism"

1.   Michael Specter, "The Extremist: The Woman Behind the Most Successful Radical Group in America," *New Yorker*, April 14, 2003, p. 60.

2.   For a thorough look at animal-rights terrorism, see "Animal Extremist/Ecoterror Crimes," www.furcommission.com/attack, accessed on August 15, 2003.

3.   Sonja Barisic, "Anti-Milk Ads Go Sour," ABCNews.com, March 13, 2000, abcnews.go.com/sections/us/DailyNews/beer000316.html, accessed on August 31, 2003.

4.   Richard Berman, "Enemies Here Threaten Food," *USA Today*, November 1, 2001, p. 19.

5.   PETA's attacks on the March of Dimes can be found on their website, www.marchofcrimes.com, accessed on May 15, 2004.

6.   Quoted in Brian Carnell, "PETA and Animal Rights Violence," CNSNews.com, November 12, 2001, www.cnsnews.com/Commentary/Archive/200111/COM20011112b.html, accessed on August 31, 2003.

7.   "PETA Roars Over Roy Incident," *Newsday*, October 7, 2003, p. 12. "The only natural thing that happened on that stage was that this majestic animal lashed out against a captor who was beating him with a microphone because he wouldn't do a trick," read part of Mathews's ill-timed missive. "No matter how much you say that you love the wild animals whom you have confined continents away from their natural homes, you are still the men who have subjugated their wills and natures to further your own careers."

8.   Quoted in Richard Berman, "Enemies Here Threaten Food," *USA Today*, November 1, 2001, p. 19.

9.   Quoted in Wesley J. Smith, "PETA-Fried," National Review Online, July 11, 2003, www.nationalreview.com/comment/comment-smith071103.asp, accessed on July 11, 2003.

10.   Quoted in Donovan Slack, "Exhibit Comparing Holocaust, Animals Decried," *Boston Globe*, May 21, 2003, p. B1.

11. Matthew Barakat, "PETA Euthanized More Than 1,000 Animals Last Year," July 29, 2000, Associated Press Wire.

12. "Animal Extremist/Ecoterror Crimes," www.furcommission.com/attack, accessed on August 15, 2003.

13. "Scores of Freed Mink Feed on Farm Animals," Associated Press, August 30, 2003. A later AP story ("Mink Eat Each Other After Animal Rights Break-In," Associated Press, October 10, 2003) detailed cannibalism resulting from the raid. Because farm workers were unable to identify litter mates and cage them together, many of the recaptured animals began eating one another—as they're apt to do in such situations.

14. Peter Singer, "Getting the Facts Right on Dutch Euthanasia," *Daily Princetonian*, April 7, 2000, www.dailyprincetonian.com/archives/2000/04/07/opinion/686.shtml, accessed on October 31, 2003; Peter Singer, "Not Right: American Apathy Influences Health Policies," *Daily Princetonian*, October 19, 1999, www.dailyprincetonian.com/Content/1999/10/19/edits/singer.html, accessed on October 31, 2003.

15. Peter Singer, *How Are We to Live?: Ethics in the Age of Self-Interest* (New York: Prometheus Books, 1995), p. 45.

16. Peter Singer, "The Singer Solution to World Poverty," *New York Times Magazine*, September 5, 1999, p. 61.

17. Peter Singer, *Practical Ethics* (Cambridge, UK: Cambridge University Press, 1997), p. 151.

18. Singer, *Practical Ethics*, p. 186.

19. Singer, *Practical Ethics*, p. 186.

20. Singer, *Practical Ethics*, p. 95.

21. Singer, *Practical Ethics*, p. 90.

22. Peter Singer, *Rethinking Life and Death: The Collapse of Our Traditional Ethics* (New York: St. Martin's Griffin, 1999), p. 130.

23. Singer, *Rethinking Life and Death*, p. 217.

24. Singer, *Rethinking Life and Death*, pp. 130, 98.

25. Singer, *Rethinking Life and Death*, p. 214.

26. Singer, *Rethinking Life and Death*, p. 215.

27. Peter Singer, *Animal Liberation: New Revised Edition* (New York: Avon Books, 1991), p. i.

28. Singer, *Animal Liberation*, pp. 83, 226–227.

29. Singer, *Animal Liberation*, p. 6.

30. Singer, *Animal Liberation*, p. 6.

31. Singer, *Animal Liberation*, p. 9.

32. Singer, *Animal Liberation*, p. xi.

33. Singer, *Animal Liberation*, p. 42.

34. Singer, *Animal Liberation*, p. 223.

35. Singer, *Animal Liberation*, p. i.

36. Singer, *Animal Liberation*, p. 117.

37. For examples of such comparisons to the Nazis, see *Animal Liberation*, pp. 83–84.

38. Peter Singer, "Heavy Petting," www.nerve.com/Opinions/Singer/heavyPetting/main.asp, accessed on March 14, 2001.

39. Singer, "Heavy Petting."

40. Jonathan Barnes, ed., *The Complete Works of Aristotle: Volume I* (Princeton, NJ: Princeton University Press, 1995), p. 316.

41. Quoted in Kushanava Choudhury, "Despite Rallies, University Defends Singer's Appointment to Faculty," *Daily Princetonian*, July 19, 1999, p. 1.

42. Quoted in Kushanava Choudhury, "Peter Singer to Join Faculty as Bioethics Professor in Fall," *Daily Princetonian*, February 20, 1999, p. 1.

43. Quoted in Kushanava Choudhury, "Peter Singer to Join Faculty as Bioethics Professor in Fall," *Daily Princetonian*, February 20, 1999, p. 1.

44. Quoted in Paul Gottfried, *After Liberalism: Mass Democracy in the Managerial State* (Princeton, NJ: Princeton University Press, 1999) p. 89.

45. Christopher Benneck, "No Place to Impose 'Immoral' View," *Daily Princetonian*, April 16, 1999, p. 4.

46. Daniel J. Flynn, "Angry Protests Greet Princeton's Professor Death; 14 Arrested," *Campus Report*, October 1999, pp. 1, 8.

47. Quoted in Richard Just, "Trustees Rip Forbes for Stance on Singer," *Daily Princetonian*, October 8, 1999, p. 1.

48. Quoted in Richard Just, "Trustees Rip Forbes for Stance on Singer," *Daily Princetonian*, October 8, 1999, p. 1.

49. To read the letter in full, see "An Open Letter to David Novak, CEO of Yum! Brands, from Russell Simmons," www.kfccruelty.com/letters/simmonsLetter. pdf, accessed on August 31, 2003.

50. Ad: "Thanksgiving Is Murder on Turkeys," www.peta.org/pdfs/ADphoenix. pdf, accessed on August 31, 2003.

Chapter 5: "And That Is My Truth"

1. Larry Rohter, "Nobel Winner Finds Her Story Challenged," *New York Times*, December 15, 1998, p. 8.

2. Elisabeth Burgos-Debray in the introduction to *I, Rigoberta Menchu: An Indian Woman in Guatemala*, by Rigoberta Menchu, edited by Elisabeth Burgos-Debray, translated by Ann Wright (New York: Verso, 1984, 1998), p. xi.

3. Quoted in David Stoll, *Rigoberta Menchu and the Story of All Poor Guatemalans* (Boulder, CO: Westview Press, 1999), p. 7.

4. Stoll, *Rigoberta Menchu and the Story of All Poor Guatemalans*, p. 12.

5. Patrick Costello, "The Guatemalan Peace Process: Historical Background," *Accord: An International Review of Peace Initiatives* (Conciliation Resources), www.c–r.org/acc_guat/background.htm, accessed on July 24, 2000.

6. *Country Reports on Human Rights Practices for 1996* (Washington, DC: U.S. Government Printing Office, 1997), p. 461.

7. Will Weissert, "Guatemala Vigilante Killings Common," Associated Press, July 11, 2000.

8. Patrick Costello, "The Guatemalan Peace Process: Historical Background," *Accord: An International Review of Peace Initiatives* (Conciliation Resources), www.c–r.org/acc_guat/background.htm, accessed on July 24, 2000.

9. Richard Wilson, "Violent Truths: The Politics of Memory in Guatemala," *Accord: An International Review of Peace Initiatives* (Conciliation Resources), www.c–r.org/acc_guat/wilson.htm, accessed on July 24, 2000.

10. "Stanford Slights the Great Books for Not-So-Greats," *Wall Street Journal*, December 22, 1988, p. A14.

11.   Menchu, *I, Rigoberta Menchu*, p. 91.

12.   Dinesh D'Souza, *Illiberal Education: The Politics of Race and Sex on Campus* (New York City: Free Press, 1991), p. 74.

13.   D'Souza, *Illiberal Education*, p. 72.

14.   Menchu, *I, Rigoberta Menchu*, p. 11.

15.   Menchu, *I, Rigoberta Menchu*, p. 60.

16.   Menchu, *I, Rigoberta Menchu*, p. 122.

17.   Menchu, *I, Rigoberta Menchu*, p. 118.

18.   Rigoberta Menchu, *Crossing Borders* (New York: Verso Press, 1998), p. 109.

19.   Menchu, *Crossing Borders*, p. 113.

20.   Menchu, *I, Rigoberta Menchu*, p. 2.

21.   Menchu, *I, Rigoberta Menchu*, p. 102.

22.   Menchu, *I, Rigoberta Menchu*, p. 103.

23.   Stoll, *Rigoberta Menchu and the Story of All Poor Guatemalans*, pp. 30–34.

24.   Stoll, *Rigoberta Menchu and the Story of All Poor Guatemalans*, p. 31.

25.   Quoted in Larry Rohter, "Nobel Winner Finds Her Story Challenged," *New York Times*, December 15, 1998, p. 1.

26.   Quoted in Larry Rohter, "Nobel Winner Finds Her Story Challenged," *New York Times*, December 15, 1998, p. 1.

27.   Stoll, *Rigoberta Menchu and the Story of All Poor Guatemalans*, p. 193.

28.   Stoll, *Rigoberta Menchu and the Story of All Poor Guatemalans*, p. 39.

29.   Menchu, *I, Rigoberta Menchu*, p. 114.

30.   Stoll, *Rigoberta Menchu and the Story of All Poor Guatemalans*, p. 93.

31.   Stoll, *Rigoberta Menchu and the Story of All Poor Guatemalans*, p. 94.

32.   The sole survivor blames the fire on an errant Molotov cocktail thrown by the rebels that missed its mark. Stoll, *Rigoberta Menchu and the Story of All Poor Guatemalans*, p. 80.

33.   Menchu, *I, Rigoberta Menchu*, pp. 172–182, quote appears on p. 177.

34.   Stoll, *Rigoberta Menchu and the Story of All Poor Guatemalans*, p. 69.

35.   Julia Preston, "Guatemala Laureate Defends 'My Truth,'" *New York Times*, January 21, 1999, p. 8.

36.   Menchu, *Crossing Borders*, p. 70.

37.   Menchu, *I, Rigoberta Menchu*, p. 38.

38.   Menchu, *Crossing Borders*, p. 227.

39.   Larry Rohter, "Nobel Winner Finds Her Story Challenged," *New York Times*, December 15, 1998, p. 8.

40.   Menchu, *I, Rigoberta Menchu*, p. 190.

41.   Menchu, *I, Rigoberta Menchu*, p. 1.

42.   Stoll, *Rigoberta Menchu and the Story of All Poor Guatemalans*, pp. 159–166. Quote appears on p. 165.

43.   Larry Rohter, "Nobel Winner Finds Her Story Challenged," *New York Times*, December 15, 1998, p. 8.

44.   Quoted in Stoll, *Rigoberta Menchu and the Story of All Poor Guatemalans*, p. 163. Also see, Larry Rohter, "Nobel Winner Finds Her Story Challenged," *New York Times*, December 15, 1998, pp. 1, 8.

45.   Julia Preston, "Guatemala Laureate Defends 'My Truth,'" *New York Times*, January 21, 1999, p. 8.

46.   Menchu, *Crossing Borders*, p. 45.

47.   Menchu, *Crossing Borders*, pp. 44–45.

48. Menchu, *Crossing Borders*, p. 44.

49. Quoted in Stoll, *Rigoberta Menchu and the Story of All Poor Guatemalans*, p. 227.

50. Stoll, *Rigoberta Menchu and the Story of All Poor Guatemalans*, pp. xi, 188.

51. Julia Preston, "Guatemala Laureate Defends 'My Truth,'" *New York Times*, January 21, 1999, p. 8.

52. Julia Preston, "Guatemala Laureate Defends 'My Truth,'" *New York Times*, January 21, 1999, p. 8.

53. Rigoberta Menchu Tum Foundation, "Rigoberta Menchu Tum: The Truth That Challenges the Future," January 20, 1999. The release can be found on the Foundation for Human Rights in Guatemala's website, fhrg.org/mench1.htm, accessed on June 21, 1999.

54. Rigoberta Menchu Tum Foundation, "Rigoberta Menchu Tum: The Truth That Challenges the Future," January 20, 1999. The release can be found on the Foundation for Human Rights in Guatemala's website, fhrg.org/mench1.htm, accessed on June 21, 1999.

55. Stoll, *Rigoberta Menchu and the Story of All Poor Guatemalans*, p. 181.

56. Phone interview of David Stoll by author on October 17, 2000.

57. Larry Rohter, "Nobel Winner Finds Her Story Challenged," *New York Times*, December 15, 1998, p. 8.

58. David Maeng, "Stanford Grad Doubts Nobel Laureate's Story," *Stanford Review*, February 3, 1999, pp. 4–5, 11.

59. Phone interview with Ann Jones by author on October 16, 2000.

60. Phone interview with Marjorie Becker by author on October 16, 2000.

61. Phone interview with Deborah Levenson-Estrada by author on October 16, 2000.

62. Quoted in Barry Flynn, "Profs Will Continue to Teach Nobel Prize Winner's Hoax as Fact," *Campus Report*, September 1999, pp. 1, 3.

63. Greg Grandin and Francisco Goldman, "Bitter Fruit for Rigoberta," *The Nation*, February 8, 1999, p. 26.

64. Quoted in Robin Wilson, "Anthropologist Challenges Veracity of Multicultural Icon," *Chronicle of Higher Education*, January 15, 1999, p. 14.

65. Phone interview of David Stoll by author on October 17, 2000.

66. Phone interview of Nina Scott by author on October 16, 2000.

67. Phone interview of Rick Livingston by author on September 6, 2000.

68. Stoll, *Rigoberta Menchu and the Story of All Poor Guatemalans*, p. 246.

69. Stoll, *Rigoberta Menchu and the Story of All Poor Guatemalans*, p. 247.

Chapter 6: "History Itself as a Political Act"

1. Author interview of Cynthia Orr at protest against war in Iraq held in Washington, D.C., on March 15, 2003.

2. Author interview of David Werier at protest of Bush administration's foreign policy held in New York City on February 15, 2003.

3. Author interview of Chris King at protest of Bush administration's foreign policy held in Washington, D.C., on January 18, 2003.

4. With one exception, this paragraph is based on my experiences and observations at various rallies. The last banner referenced was held aloft at a protest in San Francisco that I did not attend. To observe the banner, see Ken Hechtman,

"We Support Our Troops . . . When They Shoot Their Officers," FrontPage Magazine.com, July 4, 2003, www.frontpagemag.com/Articles/ReadArticle. asp?ID=8744, accessed on October 28, 2003.

5. Author interview of Michael McAvoy at protest of Bush administration's foreign policy held in Washington, D.C., on January 18, 2003.

6. Author interview of Marcy Betterly at protest of Bush administration's foreign policy held in New York City on February 15, 2003.

7. Author interview of Jim Swanson at protest of Bush administration's foreign policy held in Washington, D.C., on March 15, 2003.

8. Author interview of Frank Lombardi at protest of Bush administration's foreign policy held in New York City on February 15, 2003.

9. "Interview with Howard Zinn," DigressMagazine.com, www.digressmagazine. com/zinn/zinn1, accessed on September 22, 2003.

10. Eddie Vedder interviewed by Howard Zinn, "The Rocker and the Teacher," available at free.freespeech.org/evolution/vedderzinn.htm, accessed on November 1, 2003. "RATM.com Reading List," www.ratm.com, accessed on September 29, 2003.

11. *Good Will Hunting* (film), Lawrence Bender, producer (Miramax: 1997).

12. Dan Kennedy, "Don't Quote Me," *Boston Phoenix*, September 24, 1998, www.bostonphoenix.com/archive/features/98/09/24/DON_T_QUOTE_ME.html, accessed on September 29, 2003.

13. Howard Zinn, *A People's History of the United States, 1492–Present* (New York: HarperCollins, 2003), p. 669.

14. "Popular In," www.amazon.com/exec/obidos/tg/detail/-/0060528427/, accessed on May 1, 2003.

15. Syllabus: Larry Mosqueda, "The Political Economy of Noam Chomsky," Evergreen State University, Fall 2001.

16. Howard Zinn, *A People's History of the United States, 1492–Present: Revised and Updated Edition* (New York: Harper Perennial, 1995), p. 418.

17. Zinn, *A People's History of the United States*, p. 573–574.

18. Zinn, *A People's History of the United States*, p. 631.

19. Zinn, *A People's History of the United States* (2003), p. 647.

20. Press Release: U.S. Department of Justice Bureau of Justice Statistics, "Violent Crime and Property Crime Levels Fall to the Lowest Levels Since 1973," August 24, 2003.

21. Zinn, *A People's History of the United States* (2003), p. 668.

22. Daniel J. Flynn, *Cop Killer: How Mumia Abu-Jamal Conned Millions into Believing He Was Framed* (Washington, DC: Accuracy in Academia, 1999). To review the trial transcript, see "Trial Transcripts," www.justice4danielfaulkner.com/ index.html, accessed on September 24, 2003.

23. Zinn, *A People's History of the United States* (2003), p. 679.

24. Karl Marx, "The Communist Manifesto," in David McLellan, ed., *Karl Marx: Selected Writings* (Oxford, UK: Oxford University Press, 2002), p. 246.

25. Zinn, *A People's History of the United States*, pp. 1–5. In the first five pages of the book, for instance, the word "gold" appears more than twenty times.

26. Zinn *A People's History of the United States*, p. 16.

27. Zinn, *A People's History of the United States*, p. 59.

28. Zinn, *A People's History of the United States*, p. 59.

29. Zinn, *A People's History of the United States*, p. 215.

30. Zinn, *A People's History of the United States*, p. 228.

31. Zinn, *A People's History of the United States*, p. 354.

32. Zinn, *A People's History of the United States*, p. 400–401.

33. Zinn, *A People's History of the United States*, p. 404.

34. Frank McLynn, *Wagon's West: The Epic Story of America's Overland Trails* (New York: Grove Press, 2002), pp. 431–432. The author points out that only a few thousand Americans had trekked cross-country to California by 1848. Within twelve years, the figure exceeded 200,000.

35. Zinn, *A People's History of the United States*, p. 84.

36. John Rhodehamel, ed., *Washington: Writings* (New York: The Library of America, 1997), pp. 1022–1042. Robert Morris, who eventually lost his wealth, was the Revolutionary era's wealthiest merchant. Moses Brown, whose family's name graces a university, was another contemporary of Washington's whose wealth in the Republic's early years exceeded that of the nation's first president.

37. Zinn, *A People's History of the United States*, p. 438.

38. Richard Gid Powers, *Not Without Honor: The History of American Anticommunism* (New York: The Free Press, 1995), p. 101.

39. Quoted in Powers, *Not Without Honor*, p. 101.

40. Zinn, *A People's History of the United States*, p. 565.

41. "US Unemployment Rate; Monthly SA, Percent," www.economagic.com/em-cgi/data.exe/feddal/ru, accessed on September 29, 2003.

42. Robert Bartley, *The Seven Fat Years and How to Do It Again* (New York: Free Press, 1992), pp. 135–147.

43. Zinn, *A People's History of the United States*, p. 618.

44. Howard Zinn, "Howard Zinn: 'History as a Political Act,'" interviewed by Raymond Lotta, *Revolutionary Worker*, December 20, 1998.

45. *Good Will Hunting*.

46. Howard Zinn, "Foreward," in Noam Chomsky, *American Power and the New Mandarins* (New York: The New Press, 2002), pp. iii–ix. Quoted in Chomsky, *American Power and the New Mandarins*, p. 369.

47. Maya Jaggi, "Noam Chomsky: Conscience of a Nation," *Guardian*, January 20, 2001, p. 6.

48. Robert F. Barsky, *Noam Chomsky: A Life of Dissent* (Cambridge, MA: The MIT Press, 1998), p. 3.

49. Arthur Naiman, "Editor's Note," in Noam Chomsky, *Secrets, Lies, and Democracy* (Berkeley, CA: Odonian Press, 1994), p. 5.

50. Noam Chomsky, *Power and Terror: Post 9/11 Talks and Interviews*, eds. John Junkerman and Takei Masakazu (New York: Seven Stories Press, 2003), p. 116.

51. Noam Chomsky, *The Chomsky Reader*, ed. James Peck (New York: Pantheon, 1987), p. 53. Noam Chomsky, *Rogue States: The Rule of Force in World Affairs* (Cambridge, MA: South End Press, 2000), pp. 5, 9.

52. Chomsky, *American Power and the New Mandarins*, p. 9.

53. Chomsky, *Power and Terror*, p. 80.

54. Chomsky, *American Power and the New Mandarins*, p. 16.

55. Noam Chomsky, *Language and Responsibility: Based on Conversations with Mitsou Ronat* (New York: Knopf, 1979), p. 20.

56. Chomsky, *The Chomsky Reader*, p. 127.

57. Quoted in Bonnie Dhall, "Linguist Warns of U.S. Fascism," *Golden Gater*, April 25, 1995, www.journalism.sfsu.edu/www/pubs/gater/spring95/apr25/ling.htm, accessed on September 16, 2003.

58. Noam Chomsky, "Intellectuals," ZNet.com, August 29, 2003, www.zmag. org/content/pring/article.cfm?itemID=4107&sectionID=36, accessed on September 16, 2003.

59. Noam Chomsky, *What Uncle Sam Really Wants* (Berkeley, CA: Odonian Press, 1992), p. 18.

60. Chomsky, *What Uncle Sam Really Wants*, pp. 8, 19.

61. Chomsky, *What Uncle Sam Really Wants*, pp. 8–9.

62. Noam Chomsky and Edward S. Herman, "Distortions at Fourth Hand," *The Nation*, June 25, 1977, p. 789.

63. Edward S. Herman and Noam Chomsky, *Manufacturing Consent: The Political Economy of the Mass Media* (New York: Pantheon Books, 1988), p. 265.

64. Chomsky and Herman, "Distortions at Fourth Hand," p. 790.

65. Chomsky and Herman, "Distortions at Fourth Hand," pp. 790, 792, 793. For information on Cambodian Catholics and other groups targeted by the Khmer Rouge, see Stephane Courtois et al., *The Black Book of Communism: Crimes, Terror, Repression*, trans. Jonathan Murphy and Mark Kramer (Cambridge, MA: Harvard University Press, 1999), pp. 591–595.

66. Chomsky and Herman, "Distortions at Fourth Hand," p. 791.

67. Chomsky and Herman, "Distortions at Fourth Hand," p. 791.

68. Chomsky and Herman, "Distortions at Fourth Hand," p. 792.

69. Quoted in Courtois et al., *The Black Book of Communism*, p. 597.

70. Courtois et al., *The Black Book of Communism*, pp. 577–635.

71. Chomsky, *The Chomsky Reader*, p. 360.

72. Courtois et al., *The Black Book of Communism*, p. 663.

73. Quoted in Courtois et al., *The Black Book of Communism*, p. 650.

74. Courtois et al., *The Black Book of Communism*, pp. 648–649.

75. "Cuba: Executions of Three Alleged Hijackers," Human Rights Watch, April 12, 2003, www.hrw.org/press/2003/04/cuba041203.htm, accessed on September 22, 2003.

76. Quoted in Courtois et al., *The Black Book of Communism*, p. 649.

77. "Human Rights Watch World Report 2003: Cuba," Human Rights Watch (2003), www.hrw.org/wr2k3/americas5.html, accessed on September 22, 2003. "Amnesty International's Human Rights Concerns for Cuba," Amnesty International USA (2003), www.amnestyusa.org/countries/cuba/document.do?id=1B95A6239421DF2680256D2400379150, accessed on September 22, 2003.

78. "Human Rights Watch World Report 2003: Cuba," Human Rights Watch (2003), www.hrw.org/wr2k3/americas5.html, accessed on September 22, 2003. "Amnesty International's Human Rights Concerns for Cuba," Amnesty International USA (2003), www.amnestyusa.org/countries/cuba/document.do?id=1B95A6239421DF2680256D2400379150, accessed on September 22, 2003.

79. Noam Chomsky, *9–11* (New York: Seven Stories Press, 2001), p. 54.

80. Chomsky, *9–11*, p. 50.

81. Russell Watson and John Barry, "'Our Target Was Terror,'" *Newsweek*, August 31, 1998, p. 24.

82. Keith Windschuttle, "The Hypocrisy of Noam Chomsky," *New Criterion*, May 2003, www.newcriterion.com/archive/21/may03/chomsky.htm, accessed on October 31, 2003.

83. Interview: Suzy Hansen, "Noam Chomsky," Salon.com, January 16, 2003, www.salon.com, accessed on September 11, 2003.

84.   Carroll Bogert, "Letter: 'Noam Needs a Fact Checker,'" Salon.com, January 22, 2002, www.salon.com/people/letters/2002/01/22/chomsky, accessed on September 11, 2003.

85.   Werner Daum, "Universalism and the West," *Harvard International Review*, Summer 2001, p. 19.

86.   "Interviewing Chomsky: Radio B92, Belgrade," www.zmag.org/chomb92, accessed on September 23, 2001.

87.   Chomsky, *9–11* p. 102.

88.   "Bin Laden on Tape: Attacks 'Benefited Islam Greatly,'" www.cnn.com/2001/US/12/13/ret.bin.laden.videotape/, accessed on May 18, 2004. "New bin Laden Tape Surfaces," www.cnn.com/2002/WORLD.meast/04/15/terror.tape/, accessed on May 18, 2004.

89.   Noam Chomsky interviewed by David Barsamian, "U.S. Intervention from Afghanistan to Iraq," *International Socialist Review*, September–October 2002, www.isreview.org/issues/25/chomsky/interview.shtml, accessed on April 7, 2004.

90.   Speech: Noam Chomsky, "The New War Against Terror," Cambridge, MA, October 18, 2001, www.zmag.org/Global Watch/chomskymit, accessed on September 17, 2003.

91.   "Interviewing Chomsky: Radio B92, Belgrade," www.zmag.org/chomb92, accessed on September 23, 2001.

92.   Speech: Noam Chomsky, "The New War Against Terror," Cambridge, MA, October 18, 2001, www.zmag.org/Global Watch/chomskymit, accessed on September 17, 2003.

93.   Laura King, "AP Review of Afghan Civilian Casualties Suggests Toll in Hundreds: Taliban Inflated Count," Associated Press, February 11, 2002. For an additional discussion of the amount of food brought to, and bombs dropped on, Afghanistan, see "Air War Afghanistan," EFreedomNews.com, www.efreedomnews.com/News%20Archive/Afghanistan/Air%20War.htm, accessed on September 17, 2003; and "USAF Talking Points: The War on Terrorism," Air Force Link, December 6, 2002, www.af.mil/news/efreedom/GWOT_talker_6Dec02_.pdf, accessed on September 29, 2003.

94.   Laura King, "AP Review of Afghan Civilian Casualties Suggests Toll in Hundreds: Taliban Inflated Count," Associated Press, February 11, 2002.

95.   Speech: Noam Chomsky, "The New War Against Terror," Cambridge, MA, October 18, 2001, www.zmag.org/Global Watch/chomskymit, accessed on September 17, 2003.

96.   Chomsky, *The Chomsky Reader*, p. 60.

97.   Quoted in Gore Vidal, *Palimpsest: A Memoir* (New York: Random House, 1995), p. 148.

98.   Fred Kaplan, *Gore Vidal: A Biography* (New York: Anchor Books, 2000), pp. 556–557.

99.   Kaplan, *Gore Vidal*, pp. 661–662. Quotes therein.

100.   Vidal, *Palimpsest*, pp. 301–307. Kaplan, *Gore Vidal*, pp. 690–691.

101.   Kaplan, *Gore Vidal*, pp. 531, 544.

102.   Quoted in Kaplan, *Gore Vidal*, pp. 600–601.

103.   Kaplan, *Gore Vidal*, p. 642. Vidal's comparison of Mailer, who nearly murdered his wife in 1960, to Manson, a convicted serial killer, was clearly intended to conjure up images of a drunken Mailer stabbing his wife. This unstated premise of the comparison seems to be the real reason for Mailer's rage.

104.   Quoted in Kaplan, *Gore Vidal,* p. 710.

105.   Vidal, *Palimpsest,* p. 16.

106.   Vidal, *Palimpsest,* pp. 7, 72, 323.

107.   Vidal, *Palimpsest,* pp. 102–103.

108.   Vidal, *Palimpsest,* pp. 177, 218.

109.   Vidal, *Palimpsest,* p. 121.

110.   Vidal, *Palimpsest,* p. 95.

111.   Vidal, *Palimpsest,* p. 123.

112.   Vidal, *Palimpsest,* pp. 94, 115, 231.

113.   Vidal, *Palimpsest,* p. 231.

114.   Vidal, *Palimpsest,* p. 36.

115.   Vidal, *Palimpsest,* p. 121.

116.   Quoted in Kaplan, *Gore Vidal,* p. 330.

117.   Kaplan, *Gore Vidal,* p. 789.

118.   Gore Vidal, "The Unrocked Boat," *The Nation,* April 26, 1958, p. 372.

119.   Quoted in Kaplan, *Gore Vidal,* p. 668.

120.   Kaplan, *Gore Vidal,* pp. 624–626, 694–695.

121.   Bill Kaufman, "The Patriot," *Chronicles,* June 2003, www.chronicles magazine.org/Chronicles/June2003/0603Kauffman.html, accessed on March 21, 2004. Justin Raimondo, "Patriotic Gore," *The American Conservative,* March 1, 2004, pp. 32–33. The former book review refers to Vidal as America's "greatest living man of letters," "an exemplary citizen-writer," and a "patriot." The lovefest continues in the latter book review. "Wherever [Vidal] got his reputation as a liberal," Raimondo writes, "this polemic ought to dispel it for good."

122.   Quoted in Bill Kauffman, *America First! Its History, Culture, and Politics* (Amherst, NY: Prometheus Books, 1995), p. 133.

123.   Gore Vidal, *Dreaming War: Blood for Oil and the Cheney-Bush Junta* (New York: Nation Books, 2002), p. 11.

124.   Vidal, *Dreaming War,* p. 187.

125.   Vidal, *Dreaming War,* p. 15.

126.   Vidal, *Dreaming War,* p. 40.

127.   Vidal, *Dreaming War,* p. 23.

128.   Gore Vidal, *Perpetual War for Perpetual Peace: How We Got to Be So Hated* (New York: Nation Books, 2002), p. 118.

129.   Vidal, *Perpetual War for Perpetual Peace,* p. ix.

130.   Vidal, *Perpetual War for Perpetual Peace,* p. 117.

131.   Vidal, *Perpetual War for Perpetual Peace,* p. 47.

132.   Vidal, *Dreaming War,* p. 70.

133.   Office of Management and Budget, *The Budget for Fiscal Year 2004: Historical Tables* (Washington, DC: US Government Printing Office, 2003), p. 51.

134.   Vidal, *Dreaming War,* pp. 188–189.

135.   Larry Nowels, *Appropriations for FY2003: Foreign Operations, Export Financing, and Related Programs* (Washington, DC: Congressional Research Service, 2003), p. 12. Israel's take of U.S. foreign aid totaled $2.7 billion, which is more than that received by any other nation. The total foreign aid detailed in *Appropriations for FY2003* exceeds $16 billion. Furthermore, that $16 billion represents only about two-thirds of the U.S. budget for foreign aid. Clearly, Israel doesn't receive most of U.S. foreign aid.

136.   Vidal, *Perpetual War for Perpetual Peace,* p. 10.

137. Vidal, *Dreaming War*, p. 128.

138. Vidal, *Dreaming War*, pp. 89, 96.

139. Vidal, *Dreaming War*, p. 113.

140. Vidal, *Dreaming War*, p. 63.

141. Richard Posner, *Public Intellectuals: A Study of Decline* (Cambridge, MA: Harvard University Press, 2001), p. 175, 194–206.

142. Vidal, *Dreaming War*, pp. 7, 76.

143. Author interview of Reesa Rosenberg at protest of Bush administration's foreign policy in Washington, D.C., on January 18, 2003.

144. Author interview of John Aria at protest of Bush administration's foreign policy in Washington, D.C., on March 15, 2003.

145. Author interview of Abram Megrete at protest of Bush administration's foreign policy in Washington, D.C., on March 15, 2003.

146. Author interview of anonymous protestor at demonstration on various issues (the International Monetary Fund, the war in Iraq, the Bush administration, etc.) in Washington, D.C., on April 24, 2004.

147. Author interview of marcher who refused to give his name at protest of Bush administration's foreign policy held in New York City on February 15, 2003.

148. Quoted in Elizabeth Knowles, ed., *The Oxford Dictionary of Quotations: Major New Edition* (Oxford: Oxford University Press, 2001), p. 648.

Chapter 7: "A Truth That Lesser Mortals Failed to Grasp"

1. Richard A. Clarke, *Against All Enemies: Inside America's War on Terror* (New York: The Free Press, 2004), pp. 30–33, 264–265. Bob Woodward, *Bush at War* (New York: Simon & Schuster, 2002), pp. 49, 83–85, 88. Ron Suskind, *The Price of Loyalty: George W. Bush, the White House, and the Education of Paul O'Neill* (New York: Simon & Schuster, 2004), pp. 186–188.

2. Speech: George W. Bush, "State of the Union, 2003," Washington, DC, January 28, 2003.

3. Mitch Frank, "Tale of the Cake," *Time*, July 21, 2003, pp. 24–25. Michael Duffy, "Weapons of Mass Disappearance," *Time*, June 9, 2003, p. 29.

4. Quoted in Mitch Frank, "Tale of the Cake," *Time*, July 21, 2003, p. 24.

5. Quoted in John J. Lumpkin and Dafna Linzer, "Iraq Nuke Evidence Was Thin, Experts Say," Associated Press, July 19, 2003.

6. Quoted in Michael Duffy and James Carney, "A Question of Trust," *Time*, July 21, 2003, p. 25.

7. Quoted in Dana Priest and Glenn Kessler, "Iraq, 9/11 Still Linked by Cheney," *Washington Post*, September 29, 2003, p. 1.

8. Quoted in Priest and Kessler, "Iraq, 9/11 Still Linked by Cheney," p. 1.

9. Quoted in Priest and Kessler, "Iraq, 9/11 Still Linked by Cheney," p. 1.

10. Quoted in Priest and Kessler, "Iraq, 9/11 Still Linked by Cheney," p. 1.

11. Quoted in Priest and Kessler, "Iraq, 9/11 Still Linked by Cheney," p. 1.

12. Quoted in Bruce Auster, Mark Mazzetti, and Edward Pound, "Truth and Consequences," *U.S. News & World Report*, June 9, 2003, p. 17.

13. Speech: George W. Bush, "State of the Union," Washington, DC, July 28, 2003.

14. Nancy Gibbs and Michael Ware, "Chasing a Mirage," *Time*, October 6, 2003, pp. 38–42. Douglas Jehl, "Official Suggests Iraq Hid Weapons in Syria," *New York Times*, October 29, 2003, p. 1.

15. Quoted in Auster, Mazzetti, and Pound, "Truth and Consequences," *U.S. News & World Report*, June 9, 2003, p. 17.

16. Quoted in Michael Duffy, "Weapons of Mass Disappearance," *Time*, June 9, 2003, p. 31.

17. Quoted in Michael Duffy, "Weapons of Mass Disappearance," *Time*, June 9, 2003, p. 32.

18. Tom Zeller, "Father Strauss Knows Best," *New York Times*, May 4, 2003, p. D4.

19. Leo Strauss, *The City and Man* (Chicago: University of Chicago Press, 1978), p. 3.

20. Leo Strauss, *On Tyranny*, eds. Victor Gourevitch and Michael S. Roth (Chicago: University of Chicago Press, 2000), p. 23.

21. Hadley Arkes, "Strauss on Our Minds," in *Leo Strauss, the Straussians, and the American Regime*, eds. Kenneth L. Deutsch and John A. Murley (Lanham, MD: Rowman and Littlefield, 1999), p. 69.

22. George Anastaplo, "Leo Strauss at the University of Chicago," *Leo Strauss, the Straussians, and the American Regime*, eds. Deutsch and Murley, p. 6.

23. Quoted in George Anastaplo, "Leo Strauss at the University of Chicago," in *Leo Strauss, the Straussians, and the American Regime*, eds. Deutsch and Murley, p. 10.

24. Shadia B. Drury, *Leo Strauss and the American Right* (New York: St. Martin's Press, 1999), p. 2.

25. Robert Locke, "Leo Strauss, Conservative Mastermind," FrontPage Magazine.com, May 31, 2002, www.frontpagemag.com/Articles/ReadArticle.asp?ID=1233, accessed on October 19, 2003.

26. Shadia B. Drury, *Leo Strauss and the American Right*, p. 2.

27. Drury, *Leo Strauss and the American Right*, p. 4.

28. Quoted in Arkes, "Strauss on Our Minds," in *Leo Strauss, the Straussians, and the American Regime*, eds. Deutsch and Murley, p. 76.

29. Strauss, *The City and Man*, pp. 209, 239. Leo Strauss, *What Is Political Philosophy? and Other Studies* (Chicago: University of Chicago Press, 1988), p. 238.

30. Strauss, *What Is Political Philosophy?*, pp. 42, 238.

31. Strauss, *Natural Right and History* (Chicago: University of Chicago, 1992), p. 133.

32. Leo Strauss, *Persecution and the Art of Writing* (Chicago: University of Chicago Press, 1988), p. 118.

33. Strauss, *Persecution and the Art of Writing*, p. 186.

34. Strauss, *Persecution and the Art of Writing*, p. 161.

35. Strauss, *Persecution and the Art of Writing*, p. 25.

36. Strauss, *Persecution and the Art of Writing*, p. 32.

37. Quoted in Ted V. McAllister, *Revolt Against Modernity: Leo Strauss, Eric Voegelin, and the Search for a Postliberal Order* (Lawrence, KS: University Press of Kansas, 1995), pp. 93–94.

38. Leo Strauss, *Natural Right and History*, p. 217n.

39. M. F. Burnyeat, "Sphinx Without a Secret," *New York Review of Books*, May 30, 1985, p. 36.

40.   Leo Strauss, *Liberalism: Ancient and Modern* (Chicago: University of Chicago Press, 1995), p. 75. See also, Strauss, *The City and Man*, pp. 70–73, 82; Strauss, *On Tyranny*, p. 128.

41.   Strauss, *The City and Man*, pp. 50–138.

42.   M. F. Burnyeat, "Sphinx Without a Secret," *New York Review of Books*, May 30, 1985, p. 35.

43.   McAllister, *Revolt Against Modernity*, p. 100.

44.   Strauss, *Natural Right and History*, p. 220.

45.   Strauss, *Natural Right and History*, pp. 205, 209. Leo Strauss, *What Is Political Philosophy?*, p. 304.

46.   Strauss, *Natural Right and History*, p. 220.

47.   Strauss, *Natural Right and History*, p. 165. Strauss's basic argument holds that because Locke doesn't make the case that God exists to Strauss's satisfaction, the seventeenth-century thinker really didn't believe in God. Since Locke based the concept of natural law on belief in God, Strauss alleges, Locke couldn't really believe in natural law.

48.   Strauss, *What Is Political Philosophy?*, p. 230.

49.   McAllister, *Revolt Against Modernity*, p. 87.

50.   Larry Peterman, "Approaching Leo Strauss: Some Comments on 'Thoughts on Machiavelli,'" *Political Science Reviewer*, Fall 1986, p. 323.

51.   Steven Lenzner, "Author as Educator: Strauss's Twofold Treatment of Maimonides and Machiavelli," paper presented at the American Political Science Association 2002 annual convention, www.claremont.org/writings/02apsa_lenzner.html, accessed on October 17, 2003.

52.   M. F. Burnyeat, "Sphinx Without a Secret," *New York Review of Books*, May 30, 1985, p. 31.

53.   Jacob Weisberg, "The Cult of Leo Strauss," *Newsweek*, August 3, 1987, p. 61.

54.   Richard Bernstein, "A Very Unlikely Villain (or Hero)," *New York Times*, January 29, 1995, p. D4.

55.   Quoted in Drury, *Leo Strauss and the American Right*, p. xi.

Chapter 8: "Human Weeds"

1.   Madeline Gray, *Margaret Sanger: A Biography of the Champion of Birth Control* (New York: Richard Marek Publishers, 1970), p. 13.

2.   Emily Taft Douglas, *Margaret Sanger: Pioneer of the Future* (New York: Holt, Rinehart, and Winston, 1970), p. v.

3.   "Why *The Woman Rebel*?" *The Woman Rebel*, March 1914, p. 8.

4.   "On Picket Duty," *The Woman Rebel*, March 1914, p. 3.

5.   Gray, *Champion of Birth Control*, p. 72.

6.   David Kennedy, *Birth Control in America: The Career of Margaret Sanger* (New Haven: Yale University Press, 1970), p. 23.

7.   The article criticizing Comstock listed in the indictments is "Are Preventative Means Injurious?" *The Woman Rebel*, July 1940, p. 40.

8.   Ellen Chesler, *Woman of Valor: Margaret Sanger and the Birth Control Movement in America* (New York: Simon & Schuster, 1992), pp. 277, 361, 368.

9.   "Tragedy," *The Woman Rebel*, July 1914, p. 33.

10.   "Tragedy," *The Woman Rebel*, July 1914, p. 33.

11. Robert A. Thorpe, "A Defense of Assassination," *The Woman Rebel,* July 1914, p. 33.

12. Quoted in Lawrence Lader and Milton Meltzer, *Margaret Sanger: Pioneer of Birth Control* (New York: Thomas Y. Crowell, 1969), pp. 59–60. The larger discussion of Comstock takes place on pp. 54–78.

13. The discussion of the Comstock-Sanger battle in Douglas, *Margaret Sanger: Pioneer of the Future,* occurs on pp. 42–93.

14. Esther Katz, ed., *The Selected Papers of Margaret Sanger: Volume I: The Woman Rebel, 1900–1928* (Urbana, IL: University of Illinois Press, 2003), p. 98.

15. Esther Katz, ed., *The Selected Papers of Margaret Sanger,* p. 91.

16. Esther Katz, ed., *The Selected Papers of Margaret Sanger,* pp. 88–90.

17. Esther Katz, ed., *The Selected Papers of Margaret Sanger,* p. 88.

18. Esther Katz, ed., *The Selected Papers of Margaret Sanger,* pp. 471–472.

19. Quoted in Edwin Black, *The War Against the Weak: Eugenics and America's Campaign to Create a Master Race* (New York: Four Walls Eight Windows, 2003), p. 12.

20. Statistics on eugenics through 1946 can be found in William Richardson and Clarence Gamble, "The Sterilization of the Medically Handicapped in North Carolina," *North Carolina Medical Journal,* February 1948, pp. 75–78, and the booklet "Selective Sterilization," published by the Human Betterment League of North Carolina. Both items are included in the Margaret Sanger Collection, Library of Congress.

21. Black, *War Against the Weak,* pp. 242–245.

22. The Alan Guttmacher Institute, "State Facts About Abortion: The District of Columbia," www.agi-usa.org/pubs/sfaa/print/district_of_columbia.html, accessed on March 24, 2004. Women traveling to the District of Columbia from surrounding areas to obtain abortions might account for some of the large disparity between babies delivered and babies aborted in the capital city. The nationwide abortion rate in 2000 numbered 21.3 per 1,000 women of reproductive age. In Washington, D.C., that rate stood at 68.1.

23. Untitled speech, Margaret Sanger, January 15, 1937, p. 2 (MSC, LC).

24. Untitled speech, Margaret Sanger, January 15, 1937, p. 1 (MSC, LC).

25. A special issue on eugenics dated June 1925, and another on sterilization dated April 1933 (after Sanger ceased serving as editor) are but two examples of *The Birth Control Review*'s allegiance to such ideas.

26. Margaret Sanger, "Birth Control and Racial Betterment," *The Birth Control Review,* February, 1919, p. 11, and Margaret Sanger "The Eugenic Value of Birth Control," *The Birth Control Review,* October 1921, p. 5.

27. The motto appeared in the December 1921 issue.

28. "The Future of the *Birth Control Review,*" *The Birth Control Review,* August 1928, p. 238. Also see similar discussions in the June and July issues of that year.

29. Margaret Sanger, "A Plan for World Peace," *The Birth Control Review,* April 1932, pp. 107–108.

30. Margaret Sanger, "A Plan for World Peace," *The Birth Control Review,* April 1932, p. 108.

31. The authors are Gray, Chesler, Kennedy, Lader and Meltzer, Douglas, and Lader.

32. Esther Katz, ed., *The Selected Papers of Margaret Sanger,* p. 45.

33. Esther Katz, ed., *The Selected Papers of Margaret Sanger*, p. 363.

34. One such colleague was Lothrop Stoddard, author of *The Rising Tide of Color Against White World Supremacy*, while another, Harry Laughlin, a board member of Sanger's birth-control organization, was an infamous racist.

35. Esther Katz, ed., *The Selected Papers of Margaret Sanger*, p. 167. Emily Taft Douglas, *Margaret Sanger: Pioneer of the Future* (Garrett, MD: Garrett Park Press, 1975), p. 192.

36. Black, *War Against the Weak*, p. 127.

37. Letter: Margaret Sanger to Mr. D. Kenneth Rose, February 8, 1943 (MSC, LC).

38. W.E.B. Du Bois, "Black Folk and Birth Control," *The Birth Control Review*, May 1938, p. 90.

39. Speech: Dorothy Boulding Ferebee, Birth Control Federation of America Annual Meeting, New York, N.Y., January 29, 1942 (MSC, LC).

40. Margaret Sanger to Clarence Gamble, December 10, 1939 (MSC, LC).

41. Margaret Sanger, "The Pope's Position on Birth Control," *The Nation*, January 27, 1932, p. 102.

42. Esther Katz, ed., *The Selected Papers of Margaret Sanger*, p. 335.

43. Margaret Sanger to Rabbi Sidney Goldstein, January 16, 1941 (MSC, LC).

44. Esther Katz, ed., *The Selected Papers of Margaret Sanger*, p. 465.

45. Margaret Sanger to the Honorable Graham Barden, July 7, 1949 (MSC, LC).

46. "Editorial," *The Birth Control Review*, May 1928, p. 137.

47. "Editorial," *The Birth Control Review*, August 1924, p. 219.

48. Margaret Sanger, "The Next Step: Full Steam Ahead" (Washington, DC: National Committee on Federal Legislation on Birth Control, Inc., 1937) (MSC, LC).

49. Chesler, *Woman of Valor*, pp. 234, 455.

50. Chesler, *Woman of Valor*, p. 340.

51. Chesler, *Woman of Valor*, p. 433.

52. Esther Katz, ed., *The Selected Papers of Margaret Sanger*, pp. 268–269, 277, 287–288, 299.

53. Margaret Sanger, "The Pope's Position on Birth Control," *The Nation*, January 27, 1932, p. 103.

54. Chesler, *Woman of Valor*, pp. 300–301.

55. *The Birth Control Review*, December 1927, p. 315.

56. Margaret Sanger, *The Pivot of Civilization* (New York: Brentano's, 1922), p. 108.

57. Sanger, *The Pivot of Civilization*, p. 108.

58. Quoted in Black, *War Against the Weak*, p. 127.

59. Sanger, *The Pivot of Civilization*, pp. 114–115.

60. Sanger, *The Pivot of Civilization*, p. 115.

61. Chesler, *Woman of Valor*, p. 186.

62. Chesler, *Woman of Valor*, p. 53; Gray, *Champion of Birth Control*, p. 40.

63. Chesler, *Woman of Valor*, p. 95.

64. Quoted in Chesler, *Woman of Valor*, p. 137.

65. Chesler, *Woman of Valor*, p. 137.

66. Chesler, *Woman of Valor*, pp. 133–134.

67. Chesler, *Woman of Valor*, p. 417.

68. Chesler, *Woman of Valor*, pp. 440–442.

69. Author interview of Andrea Weaver at the March for Women's Lives in Washington, D.C., on April 25, 2004.

70. Author interview of Kostya Branwen Sudice at the March for Women's Lives in Washington, D.C., on April 25, 2004.

71. "Reader Survey Results: Winter 1999: Female Heroes," *National Now Times*, Spring 1999. Information found at www.now.org/nnt/spring-99/wintersurvey-results.html, accessed on June 29, 2000.

72. Gloria Steinem, "Margaret Sanger," *Time*, April 13, 1998, p. 93.

73. *Tell Your Story, Change the World: Annual Report, 2002–2003* (New York: Planned Parenthood Federation of America, 2003).

74. Chesler, *Woman of Valor*, pp. 149–151.

75. "What Is IPFF," www.ipff.org/about/what, accessed on March 27, 2004.

Chapter 9: "Absolutely Segregate the Races"

1. W.E.B. Du Bois, *The Souls of Black Folk: Essays and Sketches* (Chicago: McClurg, 1909), p. 3.

2. W.E.B. Du Bois, "A Vista of Ninety Fruitful Years," *National Guardian*, February 17, 1958 (Du Bois Papers, Special Collections, W.E.B. Du Bois Library, the University of Massachusetts, Amherst).

3. David Levering Lewis, *W.E.B. Du Bois: Biography of a Race* (New York: Henry Holt, 1993), p. 156.

4. A discussion of Du Bois's attempts at subverting Garvey is included in David Levering Lewis, *W.E.B. Du Bois: The Fight for Equality and the American Century, 1919–1963* (New York: Henry Holt, 2000), pp. 50–84.

5. Quoted in Lewis, *The Fight for Equality and the American Century*, p. 82.

6. Quoted in Kenneth O'Reilly, *Black Americans: The FBI Files*, ed. David Gallen (New York: Carroll and Graf, 1994), p. 84.

7. W.E.B. Du Bois, *The Souls of Black Folk*, p. 126. Blaming Jews for the problems of Southern blacks is a theme Du Bois returns to several times in the book.

8. W.E.B. Du Bois, *Darkwater* (Milwood, NY: Kraus–Thomson Organization Limited, 1975), pp. 9–10. Lewis, *Biography of a Race*, p. 31.

9. W.E.B. Du Bois, "Race Pride," *The Crisis*, April 1920, p. 107.

10. W.E.B. Du Bois, "On Being Ashamed of Oneself," *The Crisis*, September 1933, p. 199.

11. W.E.B. Du Bois, "Segregation," *The Crisis*, May 1934, p. 147.

12. Walter White, "Segregation—A Symposium," *The Crisis*, March 1934, p. 80.

13. W.E.B. Du Bois, "Segregation in the North," *The Crisis*, April 1934, p. 115.

14. W.E.B. Du Bois, "Crusader Without Violence," *National Guardian*, November 9, 1959 (Du Bois Papers/UMass).

15. W.E.B. Du Bois, "Whites in Africa After Negro Autonomy," in *W.E.B. Du Bois: A Reader*, ed. David Levering Lewis (New York: Henry Holt, 1995), pp. 686–687.

16. Stephane Courtois, Nicolas Werth, Jeanne Louis Panne, et al., *The Black Book of Communism: Terror, Crimes, Repression* (Cambridge: Harvard University Press, 1999), p. 62.

17. Quoted in Courtois et al., *The Black Book of Communism*, p. 90.

18. Courtois et al., *The Black Book of Communism*, p. 88.

19. Quoted in Courtois et al., *The Black Book of Communism*, p. 130.

20. A discussion of the subject's first trip to the USSR is found in Lewis, *The Fight for Equality and the American Century*, p. 198. A description of the trip is found in W.E.B. Du Bois, "Russia, 1926," *The Crisis*, November 1926, p. 8.

21. W.E.B. Du Bois, "Marxism and the Negro Problem," *The Crisis*, May 1933, pp. 55–56.

22. Letter: W.E.B. Du Bois to Gus Hall, October 1, 1961 in O'Reilly, *Black Americans*, pp. 126–127.

23. Lewis, *The Fight for Equality and the American Century*, p. 469.

24. Fort-Whiteman's plight is documented in Harvey Klehr, John Earl Haynes, and Kyrill M. Anderson, *The Soviet World of American Communism* (New Haven: Yale University Press, 1998), pp. 218–227. Descriptions of Fort-Whiteman's attempts at sparking Du Bois's interest in Communism appear in Lewis, *The Fight for Equality and the American Century*, pp. 196, 256.

25. W.E.B. Du Bois, "On Stalin," *National Guardian*, March 16, 1953 (Du Bois Papers/UMass).

26. W.E.B. Du Bois, "The Vast Miracle of China Today," *National Guardian*, June 8, 1959 (Du Bois Papers/UMass).

27. W.E.B. Du Bois, *The Autobiography of W.E.B. Du Bois* (New York: International Publishers, 1968), pp. 42–43.

28. Lewis, *Biography of a Race*, p. 3. Lewis, *The Fight for Equality and the American Century*, pp. 563–564. Du Bois, *The Autobiography of W.E.B. Du Bois*, p. 49.

29. Lewis, *The Fight for Equality and the American Century*, pp. 560–561.

30. Lewis, *Biography of a Race*, pp. 4–5.

31. Daniel Boorstin, *The Americans: The Colonial Experience* (New York: Random House, 1958), p. 94.

32. Lewis, *The Fight for Equality and the American Century*, p. 390.

33. Lewis, *The Fight for Equality and the American Century*, pp. 413–414.

34. W.E.B. Du Bois, "Lunch," *Pittsburgh Courier*, February 27, 1937 (Du Bois Papers/UMass). Du Bois, *The Autobiography of W.E.B. Du Bois*, p. 46.

35. W.E.B. Du Bois, "China and Japan," *Pittsburgh Courier*, February 27, 1937 (Du Bois Papers/UMass).

36. Lewis, *The Fight for Equality and the American Century*, pp. 391–392.

37. Lewis, *The Fight for Equality and the American Century*, p. 414.

38. W.E.B. Du Bois, "Japan, Color and Afro-Americans," *Chicago Defender*, August 25, 1945 (Du Bois Papers/UMass).

39. Lewis, *The Fight for Equality and the American Century*, p. 392.

40. Lewis, *The Fight for Equality and the American Century*, p. 401.

41. W.E.B. Du Bois, "Race Prejudice in Germany," *Pittsburgh Courier*, December 19, 1936 (Du Bois Papers/UMass).

42. W.E.B. Du Bois, "The German Case Against Jews," *Pittsburgh Courier*, January 2, 1937 (Du Bois Papers/UMass).

43. W.E.B. Du Bois, "The Hitler State," *Pittsburgh Courier*, December 12, 1936 (Du Bois Papers/UMass).

44. W.E.B. Du Bois, "Profit," *Pittsburgh Courier*, December 26, 1936 (Du Bois Papers/UMass).

45. W.E.B. Du Bois, "Germany," *Pittsburgh Courier*, December 5, 1936 (Du Bois Papers/UMass).

46. Data on prisoners of war can be found in Gavan Davis, *Prisoners of the*

Japanese: POWs of World War II in the Pacific (New York: William Morrow and Co., 1994), p. 360.

47. W.E.B. Du Bois, "Peace: Freedom's Road for Oppressed Peoples," in *W.E.B. Du Bois: A Reader*, ed. David Levering Lewis (New York: Henry Holt, 1995), p. 753.

48. W.E.B. Du Bois, "Cannot This Paralyzed Nation Awake?" *National Guardian*, April 12, 1954; W.E.B. Du Bois, "Peace," *Chicago Globe*, September 23, 1950 (Du Bois Papers/UMass).

49. W.E.B. Du Bois, "The Iron Curtain," *Chicago Globe*, September 9, 1950 (Du Bois Papers/UMass).

50. W.E.B. Du Bois, "Cannot This Paralyzed Nation Awake," *National Guardian*, April 12, 1954 (Du Bois Papers/UMass).

51. W.E.B. Du Bois, "Japan, Color, and Afro-Americans," in *W.E.B. Du Bois: A Reader*, ed. David Levering Lewis, p. 86.

52. W.E.B. Du Bois, "We Cry Aloud," *National Guardian*, July 10, 1952 (Du Bois Papers/UMass).

53. Quoted in Lewis, *The Fight for Equality and the American Century*, p. 554.

54. W.E.B. Du Bois, "Cannot This Paralyzed Nation Awake?" *National Guardian*, April 12, 1954 (Du Bois Papers/UMass).

55. "Du Bois, W.E.B.," *The Columbia Encyclopedia*, Sixth Edition (2001), available at www.bartleby.com/65/du/DuBois-W.html, accessed on November 4, 2003.

56. Lewis, *The Fight for Equality and the American Century*, p. 569.

57. W.E.B. Du Bois, *Black Folk: Then and Now* (Milwood, NY: Kraus–Thomson Organization Limited, 1975), pp. 177, 24.

58. Du Bois, *Black Folk*, p. 211.

59. Remarks on the blackness of Egyptians and blacks sparking the industrial age can be found in Du Bois, *Black Folk*, pp. 230, 221. Du Bois's views on the reasons behind both world wars are aired, for instance, in W.E.B. Du Bois, "The Negro and Imperialism," in *W.E.B. Du Bois Speaks: Speeches and Addresses 1920–1963*, ed. Philip S. Foner (New York: Pathfinder, 1991), pp. 150–160.

60. Sean Wilentz, "Heart and Souls: The Strange Education of W.E.B. Du Bois," *New Republic*, April 4, 1994, p. 29.

61. Quoted in Dan Flynn, "The Canonization of W.E.B. Du Bois," *New Criterion*, April 1996, p. 79.

62. Quoted in Press Release: University of Massachusetts President's Office, "UMass to Name Library in Honor of W.E.B. Du Bois," October 4, 1994.

63. Lewis, *Biography of a Race*, p. 4.

Chapter 10: "Forgery by Typewriter"

1. John Earl Haynes and Harvey Klehr, *In Denial: Historians, Communism, and Espionage* (San Francisco: Encounter Books, 2003), p. 160. G. Edward White, *Alger Hiss's Looking-Glass Wars: The Covert Life of a Soviet Spy* (New York: Oxford University Press, 2004), pp. 46–47. Whittaker Chambers, *Witness* (New York: Random House, 1952), pp. 463–471.

2. Quoted in Allen Weinstein, *Perjury: The Hiss-Chambers Case* (New York: Alfred A. Knopf, 1978), p. 415.

3. Quoted in Weinstein, *Perjury*, p. 438.

4. Quoted in Weinstein, *Perjury*, p. 379.

5. Weinstein, *Perjury*, pp. 150, 479.

6. Fred Cook, *The Unfinished Story of Alger Hiss* (New York: William Morrow Co., 1958), p. 62.

7. Weinstein, *Perjury*, pp. 41–42.

8. Weinstein, *Perjury*, p. 47.

9. Weinstein, *Perjury*, pp. 213–216.

10. Chambers, *Witness*, p. 416.

11. Weinstein, *Perjury*, pp. 214–215.

12. Chambers, *Witness*, p. 534.

13. Robert Whalen, "Hiss and Chambers: Strange Story of Two Men," *New York Times*, December 12, 1948, p. 6E.

14. Chambers, *Witness*, p. 25.

15. Sam Tanenhaus, *Whittaker Chambers* (New York: Random House, 1997), p. 291.

16. Weinstein, *Perjury*, pp. 261–262.

17. Weinstein, *Perjury*, p. 300.

18. Weinstein, *Perjury*, p. 247.

19. Chambers, *Witness*, p. 445.

20. John Chabot Smith, *Alger Hiss: The True Story* (New York: Holt, Rinehart, and Winston, 1976), p. 345. Fred Cook, *The Unfinished Story of Alger Hiss*, p. 113.

21. Weinstein, *Perjury*, p. 261.

22. Smith, *Alger Hiss*, p. 89.

23. White, *Alger Hiss's Looking-Glass Wars*, pp. 167–169.

24. John Earl Haynes and Harvey Klehr, *Venona: Decoding Soviet Espionage in America* (New Haven: Yale University Press, 1999), pp. 9, 339–370.

25. August 8, 1969, interpretation of Venona #1822, Washington to Moscow, March 30, 1945.

26. Venona #1822, Washington to Moscow, March 30, 1945.

27. Charles Kramer, Victor Perlo, and Harold Glasser appear in numerous Venona transmissions, including Venona #588, New York to Moscow, April 29, 1944. Harry Dexter White also makes multiple appearances, including Venona #1119–1121, New York to Moscow, August 4–5, 1944. Laurence Duggan is discussed in Venona #1613, New York to Moscow, November 18, 1944. Frank Coe appears in three cables, including Venona #1838, New York to Moscow, December 29, 1944. Abraham George Silverman is referred to in numerous documents as well, including Venona #655, New York to Moscow, May 9, 1944.

28. John Earl Haynes, Harvey Klehr, and Fridrikh Firsov, *The Secret World of American Communism* (New Haven: Yale University Press), pp. 309–321 detail the activities of Perlo, Kramer, Glasser, Emery, and Bachrach. Soviet documents outlining the role of J. Peters in espionage can be found on pp. 73–83. Max Bedacht and Phillip Rosenbliett are discussed on pp. 25–26.

29. John Lowenthal, "Venona and Alger Hiss," *Intelligence and National Security*, Autumn 2000, p. 119.

30. John Lowenthal, "Venona and Alger Hiss," *Intelligence and National Security*, Autumn 2000, p. 108.

31. John Lowenthal, "Venona and Alger Hiss," *Intelligence and National Security*, Autumn 2000, p. 109.

32. Weinstein, *Perjury*, p. 361.

33. Allen Weinstein and Alexander Vassiliev, *The Haunted Wood: Soviet Espionage in America—the Stalin Era* (New York: Random House, 1999), p. 5.

34. Weinstein and Vassiliev, *The Haunted Wood*, p. 7.

35. Weinstein and Vassiliev, *The Haunted Wood*, p. 7.

36. Hede Massing, *This Deception* (New York: Duell, Sloan and Pearce, 1951), pp. 164–180.

37. Herbert Romerstein and Eric Breindel, *The Venona Secrets: Exposing Soviet Espionage and America's Traitors* (Washington, DC: Regnery, 2000), pp. 131–136. Haynes and Klehr, *Venona*, p. 75. Haynes and Klehr, *In Denial*, pp. 146–150.

38. Weinstein and Vassiliev, *The Haunted Wood*, p. 294.

39. Weinstein and Vassiliev, *The Haunted Wood*, p. 295.

40. Quoted in "Hiss Dies but Not His Lies," *AIM Report*, November-B 1996, p. 1.

41. Letter: Gen. Dmitri Volkogonov to John Lowenthal, October 14, 1992.

42. Victor Navasky, "Alger Hiss," *Nation*, December 9, 1996, p. 7.

43. Quoted in White, *Alger Hiss's Looking-Glass Wars*, p. 214.

44. Quoted in "Hiss Dies but Not His Lies," *AIM Report*, November-B 1996, p. 2.

45. "Hiss Dies but Not His Lies," *AIM Report*, November-B 1996, p. 2.

46. Chambers, *Witness*, p. 790.

47. Cook, *The Unfinished Story of Alger Hiss*, p. 137.

48. Cook, *The Unfinished Story of Alger Hiss*, p. 113.

49. Smith, *Alger Hiss*, p. 346.

50. Meyer Zeligs, *Friendship and Fratricide: An Analysis of Whittaker Chambers and Alger Hiss* (New York: The Viking Press, 1967), pp. 210–213, 217, 262.

51. Zeligs, *Friendship and Fratricide*, pp. 110–115. 376

52. Zeligs, *Friendship and Fratricide*, p. 426.

53. Zeligs, *Friendship and Fratricide*, pp. 427–432.

54. Cook, *The Unfinished Story of Alger Hiss*, p. 176.

55. Smith, *Alger Hiss*, p. 416.

56. Smith, *Alger Hiss*, pp. 418–419.

57. For a discussion of the various conspiracy theories, see Weinstein, *Perjury*, pp. 569–589.

58. Joel Kovel is the Alger Hiss Professor of Social Studies at Bard College.

59. "The Alger Hiss Story: The Search for Truth," www.nyu.edu/hiss, accessed on May 18, 2001.

60. Ellen Schrecker, *Many Are the Crimes: McCarthyism in America* (Boston: Little, Brown, 1998), p. 181.

61. Haynes and Klehr, *In Denial*, p. 218.

62. Cook, *The Unfinished Story of Alger Hiss*, p. 1.

Chapter 11: "It's Totally Rational"

1. *Bananas* (film), Jack Grossberg, producer (United Artists, 1971).

2. This oft-cited factoid has almost become the obligatory preface to discussing *Atlas Shrugged* among Randians. It should be noted that although *Atlas Shrugged* placed second to the Bible, the gap in votes between the two was quite substantial. For a critical discussion of this survey, see Jessica Amanda Salmonson, "'Ayn Rand More Popular Than God!' Objectivists Allege," www.violetbooks.com/aynrand, accessed on September 28, 2003.

3.   Barbara Branden, *The Passion of Ayn Rand* (Garden City, NY: Doubleday, 1986), p. 186.

4.   Del Jones, "Scandals Lead Execs to *Atlas Shrugged*," *USA Today*, September 23, 2002, p. 1; Branden, *The Passion of Ayn Rand*, p. 422.

5.   Quoted in Branden, *The Passion of Ayn Rand*, p. 414.

6.   Ayn Rand, *Capitalism: The Unknown Ideal* (New York: Signet, 1967), p. 195.

7.   Ayn Rand, *The Virtue of Selfishness* (New York: Signet, 1964), p. 30.

8.   Quoted in Branden, *The Passion of Ayn Rand*, p. 60.

9.   Branden, *The Passion of Ayn Rand*, pp. 115–116, 126–127, 127n.

10.   Branden, *The Passion of Ayn Rand*, pp. 67–73, 92.

11.   Quoted in Branden, *The Passion of Ayn Rand*, p. 93.

12.   Ayn Rand, *Atlas Shrugged* (New York: Plume, 1992), p. 128.

13.   Rand, *Atlas Shrugged*, p. 971.

14.   Rand, *Atlas Shrugged*, p. 857.

15.   Rand, *The Fountainhead* (New York: Plume, 1993), p. 312.

16.   Rand, *Atlas Shrugged*, p. 1071.

17.   Quoted in Jeff Walker, *The Ayn Rand Cult* (Peru, IL: Open Court, 2002), p. 78.

18.   Quoted in Murray N. Rothbard, "The Sociology of the Ayn Rand Cult" (1972), www.lewrockwell.com, accessed on June 25, 2003.

19.   Nathaniel Branden, *My Years with Ayn Rand* (San Francisco: Jossey-Bass Publishers, 1999), pp. 13–14.

20.   Walker, *The Ayn Rand Cult*, p. 190.

21.   Rothbard, "The Sociology of the Ayn Rand Cult."

22.   Rothbard, "The Sociology of the Ayn Rand Cult."

23.   Jerome Tuccille, *It Usually Begins with Ayn Rand* (New York: Stein and Day, 1972), pp. 29–33. Walker, *The Ayn Rand Cult*, p. 20.

24.   Rand, *Capitalism: The Unknown Ideal*, p. 24.

25.   Branden, *The Passion of Ayn Rand*, p. 268.

26.   Rand, *The Virtue of Selfishness*, p. 82.

27.   Branden, *The Passion of Ayn Rand*, p. 363.

28.   Rand, *Atlas Shrugged*, p. 684.

29.   Quoted in Branden, *The Passion of Ayn Rand*, p. 208.

30.   Quoted in Branden, *The Passion of Ayn Rand*, p. 329.

31.   Branden, *My Years with Ayn Rand*, pp. 213–214.

32.   Branden, *My Years with Ayn Rand*, p. 214.

33.   Walker, *The Ayn Rand Cult*, p. 252.

34.   Quoted in Branden, *The Passion of Ayn Rand*, p. 381.

35.   Bjorn Lomborg, *The Skeptical Environmentalist* (Cambridge, U.K.: Cambridge University Press, 2001), p. 219. Lomborg points out that lung cancer death rates for smokers versus abstainers are now twenty-three times higher for men and thirteen times higher for women.

36.   Branden, *My Years with Ayn Rand*, p. 268.

37.   Branden, *The Passion of Ayn Rand*, p. 383.

38.   Quoted in Chris Matthew Sciabarra, *Ayn Rand: The Russian Radical* (University Park, PA: Pennsylvania State University Press, 1995), p. 101.

39.   Ayn Rand, *We the Living* (New York: Signet, 1996), p. 90. The new passage reads: "Can you sacrifice the few? When those few are the best? Deny the best its right to the top—and you have no best left. What *are* your masses but millions of dull, shriveled, stagnant souls that have no thoughts of their own, no dreams of their own, no will of their own, who eat and sleep and chew helplessly the words others put into their brains? And for those you would sacrifice the few who know life, who *are* life? I loathe your ideals because I know no worse injustice than the giving of the undeserved. Because men are not equal in ability and one can't treat them as if they were. And because I loathe most of them."

40. Walker, *The Ayn Rand Cult*, p. 251.

41. Walker, *The Ayn Rand Cult*, p. 224.

42. Quoted in Walker, *The Ayn Rand Cult*, p. 192.

43. Rand, *Capitalism: The Unknown Ideal*, p. 305.

44. Rand, *The Virtue of Selfishness*, p. 13.

45. Ayn Rand, *Return of the Primitive: The Anti-Industrial Revolution* (New York: Meridian, 1999), p. 108.

46. "About the Author" in Rand, *Atlas Shrugged*.

47. Sciabarra, *Ayn Rand: The Russian Radical*, p. 19.

48. Branden, *My Years with Ayn Rand*, p. 248.

49. Branden, *The Passion of Ayn Rand*, p. 101.

50. Rothbard, "The Sociology of the Ayn Rand Cult."

51. Quoted in Branden, *My Years with Ayn Rand*, p. 202.

52. Branden, *My Years with Ayn Rand*, p. 218.

53. Among the figures Rand attacked were Barry Goldwater, Alexander Solzhenitsyn, Ronald Reagan, F. A. Hayek, Whittaker Chambers, Ludwig von Mises, and William F. Buckley Jr. According to Rand, "Senator Goldwater was not an advocate of capitalism." The Arizonan ran a "meaningless, unphilosophical, unintellectual campaign" for the White House (Rand, *Capitalism: The Unknown Ideal*, p. 208). According to Nathaniel Branden, Rand's notes on one of Ludwig von Mises's works referred to him as a "bastard." "The margins were filled with abusive comments," Branden remembers. "It was not her disagreement that disturbed me but the savagery of her attacks" (Nathaniel Branden, *My Years with Ayn Rand*, p. 116). "As an example of our most pernicious enemy," Rand wrote, "I would name Hayek. That one is real poison" (Walker, *The Ayn Rand Cult*, p. 334). Objectivist intellectual John Hospers held that "she opposed Reagan from the beginning because Reagan was against abortion. Everything else that he had—pro-free enterprise and so on—counted for nothing, except that" (Walker, *The Ayn Rand Cult*, p. 252). Not unlike other ideologues, Rand attacked those with *competing* ideas more severely than she did those with *opposing* ideas. Was the libertarian economist F. A. Hayek really more of an enemy to her ideas than, say, Karl Marx?

54. Branden, *The Passion of Ayn Rand*, p. 313.

55. Branden, *My Years with Ayn Rand*, p. 188.

56. Branden, *My Years with Ayn Rand*, p. 137.

57. Branden, *My Years with Ayn Rand*, p. 143.

58. Branden, *My Years with Ayn Rand*, p. 330.

59. Quoted in Branden, *The Passion of Ayn Rand*, p. 277.

60. Branden, *My Years with Ayn Rand*, p. 333.

61. Branden, *My Years with Ayn Rand*, p. 331.

62. Branden, *My Years with Ayn Rand*, pp. 342–345.

63. Rand, *Capitalism: The Unknown Ideal*, p. ix.

64. Quoted in Branden, *My Years with Ayn Rand*, p. 353.

65. Branden, *My Years with Ayn Rand*, pp. 353, 355.

66. Branden, *My Years with Ayn Rand*, p. 355. Branden, *The Passion of Ayn Rand*, p. 356n.

67. Branden, *My Years with Ayn Rand*, pp. 356–357. Rothbard, "The Sociology of the Ayn Rand Cult."

68. Branden, *The Passion of Ayn Rand*, p. 357.

69. Branden, *My Years with Ayn Rand*, pp. 352, 391.

70. Branden, *The Passion of Ayn Rand*, p. 352. While Mrs. Branden penned her work in the 1980s, Leonard Peikoff's silent treatment continues to the present. Perhaps familial love will win the day, but prospects don't appear promising.

71. Branden, *The Passion of Ayn Rand*, pp. 355–356.

72. Walker, *The Ayn Rand Cult*, p. 36.

73. Quoted in *Ayn Rand: A Sense of Life* (film), Michael Paxton (AG Media, 1997).

74. Chris Matthew Sciabarra, "Bowdlerizing Ayn Rand," *Liberty*, September 1998, available at www.nyu.edu/projects/sciabarra/essays/liberty.htm, accessed on September 2, 2003.

75. Quoted in Walker, *The Ayn Rand Cult*, pp. 265–266.

Chapter 12: "Comfortable Concentration Camp"

1. Ayn Rand, *Return of the Primitive: The Anti-Industrial Revolution* (New York: Meridian, 1999), p. 148.

2. Rand, *Return of the Primitive*, p. 148.

3. Edith Ephron, "*The Feminine Mystique* by Betty Friedan," *The Objectivist Newsletter*, July 1963, p. 27.

4. Quoted in Daniel Horowitz, *Betty Friedan and the Making of "The Feminine Mystique"* (Amherst: University of Massachusetts Press, 1998), p. 203.

5. Betty Friedan, *The Feminine Mystique* (New York: Dell, 1971), p. 197.

6. Friedan, *The Feminine Mystique*, p. 294.

7. Friedan, *The Feminine Mystique*, pp. 271–298.

8. Horowitz, *Betty Friedan and the Making of "The Feminine Mystique,"* p. 18.

9. Horowitz, *Betty Friedan and the Making of "The Feminine Mystique,"* pp. 165–166.

10. Horowitz, *Betty Friedan and the Making of "The Feminine Mystique,"* p. 170.

11. Horowitz, *Betty Friedan and the Making of "The Feminine Mystique,"* p. 154.

12. Betty Friedan, *Life So Far: A Memoir* (New York: Simon & Schuster, 2000), pp. 64, 88.

13. Friedan, *The Feminine Mystique*, pp. 4 (dedication), 7, 15.

14. Friedan, *The Feminine Mystique*, p. 63.

15. Horowitz, *Betty Friedan and the Making of "The Feminine Mystique,"* pp. 38, 44, 58–61.

16. Horowitz, *Betty Friedan and the Making of "The Feminine Mystique,"* p. 93.

17. Horowitz, *Betty Friedan and the Making of "The Feminine Mystique,"* p. 111.

18. The first quote belongs to Ronald Schatz; the second, to Robert Zieger. Quoted in Horowitz, *Betty Friedan and the Making of "The Feminine Mystique,"* p. 133.

19. Horowitz, *Betty Friedan and the Making of "The Feminine Mystique,"* pp. 144, 151.

20. Horowitz, *Betty Friedan and the Making of "The Feminine Mystique,"* p. 241.

21. Horowitz, *Betty Friedan and the Making of "The Feminine Mystique,"* p. 10.

22. Horowitz, *Betty Friedan and the Making of "The Feminine Mystique,"* pp. 9–15

23. Keith Reeve, *Cheerless Fantasies: A Corrective Catalogue of Errors in Betty Friedan's "The Feminine Mystique,"* p. 5. The online monograph can be found at www.cf.en.cl.

24. Friedan, *The Feminine Mystique*, p. 370n.

25. Reeve, *Cheerless Fantasies* (Part I), pp. 2–3.

26. Friedan, *The Feminine Mystique*, p. 12.

27. Reeve, *Cheerless Fantasies* (Part I), pp. 28–29.

28. Friedan, *The Feminine Mystique*, p. 290.

29. Reeve, *Cheerless Fantasies* (Part IV), pp. 2–3.

30. Friedan, *The Feminine Mystique*, p. 154.

31. Reeve, *Cheerless Fantasies* (Part II), pp. 2–4.

32. "Digest of Education Statistics 2000," (Washington, DC: U.S. Department of Education, 2001), pp. 20, 202, 239.

33. Friedan, *Life So Far*, p. 87.

34. Friedan, *Life So Far*, p. 227.

35. Friedan, *Life So Far*, p. 224.

36. "Editors' Note," *New York Times*, May 26, 2000, p. 2. "Editors' Note," *New York Times*, June 25, 2000, p. 2.

37. Quoted in Howard Kurtz, "Abuse Reports That Smack of Unfairness," *Washington Post*, June 5, 2000, p. C5.

38. Carl Friedan, "Living with Insanity," carlfriedan.com/insanity.html, accessed on June 23, 2000.

39. Carl Friedan, "Living with Insanity."

40. Carl Friedan, "Living with Insanity."

41. Quoted in Christina Hoff Sommers, *Who Stole Feminism?* (New York: Simon & Schuster, 1994), p. 62.

42. Quoted in Sommers, *Who Stole Feminism?*, p. 28.

43. "'97–'98 Politically Correct Top Ten," *Campus Report*, May/June 1998, p. 8.

44. Quoted in Peter Collier and David Horowitz, eds., *Surviving the PC University* (Studio City, CA: Second Thoughts Books, 1993), p. 115.

45. Quoted in *Comedy and Tragedy: College Course Descriptions and What They Tell Us About Higher Education Today* (Herndon, VA: Young America's Foundation, 1997), p. 4.

46. Quoted in Eric Auciello, "Nothing Feminine About These 'Feminists,'" *The Minuteman*, May 1994, p. 4.

47. Friedan, *Life So Far*, p. 249.

48. Friedan, *Life So Far*, p. 270.

49. Friedan, *Life So Far*, pp. 200–201.

50. Friedan, *Life So Far*, p. 190.

51. Friedan, *Life So Far*, p. 313.

52. Friedan, *Life So Far*, p. 223.

53. Friedan, *Life So Far*, p. 230.

54. Friedan, *Life So Far*, p. 248.

55. Friedan, *Life So Far*, p. 285.

56. Friedan, *Life So Far*, pp. 295–296.

57. Friedan, *Life So Far*, p. 295.

58. Friedan, *Life So Far*, p. 309.

59. Gina Bellafante, "Feminism: It's All About Me," *Time*, June 29, 1998, pp. 58–59.

60. "Digest of Education Statistics 2000" (Washington, DC: U.S. Department of Education, 2001), pp. 20, 202, 239.

61. U.S. Department of Justice, *Bureau of Justice Statistics Bulletin*, "Prisoners in 2002," July 2003, p. 1.

62. Statistics in this section, which refer to trends in the United States, come from Andrew Kimbrell, *The Masculine Mystique: The Politics of Masculinity* (New York: Ballantine Books: 1995), pp. 3–13.

63. Quoted in Media Research Center, "Flagrant Feminism Thrives at Time," *Media Reality Check*, July 9, 1998, available at www.mediaresearch.org/realitycheck/1998/fax19980709.asp, accessed on April 5, 2004.

64. Sommers, *Who Stole Feminism?*, pp. 11–14, 15.

Chapter 13: "Therefore We Will Be Incoherent"

1. To read the original piece, see Alan D. Sokal, "Transgressing the Boundaries: Towards a Transformative Hermeneutics of Quantum Gravity," *Social Text*, Spring/Summer 1996, available at www.physics.nyu.edu/~as2/transgress_v2/transgress_v2_singlefile.html, accessed on October 29, 2003.

2. Alan D. Sokal, "A Physicist Experiments with Cultural Studies," *Lingua Franca*, May/June 1996, available at www.physics.nyu.edu/~as2/lingua_franca_v4/lingua_franca_v4.html, accessed on December 14, 2002.

3. Sokal, "Transgressing the Boundaries: Towards a Transformative Hermeneutics of Quantum Gravity." See also Sokal, "A Physicist Experiments with Cultural Studies." In the latter piece, Sokal clarifies much of the difficult-to-comprehend language used in the earlier hoax.

4. Sokal, "A Physicist Experiments with Cultural Studies."

5. Stanley Fish, "Professor Sokal's Bad Joke," *New York Times*, May 21, 1996, p. 23.

6. Dinitia Smith, "Philosopher Gamely in Defense of His Ideas," *New York Times*, May 30, 1998, p. B7.

7. Christopher Lodge, ed., *Modern Criticism and Theory: A Reader* (New York: Longman, 1988), p. 108.

8. Jacques Derrida, *Writing and Difference*, trans. Alan Bass (Chicago: University of Chicago Press, 1978), p. 84.

9. Jacques Derrida, *Of Grammatology*, trans. Gayatri Chakravorty Spivak (Baltimore: Johns Hopkins University Press, 1980), p. 217.

10. Derrida, *Writing and Difference*, p. 256.

11. Alan Bass, "Translator's Introduction," in Derrida, *Writing and Difference*, p. xiv.

12. Derrida, *Of Grammatology*, p. 4.

13. Derrida, *Of Grammatology*, p. 19.

14. Derrida, *Writing and Difference*, p. 28.

15. Derrida, *Writing and Difference*, p. 235.

16. Mark Lilla, *The Reckless Mind: Intellectuals in Politics* (New York: New York Review Books, 2001), p. 183.

17. Quoted in Smith, "Philosopher Gamely in Defense of His Ideas."

18. Quoted in Jeff Collins and Bill Mayblin, *Introducing Derrida* (New York: Totem Books, 1998), p. 131.

19. Collins and Bill Mayblin, *Introducing Derrida*, pp. 119–123.

20. Jonathan Walker, "The Deconstruction of Musicology: Poison or Cure?" www.boethius.music.ucsb.edu/mto/issues/mto.96.2.4/mto.96.2.4.walker.html, accessed on June 28, 2002.

21. Susan McClary, *Feminine Endings: Music, Gender, and Sexuality* (Minneapolis: University of Minnesota Press, 1991), pp. 112–113.

22. Quoted in Tom Spears, "'Outrageously Sexual' Anne Was a Lesbian, Scholar Insists," *Ottawa Citizen*, May 29, 2000, p. 3.

23. Christopher Norris, *Derrida* (Cambridge: Harvard University Press, 1987), p. 112.

24. Quoted in James Miller, *The Passion of Michel Foucault* (New York: Simon & Schuster, 1993), p. 34.

25. Lilla, *The Reckless Mind*, p. 163.

26. David Macey, *The Lives of Michel Foucault* (New York: Pantheon Books, 1993), pp. 408–411, 421.

27. Quoted in Macey, *The Lives of Michel Foucault*, pp. 228–229; Miller, *The Passion of Michel Foucault*, p. 180.

28. Macey, *The Lives of Michel Foucault*, pp. 229–231.

29. Quoted in Arthur Herman, *The Idea of Decline in Western Civilization* (New York: The Free Press, 1997), p. 355.

30. Quoted in Lilla, *The Reckless Mind*, p. 149.

31. Macey, *The Lives of Michel Foucault*, pp. 374–376. Miller, *The Passion of Michel Foucault*, pp. 204–206.

32. Quoted in Miller, *The Passion of Michel Foucault*, p. 306.

33. Miller, *The Passion of Michel Foucault*, pp. 26–29, 375, 380–382. A spirited debate exists whether Foucault *intentionally* infected others with HIV. At the same time his admirers praise him as one of the twentieth century's most brilliant minds, they seem to argue that he was somehow oblivious to his declining condition. His visits to sex clubs, some admirers argue, were thus not as reckless as they might have been had he known that he was infected. Foucault's unchecked sexual appetites, coupled with his immersion in gay intellectual circles, make it hard to believe that he stumbled through life's final act that blind.

34. Quoted in Christian Kopf, *The Devil Knows Latin: Why America Needs the Classical Tradition* (Wilmington, DE: ISI Books, 1999), p. 124.

35. Quoted in Sokal, "Transgressing the Boundaries: Towards a Transformative Hermeneutics of Quantum Gravity." Although Sokal intended his article as a satire of postmodernism, he cited real books and articles, including the one mentioned in the text.

36. Quoted in Paul R. Gross and Norman Leavitt, *Higher Superstition: The Academic Left and Its Quarrels with Science* (Baltimore: Johns Hopkins University Press, 1998), p. 80.

37. Quoted in Noretta Koertge, "Wrestling with the Social Constructor," in *The Flight From Science and Reason*, eds. Paul R. Gross, Norman Leavitt, and Martin W. Lewis (New York: New York Academy of Sciences, 1997), p. 271.

38. Quoted in Jacques Derrida, "Like the Sound of the Sea Deep within a Shell: Paul de Man's War," trans. Peggy Kamuf, *Critical Inquiry*, Spring 1988, pp. 609–610, 622–623. For a more critical appraisal of de Man's wartime writing, see Jon Weiner, "Deconstructing de Man," *Nation*, January 9, 1988, pp. 22–24.

39. Derrida, "Like the Sound of the Sea Deep Within a Shell: Paul de Man's War," p. 631.

40. Derrida, "Like the Sound of the Sea Deep Within a Shell: Paul de Man's War," p. 625.

41. Derrida, "Like the Sound of the Sea Deep Within a Shell: Paul de Man's War," pp. 625–626.

42. Lilla, *The Reckless Mind*, p. 175.

43. Richard Posner, *Public Intellectuals: A Study of Decline* (Cambridge: Harvard University Press, 2001), pp. 212–214.

Conclusion: "A Terrible Thing to Waste"

1. "Flattened," *The Economist*, September 14, 1991, p. 70. Peter Carlson, "Fertile Imaginations," *Washington Post*, August 10, 2002, p. C1.

2. Quoted in Carlson, "Fertile Imaginations," p. C1.

3. "Welcome to Crop Circle Research Dotcom," www.cropcircleresearch.com, accessed on January 14, 2004.

4. Quoted in Bob Brown, "Unexplained: Crop Circles Tell Us Something About Ourselves," ABCNews.com, August 2, 2002, available at more.abcnews.go.com/sections/2020/dailynews/cropcircles_020802.html, accessed on August 13, 2002.

5. Matt Ridley, "Crop Circle Confession," ScientificAmerican.com, August 2002, available at www.sciam.com/article.cfm?articleID=00038B16-ED5F-1D29-97CA809EC588EEDF, accessed on January 26, 2004.

6. Quoted in Carlson, "Fertile Imaginations," p. C1.

7. Quoted in Carlson, "Fertile Imaginations," p. C1.

8. Arthur Koestler, *The God That Failed*, Richard Crossman, ed. (New York: Books for Libraries Press, 1972), p. 45.

9. Aristotle, *Nicomachean Ethics* I.6 (Bekker Number 1096a, 15–16).

10. Eric Hoffer, *Reflections on the Human Condition* (New York: Perennial Library, 1973), p. 40.

Acknowledgments

Since 2000, I have tried to get this book published in various, evolving forms. Back then, the climate in the publishing industry was not particularly hospitable to conservative books. One editor actually told me that no New York publishing house would ever print my book, so stop wasting your time with the larger, Manhattan-based companies. While I may not have liked the manner in which he dismissed my book, I couldn't help but think, He's right.

Thankfully, we were both wrong. Upon ushering in Crown Forum, Steve Ross remarked that "publishers inhabit a very culturally sheltered island called Manhattan. But until we declare ourselves a sovereign state, I think we should publish for the whole country." I thank Steve Ross for having the foresight to launch Crown Forum, without which a book such as *Intellectual Morons* would have had a harder time finding a large, mainstream publisher. It's a better world that caters to the demands of the market rather than the whims of a few self-appointed liberal gatekeepers.

I appreciate my editor Jed Donahue's work guiding *Intellectual Morons* to publication. He made this book better. The careful eyes of my wife, Molly, and my uncle, Joe St. George, saved me from embarrassing mistakes, typos, and instances of bad prose. I thank David Horowitz for encouraging me to comb through Howard Zinn's *A People's History of the United States*. Judith Reisman reviewed my chapter involving Alfred Kinsey, and historian Burt Folsom gave valuable feedback on several chapters as well. To repeat the obligatory line, all errors contained within are my own.

Several organizations have my gratitude for supporting my work. At Accuracy in Academia, the organization I used to direct, I began to delve into some of the ideas and figures explored in this book. I'm currently employed by the Leadership Institute, and Billy Parker, Dan Labert, and Morton Blackwell have my thanks for bringing me on board. Since the release of *Why the Left Hates America*, Young America's Foundation has organized dozens of my lectures on college campuses. I greately appreciate the efforts of Pat Coyle and Ron Robinson in enthusiastically promoting my work to young people.

I appreciate the support of old friends Cormac Bordes and Eric Auciello, and new friend Warrior. Mike Krempasky did a tremendous job designing my site, www.flynnfiles.com, which has brought a new audience to my writings. I'm fortunate to have my brothers, Sean, Barry, Dennis, and Ryan; my parents, Janet and Ronald Flynn; and, of course, my wife, Molly.

Index

About the Author

Daniel J. Flynn is the author of *Why the Left Hates America*. A frequent campus speaker, he has faced off with book burners, mobs shouting down his talks, and officials banning his lectures. His articles have appeared in the *Boston Globe*, the *American Enterprise*, the *Washington Times*, *Human Events*, and National Review Online, among other publications. He has been interviewed on Fox News, MSNBC, CNN, and Court TV and has been a guest on several hundred radio talk shows. Before joining the Leadership Institute, a nonprofit foundation dedicated to training future conservative leaders, Flynn was the executive director of Accuracy in Academia and a program officer for Young America's Foundation. His website can be found at www.flynnfiles.com. He lives in Washington, D.C., with his wife.